The Whole GUY Thing

Books by Nancy Rue:

Fiction for Teens:

Real Life Series:

Motorcycles, Sushi & One Strange Book (Book One)*

Boyfriends, Burritos & an Ocean of Trouble (Book Two)*

Tournaments, Cocoa & One Wrong Move (Book Three)*

Limos, Lattes & My Life on the Fringe (Book Four)*

Other Nonfiction:

That Is SO Me: 365 Days of Devotions

Girl Politics

Everybody Tells Me to Be Myself But I Don't Know Who I Am

The Skin You're In: Discovering True Beauty

Body Talk

Dear Nancy

** Also available as enhanced ebooks*

The Whole GUY Thing

What Every GIRL Needs to Know about Crushes, Friendship, Relating, and Dating

Nancy Rue

ZONDERVAN.com/
AUTHORTRACKER
follow your favorite authors

ZONDERVAN

The Whole Guy Thing

This title is also available as a Zondervan ebook.
Visit www.zondervan.com/ebooks.

Requests for information should be addressed to:

Zondervan, *Grand Rapids, Michigan 49530*

Library of Congress Cataloging-in-Publication Data

CIP applied for: ISBN 978-0-310-72684-5

Published in association with the literary agency of Alive Communications, Inc., 7680 Goddard Street, Suite 200, Colorado Springs, CO 80920. www.alivecommunications.com

Cover design: Micah Kandros Design
Interior design & composition: Greg Johnson/Textbook Perfect

Printed in the United States of America

---

12 13 14 15 16 17 /DCI/ 20 19 18 17 16 15 14 13 12 11 10 9 8 7 6 5 4 3 2 1

Table of Contents

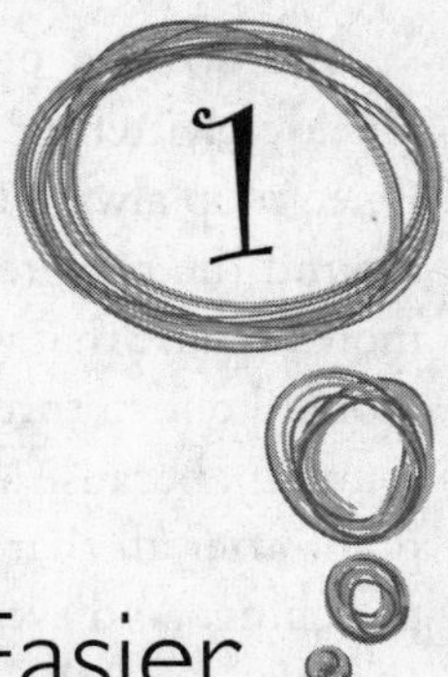

"It Was Easier When They Were Annoying Little Pests."

Take a minute to remember back when you were in, say, fourth grade. Maybe fifth.

Think recess.

The bell rang and the boys bolted out of the building already yelling — about what, nobody knew — and immediately got into an activity that involved throwing something or climbing on something or jumping from something or concocting something. Punching each other for no apparent reason was often part of that. If they stopped moving and started talking, it was either to plan the next throwing-climbing-jumping-concocting-punching thing, or to agree on how to get the most squealing out of the girls with their throwing-climbing-jumping-etc.

They were complete pains, but they were predictable. If a disagreement arose among them, they solved it with either a shove or a shout, and five minutes later (if it even took that long) they were back to throwing-climbing-jumping as if nothing ever happened.

And then there were you girls.

You strolled out of the building, sometimes arm in arm, already chattering, and you sorted yourselves out into groups. One group always formed a knot by the fence. Another gathered around the playground equipment that nobody played on anymore because that wasn't cool. (The swings and see-saw were now more like furniture.) Still another group hung out by the water fountain, because all the boys ended up needing a drink at some point after all that throwing-climbing-jumping-concocting and punching. And even though they could be little pains, there was something mildly fascinating about them to those few girls who could tolerate them for more than seven seconds.

Whether you made it your business to be around them or not, you most likely thought certain things about boys:

> "They HAVE to show off, as if people would forget they're there if they don't. Like *that's* gonna happen ..."
>
> "They're so gross! What's with that disgusting noise they make with their hands in their armpits? And burping the Pledge of Allegiance? Really? Body sounds and fluids are *that* hilarious?"
>
> "It's like making us scream is their career."
>
> "I want to stay away from them, which is pretty easy because, except for the making-me-scream part, they act like I have some weird disease they don't want to catch."

You probably complained—most likely to your father, since he was a boy once—that males were annoying, to which said father most likely told you they purposely bugged you because they liked you. You could *not* figure out the logic in that, but you didn't spend much time worrying about it, because you had more important things to concern yourself with. Like your BFF and the girl drama that was constantly taking place.

Yeah. You thought *that* was drama.

Sometime around sixth grade, give or take a year, stuff like this probably started showing up in your mind:

"I want guys as friends, but I'm too embarrassed to talk to most of them. If a guy's good looking, that makes it even harder. I had a lot more guts with guys when I was little!"

"I find myself wondering who will ask me to dances and stuff, if anybody. Is that good or bad?"

"I'm not allowed to date yet, but when I see all these happy couples together, I feel like people think no one wants to date me. Then I feel like a loser."

"I really want a boyfriend. I just want a guy to hug me and protect me. I daydream about it a lot. For hours."

"If I meet a guy and he's my age or a little older, I immediately start thinking about our wedding!"

"I want a guy to notice me. That's all."

I'm not making this up. Like all the girl quotes in italics you'll find in this book, they come directly from girls on my teen blog "In Real Life" or girls who have emailed me privately. I have dozens like them in my file, with more coming in all the time. As soon as the tween girls graduate at thirteen from their blog ("Tween You and Me"), the whole subject comes up again: "*Should I be thinking about boys this much? Shouldn't I be concentrating more on God? If there's no point in dating until I'm ready to get married, like my dad says, what am I supposed to do with all these feelings I'm having now?*"

Seriously, wasn't it so much simpler when boys did their thing, you girls did yours, and you hardly had to talk to them if you didn't want to? (And who wanted to?) Sure, they might have picked at you — knocked your pencil off your desk every time they passed, unzipped your backpack on the bus so when you stood up all your stuff fell out, laughed like a pack of hyenas when you gave the wrong answer in class. Now, you sort of *want* them to pick at you. You realize that what grown-ups told you when you were a kid was right: they do tease the girls they like. And you want to be liked.

It isn't that you didn't notice the attractive-factor in the male of the species before now. As a tween, you might have had a huge crush on the teen celebrity of the year (week, even day!). Maybe you had a "thing" for the young assistant soccer coach or that student teacher with the great dimples. Those were safe crushes, because the chances of ever meeting that media heartthrob were like a million to one, and no matter how much you daydreamed about the older guy you actually met, you knew he wasn't for you.

And then one day, as one of my bloggers put it, *"It seems like boys are finally growing up and you can totally picture yourself in a relationship with one of them. Nothing serious, but that desire for male company is definitely making itself known."*

Maybe a guy in your own age group emerges from the pack of absurd little pests looking a little less absurd than the rest. And a little cuter. Okay, a lot cuter. He has a sense of humor that doesn't include bodily functions. He uses vocabulary of more than two syllables. He actually seems to notice that other people have feelings. He shines brighter, looms larger, goes deeper than any teen guy you've known so far. Every time you see him, you may do one of a number of embarrassing things: Blush. Stammer. Lose ten or eleven IQ points. Giggle like you're five years old. Or hightail it to the nearest safe place (i.e. a restroom) to do all of the above. The mere thought of the boy is enough to send you into cardiac arrest, and that thought is ever-present—on your math worksheet, your computer screen, the insides of your eyelids. You're not exactly obsessed, but you aren't above making sure you're in the right place at the right time to catch a smile, a "hi," or—be still my heart—an actual conversation. If he accidentally touches you, you practically swoon like a character in a Jane Austen novel.

Guydlines

If you haven't felt that way around a guy, chances are you're waiting for that moment to happen. If you picked this book up on your own (as in, nobody made it required reading for you and you haven't stopped rolling your eyes since), I guarantee the above will occur at some point. You may be twenty-five before your heart hammers for someone of the male persuasion. I know women who didn't have their first crush until they were in their forties. The point is, there is nothing more normal than for you to feel drawn to a guy and crush big time. It's not even silly, though some adults who want you to put off matters of the heart for as long as possible might tell you that it is. No, this probably isn't the man you're going to spend the rest of your life with, although stranger things have happened. But for right now, it feels very real.

This almost magnetic feeling is normal because it's triggered by your hormones. Think about it: you didn't consider boys to be anything but pests before puberty, right? You didn't decide they no longer have cooties—your body did. This is how you were put together by your Creator. Granted, the pull is stronger in some girls than others, and it happens at different times for every individual, but chemically speaking, it's there. If it weren't, the human race would come to a screeching halt. So enjoying the jittery, giggly feeling or longing for the feeling or wondering why you *don't* long for the feeling is all as natural for your age as pimples, periods, and armpit hair.

And sometimes just as confusing, annoying, and downright painful.

If anything even remotely like the above is going on in your head—including, *"Why is it that every other girl on the planet who's my age is all* about *boys, and I just don't see what the big deal is?"*—you've come to the right place. Guys don't have to be "an issue" in your life for this to be an important subject for you to look at. You might not be spending every waking hour struggling over the opposite sex, but your attitude toward them is significant, no matter what it is, and you'll be thankful at some point that you got clear on it. Now's your chance.

I'm not calling this "the right place" because I have all the answers and am going to lay them out for you so that you can breeze through your teen years with this whole guy thing under control. I can't do that. Nobody can do that for you.

Nobody but you, that is.

I know it sounds almost ridiculous for me to say that *you* are in charge of your relationships with guys, even at thirteen or fourteen. Maybe the culture around you is constantly telling you what you should or shouldn't do or giving you the impression that you have no choice but to do what everybody else is doing.

On the one hand you live in a society where the clothes on the store racks sometimes border on exotic dancer or at least criminally indecent, and every secular teen magazine you pick up is telling you how to flirt, how to turn your crush into a serious relationship, and how to choose the shorts, blush, and haircut that will make you the sexiest. If you do find an article about embracing your body type and being comfortable in your own skin, it's probably placed right next to an ad featuring a skeletal model showing almost *all* of the skin she's in. Guys are under just as much pressure to be hip as you are, so you almost have to spend a thousand hours with a boy to find out who he really is. Meanwhile, our culture shrugs its shoulders and assumes that every girl in her teens is sleeping with every boy in his.

All of that is even harder when you're trying to walk in your faith. You're talking to God, getting a handle on how God wants you to live in this world, and then you go out *into* the world and people look at you like you've grown a second nose for not going with the cultural flow.

On the other hand, if you're part of a faith community that has boy-related rules, that can be confusing too. Things like:

> *"You shouldn't date until you're ready for a husband, and then you should only go out with guys you think you might want to marry. Otherwise there's no point in dating."*

What the Guys Say

"My church won't let me date until I'm sixteen, but, dude ... I want to."

> *"Christians shouldn't date; they should court."* (Or even *"You shouldn't kiss a man until you're at the altar with him, exchanging vows."*)

> *"Flirting is trashy."*

> *"You shouldn't even be thinking about boys right now. Your mind should be on God."*

Now, hear me. I'm not expressing an opinion about any of those. I'm just saying that there are so many conflicting messages, you may feel like you need to escape to the nearest all-girls boarding school and stay there until you're eighteen.

There's no need for that.

In my years as a high school teacher, workshop director, youth group leader, speaker, blogger, writer, mother, aunt, and friend, I've gotten to know many (and we're talking *many*) girls who don't want what society's telling them they ought to want, but who at the same time wrestle with the rules their church and/or parents are laying down. Like you, perhaps, they:

- really like boys and at least want to be friends with them, but aren't sure they know how
- want to get to know guys but they're afraid to, because they've been told that it could lead to sex (or that *it always does . . .*)
- enjoy having guys like them but wonder, "Is this okay? Is it godly?"

- see girls getting all strung out over boy-girl drama and wonder, "Does it have to be that way? Can I have a healthy relationship with a guy at this age?"
- want to honor their parents but don't exactly agree with their rules about boys

Those girls just aren't sure how they're "supposed" to think and feel. There's your trouble right there: the ever-lurking "supposed to."

Our society tells you you're "supposed to" be a sophisticated boy magnet by the time you're thirteen. They (whoever "they" are) tell you that, because it's your *effort* to be sophisticated that sells the movies, videos, music, makeup, clothes, hair products, magazines, and birth control they're selling.

The adults in your life may tell you you're "supposed to" put off all thoughts of guys until you're marrying age because they're afraid for you (and sometimes rightfully so) and are trying to shield you from being hurt. Their motives are a whole lot purer than the world's in general.

But what both sides tend to forget is that no one can tell you what you're "supposed to" *feel* about boys at your age, any more than anybody can tell you that you're not "supposed to" ever get jealous, or angry, or confused, or have an upset stomach. It's not just about what you feel anyway. It's about what you choose to do with those feelings.

And that ... only *you* can decide.

You.

When you get that first flutter in your stomach that tells you, "I have a crush on him," nobody is going to swoop in with the butterfly net.

When a boy plops down next to you out of nowhere and says, "Hi, I'm Jason," nobody else is going to be in your head figuring out what you want to say back.

When a guy leans in to kiss you, no set of rules is going to unroll between you with "No Kissing" highlighted.

We adults may say to you, "Do this, don't do that—and you'll be fine," but we're fooling ourselves. *You* will be the one making the decisions. *You* will be the one in charge of your behavior.

And yet not totally. You're going to find just a few **basic truths** in the following chapters, and here's the first one:

Basic Truth #1

You're much more likely to make true, authentic choices when you have a relationship with God.

You aren't in this by yourself. When you really think about it, it only makes sense that because God created the hormonal-development-normal process that put you here in the first place, God is going to be there to get you through it. God has never been known to put something in motion and then abandon the people it's happening to, expecting them to fend for themselves. (Hello—forty years in the wilderness anyone?) In fact, the Lord is so in there, it's pretty much impossible to do it without him.

That's so much of what this book is about. It's here to help you form the foundation with God, which will naturally help form a foundation for your future with men (and everything else in your life!) starting from right where you are at this moment. Here's what you'll find in these pages:

- As I just mentioned, the **basic truths you'll want to use to make your decisions**, whether you're a committed Christ-follower or still finding your way. Jesus doesn't say anything directly about teen guy/girl relationships in the Gospels, but there's still great guidance in there for you to build on, especially about the all-important, has-to-come-first connection with God we just talked about. We'll delve into that in the features called **God on Guys**.
- **Quizzes and questions that give you a chance to figure out where you are in each area**. You have to know

where you stand before you can go forward. More than that, you'll need to *accept* where you are, even if you're going to move in a different direction from here on. Look for that in **What's Going On with Me?**

- **Honest talk on the major relationship topics teen girls ask me about.** It's impossible to make wise choices without the right information. By the way, you might want to reassure your parents that you won't find explicit sex education here. I'll leave that to them. You'll find all other major guy subjects in the **Guydlines** feature in every chapter. (That's the feature you're reading now.) When you see quotes from girls in italics or I tell you a story about one of them, that's all based on true stories. I haven't created any fictional scenarios (I thought I ought to say that since I do write fiction!) or put together several girls' stories into one.
- **Suggestions for ways to apply what you discover here to your own situation.** It's one thing to read about all this and a whole other thing to actually practice it. In **Making It Real**, you'll get inspiration that will help you move forward.
- **Guidance for talking to your parents about boy issues**, especially if you disagree with them. There *is* a way to honor your father and mother, God, and your own integrity all at once. I've got your back on that in **Mom, Dad ... Now Don't Freak Out.**
- **Space to get your questions, your struggles, your inner wrestling matches out there where you can look at them.** You'll see a prompt in each chapter under **If I'm Totally Honest ...**
- **Actual input from guys I've interviewed**, so you can gain insights into what's going on with them. It's a no-

brainer that the best way to figure out what guys think is to ask them. Of course, they aren't always comfortable actually telling you, the potential girlfriend, so I've done the asking for you. Their answers are scattered in **What the Guys Say**.

What the Guys Say

"How can I tell when a girl likes me? I CAN'T!"

- **A brief recap of what each section says** just in case you need a quick refresher, or you're just not sure *what* I'm talking about. Each one is called **The Twitter Version** because it contains less than 140 characters. Life is short, after all.

Just to make sure we're clear, here's what this book ISN'T:

- It ISN'T a list of everything you should think, do, and say when it comes to boys. You'll just read honest information so you can wisely take it from there.
- It ISN'T even *my opinion* on what philosophy every teen girl should embrace when it comes to her relationships (or lack of them) with boys. You are all different. Your practice of the absolute truths will be unique to you, because that's part of God's infinite variety.
- *It ISN'T a Book of Judgment*. If you've already made some mistakes in the guy department or if you have thoughts you wouldn't tell your best friends, you won't feel like a finger is being pointed at you as you read this book. You'll have a chance to shed any shame and start fresh, which is the whole Jesus thing to begin with.

If you're still with me, let's start with a look at where you are with guys right now.

The Twitter Version

This book is about making choices, not about following a bunch of rules. Nobody can make those choices for you. Seriously. Nobody.

What's Going On with Me?

This is sort of like one of those quizzes you take in a magazine. (You may not read any of the articles, but you'll always take the tests, right?) The difference is that this one, and the ones in future chapters, are not designed to put you on a scale of good to bad, or even slide you into a slot. It's here so you can take stock of the jumble of guy-stuff going on in your head (and heart) and at the same time see that you aren't the only one who has foggy spots when it comes to boys. Even if you and a friend both take the quiz, don't give in to the temptation to compare your results and walk away feeling like you're worse than—or better than—she is. Think of it as, "It is what it is, and I want to find *out* what it is."

Each time you take out pencil or pen for one of these self-surveys, remember to give the most honest answers you can, rather than the ones you think you're "supposed to" give. We have pretty much done away with the term "supposed to" in the previous pages, because what good is it going to do you to create a false picture of yourself? If you're nervous about somebody else knowing what you're really thinking and feeling, write your answers on a piece of paper you can throw away. If you have siblings, consider shredding (the paper, not the siblings).

Read all six of the scenarios below. Then number them according to how much each one is like you—1 being closest to who you are and 6 being farthest from your mind. If any of them is nothing at *all* like you, put a 0 next to it. (Which means you could have anything from six zeroes to 1, 2, 3, 4, 5, and 6.)

Here we go.

GIRL A

_____ "Every female my age is always talking about guys. I'm never the one to go 'Oh, that boy's really hot' or 'He's so cute, blah, blah, blah.' Guys are okay. I'm just not that into them, and when everybody's going on and on about the whole thing, I feel left out."

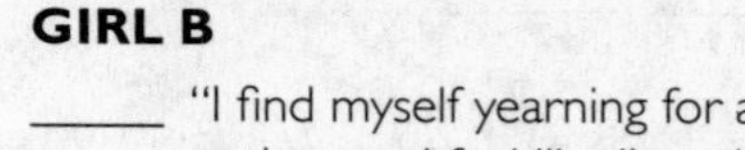

GIRL B

_____ "I find myself yearning for a boy to like me. You know, just to notice me. I feel like I'm missing out on something, but I don't know how to get their attention without looking like I'm trying to get their attention. I'm way more comfortable talking to guys online than in person. Does that make any sense at all?"

GIRL C

_____ "Right now I just want to be friends with guys because I don't think I'm ready for the boyfriend-girlfriend thing. Guys can make great buds, just to hang out with, no pressure. The problem is, nobody will leave it alone. They're all like, 'But seriously, don't you like him?'"

GIRL D

_____ "I really want a boyfriend, like other girls have. I want to be loved, to feel wanted, and to know somebody really cares. I think that would be so awesome. But then I start thinking, is it okay to feel that way? Shouldn't I just be patient and wait for the guy God has picked out for me?"

GIRL E

_____ "I'm pretty much comfortable with guys, as friends and as dates. I don't know, it just comes to me naturally. What I'm wondering, though, is how to be in a relationship without all the drama. Especially about sex. I know girls who make it sound like after a few weeks their boyfriends just expect them to have it."

GIRL F

_____ "I've made up my mind not to date until I'm ready to get married because what's the point? I want to save myself for my husband in every way. But what am I supposed to do in the years between now and then—with all this male cuteness around me? Should I not even be friends with any of them because it could turn into something else?"

What the Guys Say

"I started getting interested in girls when I was ten."

"At thirteen, I'm not ready to date."

"I'm fifteen and I've had one relationship that didn't turn out too well."

"I date but it's totally not serious. I'm only seventeen."

Now, take a look at how you scored yourself. Did you place a 6 next to one of the girls, with zeroes on all the others, or were your fields of identification more evenly spread? Hopefully that gives you a picture of where you stand on boy issues at this point and which things you're going to want to pay special attention to in this book (even though you'll want to read it *all*, of course!) A few insights that might be helpful:

If you have **GIRL A** tendencies, don't worry that there's something "wrong" with you. Everybody starts to notice guys at different times in their lives, or you just may be one of those women who will always be pretty content without them. Don't let what everybody else is doing determine your view of yourself. You're okay, girl. Read on anyway and find out what it's all about. You'll be especially interested in chapter two, "I Just Don't Get Guys."

If you have **GIRL B** in you, it *does* make sense to want boys to notice you without you having to do anything to *get* them to acknowledge your existence. It also makes sense to feel like some girls do it completely without effort, because some girls actually do. But more of them don't. More of them, like you, feel like they're all arms and legs and teeth about it at first. So, the desire for male attention is perfectly normal, and so is being absolutely sure you're never going to get it! I think you're going to learn a lot from chapter three, "I Feel Like a Geek." In chapter four, the **A Word About Guys Online** section will help you with the Internet thing.

If you see yourself in **GIRL C**, you're off to a good start in your life with the opposite sex, because whether it's romance or just friends, knowing a guy as a person is the best basis for any relationship. Chapter four, "Can We Be Just Friends?", will help you with your more boyfriend-prone friends who don't get friendship with guys.

Is **GIRL D** like you, even a little? Good for you, fessing up to that, because it's as normal to want a boyfriend now as it was for you to plaster boy band posters all over your room when you were eleven. People are meant to be loved, and you are just awakening to the fact that someday you'll want a forever love with a man. That desire doesn't just appear when you're old enough to do something about it. Otherwise you wouldn't even need this book. It's your reasons for craving a relationship that are worth looking at carefully. Chapter six, "So—Should I Date or What?", is going to be of special interest to you.

What about **GIRL E**? If she's your mirror image—or you can see a bit of your reflection in her—you have both the easiest and the hardest aspect of the boy thing going on. You're confident around guys, but that same confidence can put you in situations you aren't sure how to handle. Chapter five, "Do They Really Want Just One Thing?", and chapter seven, "Oh, the Drama," are the ones you'll especially want to focus on.

As for **GIRL F** lookalikes, it is awesome that you have such firm convictions, and that you recognize how hard it is to stick to them. You're going to find a lot of support here, and that includes safe places to look at your beliefs and make sure they're coming from God and not from fear, as sometimes (and I'm just saying sometimes) happens. After you've read the whole book, I suggest you really study chapter eight, "This Is All-Important, Because ..."

No matter where you are, the next step forward is to hear what God has to say on the guy subject in general.

The Twitter Version

Every girl's in a different place when it comes to guys. Every place is a starting place.

God on Guys

"I feel really guilty because I spend A LOT of my time daydreaming about guys, and I give God less attention."

I think it's safe to say that the majority of girls in society today would look at you like you were nuts if you said that out loud. The response would probably be something like, "*God?* Really?" Let's face it, knowing God doesn't always make life easier. On top of everything else we've mentioned—confusion, awkwardness, feeling completely clueless—you have to worry about *God* too!

So let's go there first, beginning with one of the Beatitudes—or as some of my teen friends call them, the Boy-Attitudes. As Jesus is listing the "Blessed Ares," he says, "Blessed are those who hunger and thirst for righteousness, for they will be filled" (Matthew 5:6).

Each of the beatitudes has two parts—what *we* need to do and what *God* does. In this one, *our* job is to hunger for doing the right thing, to thirst (as in find yourself dying for a water bottle) for a relationship with our Lord that goes deep. *God's* job is to fill that hungry emptiness and quench that thirsty longing so that we don't even *want* to do the shallow and the trivial, much less the heinous and the horrible.

And this has what to do with guys?

A bunch, because nobody can distract you from your hunger for righteousness like the male of the species.

"Not long ago I was at my crush's house (his sister is my friend) and while we were all praying, he was beside me, so we were holding hands. I've been going crazy ever since, just because I got to hold his hand!"

This doesn't mean you shouldn't have anything whatsoever to do with guys. They aren't put here on this earth solely to pull you away from God, no matter what some well-meaning parent may tell you. They're here, they're part of your life, and you very naturally want to be part of theirs. It's just important to put your hunger and thirst for God first, so that stomach-rumbling, dry-mouth longing for a boyfriend doesn't get out of control. The fact of the matter is, you can have great relationships with guys that actually enhance your spiritual walk. What could happen if you prayed with guys? Volunteered together at a homeless shelter? Went on the same mission trip? Actually talked about your faith — what a concept, yeah? God, in God's infinite power and wisdom, can use anything (even a former pest), as long as you're following closely.

> **What the Guys Say**
> "I know God's going to show me the girl I'm meant to spend my life with, so I'm not that into dating."

This beatitude doesn't say you have to *be* righteous every minute of every day. What it does say is that we need to be ravenous for righteousness. We need to be so hungry and so thirsty that we're trying all the time to have that need satisfied.

And here's the deal: having a guy like you isn't going to satisfy that hunger. Being the girl they all flirt with isn't going to quench that thirst. Feeling confident with your own guy-catching skills definitely isn't going to make you feel full.

There is nothing wrong with having a boyfriend, having a crush, or enjoying the fun of being attractive (without playing with people's feelings and hurting them). There is everything right with having healthy friendships with guys just as you do with girls and learning to understand them as people so you don't always feel weird and awkward around them.

What's wrong is when you forget the hunger and thirst for being close to God because you're hungering and thirsting for male attention, or for the ease with which the ever-present "other girls" draw guys to them like the poor boys are in a trance, or for the guy you're crushing on to at least know you're breathing.

So how do you strike a balance? You don't.

The scale is meant to be lopsided. God always has to be bigger, take up more of your time and your thoughts and your intentions. But — and hear me on this — God is *in* there when you like a guy because that guy is a good person, because you like the way he treats people, because he makes you laugh or makes you think or makes you want to be your real self. God's *in* there when you treat guys as people instead of mysterious creatures you have to conquer. God's present when you resist the urge to flirt with a guy you don't really care anything about, just to see if you can snag him. When you're jealous because other girls are getting all the male attention and you pretty much hate that about yourself, God's there to forgive and turn you around. When your heart gets broken because your guy falls for your BFF, God is already on it, loving and healing and moving you on.

So just like everything else in your life, it's not God OR... It's God AND. Not God OR guys. God AND guys.

How do you get there? In some ways, that's different for each individual, but one basic thing is essential for everybody.

Take time every day to talk to God about this stuff.

This is the space where you ask the questions you actually have, not the ones you think you're "supposed" to have. (There's that word again). If the guy issue is on your mind now, then for Pete's sake why would you strike up a conversation with God about what he wants you to do when you're thirty? God wants to discuss what you're wrestling with today, this instant. Because if you don't get God's help with today's struggles, you can't move on to tomorrow's.

What do you do when you talk to God? You can journal your thoughts—unless the idea of writing page after page makes you want to scale the nearest wall, in which case you might draw what you're feeling and thinking as you pray, or go for a run and pray, or make lists, or shoot baskets and pray. Anything to keep your focus so you can really get it out there where you and God can take a serious look at it.

Study the Scripture we'll talk about in this book. Read it as if God is talking directly to you in the context of what you're going through. Stop when something speaks to you and write it down (draw it, etc.) and keep it where you can go over it again. And again. And did I mention again?

Just in case you're thinking, "That's easy for you to say. You've been married for a million years!", let's look at what one of your *own* kind commented one day on the blog:

"Something that's really struck me recently is the verse: 'Love the Lord your God with all your heart and with all your soul and with all your mind' (Matthew 22:37). Everything in our lives should be focused on God. If we are fully loving God with everything we have and everything we are, then all our other priorities will just swish into place. This is a pretty hard concept for me to accept, because one of my weakest points is how I can get so crazy about a guy. The more I think about it though, the more it makes sense. Everything will fall into its proper place in our life, even a guy, if we put God as number one."

I love the idea of priorities "swishing into place." It's not about guilt. ("I'm a horrible person because I thought about the guy holding my hand instead of the prayer we were saying.") It's not about shame. ("I can't even talk to God now because I daydream about my crush instead of reading the Bible.") It's not about being so godly that guys never enter your mind. ("If I really want to be a God-follower, I have to ignore half the people God created.") It's about being so hungry for God in your life that you set aside time to feast with God every day so you're filled with the Spirit as you go out into that world, where guys are so everywhere you're practically tripping over them. Not noticing them, not thinking about them, not wanting to be accepted by them is a pretty ridiculous goal. The real goal is to be aware that God is there, helping you keep it all in perspective. You only know that by loving God with everything you have.

And that's the truth.

The Twitter Version

If you develop a close relationship with God, you're going to know God's there in everything you face. Including guys. Especially guys.

Making It Real

In this feature in each chapter, we'll be talking about ways to apply what you've found in the God on Guys and Guydlines sections. Since we're only in chapter one, let's just go over five things you'll need to get serious with yourself about before we move on. Think of it as kind of a mental to-do list:

(1) Be honest about your feelings. Do you just want a guy to like you so you'll feel better about yourself? Or are there really some boys you'd like to get to know as people? Are you really interested "hot" guys, or do you just say that because everyone else is saying it? Are you actually into a particular guy and say you're not because somebody (your parents, your church, your friends) says you "shouldn't" be? If you need to, go back to your answers in "Where Am I?" and look at them more closely. Again, nobody has to know how you feel but you. And God.

If I'm totally honest, my reaction toward the male population (and all the guy-girl stuff that comes with) is

____

____

____

(2) Make sure you know the difference between "romance" and "relationship," because most of what we're going to be talking about here falls into the relationship category. We'll touch on romance, because it's vital that you don't get them confused. For now, see if you can come up with a definition for each.

Romance means:

____

____

____

A relationship means:

______

______

______

______

(3) Take stock of your current relationships with guys. Think about who's a friend, who's a crush, who's somebody you could see yourself with five or six years from now, who's someone you'd just like to get to know better. Name names. Think faces. Your whole experience with this book will make more sense if you're thinking about individuals, rather than just the concept of "guys."

Guys I'm simply friends with (and am happy staying that way):

______

______

______

______

Guys I have a huge crush on:

______

______

______

Guys I want to know more about:

______

______

______

Guys I can actually see myself dating in a few years:

____

____

____

____

(4) And, of course, take an honest, serious look at your relationship with God. Do you feel close to God? Do you talk to God and sense the divine presence? Are you still getting there? Just starting out? Just now thinking about it? Don't put that on a good-to-bad scale. I'll probably say this fifty times: there's no judgment here. Just get a clear picture and we'll take it from there.

(5) If you don't already know, find out where your parent(s) or guardian(s) stand on the whole guy thing. Need some help with that? We're just about to go there.

Mom, Dad ... Now Don't Freak Out

"I don't want a boyfriend yet, but I do find myself liking guys more. My mom says, 'Why are you talking about boys so much?'"

It doesn't matter that your parents have known since the moment they found out you were a girl that this day would arrive — it still seems to come as a complete surprise to them that you're now interested in guys. That's part of the reason why they tend to pull in the reins when it comes to boys: either they didn't see it coming, or they're in denial. There are other reasons too, which we'll be talking about in the chapters ahead. The point is, however you may feel about the control your parents or guardians have in your life, the first thing you need to do is accept that they have it. It's a God-thing. Commandment Number Five makes it abundantly clear: *"Honor your father and your mother."* And then it goes on to say, *"So that your days may be long in the land that the Lord your God is giving you"* (Exodus 20:12). What mother hasn't said in those moments when her kid is going defiant on her: "I brought you into this world, and so help me I can take you out of it!"? Even God says, if you want to survive, you'd best be respecting your parents.

Having said *that,* let me say *this:* "Honor" doesn't mean *unquestioning* obedience, not at this stage of your life. *Eventual* obedience, yes. The people raising you get the last word, and well they should, because when it comes to the big picture they know more than you. But it is perfectly appropriate, and definitely good for your growth as a person, for you to discuss issues with your family and at least understand their decision-making process. As I've said, the decisions you make are ultimately your own; you're going to choose whether to go with their advice or do your own thing and deal with the consequences (which will inevitably include a breach in trust). But their rules and their wisdom need to be a part of your choices or, metaphorically speaking, your days aren't going to be long in the land of milk and honey.

Let's also make a clear distinction between your actions and your feelings. If your dad says you can't date until you're eighteen, you need to let the guys in your life know that and not sneak around that rule. But even if you're not allowed to date and you really, really like a guy, that attraction doesn't make you a disobedient daughter. What you are is a young person who has to make a decision about what she's going to do with those feelings without going against her parents' wishes. Will you decide to avoid that boy you like as if he were the H1N1 virus so you won't be tempted? Be his friend and keep your feelings to yourself? Get focused on other things so you won't spend all your time daydreaming about things that can't happen right now? Those are all legit ways to honor the rules without denying that you have feelings.

What all this tells you is that you need to find a way to talk to your parents about your relationships with guys and what the house rules are going to be in that regard.

Talk.

Not argue. Not get all defensive and wind up storming off to your room and slamming the door and thus ending all chance of conversation. Not this-is-what-I'm-going-to-do-and-you-can't-stop-me.

Talk. As in:

Ask your parents to be clear about their rules and why they've made them. And, yes, you do have the right to ask for clarification and explanation, as long as you do it respectfully. Make sure they get that you're going to do what they ask you to do, but that it'll go down easier if you can understand why. "Because I said so" isn't really a fair response to a thirteen- to sixteen-year-old girl on this issue, so explain to your parents that you'll be able to make better decisions yourself if you know how they make theirs.

An approach like this will take you nowhere:

"I don't get why you won't let me stay out past ten o'clock. It's stupid."

This one, on the other hand, has a better chance of bringing you the clarity you need:

"Okay, so can we talk about the reasoning behind my curfew? I'm not challenging it. I'd just really like to know."

Ask them to give you a chance to state your case. If they say, "No, we don't see the point in that," the conversation is over. But if approached in a mature, non-hysterical way (you aren't pitching a fit or brandishing a weapon, for instance), most parents will hear you out.

This probably won't do it:

"Let me just tell you why that doesn't work for me." Neither will "*This is the lamest rule in this hemisphere*" or "*This is what everybody else's parent are letting them do.*"

This, however, might:

"I'm going to follow the rules, for sure, but I'd just like a chance to tell you how I feel about them."

Just keep in mind: tone of voice and body language speak

just as clearly as your words, sometimes even more so. Folding your arms, rolling your eyes, curling your lip—you won't get too far with those.

The Twitter Version

Your parents make the rules, but discussion about those rules is totally appropriate. How you approach that will make all the difference.

Ask them to pray for you. This isn't a trick to get them to think you're Angel Child. In fact, if your request isn't genuine don't ask. Truly, though, you need all the prayer you can get on this, and who better to go to God for you than the people who love you the most? And ...

Ask how you can pray for *them*. Your parents are at the most challenging point in child-raising since potty training and tantrums (which hopefully you're no longer throwing). Trust me, they need prayer as much as you do.

However, this is guaranteed to make them suspect your sincerity:

"I need to pray for you guys, because you just don't get it."

On the other hand, if this one comes from your heart, your folks will appreciate it:

"I know you guys worry about me, so, is there some way I can pray for you?"

We'll talk more about discussing guy issues with your parents as we get into each specific area. This much is a good start, not only in terms of boys, but for your whole relationship with your folks. If you can communicate effectively with them in this mine field, everything else is going to seem like the proverbial walk in the park.

We've already covered a lot of ground. Time for a regrouping breather. Before we go on to your first "If I'm Totally Honest ...", decide whether you want to jot down your thoughts here in the book, or gather them in a journal set aside just for guy issues, or, for that matter, whether you want to write them down at all. Some people freeze when they take pen in hand, so if you can toss thoughts around while you're hiking or horseback riding or hacking away at the mess in your closet, that's perfectly fine. The goal is to spend enough focused time on the question that you get to a place of satisfaction. That could mean anything from just venting (when you're sick, don't you always feel better after you throw up?) to actually resolving something, if only in your own spirit. It doesn't matter how you do it, as long as you do it.

If I'm Totally Honest ...

My biggest area of concern (anxiety, fear, terror ...) when it comes to boys is:

"I Just Don't Get Guys."

"I don't even know the first thing to say to a guy! They're so different from girls that I just feel like I'd make a total idiot of myself."

"I sometimes wonder if the guy I like likes me back. I mean, he makes it a point to talk to me even though somebody else is waiting for him. And even when he's in a hurry he always says 'hi' and 'I'll talk to you later.' Am I being stupid? After all, he could just be being nice to me and I just want to THINK he likes me. Seriously, am I going crazy?"

"I'm pretty sure this one guy likes me as a friend, which is what I want. The only problem is I'm not totally sure what he's thinking about when we're talking. I mean, is he really into me or does he just like me as a friend? How do you KNOW that?"

Those comments are based on the emails that wind up in my in-box weekly. Clearly, feeling less than your usual confident self around boys is a common problem, and the first comment above nailed the major reason: guys are so *different* from us females.

Ya think?

Girls who have older brothers don't seem to have as many issues with being tongue-tied or babbling aimlessly when a guy shows up on the scene. They know guys are different, alright, but they're used to it. For most of the rest of the teenage female population, these mystery creatures can make them feel like somebody else is suddenly living in their body.

The questions fall like confetti:

Do they want to talk about the same stuff girls want to talk about?

Do they care about the same things you do?

Do they even speak the same language?

And then there's the energy they put off. Now, that's *definitely* different from ours. They have a certain strength that makes a young woman feel safe and yet for some reason scared spitless at the same time. It can be delicious—or it can be more dizzying than the Goliath at Six Flags.

> *"A guy can't just tell you he likes you. He either stares at you twenty-four/seven or acts obnoxious every time you come around or tries to be all cool like he's waiting for YOU to make the first move. Then if you do, you feel like a moron when he looks at you like 'Where did you get THAT idea?'"*

> *"You can't tell if a guy actually likes you, or if he's just a big flirt. There's this guy in my English class who one minute will act like I'm the only female in there, and then the next minute he's doing the same thing with another girl. What's up with that?"*

> *"Guys do the stupidest things to try to impress you. Why would anyone think that bragging about how he punched somebody in the face would do it for you? And then they spit like they're all bad . . . I mean, seriously, who goes for that?"*

The dilemma is that we like guys *because* they're so totally different from girls. And yet that's also the reason they drive us bonkers, cause us to doubt ourselves, and pretty much make what used to be a fairly sane world seem like it needs some serious medication.

What the Guys Say

"When a girl likes you, she'll stare at you and never leave you alone."

But just because guys are different doesn't mean they're impossible to understand. In fact, you have a far better chance of getting what *guys* are about than they have of getting *you*.

What the Guys Say

"I think guys are more direct than girls. Girls use more subtle tactics than guys."

One, because boys aren't generally as mature as girls of the same age. It's a scientific finding, really. The biggest difference between a girl's brain and a boy's brain is not the speed of development (girls don't get smarter faster!) but the *way* their brains develop. Girls get language and fine motor skills earlier while boys get first dibs on the targeting and spatial memory. In other words, they can get fixated on something (no kidding?) and remember how to get places, that kind of thing. (Which is why they hate to even ask for directions at the mall!) Explains a lot, doesn't it?

And two, as complicated as guys may seem, they don't see themselves that way. When it comes to relationships, they want things to be much simpler than they actually are, at least in our view. Of course they have feelings that go deep, but many, many of them don't know what to do with them yet and won't until they're at least in their late teens. For now, some guys are going to keep those feelings at bay by immersing themselves in whatever they're into: sports, video games, punching each other, and burping—not necessarily in that order.

Their seeming simplicity doesn't mean they're "stupid" or "underdeveloped." There's a richness in some guys that you may not notice for years to come. It may mean, again, that it's easier for you to comprehend them than vice versa. That puts you at an advantage. While thirteen-, fourteen-, and fifteen-year-old guys are still showing off for you and performing for each other, you have an opportunity to observe them, analyze them, and maybe

What the Guys Say

"What a lot of guys don't get is that girls and guys just think differently. That's where all the drama comes in."

even befriend a few of them. This is your time to find out what makes them tick and then go in for a closer look at a few individuals who you're interested in as friends.

So while some guys your age are just now waking up to the realization that there are even knots to untangle in the boy-girl thing, you can start untying them and make things a whole lot smoother for both of you. Let's start with your particular snarls and snags.

The Twitter Version

Accept the fact that you'll never completely get guys, because their brains are biologically different from ours. It wouldn't be that interesting otherwise. Less frustrating, but boring.

What's Going On with Me?

Check EACH statement about guys that mystifies you, or at least makes you say, "Don't you just hate that?" All of these, by the way, come right out of the mouths of your peers.

_____ "Some guys aren't even that cute, but they have flirting down to a serious art form. And, unfortunately, it works."

_____ "People will tell you a guy likes you, but he acts like you're a total pain in the tail."

_____ "One minute they're still absurd little pains, and then they'll turn around and do something totally sweet and understanding."

_____ "A guy can't just tell you he's interested in you. He has to play some kind of game with you so you don't know what you're supposed to be doing."

_____ "There doesn't seem to be any difference between them (a) flirting with you because they like you and (b) flirting with you because they can."

_____ "They do lame things to get your attention—but if YOU did the same thing, they'd laugh right in your face."

_____ "One will be all friendly to you until his friends come around, and then you're either invisible or he totally starts dissing you."

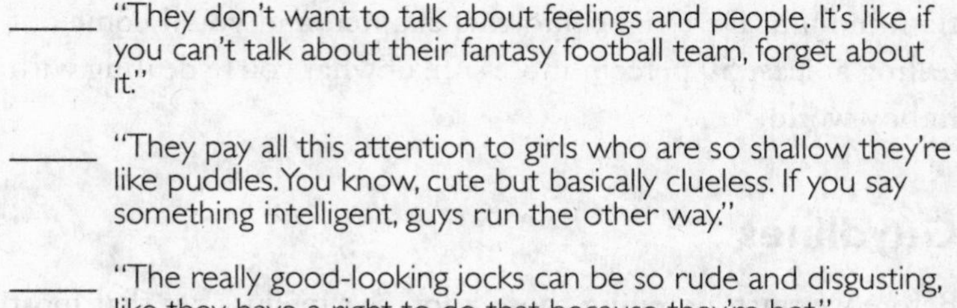

_____ "They don't want to talk about feelings and people. It's like if you can't talk about their fantasy football team, forget about it."

_____ "They pay all this attention to girls who are so shallow they're like puddles. You know, cute but basically clueless. If you say something intelligent, guys run the other way."

_____ "The really good-looking jocks can be so rude and disgusting, like they have a right to do that because they're hot."

Now count your checkmarks and see what your "score" might tell you. Remember: this is not a test you pass or fail, or a judgment call, or even an "on a scale of one to ten, here's how cool you are" kind of thing. It's just a way to see just how many mysteries you still have to solve.

If you have from **0 to 2** checks, you may have guys pretty well figured out. Or you don't see the need to figure them out at all! Do you have older brothers? Boys you've always hung out with? Do you just have a natural gift for getting along with guys? Or doesn't it bother you that guys are confusing and obnoxious at times? Consider yourself lucky, but read on. You just never know what you might learn—or where you've been misled!

If you checked from **3 to 6** of the statements, you aren't completely in the dark but you definitely have some questions. Think of it as natural curiosity and scope out the rest of this chapter for those answers you still need.

If you have between **7 and 10** checks, that doesn't mean you're hopeless when it comes to understanding guys. Your mystification probably comes from not spending much time with them in the past or from a basic personality that makes you sensitive to human behavior—especially when it seems less

What the Guys Say

"I'm not very good at being able to tell if a girl likes me. Normally one of my friends or a friend of the girl has to tell me. And they're like, 'Duh—it's right in your face!'"

than human! Dive right into this chapter, and you'll come out feeling at least 50 percent more sure of what you're dealing with in boy-world.

Guydlines

Before we start loosening those knots, let me just say that most of what you'll find here are general statements that apply to most teenage boys. Individually, they're as different from each other as you are from every other girl reading this book. If we gave *guys* a quiz . . . well, forget that. Guys don't usually do self-surveys unless it's required for them to get into college. Just know that in your experience with males, you'll find exceptions to just about everything we talk about, but when guys *do* behave in those what-is-he-*thinking* ways, it's usually for the reasons you're about to read.

Overall, guys between the ages of thirteen and seventeen have the following going on to some degree:

They're dealing with puberty and its accompanying hormones too. Before you start squalling that *they* don't have to put up with breasts and periods; take it from me, they have their own challenges on the body-changing scene. They've got voices that do unpredictable things at the worst possible moments. They're getting even hairier than you are (and on their faces). You think *your* feet are too big and your arms too long? They've got that in spades. And that's just to name a few of their issues. Yeah, they can get away with a few more zits than girls can, but they have to start *shaving* over those babies. They've got the same oily scalp thing going on, but unlike you, if they get too into hair products, their buddies are all up in their business.

They're taught practically from birth not to show their feelings, but, man, do they have them. Hormonally and developmentally they're starting to like girls, but they can't just go around saying, "I really dig you. Let's hang out and see where this goes." The thought of that scares most guys to death. If they actually do it, they never hear the end of it in the locker room, because everybody else is afraid *they're* going to have to do it. That drive to get close to girls is powerful enough. They can't get involved with the emotional stuff too.

Guys process their feelings differently than girls do. Especially as teenagers, they usually see things more in black and white. It's either good or it's bad. It's cool or it's lame. You're in or you're out. So, he likes a girl, she doesn't like him, he moves on. He likes a girl, she likes him, he stops liking her—he assumes she'll get over it. They definitely don't run to the bathroom crying with their friends when it doesn't work out (even if they're emotional about it in private).

Unlike you, the guy-girl thing isn't as much about feelings for them. The comment about it seeming like a game to find out if you like them and they like you? At this point for some guys, it *is* more about the game than the relationship. That doesn't mean they're all players. Sure it's fun (for them!), but most of that playing also involves playing it safe. A guy will hide behind the game so that if the girl doesn't turn out to be interested, he doesn't look like a fool, no matter how he might actually have felt. Basically, many are SO not ready for a relationship.

What the Guys Say

"I want to date different girls rather than have a relationship with just one. I can't see myself doing that."

Most adolescent GUYS don't have GIRLS figured out yet! Which is why a lot of guys do things like travel in inseparable groups—the whole safety-in-the-pack mentality. It's why they brag or turn everything into a joke or act bored and call it cool. They don't know what you want, so some of them fall back on behaviors that worked for them in fourth grade. That's a fact, actually. While they can look a little like men, in certain situations they may actually be less mature than they were at ten, before the hormones kicked in. They aren't really that immature all the time. Just around you.

> **What the Guys Say**
> "I admit that when I like a girl, I totally try to impress her."

Flirting isn't really much different for guys than it is for girls. It's like a test: *Do you notice me? Do you think I'm kinda cute? How long can I keep you interested?* Notice the repetition of "I" and "me." Flirting is about the flirt-ER, not the flirt-EE. That doesn't automatically make it bad (as we'll see in chapter three), but it does make it easily misunderstood. Some guys don't even know they're doing it. Others make it a career. But in the end, it's their way of reassuring themselves that they're charming and attractive.

That's the general idea. Let's move on to some specifics that apply to various guys. Do I dare group them into types? Just don't tell *them* we're doing it.

The Jock. It doesn't matter how hunky he is and how much he likes to surround himself with women: sports and the opinions of his guy friends will almost always come before girls (or anything else) until he learns that there are other priorities. Maybe in his late teens. Early twenties. Thirties ... That's not to say that athletes aren't great guys. All that teamwork and physical discipline turns a lot of them into pretty terrific men. But right now, don't count on being the football captain's number-one focus.

The Gamer. He's so into Black Ops, World of Warcraft, or figuring out how to get his hands on the next midnight release he barely notices there are girls in the world unless you're wearing an Xbox or PS3 headset as jewelry. He'll chat you up if you, too, spend hours upgrading your tank, looting treasure chests, or enhancing your armor (and even then he likely only cares about how many achievements and defeated levels you've racked up). But that virtual world is his safe place right now. Don't be offended if he doesn't seem to see you. Either he doesn't, or you're still way too scary for him.

The Scholar. You may think of him as a brain, but he's not that different from the jock. He's focused on his mind and what he can put in there, what he can figure out, what he can invent. He'll catch up on his girl skills later, but don't dismiss him; he's great friend material. It doesn't occur to him to play the game, and he can actually carry on a conversation if you get him on the right topic.

The Player. All he seems to think about is girls! That can come from a lot of different places—from a surplus of hormones to an ego that needs constant feeding because of, say, issues at home. His supposed affections are not to be taken seriously, but he can be enjoyed, especially if you see what he's up to. Try not to be judgmental, even as you give him a wide emotional birth. Sometimes that need to be the campus ladies' man comes from a place of deep pain. But don't try to psychoanalyze him or rescue him. You can't. Just know that he may not be as cavalier as he pretends to be.

The Artist. Once again, this guy is focused, whether it's on his music, his drawing, his poetry, his acting—whatever. Because he's sensitive enough to create art, he's also sensitive enough to get girls, and to be hurt by them. More likely to talk about ideas and feelings, he's also more likely to get his heart broken. While he may seem to be all about the band he's in or the theatrical role he's playing, his relationships with girls can be important to him. And they can also be more about romance and all its trappings, as part of his whole romantic persona. Just like every other teenager on the planet, he's figuring himself out. He's simply more aware of it than most guys.

The Tortured Soul. On the surface, this guy may look like a full-out loser. Drugs, maybe. Alcohol. The I-don't-care-how-I-look attire and hygiene. Can't get it together in school. No passion for anything except putting everything down, and even that he does with either boredom or anger. He's either given up already, or he just wants to get back at the world for making his life miserable—whether it actually has or not. He's got issues. He might reach out to a girl to ease some of his pain. If you're within reach, back off kindly. You can't fix him. Pray? Yes. Solve his problems? No. Besides, all that baggage makes a healthy relationship just about impossible.

The Really Nice Guy. Friendly, considerate, never in trouble—that's this guy. You can approach him without worrying that he's going to give you the "You're kidding, right?" look. You could tell him your most secret of secrets and they would stay that way. You could do something terminally embarrassing and he would never tease you about it. He's sweet. He listens. And for the life of you, you can't figure out why you're not attracted to him. That's because he has a lot of competition from guys who can act like cave men but are at the same time fascinating. This guy is going to get his share of "You're a nice guy, but . . ." from girls he falls in love with along the way, but years from now he's going to be the husband about whom other women say, "Why couldn't I find one like him?" Meanwhile this kid may be the best friend you'll ever have, so be careful with his feelings. Respect him for who he is. Let him show you that guys on the whole can be a pretty wonderful gender, once they grow up.

Whether any of these guys admits it or not, they are generally fascinated by you and the mysterious changes that are happening in you—not only your new figure and the natural swing that has swung into your walk, but your blossoming maturity and your confidence that may be way ahead of theirs. You are far more different from them than you have ever been before, and they are both entranced by that and terrified of it.

Which means that regardless how they come off, they are afraid of you to some degree—because you have an effect on them you don't even know about. Without even realizing it, you make them blush and trip over their feet and stutter like Porky Pig. You think *you* are awkward around *them*? That's nothing compared to the goofy way they feel every time you walk by with your female secrets. So what do they do with that?

Flit like crazed moths from girl to girl.

Pretend they don't notice you.

Act like men and then realize they're acting like men and scare themselves and regress into little boys.

Salivate over girls who wouldn't give them the time of day.

Look for approval from guys who are just as clueless as they are.

Spit out of car windows, wear ball caps over their eyes, walk around with their shoelaces untied.

There is no end to the romantic gestures.

You're changing too fast so they fall back on what has always worked: confusing the daylights out of you. At the same time, they want to touch you. Some of them will do it whenever possible. From "accidental" brushes in the halls to full-out hugs in the corners. From arm wrestling challenges to picking you up and carrying you around. From a poke in the side when something's mildly amusing, to an arm around your shoulders that stays there. Mostly, they're testing out their former theory that girls were just soft boys. They seem to need a lot of tests.

Day by day, though, they're maturing. More and more you'll see them breaking from their pack where they have to act according to the code and making themselves available for real conversation. You'll find out that one actually reads when his grade doesn't depend on it. That he likes the same music you do. That he isn't so much into sports as he is sci-fi or movies or camping, which doesn't exactly disappoint you. You might discover he has a sense of humor. That he cares about what you have to say. That he shares your faith.

Get him back with his buddies and he may not own up to any of the above, but one-on-one, he and others like him will become easier to get to know. Their energy won't freak you out anymore. It may make you feel softer, or glowy-er, or more confident. That's chemistry, and it's nice.

Of course, almost the minute you think guys might not have slime for brains after all, you come up against one who won't leave your complexion alone ("How's it going, Pizza Face??") or who mocks you every time you raise your hand in class, and actually talks to you as if you're a guy. ("Dude, don't you do anything but study?") But that kind does grow fewer and farther between. The good guys start outnumbering the bad.

The Twitter Version

Instead of being hard on the male gender as a whole, look at each guy as an individual. That's what you want them to do with you, right?

Then they present different problems. Not paying as much attention to you as you're willing to give them. Treating you like a treasure at church when his cronies aren't around and acting like you've become extinct when you see him at a soccer game, surrounded by his fellow belchers.

Still, there's hope for them. Though not all of them. Some will always be immune to being civilized when it comes to women. Some will take longer than others to realize they have to treat a girl like more than a good time or a casual possession if they want to have a relationship. But many of them will get it, a few even before their teen years are over, more by the time they hit their mid-twenties.

So in the meantime, what do you do with this sometimes maddening situation? Interesting enough, God has some answers for you. God did, after all, create them that way.

What was he thinking?

God on Guys

In the garden of Eden, Eve was lucky. The way the story unfolds in the Bible, she didn't have to grow up with boys becoming men. She came into being as a full-grown woman, made perfectly for a full-grown guy.

Really ticks you off about the whole eating the forbidden fruit and being thrown out of the garden thing, doesn't it? We could have had it so good! But the point is that God truly did create men and women to be completely different.

"Male and female he created them," the first creation story says (Genesis 1:27).

In the second account, God first makes the man out of dust and puts him in the garden alone. Then God realizes that's not working, which is the only time in either telling that God declares something he has done to be anything but "very good." *"It is not good that the man should be alone"* (Genesis 2:18). So God creates a woman out of one of Adam's ribs and presents her to him, and Adam is more than pleased (Genesis 2:18–24).

From the beginning, then, God intended for men and women to be different from each other. Hard as that is sometimes, it's a given. You can fight it, or you can accept it and celebrate those differences, because there it is. Unfortunately, God doesn't present your intended partner to you fully mature and say, "Here you are, bone of each other's bone, flesh of each other's flesh." You've got to go through the burping and the bragging and the baffling behavior. Fortunately, God's there to help.

One other detail of the creation-of-humans story is essential to getting through these years:

"So God created humankind in his image ..." (Genesis 1:27).

And just to be sure you don't miss it—

In the image of God he created them."

Then the story says:

"Male and female he created them."

Guys, as crass and confusing and confoundedly cute as they can sometimes be, are created in the image of God, just like you. The potential for awesome maturity and breathtaking character and splendid integrity lies deep in every one of them. Deeper in some than others, I'll give you that, but there nevertheless.

So not only will it make your life easier to try to understand guys and cut them some slack, you have an obligation to do it. Jesus underscores that much later, in the Gospel of Matthew, where he says:

"Do not judge, so that you may not be judged. For with the judgment you make you will be judged, and the measure you give will be the measure you get" (Matthew 7:1–2).

When you think about this in terms of guys, it kind of gives new meaning to the following verse about not pointing out the speck in your neighbor's eye before you remove the big ol' honkin' log in your own, doesn't it? Here we are saying, "Guys are so fickle! Guys are totally confusing! Guys are immature!" But have we noticed the stuff we do to them? A few insights from my teen guy informants:

"I'll like a girl because of the way she acts, and then when she finds out I like her, she'll act totally different."

"Girls can be so cruel when you ask them out, like, 'Uh, NO!', so if I like a girl, I just wait to see if she likes me first."

"Some girls think we're all the same, and we're not."

"A girl can totally twist your words. Like if she shows you a new dress she got and asks what you think and you say it looks nice and you go back to texting or watching a movie, the girl says 'You don't like it?' That annoys me because that's not what I said and now I sound like a jerk."

Over and over I hear that when a guy likes a girl, he'll try to help her out with things, like homework. Or he'll try to talk to her or text her frequently to get to know her better. The problem is when guys do this, girls seem to have the opposite of the desired response. As one girl put it, *"When a guy likes you, he just makes hints and hangs on you."*

Go figure.

The Twitter Version

God made guys the way they are for a reason. We may not get it, but we gotta go with it. They are a God-thing too.

Making It Real

The next logical step—and yes, there is a certain logic to understanding guys—is to do some observing. You'll want to do this unobtrusively, of course. Staring at a guy and then whipping out your notepad and jotting things down isn't the best approach. Just be intentional about noticing these kinds of things when you're around boys and see how it affects your view of them.

Their attempts at being funny—successful or not. Several of the teen guys I've interviewed said they purposely make jokes around a girl they like. If the girl likes the guy back, she'll usually laugh even though he's being "dumb and corny." (Hey, he said it, not me!) Does that make them seem less obnoxious and more, well, sort of endearing?

Their willingness to help. It can be pretty annoying when a guy acts like he knows everything and has no problem telling you, but a lot of times, if you listen carefully, he's trying to fix your problem. "You're using an outdated version of Windows" doesn't mean, "You're stupid when it comes to computers." It means, "I want to share my expertise with you because I want to impress you." Is there something so wrong about someone wanting you to notice them? Wanting you to know what's unique about him? Is that being phony, or just wanting to show himself in his best light? Don't you do the same thing?

What seems to push them away. Do you notice any guys registering this in their body language?

"Girls put on all this makeup, and to be honest, we don't care. We'd rather see their real faces."

"I hate it when a girl sends me a message on Facebook, and when I don't answer right away she sends me two more."

"It drives me nuts when girls change who they are just so you'll like them. I wish girls would just be them."

"I want to say to girls, 'Don't play mind games, because most of us can't figure you out. That's what we like about you, but don't try to rule us with it.'"

When you think about it, aren't their complaints valid? Can you see how avoiding those behaviors would give you a better chance of getting to know the real guy who's in there behind the scowling and the eye-rolling?

Give it a shot and see what happens. As you do, keep these two direct quotes from sixteen-year-old guys right in the front of your mind:

"Our minds are different, and we cannot read yours."

"We can be really stupid at times. We may even say the wrong thing and hurt your feelings accidentally. But that doesn't mean we hate you and don't care about you."

I think they speak for themselves, yes?

Mom, Dad ... Now Don't Freak Out

Keeping in mind the guidelines I offered in the parenting section of chapter one, take the next step and **ask your folks for their advice**.

No, really, I'm serious. Your mom and dad have been there, or you wouldn't exist. So, yeah, the world has changed dramatically since they were teens, but human nature is the same as it's always been. If possible, consult your dad (the former boy) on why guys act the way they do. Query your mom about her experiences with the male gender in her day. Tell them you're gathering data and want their input.

If you want them to feel respected and valued by you, this won't do it:

"Everything's different now than it was back then." (Insert *"WAY back then"* and you're toast.)

This might get you some useful information:

"You were my age once, so, like, what did you do when ______?"

Obviously if you just do it to lull them into a false sense of security while you go ahead and do whatever you jolly well please, this won't be effective. Your parents weren't born yesterday. They're going to see through insincerity and you'll be worse off than you were before you tried to have this conversation. Jot down some questions you really want answers to that your parents' past might actually give you some insights on.

How did you two meet?

What was it like when you were dating?

Did your parents approve?

Did you like each other at first sight?

When did each of you start to get interested in guy/girls?

Were you ever as clueless as I feel?

Then prepare to be surprised, if not delighted. You might actually see your parents in a whole new light—one that might even enlighten *you.*

The Twitter Version

Parents can be a great source of advice about guys if you get over yourself and ask.

If I'm Totally Honest ...

There is at least one change I could make in my attitude toward boys in general ... okay, maybe two ... which is:

____

____

____

[illegible] some [illegible] information.

[illegible] a [illegible] the [illegible] good [illegible]

Obviously, if you feel too [illegible] all [illegible] [illegible] take [illegible] [illegible] [illegible] do whatever you [illegible] [illegible] [illegible] [illegible] [illegible] [illegible] [illegible] [illegible]

[illegible]

What was it like when you were little?

Did you ever long [illegible]?

Did you like [illegible]?

[illegible] to get [illegible]?

What do you [illegible]?

[illegible]

Hypnotically Honest . . .

[illegible] generally [illegible]

3

"I Feel Like a Geek."

Understanding guys — as much as any girl is able to, right? — can help you feel at least a little bit less like an alien around them. But "a little bit" doesn't really cut it in situations like these from the lives of your sisters in confusion:

> *"I was at this church fun night thing, and me and the guy I sort of like were there. I think I lost my head and went a little wacko. I was giving him hugs (I wanted to kick myself) and following him and yelling while I was looking for him. I was so embarrassed, especially when I found out he doesn't even like me. Ugh!"*

> *"There's this new guy at church, and I'd like to get to know him just as a person because he seems interesting. He's not like all the other guys and is kind of a geek, but he seems comfortable in his own skin, which I think is pretty cool. He doesn't try to dress and act like the typical teenage boy, you know what I mean? My problem is I don't know what I should say. When I talk to my friends, I usually tease and joke with them, but I'm not sure how much of this I can do with him without seeming like I'm flirty or something."*

"Why is it that some girls are completely comfortable hanging out with guys? There's a girl in my youth group who's definitely like that. She doesn't really flirt, but guys seem to want to talk to her anyway. She's skinny and pretty and has shampoo commercial hair. Do you think guys hang out with her for that? Should I watch her and try to do what she does?"

The girls who posted these comments on my blog are ordinarily independent, confident, put-together young women. Get a guy in there, though, and suddenly they freeze up or go in the other direction and freak out. In short, they just can't seem to be who they usually are.

Sound familiar? Girls have confessed to all of the following. Maybe you can relate to ...

- fainting in front of the guy you like. (That's one way to get his attention.)
- generally jabbering on about nothing (and later feeling like an idiot).
- giggling hysterically for no apparent reason (while wishing something large would fall on your head and stop you).
- clamming up for fear of looking like you're flirting (even though, really, you just want to be friendly).
- staying totally away from a guy you actually like because you're afraid of getting too attached (even though you stood up in front of the whole class in third grade and announced which boy in there you were going to marry).
- never being able to think fast enough to say something smart or witty. (Ten minutes later, of course, when he's long gone, you're practically Tina Fey.)
- feeling your heart rate go up, unable to make eye contact with anything but the ground (and if other people are there watching, you're basically headed for a coronary).

- falling over a trash can while watching your crush out of the corner of your eye (or landing in his lap in a camp chair because your legs gave out at the nearness of him).

Seriously, what is up with all the klutziness around guys? They're just people, right? Why can't we just act normal around them?

How much time ya got?

Actually before we go into reasons (there are many) and solutions (there are a few), let's check out what your comfort level is when it comes to guys.

What's Going on with Me?

Read each of the following statements and choose the response that best fits you. Don't forget to be completely honest with yourself. Your answers won't be good or bad; they'll just be you.

1. When I'm in a group of people I know that includes guys I ...

a. love it!

b. can actually speak without being convinced that some guy is going to say, "Where did you come from?"

c. stay quiet and hope nobody thinks my breathing is weird.

d. wouldn't be there. At all.

2. When I wind up being one-on-one with a guy I ...

a. am jazzed.

b. know I'm going to say something stupid, but give it my best shot anyway.

c. might be able to get out an entire sentence without hyperventilating.

d. am out of there.

3. When I like a guy as a friend I ...

   a. hang with him the same way I do with a girlfriend (except maybe for the conversation topics!).

   b. am a little bit on guard because I don't want him to think it's something else.

   c. wouldn't even know where to start making friends with him.

   d. don't know any guys I would want as friends.

4. When I have a crush on a guy, I ...

   a. turn on the charm and see where it goes.

   b. suddenly can't think of a thing to say to him—or say ridiculous things I can't believe came out of my mouth.

   c. avoid him, because liking somebody that much freaks me out.

   d. Crush? You're kidding, right?

5. My crush ...

   a. knows I like him; I make sure of that!

   b. thinks we're just friends (acquaintances?), because I'm scared for him to know I like him. I mean, what if he doesn't like me back?

   c. doesn't know my name; make that my first initial.

   d. doesn't exist. Ew.

6. To me, the difference between flirting with a guy and just being friendly is ...

   a. not there; they're the same thing, aren't they?

   b. flirting is for somebody you have a crush on, and being friendly is for friends.

   c. flirting is fake and being friendly is real.

   d. nothing. They both sound like trouble to me.

7. When it comes to a boyfriend ...

a. I've already had one (maybe two).

b. I'm so not ready.

c. I can't imagine a guy wanting to be my boyfriend.

d. Don't even take me there.

Count up your a's, b's, c's, and d's, and let's see what they tell you about how this chapter can work for you.

If you had a number of a's (at least three or four), you're pretty much at home in guy world, and you probably make guys feel at ease around you too. You might be tempted to skip this chapter, but don't. Your natural boy-magnet status has some potential to lead you into situations you don't mean to get into, and the following chapter can point out the warning signs. It will also give you info for helping your more guy-challenged friends.

If you had a number of b's (at least three or four), you may feel like a geek a lot of the time, but you're farther along than you think. In fact, the caution you feel can serve you well. Still, you may be missing out on some of the fun of having guys as friends or enjoying a crush, so read on. A little confidence-building can go a long way.

If you had a number of c's (at least three or four), being around guys still paralyzes you. But that doesn't mean your social life is doomed. In this chapter, you'll see how to relax and find friendship among those formerly absurd boys, without getting into the romance that currently freezes your personality. There's plenty of time for romance later.

If you had a number of d's (at least three or four), you avoid guys whenever possible, either because all the ones you know have the maturity of newborn weasels, or you've had or seen some things go down that make you want to have no part of anything boy related. It's actually impressive that you've gotten this far in the book! Keep reading. You'll need this info eventually, and

What the Guys Say

The ways you can tell a girl feels awkward are:

"She doesn't talk to you. At all."

"She changes the subject a lot."

"She doesn't finish her sentences."

"It's easy to get her to blush and look away."

"Her cheeks go to bright-red-tomato stage."

when that time comes, you may be able to skip the awkward stage completely.

Wherever you are, you don't have to stay there. The why and the what next can help you move into a more confident place.

Guydlines

There are as many reasons for becoming a complete ditz around a guy you like or amid a bevy of boys as there are girls experiencing that annoying phenomenon. A few general principles might be of help to everybody:

1. The early teen years are generally awkward anyway. While some girls escape it (the luckies), most have trouble from time to time keeping fast-growing legs, arms, and feet under control. Your center of gravity is changing and your body doesn't move exactly the way it always has, so there's that to get used to. And then you have all this stuff that you're not entirely comfortable with yet. Budding breasts. Spreading hips. More curves in general. Not to mention the things you're sure you'll never be at ease with, that make you feel like an extraterrestrial: Skin that makes YOU think you look like you've been nailed with a double pepperoni (though nobody else sees it that way). A nose that suddenly seems out of proportion to your face (that was my issue). Trouble finding clothes that fit because your weight and height haven't equaled out yet. Hair that needs to be degreased like three times a day. Whose idea was it to have all this start just when you actually want to look cute for the opposite sex? Even if you're magazine-cover-girl material, you're probably still ultra-critical of your appearance, which can't help but make you self-conscious. Feeling self-conscious then manifests itself in acting like a klutz.

2. Boys seem to bring that basic awkwardness out in girls like the sun brings out freckles, puberty brings in pimples, evil brothers bring on fangs—you get the idea. Guys' new energy is unsettling, and you don't know what to do with it yet. It's not that much different from learning a new dance move or soccer skill or cheerleading routine. Just about everybody struggles with it at first.

3. You don't know what the results of your actions are going to be. Kind of reminds you of walking down a dark street at night. Something unexpected could jump out at you or come up on you from behind, so you creep along all crouched, looking over your shoulder, startling at every sound. You can't relax and take it in stride because you have no idea what's going to happen in this potentially dangerous situation. Not to make guys out to be stalkers, but for some girls the feelings of not knowing what will happen are similar.

"What if I let a guy get to know me and then he asks me out? I'm not allowed to date yet and I'm afraid I'll hurt his feelings or he'll think I led him on."

"What if I'm just friendly and some guy thinks I'm flirting, then he tells everybody and I get a bad reputation?"

"What if I try to talk to a guy and he ignores me?"

"What if I start a conversation with a guy and he looks at me like, 'Why would I want to talk to you?'"

"What if I say something totally dumb, and I have to just . . . change schools or something?"

> **What the Guys Say**
> "I can't tell if a girl's flirting with me. I feel stupid when I think she is and then find out she isn't."

4. It seems to matter so much. When you were younger, most of your self-esteem came from being accepted by your girlfriends and knowing that you belonged. You also had your parents and siblings, your activities, maybe your church family, and you were good to go. Now it seems like a lot of the girls you know are turning to guys to make them feel worthy and accepted. It's like the ones who have boyfriends are on a higher plane than the ones who don't. If a guy has a crush on you, then you must have something going on. If a lot of guys are friends with you, that means you're cool, and we gotta be cool or die, right? Whether having relationships of any kind with guys actually matters to *you,* it matters in the world you live in. And when something is significant, it tends to make us nervous.

Think about the way you feel when you go into a championship game or take the stage for your solo or sit down for a final exam. How you perform matters, and consequently the potential to choke and fail goes up about five notches. You like the boy, and it matters whether or not the boy likes you, which makes you anxious, so you do whatever it is you do when you get nervous (giggle, babble, pull in like a turtle), and, *voila!* . . . you feel like a geek.

It happens so fast you don't even have time to think about it. Until an hour later when you're beating yourself up and thinking you will die a spinster, *blah, blah, blah.* It's a wonder you can even squeak out a syllable in the presence of testosterone.

Obviously, the first thing to get a handle on is the mistaken idea that your whole worth as a female is wrapped up in whether or not guys find you appealing. That's really the most ridiculous thing I can think of. Seriously. The world you're living in right now may be telling you it's so, but in that respect, the world is totally lying through its teeth. The world doesn't get to decide the truth of that for you. You get to decide that. You get to decide to believe in and live by a basic truth, and here it is:

Basic Truth #2

Your true worth as a person comes from being loved by God as the unique individual you were made you to be. Nothing the world tells you can compare.

Don't even think about saying, "Try telling that to the kids at my school." Or, "You don't know what it's like to feel like a loser." First of all, you think I haven't been there? Me and about 90 percent of the women who've gone through middle and high school since I was a teenager? Talk about your nerds—my picture was next to the word in the dictionary. And yet, like so many people like me, somehow I had guy friends and then boyfriends, and eventually married an amazing man. You can too. But it won't be because you develop flirting skills or find a way to "fake it 'til you make it" or have a complete makeover.

It will be because you find your worth in who God made you to be out of total and unconditional love for you. Anything else is like plastic surgery on your soul.

Did I mention that it probably isn't going to be easy? That you might not truly blossom until you're in your twenties? That being the Scarlett O'Hara of the 21st century may not be a role you'll ever play? (You've heard of *Gone with the Wind,* right? About the chick who turned getting any man she wanted into an exact science?) Finding out who God made you to be and being that (instead of the false self we all tend to put on to try to cope with soul-stripping things like bullies, exhausted teachers, and a toxic culture) is a lifelong process. The beginning, now, is the hardest because teenagers can be critical, judgmental, narrow-minded, and thoughtless—present company excepted, of course. If you feel "different" you might think there is nowhere to run, nowhere to express that, no place where that's okay. But you can still do it. In terms of the guy scene, here's what that looks like:

What the Guys Say

"When a girl just happens to be sad and needs a hug when you walk by, that's flirting. When she just acts like a normal person and laughs with you, she's being friendly."

- Work on getting to the place in your mind where you can say, "Whether that boy (or boys in general) likes me doesn't make me or break me as a person. I'm pretty cool just being me. Really. I am."
- Stop watching TV or reading magazines for a while if you have to, and avoid conversations with friends about who likes who. Getting yourself clear often means dumping all the influences that muddy your thinking.
- Start looking at boys not as dangerous creatures you have to stay unattached from so you won't get in trouble or get your heart broken, but as potential friends, just the way you see girls as potential BFFs.
- If even thinking about a guy as a friend ties your tongue into a square knot, start small. Is there some guy you'd like to get to know, just because he's a great person? What is it about him that interests you? Ask him about that. Tell him why you find that fascinating. The fact that boys love to talk about themselves definitely works in your favor! If he acts like you're bothering him or like he thinks you're trying to flirt with him, you don't need him as your friend. That behavior says nothing about you and everything about him—as in, he has an ego the size of Montana. Move on.
- Watch the girls who seem completely comfortable hanging out with guys. What do they do that you think is appropriate and fun and something you'd like to be able to do? On the other hand, what do they do that makes

you think, "I could never do that. I don't even *want* to do that." For instance, you may admire the girl who can say to a guy without stumbling over her words, "Okay, it's obvious you're the only one in class who's getting this algebraic equation thing, so here's the deal—will you tutor me?" But you may be completely turned off by the girl who snuggles up to the guy in the cafeteria line and says, "I need you to be my protector today." I mean, *really?* Your best instincts will tell you to steer clear of the Miss I-Need-Your-Protection approach. A guy may seem to like the shamelessly flirty approach, but the relationship usually doesn't go too far from there. It's based on a game that can only be played for so long. But watching the genuine girl will demonstrate how to relate to guys according to your own authentic personality. If you're bubbly and fun, there's nothing wrong with telling him something hysterical you just saw go down in the hall. If you're more scholarly and he is too, strike up a conversation about the upcoming midterm. If you share a sarcastic wit, compare websites that cause LOL reflexes to kick in. He's a unique person, so are you. How else are you going to get to him know him if you don't show him who you are?

What if you have an actual crush on a guy, somebody you feel different around than you do the guys you just want to be friends with? A crush tends to bring out a girl's most bizarre behavior. The proverbial butterflies in the stomach seem to have a direct link with the blush reflex, the immobilized or runaway tongue, the loss of cognitive function. Just when you really want to show him what you're made of, suddenly what you're made of is Jell-O. What then?

As with guy friends, try to keep it in perspective. Ask yourself where

What the Guys Say

"When a girl's flirty, she's more touchy. You can't joke around with her the way you can with a girl who's your friend."

you really want this to go. Are you ready for a boyfriend? Do you hope this crush morphs into a relationship? Do you know what that will involve? Would your parents even approve? Or do you just want to enjoy the feeling and admire Crush Boy from afar and giggle about it with your friends? (The ones you trust with your life, unless you want your feelings broadcast with the morning announcements.) In either case, remind yourself that this cutie you're crushing on is 99 percent sure *not* to be the guy you spend the rest of your life with. As aflutter as you feel around him, you're not in love with him. The this-matters quotient is not very high. See these feelings and gentle flirtations for what they are: a fun part of being a young girl. Enjoy the glow.

By the way, for those of you determined to save not only your body but your heart for your future husband ... if you do develop a crush on someone who obviously isn't going to be your life partner, don't tell yourself you're "cheating" on the one who someday will be. I can't tell you how many girls have emailed me, feeling guilty because they get weak-kneed over a guy at thirteen or fourteen. "Shouldn't I be guarding my heart?" they want to know. Yeah, you should. But "guarding" it means don't give it away. Having a crush is more like feeling your pulse race, not offering up your still-beating coronary organ on a platter. Once again, don't fight how you feel. Just make wise choices about what you do with those feelings.

Some advice on handling a crush:

Get to know him as a friend. A crush can be blinding. While you're checking out those great shoulders and dreamy eyes, you might miss the fact that he's rude to teachers or always grabs the biggest piece of pizza at youth group. A crush is just infatuation if you don't really know the guy.

I advise against chasing Mr. Hottie. It's one thing to conveniently arrive at math class the same instant

What the Guys Say

"When a girl flirts, she compliments you on every little insignificant thing you do. It can seem really fake."

he does. It's another to text him every possible minute and plant yourself outside the locker room door when he's going out for soccer practice. Let the time you spend together happen naturally. Even though these days it's accepted that girls call guys, teen boys don't always like for the girl to take the lead, old-fashioned as that sounds. You could take your own survey among boys who are your friends, or your older brother's friends, and see what they say. Count on at least one of them to come up with, "It depends on the girl." He's no help. The days of waiting by the phone for the boy to call might be over, but the pursuing ought to be at least equal. If he isn't texting back, give it up.

Complicated intrigue isn't a good idea either. Like asking your friend, who is a third cousin to a guy that used to be your crush's best friend, to find out if your crush likes you. Or getting him to notice you and then pretending you don't notice him to see if he really wants to get to know you. Seriously, at this age, most guys aren't going to work that hard. Besides, if you really want to have a good friendship with him, why mess with his head? If you're bored, find a hobby! Surely you've seen games played, and seen them mess up what could have been a cool relationship. It doesn't have to happen.

What the Guys Say

"It really bugs me when a girl follows me everywhere."

About the worst thing you can do with a guy you're crushing on is try to act the way you think you need to act to get his attention if it isn't who you really are. If he seems to go for outgoing girls and you're the quieter type, then suddenly laughing uproariously in the lunchroom or trying to do a stand-up comedy routine in the middle of youth group might get him to notice you, but what are you going to do after that? Keep pretending to be the life of the party when you'd actually rather die than be in the spotlight? The truth's going to some out sooner or later. The same goes for playing the part of the helpless female when you're feisty and independent, or dressing like a hoochie mama because you've seen him drool over girls in jeans that fit like a second skin. Okay, so, no, you don't totally know who you are yet, but you do know who you're not. Don't go there—or he'll be noticing a girl who really isn't you.

It's so delicious to think about him, flirt with him, tell your girlfriends what he said and what you said. Those will be feelings you've never had before and you'll savor them. **But if you find that they're keeping you from, oh, doing your homework, spending quiet time with God, sleeping ... you'll definitely want to pray for God to help you refocus in a healthy way.** Think about it. Married people who are crazy in love and have committed their entire lives to each other still go to work, nurture other friendships, and go for hours without contacting each other on Facebook. Boys are just one part of your life. You don't *have* to do anything at all if you have a crush. If you leave it alone—or even if you don't!—I guarantee it will fade eventually. Many times, if a girl has a crush on a guy, it's because she senses that he likes her too, which can lead to a friendship that'll last or an attempt at a boyfriend-girlfriend thing that usually dies out at some point. We are not talking serious here. Keep that in mind.

If you do want to get to know your crush and find out if he has the same feelings for you, one of the things you'll want to understand is the concept of flirty vs. friendly. That also goes for those of you who like to hang out with mixed groups. The question always arises: *Is it all right to flirt and joke around with guys? Or is that leading them on?*

What the Guys Say

"Whether it's flirting or being friendly depends on the girl's intention. Friendly girls are everywhere, and just because they smile and are polite doesn't mean they like you. Flirting is a step beyond friendly, where you hold each other's gaze, talk in a way that shows you're interested, and smile a lot."

Some definitions can help you here.

To flirt, according to the dictionary, is to "throw quickly and jerkily" or to "wave back and forth quickly, as the bird *flirted* its tail." It isn't hard to see how the next definition developed: "to play at love without serious intentions." Ya gotta love that. When a girl flirts, she's like a bird, waving her little self back and forth. A quick dive in and then just as quickly back out. Nothing serious. Just play.

Looking at it that way, flirting could be a harmless, fun thing. Grabbing his ball cap and running off squealing while he chases you, the same way he pretends to bump into you as he's getting on the bus and then grins in that sort of heart-melting way. You're both throwing a cute little piece of yourself out there just to see what happens.

Or you could see it as dangerous. Toying with something shallow and meaningless. Just trying to get attention. Starting something you have no intention of finishing.

The word "intention" is the word that'll help you out here. It all comes down to *why* a person flirts. I can think of five reasons why girls do it. (I'm not sure if these apply to boys too. They probably aren't sure either, to tell you the truth.)

Girls may flirt because:

1. They like attention from boys.
2. Depending on how guys respond, they'll find out if they're attractive to the opposite sex without getting into heavy heartbreak.
3. It keeps things light. They want to have fun with boys without all the trauma and drama of a relationship.
4. They hope it'll lead to something more.
5. They have no idea, except that it makes them feel good.

Those reasons can be looked at in a number of different ways. Take getting attention from boys, for instance. Is that necessarily a bad thing? Is there something wrong with wanting to be noticed? Does it say somewhere in the Bible that the good people sit in a corner and try not to be looked at? If you have the urge to say, "*I don't want to have to flirt and play games to get some guy to notice me,*" then flirting isn't for you. Just be careful about judging the girl who does flirt when she interacts with boys. Quite frankly, drawing on a guy's arm with a Sharpie while he pretends to protest and is obviously loving it is not comparable to making out with the guy in the lunch room. The flirter isn't lowering herself. She's having a great time. So is he. A Sharpie war isn't leading them into a serious relationship they aren't ready to handle. It's a drawing with a permanent marker, not the road to marriage.

What happens sometimes is that those who aren't good at flirting don't get that it comes naturally to some girls. They don't understand that inherently flirtatious girls aren't consciously scheming to snag a guy who doesn't want to be snagged. Yeah, some girls *do* make absolute fools of themselves chasing after boys who couldn't care less. Those girls have a self-esteem thing going on and need our prayer, not our condemnation. But those girls who just enjoy the company of boys in a playful way are not committing a sin. Not having "serious intentions" is exactly where you *want* to be at thirteen, fourteen, fifteen, and sixteen!

What about the testing aspect—the finding out whether you're attractive to the opposite sex? It is normal, natural, hormonal, and God-ordained that you want boys to think you're pretty, fun, and great to be with. If we stop caring whether men want to be with us, humanity will die out. Whether you're interested in dating or have decided to wait until you're older to court or whatever, you probably wouldn't feel horrible if you found out a boy liked you. You've probably had some doubts about whether you're "going to be able to attract a (future) husband." That need to know is in there, and it's human.

So as we've said, flirting isn't good or bad in itself. It's all about what you intend by doing it. There are other behaviors that people confuse with flirting that just aren't—and they need to be avoided. I've narrowed them down to three:

Acting sleazy with boys. That means body language, actual language-language, ways of dressing, and intentions that suggest the girl has sex on her mind. It's the kind of thing that makes me want to go over and say, "Honey, you're so much better than that. Can we go to God with this right now? Oh, and would you put some clothes on first?" That isn't flirting, it's seduction. There's never a place for that when you're an unmarried woman. And definitely not when you're a teenager. Yikes.

Being fake with boys. This involves doing things that so aren't you, just to make a connection. Actually, fake is never a good idea in any kind of normal interaction with people. Some girls are more comfortable getting to know a guy by starting with something light and on-the-surface before they get to their shared interests, but that something light should always reveal a true personality trait, not one you're pretending to have.

Leading boys on. This is purposefully giving a guy the impression that you *like* him, when you have no intention of doing anything but playing with his affections. Never a good thing. That seems to happen when a girl is not so much interested in getting to know a boy as she is proving that she can have any guy she wants. Ya gotta have deep compassion for that, because usually it means there's something painful or empty happening inside.

Flirting isn't any of those. Nor is it an absolute essential. You are not less-than-a-real-girl if you don't flirt, and you are not a phony if you do. It's all about keeping your motives pure and your actions true to who you are, not who the world says every girl has to be.

What if as you're reading all this you get that funky, sinking feeling that some of applies to you? Maybe you're realizing that you try to shape yourself to be some guy's ideal, or you are sort of "addicted" to getting

What the Guys Say

"To me, it goes beyond flirting when a girl starts wanting to know you personally—starts showing you that she wants to know who you are."

male attention just because you can? If that's the case, don't beat yourself up. Go to God with it. Ask for God's help with being more real. Being aware is half the battle won. God can assist with the other half, which is exactly where we're going next.

The Twitter Version

Being as close to your true self as possible is what guys really like and what God likes. You'll like it that way too.

Hopefully you're feeling less awkward and unsure already. To really bring it home, we need God. Let's go there now.

God on Guys

I hope those insights and that advice take the edge off of your nervousness around guys. Some of it simply involves a shift in thinking. More of it has to do with what you really know, what beliefs determine how you behave. Not head-beliefs, but heart-knowing.

That is so hard. Even Paul had issues with it.

"I do not understand my own actions. For I do not do what I want, but I do the very thing I hate" (Romans 7:15).

He totally gets the concept of knowing in your head but not being able to act on what you know. In fact, he goes on for nine more verses making sure *we* get it. Fortunately, he offers a solution, which I think applies to the guy-things we're talking about. He says in verses 24 and 25:

"Who will rescue me from this body of death? Thanks be to God through Jesus Christ our Lord!"

Much as it may feel like it at times, your relationship with guys doesn't constitute a "body of death," but we've established that it does matter and can mess with your mind. The rescue comes from our Lord. Okay, no, he doesn't swoop in and put the right words in your mouth or give you a flash of what the object of your affections is thinking or steer you away from making a spectacle of yourself in front of Mr. Cutie . . .

Or does he? Paul goes on to point out that you don't have to be ruled by your "flesh" anymore. You don't have to obey the sweaty palms and the desperate dry mouth that come from being afraid you'll be rejected and forever unloved. He says, and ya gotta love this:

"You are in the Spirit, since the Spirit of God dwells in you" (Romans 8:9).

God has already "swooped in" and *will* give you the words if you're paying attention. Maybe not audibly, but by showing you the real person you've been made to be. It's like this:

You spend time everyday focusing on God. As a result, you see who you are. That means you behave more like you. And more like you. And more like you. So that when a new, oh-this-matters situation comes up, you barely have to think about what you're going to do or say. It's there. The Spirit of God dwells in you.

This obviously doesn't mean you'll never make a mistake or blurt out something inane or realize you've daydreamed yourself into iffy territory. It does mean that it will be natural for you to scurry back to God and get centered again on who God made you to be.

And that's going to be absolutely essential, because the only person you have any control over whatsoever is you. Being indwelt with the Holy Spirit isn't going to change how guys generally behave around you. It isn't going to alter the culture's attitude about all things male and female. You're going to have to take cover sometimes and remember God's only a breath away.

However, and this is good news, the more you are your authentic God-made self around the individual guys that you know, the easier it's going to be for them to be who *they* really are. They might not know why, mind you, but it's a start. One of my favorite quotes of all time is attributed to Francis of Assisi, who was reported as saying, "Preach the Gospel at all times and when necessary use words." Just by being who you truly are, you spread this good word:

"Whoever did want him, who believed he was who he claimed

and would do what he said, He made to be their true selves, their child-of-God selves" (John 1:9, *The Message*).

God's got your back on this. And your front. And your inside. The more you hang with God in concentrated chunks of time, the more deeply you're going to know that. And it's going to show. You won't necessarily become prom queen (although you can't rule that out . . .), but you'll be comfortable with who you are. And even if not every guy will realize it, there is nothing more attractive than an authentic human being.

Know it. It is a basic truth.

Basic Truth #3

The only power you truly have is the power to be who you were made by God to be.

Making It Real

"The whole guy thing with me is WAY better than it used to be. I don't have any desperate crushes on any guys. I don't think about guys 24/7. And I'm not all freaked out when I have to talk to a guy like he's an alien. I used to not talk to guys at all. But now that's all fine . . . I mean, sometimes I still find myself slipping, and I have to ask God to help me focus on him. But my attitude towards guys in general is way better than it used to be."

What a great place to be, huh? Every girl can get there. It's a matter of taking one step at a time. If you want to inch forward, you can try any of the steps below that apply to you. Or just think about them and pray about them for when you're ready.

If you feel like you completely lose your personality when you're around a boy, name one reason why the real you, the you that you're most comfortable being in other situations, wouldn't be accepted by that boy. Just one reason. I bet you can't do it. What does that tell you? If you *can* name one trait that a particular guy would snicker at, consider whether he's somebody you want to be friends with anyway.

If you have a crush a mile wide on a guy, but you either turn into a zombie when you're with him or can't stop running off at the mouth about nothing, imagine him saying to you, "Let's be friends. You wanna hang out?" (Remember, I said "imagine"!) How would you act around him then?

If you find yourself developing an instant crush on any guy who looks your way, make a list of the characteristics of the perfect guy to spend time with as a friend. You might include something like, "A sense of humor that isn't based on putting people down," or "Is pretty much friendly to everybody, not just 'the cool kids.'" If a crush comes close to that list, think about being friends with him. If he doesn't, you might be more in love with love itself. Watch a chick flick instead!

If guys fall for you even when you're just being friendly, get a trusted friend to tell you what she sees when you're around boys. Does your friendliness look like flirting? Like you're interested in being a girlfriend? Is there anything you want to change? Or do you think guys just need to get a clue? This is going to require some big-time honesty from both you and your friend.

If you're convinced all guys are jerks, choose one guy you know of and study him (without him knowing it, obviously). See if you can come up with one thing about him that doesn't totally annoy you. Got that? Try another one. This exercise isn't designed to make you boy crazy. It's to help you see that guys are decent human beings inside there somewhere.

Remember, these are just baby steps, not magic solutions. Every road is traveled by putting one foot in front of the other.

Mom, Dad ... Now Don't Freak Out

One of the hardest things about the awkward-with-boys stage is that it often feels so lonely. You can become convinced that you're the only girl who isn't beating guys off with a stick, which leads to being too embarrassed to talk to your friends about it, especially if they seem to get male attention just by showing up. Before you know it, you've lost all perspective and have come to the conclusion that no guy is ever going to look your way. If you're a boy magnet yourself, it might be hard to discuss your issues with your friends because all they can say is, "You can have any guy you want. Don't even go there with me!"

What you need is someone to talk to who loves you unconditionally and has probably been there before you. Who meets those qualifications better than your parents?

Before you protest, hear me out.

We've already established that some parents get nervous (okay, they freak out) when daughters get interested in boys. Moms and dads simply want to protect their girls from getting hurt and messing up their lives. They sometimes make quantum leaps, in this case from "She thinks guys are cute" to "She is going to get pregnant and all our dreams for her will go down the tubes." That's no different than you going directly from "I just don't know what to say to boys" to "I'm going to be alone for all time."

I maintain that you can help each other out with this. See if this makes sense to you:

Your parents need to be reassured that your interest in guys is a normal, healthy part of your development. They need to know what you're thinking right now—whether you just want some guys as friends, or you want to feel comfortable in a group that has guys in it, or you really, really like a guy and he likes you but you're not sure where to go with that. They won't flip out if you go to them with that information, as long as you present it in a way that says, "You're my parents and I trust you. You're the people I want to be able to come to with this stuff." It's doubtful that anything you tell them is going to be as disturbing as what they fear, believe me.

They may also have some great insights. Maybe your mom

was a basket case with guys when she was your age too, and then she gradually found her self-confidence. Just hearing her story could be a huge boost for you. Your dad (previously a teenage boy) could undoubtedly tell you what things made him go "huh?" about teenage girls. He's the man who loved you first. Once you get him beyond, "No, you don't like boys. I'm forbidding you to," he might want to help. Ask him some direct questions. Give him a scenario and see what he thinks.

If the chances of you having a conversation like that with either of your parents are as good as you winning the lottery, start with a different topic. Approach them with something not so close to your heart, like the girl drama you've observed or the math teacher who's giving you nightmares. Show that you really want their wisdom. Give mature feedback when they ask about the things going on in your life. It'll pave the way for a later discussion about guys.

Parents don't willingly stop thinking of their offspring as children. It's up to you to show your parents that they're ready for the next level in your relationship. Do it in your most respectful and authentic way, and Mom and Dad will hopefully be ready too.

> **The Twitter Version**
> You can change parent talks from lectures to discussions. Just ask the right questions.

If I'm Totally Honest ...

I think if the right guy knew this about me, he would really like me:

____

____

____

"Can We Just Be Friends?"

"Here's what I want: good guy friends that treat me with respect and just want me to be me."

I hear that above quote from girls a whole lot more than I hear, "I just want a boyfriend!" And why not? One of my bloggers puts it this way:

"My thing about guys is that I don't want to get romantically attached to someone at this stage of my life, and there's a big difference between being romantically attached to a guy and just being . . . well . . . attached to him. Kind of like your brother. You're not attached to the boy romantically, but you're still mightily attached to him whether you like it or not—whether you even know it. For me, it's easier to be around guys when you think of them as a bunch of your crazy brothers. You can enjoy them for who they are, because as we with brothers know, it's impossible to make a brother quit doing the things that drive you utterly insane. You just learn to live with their insanity and have fun with them all the same."

She makes it sound so reasonable, so simple. So fun. And yet like everything else about guys, somebody somewhere made it complicated.

"The boys in my grade at church aren't allowed to mix with the girls, and that's a tad annoying because some of the best friends anyone can have are boys."

What the Guys Say

"At least half my friends are girls."

"I've always had a lot of guy friends, and I don't see what the big deal is. But other people think I have all these crushes, especially if I ask a boy for his email address so we can chat back and forth now and then. They make me wonder if it's even okay to have FRIENDS!"

It *is* okay. It's just different from friendships with girls—big surprise, right? If you want guy friends, you can have them. It really is as simple as that. Let's start with where you are when it comes to boys as buds.

What's Going On with Me?

After reading each statement, choose the number that matches how true it is for you. There are no right or wrong answers—just honest ones.

5—totally true
4—kind of true
3—I want it to be true
2—never true
1—never going to be true

_____ 1. I know from experience what kind of friendships you can have with guys.

_____ 2. Friendships with guys are great.

_____ 3. In some respects, friendships with guys are sometimes better than friendships with other girls.

_____ 4. I have friendships with guys no matter what other people say.

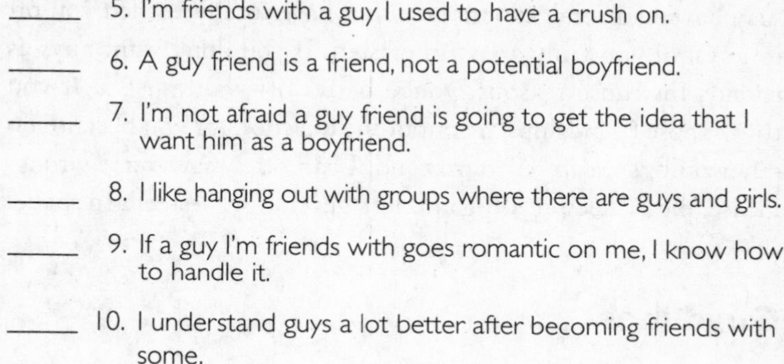

_____ 5. I'm friends with a guy I used to have a crush on.

_____ 6. A guy friend is a friend, not a potential boyfriend.

_____ 7. I'm not afraid a guy friend is going to get the idea that I want him as a boyfriend.

_____ 8. I like hanging out with groups where there are guys and girls.

_____ 9. If a guy I'm friends with goes romantic on me, I know how to handle it.

_____ 10. I understand guys a lot better after becoming friends with some.

Add up your numbers and jot down your total: _____ Remember, this is not like a score on the SAT. It just tells you how much you can learn from this chapter.

If your total is between 50 and 43, being friends with guys is as natural for you as breathing. Consider yourself blessed. There are still some things to be aware of so give this chapter a thorough reading. You never know what you might add to your current wisdom.

If your total is between 42 and 35, you're probably working on it, but you may still have a few doubts. This chapter will help you start to smooth those out. Pay close attention to the sections that focus on your particular questions.

If your total is between 34 and 22, you may dream of those friendships that seem to come so easily to some girls, but you're still at the wishing stage. If you're not sure how get beyond that, you'll find ways to change your thinking so you can count a guy or two among your besties.

If your total is between 23 and 16, this is all still pretty foreign to you. Don't feel socially challenged! This is just strange new territory, and this chapter can be something of a map. Remember, one step at a time.

If your total is between 17 and 10, chances are you're squirming in your seat and thinking about not finishing this book! You may have had some experiences that have totally turned you off to guys, or you truly aren't interested. If you don't want guys as friends for those reasons, you're better off waiting. But if you think those friendships are out of the question for you because no guy would want to be your friend, I can safely say you're wrong. Please, please keep reading and let's get that self-esteem in shape.

Guydlines

Before we move on, I want to make sure you understand that having guys as friends isn't a *requirement* for being a real girl. You're not a social reject if you choose not to take one on as a buddy. This is all about opening up the *possibilities* for friendships that could add a whole new dimension to your life.

Why is that? Your peers can tell you.

- "*I like hanging out with guys because they aren't as fussy and dramatic as some of my girlfriends. They're straightforward and honest.*" Girls who've befriended guys their age say they can talk to them about some things their girlfriends just don't get. They don't have to worry about gossip or having every word they say picked apart, because for all their other faults, guys aren't usually into either of those. There's very little "walking on eggshells," as one girl puts it. You're not going to compete with him for other guys' attention or for the coolest outfit or the best hair, so there isn't that to deal with. If you swear him to secrecy, it's like he's under oath in a court of law. And as for grudges, some girls say guys don't hold them. *"Have you noticed that's something girls are particularly good at doing? We hold a grudge against our friend for three days after they get mustard on our fave T-shirt, whereas between guys it seems to last a total thirty seconds!"* Basically, most of boys' lingering absurdity disappears when you let them relax and simply be.

- *"The more you hang around with guys, the more you'll get used to just talking. One guy came up to me the other day and said, 'Do you actually like people this much or are you not normal?'"* If you practically go into a catatonic state when it comes to boys, thinking of one as just another person to be around can do wonders, especially when you discover (and you will) that they can be funny, caring, smart, dependable human beings.
- *"I'm glad I've had lots of experience with guy friends, because I have the ability to just say 'I'm not impressed' when other boys flirt with me inappropriately, which throws them off guard and gives me a chance to get out of there!"* What you can learn about guys in general from your friendships with a few goes beyond just being able to stand up to players and other assorted guys-acting-like-jerks. An honest friendship with a guy can let you in on how they think (and, yes, they do think), what they enjoy in a girl, what females do that makes them crazy. If you store up that information now, you'll have it to draw on when you reach the age to be serious about a relationship.
- *"I often wonder if I seem stupid or immature or if my appearance is just totally dorky. But when I look at my guy friend I realize he's not afraid to act or look like a fool around* me!*"* An authentic guy can teach you a lot about being genuine. He can bring out the best in you, the real you.

The only drawbacks to having friendships with guys seem to be the ones other people create—people who just don't get that you *can* be buddies with a boy.

- *"Sometimes my girlfriends drive me nuts because they tease me every time I talk to a guy I'm friends with. If I strike up a casual conversation with him, I get the look from them and the little eyebrow thing that clearly says they think I LIKE him. He's just a friend!"* There are people who think it's impossible for a girl and a guy to even have a conversation without it turning into a scene from a romance novel. Most of them are other girls who haven't had the experience themselves or who see every guy as a possible boyfriend (and can't see why you don't too).

> **What the Guys Say**
> "Friendships with girls are cool as long as you both agree that you're only friends. Otherwise, it gets awkward."

- *"My parents—well, mostly my dad—don't even want me to be friends with guys. They say it's a 'slippery slope,' whatever that is."* People correctly use the term "slippery slope" for things like cheating, as in, "once you start borrowing somebody's homework to check your answers, it's a slippery slope to just flat out copying it." It gives you the image of starting something you can't stop. While guy friends have been known to become boyfriends, those friendships are not automatically destined for something serious. They aren't "starter relationships."
- *"I once liked this really nice boy. He tried to make friends, but my church doesn't believe in dating so I got freaked out and kind of pushed him away. I pretended to ignore him and never even said hi to him and now I feel bad. I think I missed out on a good friend."* Yeah, some churches don't think guys and girls should be friends until they're old enough to think about courtship and marriage, and that can be a problem if you don't exactly agree. The thing is, most of them don't "absolutely forbid it."

So if you'd like to have guys in your circle of friends and there's freedom for you to make that decision, I have some suggestions for you. For those of you who already enjoy those relationships, these might help with any speed bumps you're encountering.

Start with the right mindset—and "be afraid" isn't it. If you're scared to have a friendship with a boy because you think it might go too far somehow, remember that you don't see a guy, decide he's your future husband, and go after him the way you do a college degree or first chair in the orchestra. Instead, your long road toward marriage is a process of learning what boys are about, what you want in a partner, what's attractive about you, and what it feels like to have the kind of friendship that should be the foundation for any long-term relationship. The very safest and healthiest way to do that is to be friends with guys. If you do, then when you meet HIM, you will still be pure, as so many of you want to be, but not so hopelessly terrified that you have no idea what to do.

So look at boys as people, the same way you do girls. One of my bloggers says she doesn't "draw an imaginary line" between girls and boys, and I like that. Rather than stating your goal as "I want to be friends with guys," it makes more sense to say, "I want to get to know that particular guy because I think we'd have a good time together." If there's actually a guy, or several, who seems like he'd be cool to just hang out with, you're onto something. If not, it's better not to look for a boy to befriend just because he's male. Says one girl who has a bunch of guy friends, *"Sometimes it's hard to control the whole unintentional-flirting thing with them because, well, I'm a fifteen-year-old girl! But I just try to think of them as brothers, not as possible future husbands."* You can bet the *guy* isn't going there!

Remember that a guy is a mere mortal. Just because he's taller, stronger, and exudes that eyebrow-singing energy doesn't mean he's powerful. He actually has no more power than you do. Remember Basic Truth #3: the only power any of us has is the power to be who we were made to be. I'll say it again: what's the guy going to do if you say hi to him or ask how he thinks he did on the algebra test? If you're sure he's going to guffaw in your face or immediately think you're trying to flirt with him, he's

What the Guys Say

"There's a relational attraction that makes a guy and a girl friends to begin with. But that can jeopardize the friendship so you have to be aware of that."

not the guy you want as a friend anyway. That kind of response tells you he's operating under a gigantic sense of his own importance. This mere mortal can't hurt you. The only one he's hurting is him, by depriving himself of your amazing company. Chances are a guy you feel comfortable enough to strike up a conversation with isn't going to blow you off. If he's the decent guy you have him pegged for, he'll be friendly right back at ya.

The way you get things rolling comes from whatever it is that makes you want to be friends with the guy in the first place. He plays soccer (tennis, field hockey, or video games) and so do you? You have a ready-made conversation starter. You guys go to the same church and have exchanged eye rolls across the room when everybody else is acting like youth group is a singles mixer? There you go—instant connection. Did you see him reading *Lord of the Rings*, which you practically have memorized? How can you *not* talk to him? That's the whole idea; a friendship, any friendship, unfolds naturally. Be friendly and honest and interested because you genuinely are. That's hard for anybody to resist.

Don't worry about your friends wanting to pair the two of you up or accusing you of being a shameless flirt. In fact, don't even get into that discussion with other people. If friends is what you and this guy are, that will become obvious and people will find something else to whisper about. When you get right down to it, it truly doesn't matter what people think when you're behaving with honesty and integrity and sisterly love. If you don't want their gossip to ruin your thing with your boy buddy, tell him what they're saying and laugh it off together. And don't be shy about telling your girlfriends to back off and get a clue. (Okay, so you'll be nicer than that ...) Honestly, if those BFFs can't respect your feelings, they aren't BFFs.

If as you get to know Friend Guy you find yourself developing a crush on him and you don't want that kind of relationship, don't think you have to stop hanging out with him. Usually the urge to talk about naming your future children will pass, especially if you don't dwell on your feelings—daydreaming about the two of you walking along the lake holding hands, etc. That part will probably fade and you'll still have the friendship. Crushes are fleeting. Friendship is a whole lot more enduring.

What the Guys Say

"I think if a girl you're friends with wants more than just friendship and you don't, you shouldn't start dating her just because you feel bad."

None of this is about needing guys in your life. It's about needing good healthy *relationships* in your life, whether they're girls, guys, adult mentors, family members, or the little kids you babysit. All the same principles apply. If it's real, you're good to go. Follow the lead of one of your same-age sisters:

"I have to be 100 percent me around people, otherwise they might be disappointed if I act as someone else and they like that more. If they accept my geekiest and klutziest, it can only get better!"

A word (or more!) about guys online. Girls frequently confide in me that it's so much easier for them to establish a friendship with a guy on Facebook or via email or even texting.

"I met this guy on a website for kids with the same chronic illness I have. We chat a lot and he seems like a really nice guy. I'm just not really sure what to do about any of it. I mean, I really like him, but he lives so far away . . . I'm just really confused."

"I've been talking to a guy I know on Facebook for the last few nights and he's very interesting. He's eighteen and I'm fifteen, but I like that he actually uses intelligent-sounding words and is smart. I wouldn't want to go out with him, but as a friend he seems cool. And yet, do I really know him?"

"I was talking on Facebook to a guy I've only met once in person and he invited me to come see him in his school's band

The Twitter Version

Being just-friends with a guy has way more benefits than drawbacks. As long as you're honest with each other, there are no negatives.

on Friday. What do you think he meant by that? I am of course obsessing and analyzing everything he said before and after that. I think he was just being friendly, but it kinda caught me off guard. Am I freaking out over nothing?"

"I usually start my friendships with guys on Facebook, like this new guy in our class. I didn't talk to him because I'm shy around people I don't know well. But on Facebook we talked for like an hour. It just helps to break the ice."

Social networking can be a total blast, and, as some of your sisters have pointed out, it eliminates that awkward "what do I do with my arms?" and "I bet my face looks red as a beefsteak tomato right now." If both you and a guy you're chatting with on Facebook are being real, it can be a way to start getting to know each other. And if he lives far away, you've taken your friendships global.

There are benefits to online friendships, but the issue with the Internet is that it can also be totally used in the wrong way as well. It was created to give everybody a voice, but there are some voices you don't need to hear. Doesn't it seem like there are always folks out there who can take any good thing and twist it until it's no longer recognizable?

That doesn't mean you shouldn't use the social network to develop friendships. You just have to be super careful. Some guidelines:

- **If you have never actually met the guy you're Facebooking with** (as in, you haven't seen each other's *real* faces!), don't give away any personal or contact information. (Which means keep all of that out of your profile too.) Let your conversations be light and focused on interests you share, rather than on your virtual feelings for each other. Not to make you paranoid, but you really don't know who this guy is and whether anything he's saying is the truth. Definitely do NOT agree to meet with him, and if he asks, make sure you tell an adult you trust.

- **If you have met the guy and you're keeping in touch because he lives someplace else**, take the same approach as if you'd never seen him in person. Unless you know you're going to get together again, under safe circumstances, there's really no point in going for deep soul-sharing. Becoming emotionally involved with someone you've barely met is never a good idea. Girls have been known to make some pretty crazy choices thinking they've found love online. Have fun but stay unattached.
- **If your text/email/Facebook guy friend is somebody you see often** (church, school, sports, that kind of thing), talking via the Internet can indeed help you get past the initial shyness and keep you from turning into a sweaty mess the minute he looks at you. It will be like picking up the conversation where you left it when you signed off. Obviously, you're going to balance online time with all the other stuff you have going—uh, like schoolwork, quiet time … sleep. Right? Things like Facebook can be addictive, especially if you know there's somebody you like waiting for you to post a comment on his comment, which was a response to your comment. Decide what's a reasonable amount of time to spend sitting in front of your computer and try to stick to that. Parents can be very helpful there.
- **No matter what the situation is with an Internet friend**, remember that everything you post is potentially public. That's actually a good thing. It makes you think before you hit Enter: Is this something I'd want my mom and dad to see? Is this something that could be misinterpreted? Do I actually want the entire world to know this? Not a bad thought process at all.

One girls sums it up beautifully: *"I used to have all these guy friends on Facebook. But then I realized it was kind of a problem for me because, like ... I didn't know who they truly were. They could say all this stuff about themselves and then not act like it in person. And you'll say stuff you would never would to someone's face. People are so different on the computer than in real life — they'll say nasty or intimate things they would never say in person. So now I don't do involved talking over the Internet because it has ruined a lot of friendships."*

The Twitter Version

An Internet connection can break the ice, but genuine, slow-growing, face-to-face friends are the best.

What will that look like? That depends on your personality and his, though God does give us some basics to go on.

God on Guys

I can't even begin to guide you to God's Word on this subject as well as two of your own peers. Check out this insight.

"So you know how sometimes you're friends with a guy and get that friend-crush thing? I used to feel bad about it, but then I found this verse: 'Love one another with brotherly affection. Outdo one another in showing honor' (Romans 12:10 ESV). OH MY GOODNESS GRACIOUS!!!!!! That is the awesomest thing. Do you get it? You don't have to feel BAD about liking someone. In fact, it's good to love. Furthermore, have a love that isn't shallow. Love with a love that just wants the best for the other person, even if that's just being friends. Love is not a bad thing. It's the GREATEST THING EVER."

And this one:

"My twin brother has a best friend who's, like, a year older than us, but we hang out with him ALL the time. This guy is a Christian, he's nice, he's funny, he looks good ... so naturally after spending a LOT of time with him and my brother I started to get a 'friend-crush.' I tried to shove that feeling away and just be friends and act

normal, but if you've tried that before you know it doesn't really work. And then I realized he's my brother in Christ. I don't have to love him with a shallow flirty 'love' that would probably mess up our friendship. I can love him as a brother, with God's love, through his Spirit that lives in me."

Where did these two teenagers get this concept that many women three times their age have yet to grasp? Knowing them, I strongly suspect it came from the kind of relationship with God we talked about in chapter one. So in your next quiet time with the Creator of all guy-kind, you might want to wrap your mind around a well-known passage from 1 Corinthians. It's the one you'll hear at weddings because it describes the ideal love relationship, but when he wrote it, Paul wasn't talking about just man and wife. (As far as we know, Paul wasn't even married!) He was addressing the whole body of Christ and how its members need to treat each other. Why wouldn't this apply to you and the guys you love like brothers?

As you read 1 Corinthians 13:4–8, see if you can envision the picture as it applies to you. A list might look something like this:

- Love is patient when your best friend insists you're in love with the boy.
- Love is kind when a guy sharing a single brain with his cohorts blows you off.
- Love is not envious when other girls seem to do the boy-girl thing so easily, or boastful or arrogant when guys swarm around you like gnats, or rude when someone says, "You guys are going out, right? I know you are!"
- It does not insist on its own way when parents say, "No you can't invite your boy BFF on the family camping trip."
- It is not irritable or resentful when even a guy *friend* occasionally behaves like a jackal.

- It does not rejoice in wrongdoing but rejoices in the truth when that sort-of-a-computer-geek everybody disses turns out to be the best friend you've ever had.
- It bears all things when you help your boy bud through a rough time.
- It believes all things, like that friendship is possible even with Mr. I-Can-Have-Any-Girl-I-Want.
- It hopes all things, like "some guy will see me for who I am and want to spend time getting to know more of my amazingness."
- It endures all things, like how long it takes you to figure this all out.

The best part of the passage is verse 8: *"Love never ends."*

If you have a boyfriend-girlfriend thing, the chances of it lasting forever at this point are about the same as being struck by lightning, which—by the way—is what it can feel like when you break up. But a friendship can go on for the rest of your lives. You can be homecoming queen, student body president, and captain of the state championship volleyball team—and what you'll treasure most is that guy who celebrated with you and cried with you and helped you find yourself, just the way you did for him.

The Twitter Version

1 Corinthians 13 is like a guidebook for a friendship with a guy, so love that buddy like a brother. It's biblical.

"Love never ends."

Think you can memorize that one?

Making It Real

As simple as all this may sound, you probably have the same questions girls have asked me. Let's look at a few of them:

How do you find guys with your same standards and stuff; one that'll treat you with respect and not make you feel stupid?

The younger you are, the harder that is to do. You recall what we said about guys not maturing as fast as girls. If you're thirteen or even fourteen, the pickings might be slim right now. But as boys start to catch up, more of them who share your faith and your values and your basic tendency not to act like a bozo will rise to the surface. Meanwhile, hang onto that standard and settle for nothing less. Even a guy who gives you respect but puts other people down isn't a good candidate for your friendship. Do remember, though, that no guy is perfect. Part of being friends is to help each other with the places where you fall short. Choose a guy friend whose faults you can live with.

How do you send the message that you just want to be friends and think the boyfriend-girlfriend thing is not for you right now?

First of all, guys don't tend to go there in their minds as much as we do. Can you even imagine yourself saying to a boy, "Before we get to be friends, I just want to make it clear that I'm never going to date you"? You can probably count on that friendship never getting past the first five minutes. If it comes up in conversation, you can say, "Yeah, I don't date" (if that's true) and let it go at that. Otherwise, just enjoy each other. If he gets a total crush on you and says so, be honest — the way you always have with him — about what you want and don't want and leave the decision up to him whether he can still be just friends.

What the Guys Say

"If the relationship gets funky, talk about it. Be honest. Come to a decision. Don't just let the weirdness hang there."

My best guy friend knows a lot of stuff that not many other people know about me. I know he's fine with being friends, though I think he'd like to be something more. Is it okay that

we talk this much just as friends? Or should I try to maybe hold back some?

Trust is a huge gift to give someone. It's a good idea not to hand it out carelessly. But if you have a guy friend who listens to you and supports you, it's worth considering whether you want to share that trust. You aren't sending the message that you confide in him because you think of him as a boyfriend. If he tells you he's interpreting it that way, you're already in an honest enough relationship that you can say, "I love being your friend and I want to keep it that way." Then the choice is his. You're not in the business of reading his mind. (Not that you could anyway!)

How do you keep yourself from getting a crush on a good friend and ruining the whole thing by getting too involved?

Quite frankly, I don't think girls trust themselves as much as they could. Just because you end up feeling something for a guy doesn't mean, to be blunt, you're going to hop into bed with the kid. If you don't spend hours alone with him, for instance, you don't have to worry the way you think you do. You can miss out on some great friendships by being afraid of getting too attached. We're human beings. We're supposed to get attached to each other. Generations before you managed to have guy friends without it becoming physical. There's no reason why you can't either. Okay, yeah, you may get your heart bruised a little. Who hasn't? We learn from our losses. If we never have any, do we become the inwardly rich human beings we might have been? That's up to you to decide. If the risk is too great, then by all means stick to your girlfriends. You have to do what's right for you.

Mom, Dad ... Now Don't Freak Out

All of this may be a moot point if your parents aren't totally on board. More than one girl has told me that her mom and dad don't want her to be friends with boys because it "always leads to something else." Or that there isn't any reason to have relationships with guys because they aren't even close to marrying age. Then there are the parents—often dads—who say they trust their daughters, but they just don't trust other people's sons. They feel it's better just not to go there and avoid all problems.

I'll say this in every chapter: you are obligated to honor your parents' final decisions. I would never advise you to go against their rules. However, that doesn't mean that you shouldn't ask to discuss their choices for you, and we've already talked in chapter one about how to approach that. Since the topic of guys-as-friends may be more of an issue for you than dating or sex, I think some specifics are in order.

Always lead off with something like:

"Can we just talk about this? I'm not going to argue, I promise."

"I have a couple of questions—just some things I'm curious about."

"What you guys say goes. I just need some clarification."

I guarantee that nothing like this is going to work for you. (Ever.):

"I do NOT get this. You guys are, like, living in the dark ages."

"Could you just listen to me for once? You never let me say my side of it!"

"I totally disagree with you, but whatever . . ."

Just incidentally, "whatever" never flies with parents. And "whatev"? Even worse.

Once it's been established that there's going to be a conversation, these are some possible questions you might ask:

Can you tell me exactly why you don't want me to be friends with guys?

Are you afraid I'm going to get hurt somehow if a boy and I are friends?

Is there a way that would make both of us happy? Like I can hang out with guy friends as long as we're with a group? Or only make friends with boys from church?

What do I need to do to show you that I'm mature enough to handle a real friendship with a teenage boy?

If your parents are okay with you being friends with guys but have reservations about which ones, you might suggest inviting that possible friend over with a whole group of your buddies (boys *and* girls) so your parents can see how he interacts with you (that way Guy Friend doesn't feel like he's being staked out!) or just introduce them to him at church or a game with, "I want you to meet my friend __________. We're both into __________."

As we've said before, no one, not even your parents, can determine how you feel about someone, but whatever you do, don't try to sidestep their rules for you. In fact, the more gracefully you follow those rules, even while respectfully making it clear (once!) that you don't agree, the more likely they are to see your maturity and perhaps loosen the reins. After all, that passage from 1 Corinthians 13 applies to your love for *them* too. (Sigh.)

The Twitter Version

It helps to ask your parents specific questions about their philosophy on guys as friends, even while you're following their rules. Just don't take a tone with them.

If I'm Totally Honest ...

I would be really comfortable with having a guy as a friend if:

____

____

____

"Do They Really Just Want One Thing?"

A couple of things before you start this chapter:

We'll be talking about the issue of sex, but we're not going to discuss any of the actual details of the act. I'm assuming you know the basics and won't be going "Huh?" the whole time. If you're at all squeamish on the topic, I can assure you that nothing I say is likely to embarrass you. However, if you've never received any information about those basics (from your mom or another adult woman you trust), you might want to get that first. Then read on.

If you've already had some experience with sex, know that I'm not going to scold you, judge you, or tell you that you've ruined your life. You haven't. But you can make life better, and hopefully you'll find help for that here.

With that said, let's look at the reason we're even talking about this in the first place. One girl—a girl like you—cuts right to the root of it:

"The girls I know who date all seem to be having sex—or at least, that's what they say. But I don't think it has to be that way. Am I naive?"

What the Guys Say

"There are guys who do only want sex, but not all of us. Some guys want sex and a relationship. Some guys want to wait until marriage."

That seems to be the whole reason parents don't want their daughters to date, have guys as friends, or even think about the opposite sex until they're ready to look for a husband. It isn't that they don't trust you. They've just accepted what would *appear* to be the truth: that every teenage relationship that goes on for any longer than a couple of months is destined to wind up in the sack.

"Appear" is the operative word. If you just relied on teen magazines, for instance, you'd be convinced that once you hit puberty it's only a matter of time. They're filled with articles that tell you how to determine *when* you're ready to sleep with your boyfriend, not *if.* They fill you in on birth control, sexually transmitted diseases, and even how to be your sexiest self for the prom. Sure, they always warn you of the dangers — pregnancy, disease, and hooking up with Mr. Wrong. But they always offer having "safe sex" as one of your many acceptable options.

If you go to school outside the home — public, private, or even Christian — you'll likely hear kids talking about sex like it's no big deal. I myself have had girls tell me:

"I knew I was going to lose my virginity sooner or later, so I thought I might as well get it over with."

"I want to date but I don't, because all guys expect you to have sex. At least that's what my friends say."

"I don't even feel like I can wear cute, trendy clothes, because guys just stare at you openly, like you're a thing instead of a person."

It is true that there are a whole lot of teenagers having sex. Recent statistics show that while only 13 percent of teens have had sex by age fifteen, by their nineteenth birthday seven in

What the Guys Say

"No respectable guy just wants sex. We do want relationships."

ten teens of both sexes have had intercourse. On average, young people have sex for the first time at about age seventeen. Those figures tend to get translated into "EVERYBODY is doing it."

But those same studies show that 87 percent of teens fifteen and under *aren't* engaging in sexual activity. And who's to say that some of the respondents aren't lying and saying they are when they're not, because they don't want to come off as "nerdy" and "uncool." It used to be that only guys would be guilty of that, but now there are plenty of girls who are embarrassed by their virginity. The label "never been kissed," which used to deem a girl some kind of loser, has been replaced.

What the Guys Say

"No way guys only want sex from a girl! Girls are more than that. They're a companion. They someone to just hang out with."

If you do hold fast to a commitment to remain pure until marriage, there isn't much in our world to support you. Society in general sure won't do it. Judging from movies, videos, songs, and TV shows—all created by adults, mind you—our culture just doesn't see what all the fuss is about. One sign of that is the whole issue of teen pregnancy. In the 40s, 50s, 60s, and even the early 70s, girls who became pregnant "out of wedlock," as they called it then, were usually sent away to a "group home" to have their babies secretly and give them up for adoption. Those programs—not the healthiest places mentally, emotionally, or spiritually—are all but nonexistent now because (in addition to the availability of abortion) most families don't see the need to hide the fact that a daughter has had sex. They shrug their shoulders and say, "They all do it. She just got caught." No, I don't believe a teenage girl should be shunned and sent away because she's with child. My point is that it is less and less a cause for concern in today's society. Least of all your peers. Even some of your Christian peers.

"How can you be a 'good girl' when it seems like everybody else is making out like crazy behind the church after youth group?"

"I go to a Christian school and guys are pinching girls' butts in the halls and couples are all over each other at the lockers. What do I have to do to get away from that? Go to an all girls' academy?"

Before you get too depressed, just know this: not *every* teenage girl and guy in the world is having sex. And plenty of those who aren't are still enjoying guy-girl friendships and even dating. Yeah, it's hard to remain pure these days, but that doesn't mean you have to give up all interactions with the male species — what for some girls is one of the most fun parts of *being* a girl. It just means you have to be wise and savvy. It means you need to be even closer to God than you ever imagined. And it means you need to know your own mind, inside and out. Let's start there.

What the Guys Say

"There are times when my mind goes out in temptation land, but not every time I see a girl or am with one. Sex is not always the thing that pops into my mind."

What's Going On with Me?

Check ALL of the statements below that apply to you:

_____ 1. I want to save my first kiss for my wedding day.

_____ 2. I want to be engaged to a guy before I kiss him.

_____ 3. I might kiss a guy I really like, but he's going to have to be somebody special to me.

_____ 4. I don't see anything wrong with kissing when you're dating, but all-out sex or any of the things leading up to it — not for me.

_____ 5. I'm not going to have sex before marriage, but I think there are a lot of other things you can do that aren't really sex that might actually keep you a technical virgin.

_____ 6. I think if you're with a guy you're engaged to, it's okay to have sex because you're going to get married anyway.

_____ 7. I think if a guy is someone you'd totally marry, then why not sleep with him as long as you use protection?

_____ 8. Sex doesn't mean the same thing that it used to; it's more like what making out was a long time ago. I would totally do it if I liked a guy and it seemed right.

_____ 9. I've already had sex.

_____ 10. I think every girl should go ahead and do it before she ever settles down. Guys do it so why not us?

Your "scoring" will be a little different this time. Count how many checks you had in each of these **sets** of statements:

____ Set A—Statements 1 through 4

____ Set B—Statements 5 through 7

____ Set C—Statements 8 through 10

It's **really** important that you not look at your results as any kind of finger-wagging, OR as proof that you're virtually an angel so you can skip this chapter. This is just a way for you to see what's really driving your thinking. That will make it possible for you to get where you need to be: in the driver's seat.

If you had the most checks in Set A, you are truly a purist. Some of your convictions may change as you have more experience around guys, but hopefully you'll be able to stick to the one that really is important. This chapter will help you see that it doesn't have to be as hard as you might think.

If you had the most checks in Set B, you're in a bit of a gray area. You know having actual intercourse isn't a casual thing, but you're thinking that there are ways around the hard-and-fast rule. That could take you someplace you don't really want to be. Really study this chapter to get clear.

If you had the most checks in Set C, you'll benefit most from the sections below that talk about *why* having sex outside of marriage is "such a big deal." Again, I won't be chastising you. I'll just give you ways to make some better choices.

This time we'll start with what God has to say and then build from there.

God on Guys

The only thing Jesus said in the Gospels about female-male relationships was in response to guys dumping their wives because somebody younger and cuter came along. There was apparently a lot of that going on. He said that the only reason for a divorce was when one of the spouses was unfaithful to the marriage vows. Basically, that meant adultery—having sex outside of marriage (Mark 10:1–12).

Later on, Paul fleshes that out in 1 Corinthians 6:12–20, so that it becomes pretty clear even if you aren't married, sleeping with a guy without being married to him is not okay with God. And when you get right down to it, who is it that you really have to answer to?

Basic Truth #4

Sexual intimacy was created by God as a precious treasure for married people to give to each other.

But like every command Jesus gives us, this one isn't just something he made up to keep you from having a good time while you're young. Why would he do that? He came that we might have life and have it abundantly (John 10:10). It's based on God's love for you. He isn't saying, "I want you to be miserable while everybody else is having all the fun." He's not even saying, "Obey this and you'll get to go to heaven." He's saying, "I don't want you to get hurt *now*, and if you ignore this, you definitely will."

Abstinence isn't just about not getting pregnant or preventing STDs. And it's definitely not about sex being the root of all evil; God himself created it. It's about protecting you from the inevitable emotional pain that you can't cure with an antibiotic.

Hear me, now; the following is not a put-down of boys. They themselves will tell you the same thing: for guys at this age, sex is almost purely physical. Some of them may call it love, but what it is for them is hormonal, biological, and sometimes even egotistical. There's power in seducing a girl, no doubt about it. Basically, the typical teenage guy doesn't have sex to show a girl he loves her. He may actually care about her, but those feelings aren't very connected to what happens with her in bed or in the backseat of his car. They're two entirely different things, not because the boy's a beast but, because as we've mentioned before, his brain is developing differently from yours. (And he will probably catch up later.) For a girl, physical affection is sometimes the way she shows her feelings, and the deeper the physical, the deeper the feelings. Having sex with a guy is typically part of an emotional commitment. She's his, body and soul. There is no separation of the relationship and the sex.

What the Guys Say

"When you have sex before marriage, it's like sticking two pieces of duct tape together. You can't get them apart without tearing the tape."

At best, that creates a lopsided relationship while it lasts. At worst, when it's over, and more likely than not it will be, the guy can walk away almost unscathed because he hasn't given anything up. The girl has. She gave him not only a piece of her body but a piece of her heart, and that leaves an empty place that usually fills up with guilt and shame and regret and pain. Girls I've talked to use words like "cheap," "dirty," and "damaged" to describe how they feel. They aren't authentically any of those things but the sensation is as hard to get off as a big, sticky cobweb.

That's it, seriously. Jesus never said sexual sin was the worst possible sin. He just warned us against it because it's probably the most painful. He was (and is) all about love, real love, pure love. He doesn't want us to misuse it or abuse it or take all the dignity out of it. He doesn't want it to hurt.

Twitter Version

Just don't do it. You'll hurt yourself. You will.

Guydlines

That presents a problem, doesn't it? Here you are with this marvelous natural urge to get close to that cutie who has his locker next to yours — at age thirteen or fourteen or fifteen — and yet you aren't supposed to get *that* close to him until the two of you are married at age twenty-one or twenty-two or twenty-three or even older.

So what are you supposed to do until you've walked down the aisle? Are people right when they say you should just stay away from boys completely so you aren't even tempted?

You will decide that in your heart, and you can do that wisely if your head is also engaged. Below are three things you'd do well to press into your mind as *well* as into your feelings.

"Okay, so I have a question about being pure. Is it still pure to think about guys as long as we don't think anything bad? I mean, really — it would be pretty hard to not think about boys at all because of our hormones affecting us."

(1) You are not "bad" if you think about sex. Is it "bad" to have breasts, get your period, and discover that your eyebrows suddenly resemble a blackberry thicket? Becoming a sexual being is as much a part of puberty as any of those things. You can't just turn it off. But you *can* turn it down. You have control over the volume in your head.

Low decibel: I wonder what it would be like to kiss him. I bet it would be kind of wonderful. What am I saying? I bet it would be amazing!

High decibel: I wonder what it would be like if we were both totally naked ...

A little daydreaming about a kiss is a far cry from fantasizing your entire honeymoon. You're far more likely to do something you've imagined yourself doing in detail. That doesn't mean you *will*, but why tempt yourself? So go ahead and enjoy the occasional thought of a sweet kiss. Drift too far beyond that, though, and by the time you do kiss a guy (if you haven't already) it's going to pale in comparison to what you've dreamed up.

"I definitely don't want to have sex before I'm married but I do want to really get to know guys. How do I handle that?"

(2) There are a number of things you can do that will help you resist the temptation—and in fact not have the desire to have sex be an issue at all.

Stay away from movies and TV and music that have a lot of sexual content, especially if it's explicit. You don't have to totally stick to Disney and Pixar, but if an R-rated movie looks like it would be good, get parental approval. If your folks see it first, they can tell you whether there are images in there you won't be able to erase from your brain. The less you fill your mind up with how easy producers make casual sex look, the easier you'll make it on yourself.

Try not to engage in long conversations with your friends about sex. Sleepovers can be breeding grounds for that. In the first place, you're probably going to get a lot of misinformation from people your own age, everything from "You can get a disease from a toilet seat" (uh, probably not) to "If you have sex with a guy right after your period, you won't get pregnant" (sorry, but it happens). And secondly, people tend to exaggerate in those kinds of discussions, so that before the sun comes up, you're convinced you're the only virgin left in the club. You'll definitely be wise to avoid talking to *guys* about sex, even your close guy friends. They're not experts, for openers, and just having the conversation can be titillating. Really, how are you going to keep your mind from going, "What would it be like with *him*?" when he's explaining french kissing to you?

You'll do yourself a favor if you avoid spending time totally alone with the boy you like. Dark, romantic places where there's no one else around—a car parked at the beach, the back row of the movie theater, behind the robes in the choir room (okay, maybe that's not that romantic ...) can set you up for mistakes you'll regret later. If you're already picturing yourself in his arms, why put yourself in a situation where you're liable to end up there? Trust yourself—but don't test yourself. Trusting is *I can have a relationship with this guy because we really like each other.* Testing is *We can sneak out of our camp cabins and meet by the lake and spend the whole night together, and nothing will happen because we're both committed to purity.* Most *adults* don't have that kind of willpower! A healthy respect for your own weakness as a human being is a wise thing.

What the Guys Say

"Do all guys just want sex? I don't."

If you and a guy like each other, as friends or otherwise, there ARE other things to do besides sit around trying not to touch each other. You were attracted by something other than your potential sexuality (and if not—find somebody else!), so focus on that. Make pizza together, volunteer side by side at a soup kitchen, challenge each other to one-on-one basketball, enjoy each other as whole people.

Teasing guys, letting them think you're going to do things you're not—very bad idea. To be blunt about it, if it's not for sale, don't advertise it. A guy is not going to get the wrong idea if you don't give it to him, and you can serve it right up on a platter by dressing to give the impression that you'd like for him to discover what you're barely hiding, luring him into a suggestive situation, and then making him guess whether you're serious or not (even if you aren't), or tossing sex talk back and forth. He's responsible for his own purity, but you're also responsible for making sure you're not leading him to the wrong conclusion, and even for making staying pure more difficult for both of you.

Be very cautious about relationships with older guys. You're thirteen and you like a guy who's sixteen; you're fourteen and you're into an eighteen-year-old; you're fifteen and the man of your dreams is twenty. They're so much more mature than most of the guys your age, it can be hard not to fall for one like a wall of bricks. But here's why that's an issue:

- Even if you're really grown-up for your age, a guy three, four, or five years older than you is probably more experienced than you are in the whole guy-girl thing and he's likely to want things you're not ready for, no matter how mature you are.
- You're totally in different stages of life right now, so you won't be in sync. The depth of the relationship and the possibility of long-term commitment are more intense for the older guy than for you.
- If a guy way older than you wants to date you, there's a good chance he has immaturity issues. If he *were* mature, he'd wait until you were older to pursue anything romantic.

Sure, when it's time to date, a lot of girls go with guys a few years older than they are because the maturity level matches better. Right now, it's just safer to admire them from a distance or enjoy them as casual friends. They do make good big brothers.

Let's just be clear on this. A decision to completely stay away from guys shouldn't be based on fear of sex. If you're just not interested in guys or you don't know any you think are worth the time of day, that's one thing. Being afraid of what might happen is another. I'm talking about fear that you're going to get into a situation that you can't handle. Being afraid you won't be able to hold up the commitment you've made. Fear that you won't be able to control yourself. Fear just isn't a good foundation for this choice. Why are you spending time with God, realizing how much God loves you, how much good God wants for you, getting to know yourself the way God sees you, if you're still going to hide out because you're afraid of being hurt—maybe because someone has hurt you before? Do you really believe your Lord wants you to live in fear, rather than faith? Does God want you to be suspicious, fearful that if a guy asks you for the geometry homework he's got something sinister in mind? What we're talking about here is getting things in perspective and being realistic so you can have healthy relationships with all the people you care about, including guys.

(3) Keep in mind that just because guys in general have a physical, rather than an emotional, attitude toward sex, it doesn't mean they all want that and nothing else.

When you flirt with them, there is no knee jerk reaction that makes them think you want to have a physical relationship. Some seem to have that, yeah, but you know who they are. They're the ones always giving the power stares, constantly getting in your space, taking (or making!) every opportunity to touch you. Give them a wide berth. But there *are* guys who are just as nervous around girls as girls are around them. There are boys who don't want the responsibilities of anything serious, but they'd like to get to know some girls as people. There are still boys who know nothing about sex and, though curious, are not out there trying to seduce every female who offers them a piece of chewing gum. Just because sex outside marriage is pretty much acceptable in society today doesn't mean everybody is buying into it, not even all the guys. And just because *you* like boys, like to spend time with them, even flirt just a little, that doesn't mean you buy into it either. Guys know that. They might not admit it to their buddies, but they also respect it.

A word about forced sex: Consensual sex (as in, we both agreed to it) is unfortunately not the only issue girls your age have to deal with. One in five girls become victims of date rape in their teens. That's not meant to scare you. It's meant to alert you to the reality that some guys do see sex as their right and will push it with force if necessary. Rather than get yourself to the nearest nunnery until you're twenty-five years old and a marriage has been arranged for you (like that's gonna happen!), just follow some safety guidelines:

If a guy has a reputation for a one-track mind, don't flirt with him, don't date him, don't even befriend him. If he happens to be in a group you're in (band, youth group, drama club), you don't have to be rude. Just keep a lot of space between you and him. You might want to pray for the kid too. He's got issues.

Really get to know a guy before you spend any time alone with him, whether you're friends or starting to date. And even at that, make sure other people are within earshot until you're convinced he knows right where you stand on sex. And even at *that,* don't put yourself in a tempting situation. *You* may not be tempted, but *he* might, and once he has his mind set on what he wants, no could be hard to accept.

Don't wait until you're right on the brink of going too far to say no. In fact, don't even get within a breath of that. A no from you always means no, but the further you've gone physically, the harder he's going to be to convince that's really what you're saying. If he doesn't take that no for an answer and pushes you into sex, it isn't your fault, but why even let it be a possibility?

It probably goes without saying, but do not consume alcohol around guys. For that matter, don't consume it anywhere, anytime when you're underage. I would be remiss if I didn't emphasize that alcohol consumption lowers inhibitions and clouds judgment. Even if you're not drinking but a guy at a party is, call your parents or a cab and get out of there.

Brand this into your brain: no one, NO ONE, has the right to touch you in any way that is unwelcomed by you. That means uncles, cousins, brothers, stepfathers, or steady boyfriends. If someone is forcing himself on you in any way, or has done it in the past, put this book down and go to the nearest adult you trust and tell that person.

- An adult female will be easier to tell. Even talking to a male pastor can feel humiliating.
- A doctor or a teacher or a counselor is required by law to report the abuse, which would mean great support for you.

- An adult who doesn't know your abuser is also a good idea.
- If you don't know anyone, there are numerous rape hotlines and organizations that you can contact. These people will make sure you get the help and support you need.

You've experienced sexual assault, which is a crime. You are the victim. If no one believes you or you're told it was your fault, that you "asked for it," go to someone else, and someone else after that, until you find somebody who gets the FACT that your body is your own private property and no one has the right to touch it unless you give permission. You understand that, right? No one.

Basic Truth #5

No one—NO ONE—has the right to touch you sexually. Period.

If you've already had consensual sex or are only what some call "a technical virgin" (you haven't actually had intercourse but you've gone way past kissing, hugging, and holding hands), please don't feel like you're damaged goods. You're a human being who has made a mistake, and who among us hasn't messed up somewhere? When you turn away from it, toward God, that's repentance. You're now headed in a new direction and God has forgotten about the old one. That's forgiveness. Everybody else might have a different opinion. You may not change that. But you know you can change your own opinion of yourself, to match the one God has of you. You have a clean slate. You're no longer a non-virgin or a technical virgin. (Who came up with that term, anyway?) You're pure in your soul. You can start over.

Maybe you don't see it as a mistake, even if you got hurt. Perhaps you're thinking it was worth it, or that it will turn out better next time. Could be you're still in the middle of it and it feels pretty good to you right now. Those are things you'll need to work out with God, and if you stick to those quiet talks with

God, you will. Give some deep thought to what you really want. I suspect it's love, acceptance, and security, not sex. And just so you know, sex can't give you any of that. If this seems too big to face, get someone to help you; an adult you trust, someone who won't waggle a chiding finger at you. If you have no one like that in your life, you can go to my website to contact me.

> **The Twitter Version**
>
> Sex doesn't happen just because you spend time with a boy. But it's still important not to put yourself in situations where it might.

Making It Real

I hope at this point you're saying, "Yeah! I get it. That's what I'm going to do."

I'm also a realist and I know how hard this can all be to put into practice. It kind of makes you wonder why God gave us these desires and urges so young when our ability to really handle it doesn't come until so much later.

I may be able to help you with that one. In 1900, the average age of the onset of puberty was fourteen. That was the *onset.* Girls' periods didn't start until eighteen months to two years later. They could be sixteen before they broke out the maxi pads (which they didn't actually have, but you get my drift). In those days, since most girls didn't go to college or train for jobs, because most women didn't work outside the home, they married a whole lot younger than young women do now. It wasn't uncommon to become a bride at seventeen, and if a girl hit twenty-five and still hadn't taken a husband, she was considered an old maid. So what was that, a year, maybe two, to stay pure while battling hormones? Plus, there was no dating as we know it. Any contact with young men was done under the supervision of chaperones, so if a couple did want to get physical, they had to go to great lengths to make it happen.

In the 2000s, the average age for the onset of puberty for Caucasian girls is *nine years old,* and *eight* for African Americans. No one is entirely sure why, but some scientists are studying whether it has something to do with all the hormones that are put into our food, particularly meat and poultry products. (Not exactly a God-thing.) At the same time, because girls pursue college and careers and know they need to be able to provide at least half of the support of a future family if not take care of themselves entirely (because remaining single *is* a godly option), the typical marrying age is no longer in the teens. In fact, if a girl marries at seventeen, everyone shakes their heads and says, "It'll never last." So that comes out to fifteen, sometimes even twenty years or more of maintaining abstinence. Even as an adult looking back, I have to say that's asking a lot of young people, especially in a society that says, "What are you thinking? You're crazy to even try."

What that means is that if purity before marriage is your goal (because according to Jesus, it's God's goal), you're going to need to do more than believe in it. You're going to need a plan. Just as with almost everything else we've talked about, your plan for your physical relationships with guys will have to be shaped around your unique personality. You all have the same goal—you'll just get there in different ways. This template might assist you.

Step One: Write down what you want in detail. (In a safe place, obviously. Under industrial-strength lock and key is best if you have siblings.) Do you want your first kiss to be at the altar? (And by the way, I've heard that some people have fulfilled that goal, and I respect that, but don't beat yourself up if that doesn't turn out to be your experience. The Bible doesn't say, "Thou shalt not kiss before thy wedding vows." Just saying.) Do you want no physical contact with guys beyond friendly hugs until you're engaged? Do you just want to abstain from physical intimacy and sex until your wedding night? Whatever it looks like in your mind, write it down—even if right now it's "I just don't know what I want and here's why."

Step Two: Take it to God. Lay it all out. Pray. Listen. Journal what you hear or sense. Complain in writing if you hear nothing. Keep at it. (This isn't a one-day thing.) What you sense God saying may differ somewhat from your goal, in which case, adjust the goal. After all, it's God's will be done, not yours. Most of the time, after this kind of committed communication, the two become the same.

Step Three: Make an honest list of what reaching that goal is going to involve. Hopefully what you've read in this chapter will help you. The answer to these questions might be included:

- Will I date?
- Will I leave myself open to deeper-than-friendship relationships?
- Will I give hugs? Hold hands? Kiss?
- Will I have to change the way I dress?
- Will I need to take a look at the way I behave? Do I flirt? Lead guys on? Fall in love every time a guy pays any attention to me?
- Will I need to look at the people I hang out with? Do they share my views and values? Am I going to get support from them or be the misfit? Do I need to think about making new friends?
- Will I need to consider the kind of guy I'm attracted to? Is his type going to make it easy to achieve my goal, or way too hard?

Step Four: Make any changes in your current lifestyle that you know you need to. You don't have to stop volleyball practice, for instance, and announce to your female teammates that you're no longer going to laugh at their sexual innuendoes in the locker room. Just stop laughing. In any of the adjustments you're making, remember that it's you you're working on. It isn't up to you to judge and try to fix the kids around you who in your view are making a total mess out of their lives. Set the example. Pray. Tell them the truth if they come to you and say, "So what's going on with you?"

Step Five: Imagine and practice. Think of scenarios in which your commitment could be put to the test. Imagine yourself in those situations, doing and saying what you hope you'd do or say. Practice out loud if it doesn't make you feel lame (and if annoying brothers are out of the house ... *way* out of the house). You could even run it past a woman you trust. "If a guy does this and I say this, how do you think that's going to work out?"

Step Six: If you're dating, be prepared to state your case clearly as soon as you start seeing someone. By the time you get to that point, hopefully you're comfortable enough with the guy to be able to say *before* he makes a move, "Just so you know, here's how I feel." Why wait until something's about to happen and then put the brakes on? If you're not going too fast to begin with, there will be no need for an awkward squealing of tires.

Trust me, ya gotta have a plan. Even if you have convinced yourself that Godzilla is more attractive to guys than you are. Even if you're every guy's little sister and can't imagine any of them wanting to touch you. Even if you haven't spoken to a boy since third grade—make a plan. Better to have one you won't use for a while than be suddenly caught wondering, "What am I supposed to do *now?*"

Mom, Dad ... Now Don't Freak Out

Even the calmest of parents tend to flip out (at least internally) when their teenage daughters talk about sex in anything but the most general, this-is-something-that-happens-to-other-people terms. Most dads especially don't want to even think about some pervert (which to him may be any teen boy) touching his little girl.

So don't let your folks go there. Before the worrying even starts, take the initiative. Tell them about your goal. Assure them you're serious about it. Explain how you plan to stick to your commitment. Ask for their prayer and support.

The Twitter Version

Sex is a one-case issue with parents: They don't want you to have it, you've decided not to have it? Case closed. All they need is reassurance.

After they recover from the shock (or dead faint, loss of teeth, etc.), they will be proud and impressed. That's all the discussion you'll really need to have. What is there to talk about when it comes to sex? They don't want you to have it, you're determined not to have it. You can move on to whether you can paint your room lime green or why your older sister still acts like she's your other mother. So much of relating successfully to parents is about choosing your battles. This is one you just don't have to fight because you already agree.

You may still run into the argument that if you have anything whatsoever to do with boys you're tempting the sex devil. Feel free to show your parents this chapter. That website address is here for them too.

If I'm Totally Honest

I have some fears about sex that I'd like to talk to someone about but I'm embarrassed to …

____

____

____

____

____

____

"So, What About Dating and Boyfriends?"

"I try to stand up for my parents' belief in not dating. When I tell people that, they look at me like I'm strange. It can hurt sometimes."

For some of you, the dating decision has been taken out of your hands. Your parents have said not until you're sixteen ... until you're eighteen ... until further notice. Or your church has taken a position on teen dating and everybody has to wait until they're nineteen to court (not date).

Others of you haven't given it much thought because you think no one's ever going to ask you, or because you don't know any guys you'd want to borrow a pencil from, much less go out with.

"I haven't even run into a guy who's worth a second look. Most of them don't seem to have enough brains for anything deeper than today's weather or can actually have a real conversation for longer than five minutes."

Still others among you already have boyfriends or have reached the age where you're allowed to date and are waiting for the whole thing to start.

> **What the Guys Say**
> "I'd rather be friends with girls and go out in groups than actually date."

"If you don't date or put any interest in boys until you're ready to marry, you won't know what you like. I'm not saying move IN with them, but it seems like being a little more than friends would tell you some things about relationships."

And then there are those of you who have decided for yourselves that you're not ready and don't know when you will be.

"I'm cool with other girls having boyfriends, but I would rather wait a little bit."

Which is why this chapter is not designed to give you rules for when you should date and whether you should have a steady boyfriend. Now, if you were younger, there would be no discussion. When girls ten, eleven, or twelve say they're "going out," I always wonder where they're "going" and how they plan to get there. Usually what they really mean is that they're passing notes and having their BFF ask their crush's best friend to ask him if he likes her.

Since you're way past that, this chapter is just here to present some of the questions girls like you ask me and to provide answers for you to consider. As always, whatever your parents say on the subject is the law for you right now. But even if they've said no dating, no boyfriends now, period, when you do get the go-ahead to make that first date you'll want to be prepared. You'll need to go into it knowing what you want and what you don't want from a relationship *and* what you want to put into it. Hopefully this chapter will help you reach that point.

For starters, let's see what your uncensored views are.

What's Going On with Me?

Choose your answers to the following as if the decision to date and/or have a boyfriend were entirely up to you.

1. If a guy moved from sticking gum in my hair to emailing me for the homework assignment (when I know perfectly well he's already done it) I would:

   a. be totally annoyed.

   b. think, "Oh, guys are finally starting to grow up. Awesome."

   c. realize he probably liked me.

   d. start dreaming about our first date.

2. If a guy I liked had a conversation with me that lasted more than ten minutes and wasn't about something totally lame, I would:

   a. wonder if somebody dared him to do it.

   b. be mildly amazed.

   c. hope we'd talk again—soon.

   d. text him or Facebook him later that day.

3. If a guy I liked asked me out, I would:

   a. ask him if he was on drugs.

   b. be surprised and tell him I'd have to get back to him.

   c. smile and say yes.

   d. smile and ask what took him so long.

4. If a great guy I went out with a few times said he wanted to be my boyfriend (wanted us to be an item, wanted us to only date each other, etc.) I would:

   a. not ever be in that position.

   b. tell him I wasn't ready for a serious relationship but I'd still like to go out with him.

   c. say yes and suggest we discuss some ground rules.

   d. start looking at engagement rings.

5. If there was a guy I wanted to have a more-than-friends relationship with, I would:
   - **a.** go, "Oh, well, not gonna happen."
   - **b.** wait to see if he liked me that way too.
   - **c.** be the best friend to him I could be and see how it went.
   - **d.** go after the boy with everything I had.
6. If I met a guy my age who was everything I want in a future husband, I would:
   - **a.** get depressed.
   - **b.** hope he'd still be around when I was ready to get married.
   - **c.** get to know him and enjoy being around him.
   - **d.** tell him he's husband material.
7. If I liked a guy and found out he'd already dated a bunch of girls, I would:
   - **a.** not ever want to get involved with him.
   - **b.** wish I'd been one of them.
   - **c.** find out who those girls were and how he treated them and what their relationships were like.
   - **d.** not care as long as he was mine now.
8. To me the biggest drawback to having a steady boyfriend is:
   - **a.** all the drama, because guys are still so immature; girls too, for that matter.
   - **b.** getting hurt if a guy breaks up with you.
   - **c.** having it get too serious.
   - **d.** Drawbacks? What drawbacks?

You know the drill. Count up your a's, b's, c's, and d's. Then check out what your results might mean.

If you had mostly a's, it looks like you have a fairly negative view not only of dating, but of boys in general and possibly even of yourself. There is nothing wrong with not wanting to become involved with guys right now, especially if the ones you know are still acting like chimpanzees. But if your big-time disillusionment with boys comes from the belief that you're never going to be "good enough" for a guy to like you, we'll work on that. It's hard to be happy when you don't like yourself, with boys or without them. For now just know that you were made beautiful. It's all a matter of discovering that self.

If you had mostly b's, you're probably not ready for a steady relationship at this point because guys are still a bit of a mystery and you're not quite sure how to be around them. That's okay, though, because your attitude is pretty positive. Let's build on that so when the time comes for dating, you'll be wise and confident.

If you had mostly c's, your dating 'tude is quite healthy. You don't have a lot of experience, but you have the blossoming maturity to be able to handle what comes along, even if that means knowing when to run the other way. You may have some lingering questions, which hopefully will be answered in this chapter.

If you had mostly d's, you're ready to jump into the whole relationship thing with both feet and may already have. No one's going to accuse you of being afraid of guys! Your challenge is to think carefully with your head before you completely open up your heart. You'll learn about areas of caution in the pages ahead that will help balance that bring-it-on enthusiasm.

God on Guys

"Is it, like, biblical, that I have to wait until I'm marrying age to even date?"

Actually, the Bible doesn't make a clear statement about having a boyfriend. Jesus didn't say, "Consider the lilies, how they don't date until they're sixteen." Of course, dating hadn't been invented then. Fathers were in charge of making good marriages for their daughters, and until the wedding day guys were off limits. The custom of courting has been reinstated in many Christian communities by parents who feel God has always intended for it to be that way.

The Twitter Version

God's more concerned about the way we treat each other than about the customs we follow. The Sermon on the Mount is a good instruction manual for that.

If parents have been led by God to believe that to be true for their daughters, it's obviously what needs to happen in their households. However, there are many customs and rituals in the Old Testament that we no longer observe, from sacrificing goats on the altar to separating women from the household while they were menstruating (although I'm sure you've wished some months that someone would do that for you ...). The truth of God's love and power is remains the same, and that manifests itself in so many different ways—in the parents who help their daughters decide when they're ready to go out with boys in groups as well as in those who put a firm age on dating. Whatever is decided prayerfully and with love is what God wants you to honor.

In the Bible, God seems far more concerned with how we treat each other than about what dating customs we follow. Just read the Sermon on the Mount (Matthew 5:1—7:27) and you'll see that Jesus never *stops* talking about how we are be in relationship. We'd do well to focus on that, with all the people in our lives.

If Jesus had given tips on dating, they might look something like this:

"You are the light of the world, so if you decide to date, be sure you're reflecting me in everything you do out there."

"If you're totally focused on how great it would be to be in bed with the guy you're dating, you're already in dangerous territory. You need to stop that, my dear."

"Enjoy your time with this great guy, but keep it in balance.

My words about storing up for yourself treasures in heaven totally applies here."

"If you feel like nobody will ever *want* to date you, don't worry. God takes care of the lilies of the field and God will take care of you. Seek God first."

Kind of makes you want to keep talking to him, doesn't it?

Guydlines

So what *is* the big issue with dating and boyfriends?

On the one hand, there's the point of view that since teen relationships seldom last, it's ridiculous to have them in the first place.

"I've seen girls date a guy, and then he does some heinous boy-like thing and she doesn't like him anymore, or he gets tired of her and they break up after, like, two weeks and she moves on to somebody else. Who needs it, right?"

It's true that if taken too seriously, a boyfriend-girlfriend thing can lead to a deep hurt that no young person is emotionally equipped to handle. And as we said in chapter five, if sex is involved, the heartbreak can be even more painful. The thinking is that if you run a chance of having your heart broken, why even go there in the first place?

"Even if a relationship doesn't work out, you've still learned something."

The opposing argument is that a dating relationship can be a great teacher. Getting to know boys, the proponents say, is a good way to learn what a healthy boy-girl relationship is and what it isn't, which is something you can only truly learn by doing. The question is, is anybody in her teens mature enough to figure that out, especially when she's dealing with a man-boy who by nature probably loves his soccer cleats more than he loves her?

What the Guys Say

"Guys take things faster than girls. Girls like to get things going at first, but then they slow it down a bit."

What's the answer? Be safe—and possibly unprepared for the future? Or take some risks and chance being hurt, perhaps even badly?

"Is it okay to have a boyfriend? Some Christian girls I know are against that, but if you just hang out together in groups and text and email and talk on the phone, what's wrong with that?"

Perhaps there's a middle ground that looks like this:

If you aren't that into guys and would rather eat large quantities of Brussels sprouts than go out with one, you are not abnormal. Readiness to date happens to different girls at different ages. If your aversion to dating is because guys are horrible to you, forgive them, ignore them, and focus on being your best self. Let everybody else play the dating game if they want to. There is nothing wrong with you if you don't.

If you want to get in there and see what this whole boy-girl deal is about, develop some friendships with guys who have emerged from their purely annoying days. Get to know them as people. If you crush on one, that feeling is also normal.

The crush—the fluttering stomach when you see him—the inability to speak anything coherent when he says hi to you—that's the fun part. It's okay to enjoy that. It's part of being a girl. Admire him. Figure out what it is about him that makes you want to know his class schedule so you can just happen to be there when he walks by.

"In my mind, someone who would let me be myself would be a good boyfriend."

We've discussed all of that already. Now we get to the part where he shows his hand—he has a crush on you too—and the question arises whether to "go out" (a term that makes more sense

What the Guys Say

"Although going out with multiple girls can teach you things about dating, why would you need to learn how to date if you can have one successful relationship?"

now that you're a teenager!). I suggest that instead of making it an either/or decision, you decide what "boyfriend" really means to you. A healthy picture might look like this:

You like each other.

You have fun together.

You hang out with groups.

You keep it light, never letting it get so heavy and serious it looks like it could be on a daytime drama.

The minute you start fighting or playing jealousy games or considering sneaking off for a make-out session, it stops being fun.

If you can work it out and get back on track, great.

If not, you agree to stay friends and let it go at that. Knowing you're not mature enough to deal with all the drama is maturity in itself.

"It can't be as simple as that," you say? Actually, it can if you keep the thing just fun in the first place. Friends—good friends—don't really "break up." If you're so far into a relationship with a guy that not being his girlfriend anymore would mean never speaking to each other again, that isn't a relationship you're ready for. Maybe nobody is. The mistakes you make with a boyfriend can help you tremendously in the future, as long as going in you don't ignore what you already know, and that is that the goal is to enjoy.

That has to start, of course, with dating someone you really like. Too many girls make the mistake of going out with somebody just so they won't feel left out of the dating circuit.

"I didn't really want HIM, but I liked the idea of having what so many other girls seem to have going."

You may know how that is. You see a couple laughing together over a private joke or you watch your older sister blush when she gets a text message from her guy or you see a bevy of boys and girls going into a restaurant in their prom clothes and you think, “I want that!”

Of course you do. We all want to be loved, first of all.

Second of all, as females we’re hardwired to want to be swept off our feet in a whirl of romance, which can be anything from the two of you shooting baskets in the moonlight on your driveway to playing Juliet to his Romeo in the school play. The only danger is in wanting that experience so much that you’ll have it with just any old guy who shows some interest. Trust me, it really isn’t any fun when there’s no feeling behind it.

As for thinking it’s never going to happen to you if you wait for the right guy, don’t even go there. If you’re concentrating on becoming your true self, your day will come. You’ll have satisfying relationships, even if they don’t involve candles and I-love-you emails.

And really, high school isn’t the only chance you’ll have. This is the time when all the clumsy, immature, I-can’t-believe-I-said-that stuff goes on. The best is yet to come when the hormones settle in and the guys figure out the world isn’t all about them and you yourself become more poised and confident. Ask anyone who’s ever been to a class reunion: Which formerly popular kids obviously peaked in high school and which band geeks and wall flowers have become so intriguing they took everyone’s breath away? You really don’t know who you’re going to become. This is only the very beginning.

“What should you do when you really, really want a boyfriend, but you know that dating just because you want to feel loved is not the right reason?”

Most important of all—and you haven’t heard me give many this-is-the-way-it-is statements, so listen up—do not *ever* accept the current idea that if you don’t have a boyfriend, or if a whole mob of boys isn’t clamoring for your cell phone number, your email address, and your presence in the seat next to them at youth group, that you are someone “less than.”

Basic Truth #6

No guy can ever define who you are, or determine your worth.

No guy should ever define who you are or determine your worth, even if you marry the man. The only "guy" who does that is God. Since when did the opinion of a kid who still thinks flatulence is hilarious matter more than the One who actually made you? That's like taking beauty tips from your little brother. It's great to have a guy like you, there's no denying that. But to have one you can call your boyfriend just because not having one means you're nobody?

I'll let you answer that one.

The Twitter Version

It isn't unbiblical to date. What's unbiblical is to do it for any other reason than that is authentic for you.

Making It Real

Now that we've explored the whole concept of dating, it might be helpful for you to return to the questions your fellow sisters in bewilderment asked and shed some light on them for yourself. Again, imagine that you're free to make your own rules (even if that's a stretch right now) and give each of these some serious thought. Journaling your thoughts really works, but remember that we've talked about other options as well. As long as you can go deep, this will be effective for you.

Consider these questions:

- What is God saying to me personally about dating?
- Am I emotionally ready to date?
- Do I really know any guys I'd want to go out with?
- What would having a boyfriend look like for me?
- Could I keep a relationship in balance with the rest of my life, especially my relationship with God?

- Do I really want a boyfriend, or do I just want what everybody else has?
- (If applicable) Is the relationship I'm in right now a happy thing? Am I learning from it?

Don't try to answer all those in one day. Think of each one as a conversation topic for you and God. You bring the café mochas.

Mom, Dad ... Now Don't Freak Out

Everything we've said in other chapters concerning how to talk to your parents about guy issues is certainly true for this one. So let's take a little different approach this time. In addition to the above, if in fact you disagree with your parents' dating rules, ask them to tell you what they think makes a successful relationship. Either they have one or by now they've learned what doesn't work, but in any case they do have wisdom to share. Why not get some of that for future relationships of your own, while at the same time creating some common ground with your parents? (This is not, incidentally, a trick to soften them up for the next argument.) Just because under their rules you can't pursue a relationship right now doesn't mean you can't prepare yourself for one when the time comes.

Prepare to be surprised.

The Twitter Version

Ask your parents about THEIR relationships—past or present. Don't assume staying together doesn't take some skill on their part. You can totally tap into that. Sweet.

If I'm Totally Honest ...

I think I'll be really ready for a serious relationship when I ...

____

____

____

"Oh, the Drama."

It has to be easier for the non-human mammals when it comes to male-female interactions, don't you think? Most get together, have some babies, move on. The guy cats don't seem to care whether the girl cat is overweight or has funky markings. She'll do just as well as any other feline, even if all the toms aren't crowding around her or she doesn't look fabulous in a flea collar. It's just, "You're a cat, I'm a cat—let's get together."

But, alas, we're the unhairy mammals, the ones God gave the smarts to select our mates and live meaningful lives that go beyond catnip and naps on the windowsill (although that actually sounds kind of lovely at times . . .). Which leaves us with the task of untangling yet another boy knot: why do there always have to be issues?

It was bad enough when you were in your tween years and some girl was always running to the bathroom crying. Sometimes even you. You could have a fight with your BFF, make up, vow your undying friendship to each other, and have another knock down drag out, all within twenty-four hours. If that only happened once a week, you were doing good. Then of course there were the RMGs (Really Mean Girls: this is tween lingo—try to keep up) whose main purpose in life seemed to be to wreak havoc on the emotions of the girls not deemed worthy of their clique.

Sure, the boys were pesky, but they only accounted for about two percent of the drama you endured before you were twelve.

Just when you were starting to learn how to choose your battles with the other girls and not turn every minor slight into a soap opera plot, boys got in there and the crises picked up again. But it's not just the guys who are stirring it all with a stick. It's the girls yet again. That BFF who swore she'd be your maid of honor one day if you would be hers? It seems that all bets are off if you both like the same guy. Aren't there some days when you look back at the secure, all-girl life you once had and wonder how it got this crazy?

"The worst part about guys is when you just want to talk to them and hang out with them, but they like your best friend and just talk to her."

"One of my best friends has been going out with a guy for over a year now. They're really close and show no signs of breaking up any time soon. I'm immensely jealous, both because she shares with him all the things she used to share with me and because I don't have a relationship like that. Then I feel bad about myself."

"There's this obnoxious boy who has liked me for the whole school year. In class he stares at me and then between classes talks endlessly to me. He sits next to me on the bus every time we go on a field trip and somehow gets partnered with me in every activity. No offense, but he's a little weird and I don't like him. I'm not sure how to get out of this situation."

"I've had this thing where I meet a guy, start thinking about him a lot, hang out with him, and then realize the more I get to know him he's not that great."

"I just got an email from the guy who broke my heart. I'm just not really

What the Guys Say

Guys say the drama comes from:

"Not knowing how to talk to each other."

"Not having the guts to ask a girl out."

"Not understanding what girls want."

"Not understanding a girl's behavior."

sure what to do. I tried to be friendly but I'm pretty sure I came off upset and mad. I guess I haven't really forgiven him."

All of the above and other situations like them are the main reason people, including some teen girls themselves, think being involved with boys at your age is a bad idea. With his well-known book *I Kissed Dating Good-Bye,* Josh Harris started a whole movement of people who agreed with him that all the conflict and heartache connected with boyfriend-girlfriend relationships actually interfered with eventually finding a life partner in a healthy way. He said dating too young was a big obstacle to growing in Christ. Josh's book didn't become a bestseller because he was spouting off nonsense — he was right that avoiding serious, unhealthy dating really is a good plan for young people.

That's where I think we need to make a distinction, in the "serious, unhealthy part." Here's what I mean.

Conflict in relationships is a part of human existence. Part of your job growing up is to learn the basics of how to deal with it, and nobody gets that solely from being given instructions. You definitely need on-the-job training, and that's most assuredly what you'll get when there are boys in your daily life. And not just boys but the other girls who also play, worship, and go to school with them. Yeah, you'll be more mature in general when you're eighteen or nineteen than you are now, but if you have had zero experience with the special kinds of conflicts that seem to billow around boys like the cloud of dirt around Charlie Brown's friend Pigpen, you'll still have a deficit in that part of your growth.

I hope you know by now that I'm not saying everyone needs to throw themselves into the fray and stay in there until they figure out … whatever it is that needs to be figured out. What I *am* saying is unless you're growing up like an orchid in a hothouse, guy-related issues are pretty much unavoidable. Even if you're guyophobic and avoid voluntary contact with them, they're still in your classes, worship at your church, and pass you in the halls. Seriously, they're ubiquitous. If you have some as friends, are dating one, or have a steady guy relationship, then it's no news to you that issues come with the territory.

> **The Twitter Version**
> The boy-girl drama can be a bad scene, but if it's kept in perspective, it can actually teach you a lot about handling conflict.

This chapter is about how to deal with some of the common struggles that girls talk to me about. From that you'll be able to gather some general guidelines that apply to the personal things that come up in your experience, whether that experience is now or later. As in the rest of the book, the stories you'll read about are real—no fictional scenarios, no composites. Your concerns are too. Some adults may say to you, "You think these are problems? Wait until you grow up—then you'll know what trouble is." I hate that. The things you're facing today affect your life today—your mood, your self-confidence, your growth as a young woman. Even as I try to help you keep it all in perspective, I won't minimize any confusion or pain you're feeling.

Before we delve into the drama, take a few minutes to discover what your conflict resolution style is.

What's Going On with Me?

Read the following true story written by a teenage girl. Only a few details have been changed to protect her privacy:

"He was dark and gorgeous. I was klutzy and could never seem to keep my mouth shut. I liked him. Like, a lot. My friend told me to tell him because I was flipping out, so I did. And he told me he liked me. For three months (exactly three months yesterday) I had that high feeling. We flirted, we laughed; he made me smile and made me forget to breathe. I was totally taken by this guy. I knew it probably wouldn't end up in long-term dating or marriage, but I was in love with being in love. We were talking yesterday, and I got the news I never expected. He told me he lied. He told me that he didn't like me and that he never did.

He led me on for three months, flirted with me, told me all those sweet things and played with my heart, only to tell me he was lying and that he didn't mean any of it. He said he didn't think I was worth the truth."

After you finish muttering a few words about this creature and get that out of your system, write down what you would do if this happened to you. Get past, "It would never happen, because I am never going to get a crush on a boy like that, etc., etc." Just put yourself in her place and answer honestly.

____

____

____

____

____

____

____

Now read the following types of conflict resolution and see which one comes closest to what you wrote down.

Lock Up. "I would totally shut down and not let anyone, least of all him, see how I felt. I would tell myself it didn't matter and that *he* wasn't worth *my* truth either. In fact, I would know that I can't trust any guy from this point on. That's okay. At least I'll never have to go through that again."

Smooth Over. "I would tell him that I was fine with it, that at least he was telling me the truth now before we got in any deeper. I would say, 'I know this stuff happens with relationships and maybe we could just be friends from now on, although I would appreciate it if you would be honest with me in the future.' I would rather do that than make a big scene out of it."

Smack Down. "I would totally blow up and tell him that I was so mad I really wanted to punch him in the face. It would be hard not to call him some serious names, but I would definitely let him know that what he did was despicable. Yeah, by that time I would be screaming at him. I wouldn't care if he never spoke to me again. He would deserve it. I just have to get things like that out."

Break Down. "I would be so devastated, all I would be able to do was cry. I'm not sure I could wait until I'd walked away from him. I would be depressed for, well, for a long time. I would have to go to my best friends and have them talk to him and find out what was going on all that time, why he would do that to me. I couldn't face him myself, but I would have to know. And I would totally tell other girls not to ever be taken in by him."

Turn In. "I would be so upset, of course, mostly because I didn't see it coming. Why was I so stupid? Why didn't I know he was playing me? I wouldn't have conversations with *him*—I'd have them with *myself.* I'd be yelling at me for being such a total fool. Yeah, I'd have to figure out on my own what I did wrong to make him hate me like that."

Face Off. "Once I got done sobbing in my room, I would think it through, maybe talk to my mom about it, and then I'd figure out a way to go to him and say, 'Look, you really hurt me and that's not okay. I hope you never do this to another girl.' I might even say, 'I thought you were better than this.' It would be hard not to talk him down every chance I got, but I hope I wouldn't. He obviously has issues."

If your response is to **Lock Up**, you probably react to conflict, especially when you're hurt, by closing off your feelings. You chase the pain away. The problem is, you chase all your other emotions off with it, even the positive ones. Nothing is really resolved, and you wind up feeling numb.

If your tendency is to **Smooth Over**, you hate conflict so much you'd rather pretend it didn't happen. You might even convince yourself it doesn't matter, just as long as you don't have to talk about it. Trouble is, resentment builds up and eventually you'll blow, which creates a bigger conflict than the one you started with.

If you're one to **Smack Down**, your emotions go right into gear and you speak your mind, probably at the top of your lungs and possibly with your claws out. You attack the issue head on. Unfortunately, that often happens before your brain has a chance to engage. You definitely make your feelings known, but you also run the risk of making things worse than they were to begin with. One thing is for sure, the chances of the attackee wanting to work anything out go right down the drain.

If it's like you to **Break Down**, you do know how to own your feelings, which is healthy. It's just hard for you to talk about those feelings directly to the person who has done you wrong. You're more likely to discuss them with other people and get them involved. The perpetrator may never know how you feel, but everybody else will. There's no resolution in it for either of you, and in fact, a new conflict has been born.

If your reaction is to **Turn In**, you put the fault on yourself when conflict arises. If you can't find a way to take the blame for what happened, you beat yourself up for *letting* it happen. You're mature enough to know you need to think things through, but that's usually as far as it goes. It's difficult for you to confront the other person about his share of the blame because you feel so guilty about your own, whether it really exists or not. As a result, people practically get away with murder with you.

If to **Face Off** is your operating system, you let yourself feel the pain and move through it and then, when your head is clear and maybe you've gotten some input from wise people, you go to the person you're having issues with and lay it on the line. If there's another side to be heard, you'll listen. In a case like this one, where there's clearly nothing to be "worked out," you express your feelings with as much self-control as you can muster and then you're out of there. You might still sting from the experience, but it's a non-issue now.

Obviously **Face Off** is the approach that actually resolves conflict, even if the resolution is just in your own soul. I wish I could tell you that reading the rest of this chapter will make you a pro. The fact is nobody is totally perfect at it. If you were, the United Nations would hire you. But what you *can* do is take the best from your natural response and combine it with the Face Off. Locking down your feelings can get you through the confrontation so you don't pinch somebody's head off. The nice factor in Smoothing Over can prevent the face off from turning into a shouting match. The feistiness of wanting to Smack Down can give you the energy and passion to stay with it until the thing gets resolved. The let's-get-everybody-involved thing in Break Down will give you support as you go to the person yourself and put your cards on the table. And the analytical side of the person who tends to turn in can be a huge plus in getting your head clear before the big talk.

The point is that no matter what your style, you can tackle conflict without doing a number on yourself or anyone else. And when it comes to the issues guys can put out there, you're going to need to.

Guydlines

While the kinds of issues that surround the very presence of guys are more numerous than actual guys, I'm only presenting four here. Otherwise we'd need a miniseries. With each one, we'll talk about **why it happens** (if there is indeed a reason beyond "Guys do stupid things and we do too"), **how you can approach it**, and what, pray tell, you might learn from it. Then we'll sum it up so you can hopefully apply it to other situations that snag you.

Guys being fickle.

Do you still use that word? If not, you should, because it so perfectly describes this kind of behavior on the part of guys.

What the Guys Say

"The drama comes from guys not treating girls with respect."

"I liked a guy my friend was dating, and he knew I did. I told him I wanted nothing to do with him except be friends, because I didn't want her to get hurt, but he was like, 'No, I like you way better.' So he dumped her for me, and now she hates me."

"What do you think I should do if a guy that just broke up with my friend is now talking to me a lot and acting like he likes me? I like him too, but they had a really bad breakup and I'm afraid it'll be a mess if I go out with him."

Why on earth? There are like a bajillion girls out there. Why does he have to pick you, the best friend to the girl he just dumped? Are they just brainless, these guys? They aren't, but it can seem that way. It's mostly because he likes a certain "type" of girl, and who's going to be more like your BFF than you? And then there's the fact that in getting to know her, he's gotten to know you, and now he wants to know more. Not to mention that some guys just like to throw stones at the hive and see what kind of nasty confusion they can stir up. It's like an ego thing, you know? If he can get two girls fighting over him, that's a rush for him, because he's a cad. I know that sounds heartless, but remember that guys don't always view a relationship at this stage the way you do. To you it's an emotional attachment. To them it may be more of an experiment. When it's over, you grieve. They may go on to try another experiment. The good news is that does change as they mature, but right now for the fickle type it's a game called "How many different girlfriends can I have before I'm sixteen?"

Come to think of it, don't you know some girls who seem to be same way about boys?

So what do you do about it? My best advice is to put the friend first. Think about it: you don't go through girlfriends the way boys go through girlfriends. There's a good chance you and your current CFFs (Close Friends Forever) will remain close through high school and maybe even beyond. The guy you have a crush on right now—including the one who just ditched your best friend?—you may not even remember his name a year from now. Look at his track record. How many girls has he thrown over for somebody else this semester? Do you want to risk a great friendship just to be on that list?

As for the Face Off, involve your girlfriend as little as possible in this drama. You don't even have to tell her he's hitting on you. Why let her feelings be hurt any more than they already are? There's a little pride thing in all of us that wants other people to know we're wanted and pursued, but deny that and keep this one to your yourself. And if you can't trust your other CFFs not to be all Chatty Cathy about it, don't tell them either.

If she knows, that's another story. The issue there is usually that she doesn't believe you didn't go after him and didn't flirt him into falling for you. Tell her you've passed on his offer and then don't bring it up again. If she simply finds it easier to blame you than accept the fact that he just flat doesn't want her, maybe the friendship wasn't that strong after all. Maybe she never did know who you really are—a person of integrity and loyalty. Grieve, and then find some friends with a little more maturity.

It's Fickle Boy you really need to confront, calmly and firmly. "I don't think so, pal" should do it. If he can't get any turmoil going, he'll move on. Most guys this age just aren't going to work that hard.

What can you learn from going through a situation like that?

- Most guys aren't ready for long-term relationships (meaning longer than their attention span).
- If you have to make a choice, it's best to go with the deeper friendship, the one that brings out the best in you (as opposed to the one that feeds "Am I irresistible or what?").
- Honesty doesn't always mean confessing everything. Be mindful of people's feelings and don't hurt them unnecessarily.

Breaking a boy's heart

Or at least bruising his pride. In situations like these, wouldn't it be a whole lot easier to be like guys and not put too much thought into how you turn somebody down?

"This one guy likes me a lot and I can't do anything without knowing he's staring at me. Double worse, I've gotten to be friends with another boy and the one who is crushing on me is, like, all annoyed."

My next-door neighbor has this HUGE crush on me! He would do anything and everything for me and I don't like him the same way."

For a lot of girls, this wouldn't be a big deal. They'd just say, "In your dreams, pal," and walk away without a thought to his feelings. When I was teaching high school, I saw girls do that kind of stuff all the time, as if the less-than-hunky guys didn't have hearts. You, I'm sure, are of a different sort—as in, you care about how that poor guy is going to feel when you reject him. Being a Christian does that to you. It's part of the "love one another as I have loved you" thing Jesus told us we had to do. (More on that below.) Which doesn't solve the problem of how to handle it when Mr. Wrong is staring at you, waiting for a word, while you have eyes for Mr. Right over there—or nobody at all right now. If you love that boy the way Jesus says to, won't he be drooling in your direction forever?

Why does this even happen? Why can't guys get a vibe from you or read your body language or something? For the same reason you can come to the dinner table puffy-eyed, tears streaming down your cheeks, and about the time dessert is served, your father says, "Is something wrong?" They just aren't always as tuned into other's people's emotions as you are, especially at this age. Besides that, if you're the kind of person who wants to let him down easy without bruising his feelings,

What the Guys Say

"Drama gets started when a guy wants to date a girl and pushes it on her whether she wants to go out or not."

What the Guys Say

If she's going to let me down:

"I want her to be honest with me."

"I want her to tell me in a courteous but honest way that she doesn't feel the same way I do."

"Just keep it plain and simple. Just tell me she's 'talking' to someone else."

"I want her to just say it: she doesn't like me."

"Honestly, I'd want it put right out there. It would hurt, but with time I would get over it. It's better to stay friends."

that explains why he likes you in the first place. Guys who don't fit the total-babe-on-the-football-field mold are especially susceptible to crushes on girls who are nice to them. That's what you get for being a decent human being!

So, you handle this how? Love the kid. Obviously not romantically or even necessarily as a friend. We're talking spiritual love, which has nothing to do with *liking* the person. It's about:

- doing him no harm (and that includes gossiping, telling everyone he's a dork, laughing in his face).
- realizing he's one of God's children too, and therefore deserves your respect (which means not looking at him like he's invisible, acknowledging his good points, resisting the urge to say, "What exactly is it that you're staring at, buddy?").
- helping him out if he needs it and you're the one to do it (as in, squelching the false rumor everybody's spreading about him, letting him know he sat in the ketchup some moron put in his chair, praying for him).

If the Face Off is necessary (he's just not picking up what you're putting down) be honest (though kind) and tell him you're just not into him. There's no need to go into why ("You drive me crazy talking about your video games" or "Seriously, it's your breath."). He may be crestfallen, but it's better that he hears it straight, rather than your making excuses ("I have to go floss," for instance), or watching him suffer and hoping he'll go away, or getting somebody else to tell him to back off, especially another guy.

> **What the Guys Say**
> "Don't accept a date with me and THEN tell me you aren't interested."

What if he doesn't give up? Bless his heart. Tell him as often as you need to, and be sure you aren't doing anything to encourage him because, after all, it doesn't hurt your self-esteem any to have somebody swooning over you. Even if you're going all out to guard his feelings, they're going to be hurt, just like yours are when somebody you're crushing on makes it clear the feeling isn't mutual. You can't help that. But you can do a lot to make sure his ego isn't smashed and he doesn't end up thinking he's a complete loser.

What can you learn from that squirmy situation?

- You can't please everybody. (Hard for you soft-hearted ladies.)
- Honesty can be hard, but you owe it to someone who sees something in you he likes.
- Once you've had to turn down a guy's affections, you gain some pretty interesting insights into how you are with the boy *you* like.

Being dumped

"When he told me it was over, it's safe to say I was devastated. I trusted him and he threw it back at me. I'm still not totally over it."

If a relationship, even a friendship, means anything at all to you, you're going to be upset when it's over. That's not just because you'll miss the fun you had with the guy or the talks you shared. It also hurts because it feels like a rejection of you, personally. Who you are, it would seem, was not good enough. Not only that (as if we needed more!), but you may feel sort of stupid. Why did I believe him? Why did I trust him? Why did I show him how much I liked him? Needless to say, the more involved you were in the relationship, the worse the breakup is going to feel.

Why do guys do that, anyway? Why do they act like you're their princess one day and then totally dethrone you the next? Are they cold-hearted beings, or are they just determined to break every female heart in the class by graduation so they'll feel like Mr. Man?

Maybe there are some who think they're Don Juan, but if you're paying attention at all you'll pick up on the ones who are just racking up a body count and you'll steer clear. But most guys don't go into a relationship with a girl planning to break her heart. It's just that their dreams for the relationship may not be the same as yours. I asked the guys I interviewed if they ever daydream about marrying their girlfriend and I got a unanimous, "Are you *serious*?" But they do look for the fun, the talking and listening, the satisfying feeling of being seen for who they are. That's why they ask you out.

So they break if off why? That depends on the people in the relationship, but more often than not the reason falls into one of four categories:

1. Restlessness. "I've seen all there is. I'm ready to move on."
2. Too much responsibility. "This relationship is getting too serious. I'm not ready for this."
3. Distraction. "I like you, but I just noticed this other chick over here ..."
4. Incompatibility. "I didn't see this at first, but now I get that you and I are not going to get along."

Notice that none of that has much to do with you. Yeah, maybe you pushed a little too much for a steady commitment or you took him for granted or you wanted to watch a chick flick when he wanted to watch the playoffs. But those are mistakes. They aren't flaws in your personality. Let's face it, most teen relationships don't last into eternity—or even until graduation. Mostly, breakups happen because the two people in it aren't ready for the serious stuff yet. And there is nothing wrong with that.

What the Guys Say

"I broke up with a girl because she was always whining and saying I was cheating on her. I totally wasn't."

How do you deal with it? I don't think I can give you a better answer than the one Corrie ten Boom's father gave her when as a young woman she was in a relationship with a guy who then married another girl. In her book *The Hiding Place,* she says this is what her father told her:

> "There are two things we can do when this happens. We can kill the love so that it stops hurting. But then of course part of us dies too. Or, Corrie, we can ask God to open up another route for that love to travel. God loves Karel *(the man Corrie loved)*—even more than you do—and if you ask Him, He will give you His love for this man, a love nothing can prevent, nothing destroy. Whenever we cannot love in the old, human way, Corrie, God can give us the perfect way."

If Corrie could learn to love with God's love a man she truly expected to marry, seems like it could be done over a short-lived guy-girl thing that just didn't work out.

As for the Face Off, once you've been told it's over, it's not good form to ask why or beg for another chance. You're already miserable enough. You probably don't want to add desperate on top of that. Your guy may not even know why, or at least he can't explain it. You'll come out of it with your self-esteem still intact if you don't act like this is the end of life as you know it.

If he has behaved like a complete jackal, however (he broke up with you in a text message, posted his intentions to the world on Facebook, had his best friend give you the news, that kind of thing), he needs to know that the way he's handling this thing is not okay. Using the Face Off style we talked of earlier, go to him — unarmed — and be straight with him. Then it'll be your turn to walk away, head held high.

What the Guys Say

"When I caught my girl hugging on some other guy, that was it. I told her it was over."

What could you possibly learn from being tossed aside, besides that love can hurt?

A breakup doesn't determine your worth as a person. Seriously, we're talking about a person who can't seem to get his pants size right. He gets to decide if you're "good enough"? Really?

You now know how to deal with loss, at least on a small scale. The fact that you survive it and get over it is reassuring, isn't it?

You'll know the signals when you have a girl-of-the-week kind of guy on your hands. You're sadder-but-wiser now, and that's called maturity.

Being in constant turmoil

You start off being with a guy, even as friends, because you like each other, you make each other laugh, you like yourself when you're with him. You're thinking, "What is so hard about being in a relationship?" Then one day you realize you haven't felt like that in a week because he gets jealous every time you mention another guy's name (good grief, you're talking about your brother!) or he ignored you during the entire World Series or you forgot to text him when you promised you would. You argue, you make up — which is great — and then a day later you're at it again. What happened to holding hands at the duck pond like you did on your first date?

Several things could have happened. You aren't as meant for each other as you thought. You haven't figured each other out yet. You're expecting too much. I could go on (ad nauseam) but you see what I'm getting at. Because you both have little to zero previous experience in being in a relationship with a person of the opposite, confusing, mysterious sex, you're bound to have issues. People who don't get married until they're thirty-five have issues. Why wouldn't you?

So — what do you do? Do you decide you're not ready for all this and call it quits? That's definitely an option. If it's not going well, why keep at it? It's not like you're saving a marriage. But if you really do care about each other and you either have only the occasional spat (what couple doesn't?) or your battles are always about one thing (him teasing you in front of his friends, for example), it might be worth trying to work it out.

That calls for a mini Face Off. Get clear in your own mind what you think the problem is. Let him know you want to talk about it soon. Not while he's watching the Super Bowl or studying for his American history final, but at a time when you can both focus. Be direct and brief about what you think and how you feel. One thing guys hate is a lot of prologue and repetition. As one guy asked me, "Why can't girls just say it?" Then — and this is huge — listen to what the boy has to say. It's going to take him a minute (or fifteen) to respond, so don't decide his initial silence means he didn't hear you and or doesn't care what you said. He's processing. Once you both have it out there on the table, suggest some options for solving the problem. Important: don't go back to "You do this and it drives me up the wall." That part's done. You're into solutions now. Keep it simple. This is not marriage counseling. You're just trying to get back to enjoying each other. If it looks like fixing this is going be like a new career, be honest with each other about whether it's how you want to be spending your youth. Dating just shouldn't be that hard.

There are some signs that it *is* too hard, that you're in over your head. Don't consider yourself a relationship failure if you bow out because of one of these:

- You fight more than you laugh.
- Your arguments upset you for more than a very short time.
- The relationship isolates you from your friends and activities.
- You feel like you have to tiptoe around your guy so he doesn't get mad.
- You ever feel threatened by your guy. (Ever.)
- He's pushing for sex even though you've said no.
- You're depressed because of the relationship.
- Other guys are looking really good to you.
- Your friends are commenting that you don't seem happy.

Those are things that go on in a relationship just before it becomes abusive. Knowing what they are and getting out as soon as you see them may protect you from a really bad scene. If you have ever been afraid that your boyfriend was going to hit you, don't break up with him alone. Do it over the phone. Better yet, do it in person and take your dad or another adult you trust with you. Potential abuse is nothing to fool around with. Care not what the other kids are going to say— "She's overreacting. He would never do that." Trust your instincts.

If the guy you're seeing ever has hit you, grabbed you roughly, pulled your hair, or done anything else physically that hurt and or frightened you, go to the nearest adult you trust right now and tell her. You aren't being a snitch. You are protecting yourself and every other girl he might become involved with. And in a way, you're protecting him from hurting his future wife and kids someday. Please don't be one of the victims. Speak up.

On that cheery note, what can you learn from mucking your way through boyfriend issues?

> **What the Guys Say**
>
> "It gets messed up when you have trouble controlling your emotions or your hormones as a guy."

- It's okay to walk away. Life is wa-a-a-y too short to waste on a temporary duo that just isn't going to work out.
- If a relationship is worth working on, there's a simple (though not necessarily easy) way to do it.
- You aren't perfect. There's always something you can focusing on that will make you a dream to be with when it *is* time to get serious.

The Twitter Version

Conflict is inevitable. Being miserable is optional. There is a way to deal with everything, even it means walking away.

Before you decide, after reading all this, that you're *never* going to get involved with a guy if it's this much trouble, let's go to God. There's a whole lot of divine reassurance there.

God on Guys

Jesus is your go-to guy when it comes to resolving relationships. You've got:

"If your brother or sister has something against you ... go ... be reconciled. Come to terms quickly with your accuser" (from Matthew 5:23–25).

If someone gets in your face, don't get in his face back. Turn to him (or her!) and say, "I'm not doing it this way" (paraphrase of Matthew 5:39).

Don't just be decent to the people it's easy to be decent to. Treat everybody that way. Even the jerks (paraphrase of Matthew 5:43–48).

The one thing underlying all of them is the thing that's hardest to do.

"I try to forgive and move on, but I just can't get over what he did."

"The biggest reason I'm having trouble letting go and forgiving him is because he hasn't even admitted he did anything wrong. He just goes on."

"How do I just get rid of this I-hate-you feeling forever?"

Jesus says we have to (as in, it isn't optional) forgive other people exactly the way God forgives us (Matthew 18:21–35). So you make up your mind you aren't going to hold a grudge against Mr. Fickle anymore for treating you like one of his harem. You decide it's time to stop being resentful of that guy who said "We're history," or the one who doesn't understand any part of no. You even try to forgive yourself, for breaking Nice Guy's heart or for putting up with the twisted-up guy who tried to cut you off from all your friends. Okay. Clean slate. New day. No more gnawing on this thing. It's yours, God.

Seven seconds later (or sooner) you're back at it again, and it colors everything gray. If Jesus would just give some how-to instructions to go along with that command ...

Actually they're there, right there, in your relationship with God. God shows us all the time in the way *we* are forgiven. Just consider these questions:

Does God wish you harm because you've messed up countless times?

Does God keep wanting you to provide some kind of payback for all the times you've disappointed him?

Does God keep throwing your mistakes in your face?

Does God stop loving people in general because at times you haven't loved him with your whole self?

The answer is no on all counts. That's the way God forgives and that's what forgiveness means for us as well. You want to forgive the guy who made you feel like a loser or the friend who betrayed you over some boy?

Don't hope bad things will happen to him. Refuse to wish that something heavy would drop on her in her sleep. And don't put harm in motion by bad-mouthing him all over campus or jumping at the chance to dis him to his new girlfriend. God doesn't seek revenge. Neither should we.

Don't hold him accountable for your pain. The old version of the Lord's Prayer says, "Forgive us our debts, as we forgive our debtors." Release him from any debt to you. Don't expect him to ever make up for the hurt he's caused. Clear the books. When you stop waiting for him to pay up, you too are free. Besides, even if he did, it wouldn't make you feel any better.

Don't bring the travesty up every time you have a chance, whether to the ones who betrayed you or in conversations about them. When it comes up in your mind, tell it to get lost. Eventually it will give up and go away. As soon as you repent to God of any wrongdoing, it's forgotten in the Divine mind. Stop holding it over everyone's heads, including yours.

Don't let one person's bad treatment of you make *you* less loving. If you become all bitter and suspicious, you cut yourself off from the possibility of real love in the future. And since God *is* love—well, there you go.

Forgiveness doesn't mean, "Hey, it's all right. It doesn't matter that you hurt me. Matter of fact, come on over here and I'll let you hurt me again." It just means the hurt no longer controls you. That could take time, but in the end, forgiveness is the ultimate resolution to conflict.

That Jesus, man, he has an answer for everything. Come to think of it, he's a guy, so they can't be all bad!

Basic Truth #7

Forgiveness isn't a suggestion. God forgives us, and we have to do likewise.

Making It Real

What's the biggest guy-issue you're involved in right now? What keeps you tossing in bed until the covers are in a giant wad? What makes you bite your fingernails or twist your hair or whatever else you do when you're stressed out? What's making you snappier than usual with your siblings? What are you frantically texting your friends about or bringing up every time you have a phone conversation? (Come to think of it, they've stopped returning your calls.)

It doesn't have to be potentially heartbreaking. It can be anything from being annoyed with your best guy friend for teasing you about your cluelessness in chemistry to your best friend flirting with the guy she knows you like. It can even be wanting your secret crush to even know you sit next to him in English.

Write it down. Go ahead. It doesn't have to be a three-page essay. A sentence will do. Couple of words maybe.

Take it someplace where you can usually think clearly and without interruption (although in some households, good luck with that, right?). Bathtub maybe? Your room after everyone's asleep? Some outside spot where you always seem to run into God? That's where you're headed, to a place where you can run that issue past God and see what happens.

You may get the courage to have the Face Off that's called for.

You might get some clarity on why your current conflict management style isn't working out for you (bursting into tears every time your boyfriend mentions his ex-girlfriend's name, for instance).

It could be that you'll realize it's time to end that relationship or get over yourself and make friends with that artsy guy who fascinates you, even though your friends think he's "odd."

In the silence you may hear that still, small voice that tells you it's okay to let go and forgive, because there are better things ahead for you.

You could come away feeling no different than you did when you started. Give it some time. The answers may come in some pretty far-out ways (a song lyric, a billboard, an off-handed comment from your brother … now *that's* far out.)

Maybe you won't feel like you've gotten any help at all. But if you don't go there and ask, you definitely won't. Besides, is there some time limit on when God can answer?

When you get even a small inkling from God on what to do about that issue, put it together with all the information you've learned here and all you're finding out about your own self and take one small step in that direction. There's power in that. The issue will no longer run you. Who knows? Your nails might even have a chance to grow.

Mom, Dad ... Now Don't Freak Out

It may seem to you that your parents are the last people who would understand what you're going through in guy-world. If they do, great. That's one issue you don't have to deal with, right? But in many cases, girls know from experience that if they bring up some deal they're having with a boy, they're going to hear:

"I said you weren't ready for boys."

"This is why we don't want you dating. There's too much drama."

"You're spending too much time on all this. You have more important things to think about."

"I don't know what you're going to do when you have real problems to face."

Some people sure know how to shut down a conversation, don't they? Kind of makes you not want to mention it at all—except that it sure would be nice to be able to talk to your parents about the things that are really bothering you, even if they don't *think* that stuff should be bothering you. I keep telling you that they have both the wisdom of experience and your best interests going for them, that they're a veritable treasure trove of things that could help you through this milieu you're trying to navigate.

But if you can't get past, "Oh, for Pete's sake, don't make such a big deal out of this silly stuff," how are you supposed to find that?

For starters, it might help to understand what's going on with them. We've said it before, they love you and they don't want you to be hurt. In the past they've always been able to divert you from harm by saying, "Don't do that. Don't go there." That's what they're still trying to do. Except that there's a difference between hurt and harm.

Harm is of a more permanent nature. There's harm in staying out all night. Running around with a kid who does drugs. Getting so strung out over a guy you stop eating. Keep participating in harmful behavior and you'll be damaged as a person. Parents can't let that happen.

Hurt, on the other hand, is more temporary. It hurts to like a guy who doesn't like you back, or to find out a friend is talking trash about you and your guy friend, or to back out of the dating scene because it's turned into a mini version of *Survivor*. It could be avoided, sure, but it also teaches. Strengthens. Builds that character everybody's always talking about.

Parents don't want you hurt, either. The only one who can convince them the experience is okay is you. As always, there are ways to go about that which are going to get you grounded until you're *past* marrying age.

"I'm the one who might get hurt, not you, so why can't you just let me do my thing?"

"While you weren't looking, I grew up. I can handle this, okay?"

"I just want to be able to ask you for advice without you telling me to just go study or something."

It's the "you's" that get you into trouble. Not to mention the "I know more about this than you do" attitude. Neither is going to get you where you want to be. Do an attitude adjustment — "I have a thought I'd like to share with you"—and turn everything into an "I" statement.

> "I really want to talk to you guys about something. It might seem silly, but it's important to me and I'd like some input."
>
> "I know you think I get too worked up over all this relationship drama, but really, I'm trying to work it out so it *isn't* drama. I thought maybe you could give me some advice."
>
> "I need to just vent to somebody and you're the only one I can really trust right now."

Can you honestly imagine your parents saying, "You're right. It is silly. Come back when you have something significant to say"? Come on. They're going to come back with, "I have no advice for you," or "Go find somebody else to trust"? Not on their worst day!

Once you get the conversation going, you can reassure them that you aren't about to go off the deep end over some guy or devote all your time to Conflict Resolution 101. A clear picture of what's really going on is probably a whole lot less dramatic than what they've dreamed up. Again, you're the only one who can provide that picture. And it isn't going to take a Face Off to do it. After all, these people are way more mature than the ones you're *used* to dealing with!

> **The Twitter Version**
>
> Parents are the perfect people to go to when you're hurting. Really.

If I'm Totally Honest ...

The one issue I wish everybody would just get OVER is:

____

____

____

"And All of This Is Important Because ...?"

Let's face it: life would probably be much simpler for you right now without guys in it.

That throwing-climbing-jumping-concocting-punching thing they were into as little boys is all but over—but the flirting-hugging-strutting-confusing-the-snot-out-of-you thing that has replaced it does an even more thorough job of frying your brain.

If you just didn't have to cope with their bewildering behavior, you could probably, oh, I don't know, get through a day without wondering if that one will throw a glance your way or if that other one will finally stay *out* of you way or if any one of them will ever realize that you are not as invisible as a piece of Saran Wrap. Whether you really care about a date to prom or even think you want to complicate your life by saying, "So—how do you like your Droid?", teenage males are there to be dealt with. And the fact that you've just read an entire book on the subject tells you it definitely isn't easy. There are probably days when the next adult who tells you that guys aren't that important to your life right now is just asking for an eye roll.

I'd be right there rolling with you. Of *course* guys are not *the* most important thing. But they are undeniably a significant part of your development into a young woman — not so you can check "having a boyfriend" off on some list of milestones to becoming one. (In the first place, what list? But that's for another book ...) The importance of guys to your development is not the guys themselves and whether they adore you or ignore you or think of you as their little sister. It's what you learn about yourself when you're dealing with whatever they throw out there. (Huh. I guess they *are* still throwing ...)

If you didn't have to decipher their language and their mental processes and their body language (Is he trying to impress me or is there some other reason why he does a chin-up on the door frame every time I walk by?), you wouldn't become a shrewd observer of people as a whole.

If you didn't have to become comfortable enough to talk to one without sweating like a prize fighter and losing your entire vocabulary, you'd have a harder time becoming a poised, confident young woman across the board.

If you didn't discover that being friends with one isn't like befriending a creature from another planet, you'd be slower to learn that there is something potentially valuable in every human being.

And if you didn't have to work through the issues that are as much a part of guys as their ball caps and cell phones, you'd be slower to become compassionate and assertive and just plain forgiving.

As infuriating as they can be, teenage boys have as profound an effect on who you become as just about anything else. Fortunately (ya gotta love that word right now!), what effect they have depends entirely on you.

And, of course, God.

God on Guys—and the Guydlines That Follow

I've said that in the Gospels, Jesus didn't directly address "what should a girl do about boys?", but I have to say I think he came pretty close with this verse:

"The kingdom of heaven is like a merchant in search of fine pearls; on finding one pearl of great value, he went and sold all that he had and bought it" (Matthew 13:45).

Okay, so I know that the pearl of great price Jesus is talking about means salvation, the Kingdom of God. That's the first layer. But you are a pearl worth saving. Each of you. Whether you're voted Most Likely to Break Every Heart in the Freshman Class or the girl who's taking it all in from behind a copy of *Pride and Prejudice*. You are—all of you—pearls of great price *in* the kingdom of God.

Some of you have already realized that and are taking great care of your pearl-ness. You know the difference between flirting and being friendly, and if you flirt at all you're cautious about who you bat those baby blues (or browns or greens or hazels) at. You understand guys because you're friends with some, and you know enough to make sure none of them are going to make off with that pure, perfect treasure that is you.

Whether you have that down or not at this point, I'm sure that the very fact you've read this book means you aren't careless with your affections. I have a feeling you're not succumbing to the, "Boy? Where? Is he cute?" mentality that a lot of girls are operating under.

Just consider this about protecting your pearl-self—the wonderful, feminine, growing-into-a-woman you.

Do you think the jewel merchant is so afraid the pearl of great value is going to be stolen that he hides it in a safe deposit box at the bank so no one knows it even exists? What good would it do him—or anyone else—there? He would be wise to let people see it and appreciate it, even while he was protecting it from harm.

The smart jewel merchant would see how it could best be displayed — in a tie tack? A necklace? An earring? He wouldn't let fear drive him to bury it in a chest in the ground. Again, what would be the point?

What I'm trying to say is that as you're figuring out how you want to be around these boys-who-are-soon-to-be-men, fear is not your friend. Going into a panic about these kinds of things is not protecting — it's paralyzing:

"What if I get to be friends with a boy I really like and then he thinks I want to have a girlfriend-boyfriend thing?"

"What if I'm friends with a really cool guy and then I get a crush on him and have to stop being friends with him?"

"What if we're just friends and everybody thinks we're a couple and it ruins the friendship?"

"What if I become his girlfriend and it gets too serious?"

I haven't lied to you. Any of those things could happen. Maybe you've already experienced them. But you're still here, aren't you? You're still a beautiful pearl of a girl. Maybe an even more beautiful one because you've learned and grown and, most important of all, you've loved.

So, one more word of advice from someone who, yes, had her young heart broken and broke one (or two) herself back when — but who wouldn't give up the deep friendships with guys that I still count as treasures in my life. Here it is:

Protect yourself out of **wisdom**, not out of **fear**. Don't let the near-terror of what-if-what-if-what-if deprive you of godly relationships with *anyone.*

Fear is thinking you'll be swept away by the tide of peer pressure if you even dip your toe in the water. **Wisdom** is simply being aware of how strong peer pressure can be.

Fear is being convinced that other people will consider you Uncool for not having serial romances like the Very Cool. **Wis-**

dom is caring more about what you and God think and letting that determine your choices.

Fear is refusing to even get to know a boy as a person because there's the chance-in-a-million that one of you is going to get a crush on the other one and . . . and who knows what then, but it can't be good. **Wisdom** is letting a guy friendship be the beginning of learning what relationships are all about and how to be honest and express your feelings and enjoy somebody's company without worrying if "something" is going to happen — because *you* get to decide what happens.

If you bury your precious pearly self, you let fear make your decisions for you. That isn't going to take you anyplace you want to be. Yes, if you're not comfortable around boys yet, by all means stay away. But promise yourself that you will pray to be released from fear if that's what's keeping you from showing *anyone* what a priceless pearl you are. Don't live anxious because you're afraid to do life "wrong." One thing Jesus did *not* say was, "Be afraid. Be very afraid." He said to have life and have it abundantly. (Again, that's John 10:10.) That doesn't mean have 208 pairs of shoes. It means celebrate your pearl-ness. Share it with people you sense you can trust.

Be clear on this: the pearl we're talking about is not your virginity — it's a given that your goal is to give that only to the person you marry. *This* pearl is your true and beautiful self, a self you can never really know until you share it. The pearl that is worth being saved. It sure looks better next to the other pearls on the life-necklace than it does in the fear-box with the lid on.

> **The Twitter Version**
>
> Don't hide your pearly self out of fear. Wisdom is a far better guide to making good decisions.

What's Going On with Me?

This is our eighth "quiz" together. I hope all the checking and circling and scoring we've done has helped you see what you're doing that is so very right-for-you as well as what you might want to work on. In fact, let's take a look at the big you-picture at this point and see where you are now that you've had a chance to spend some focused-on-guys-issues time with God and maybe tried out the "guydlines" on your own stuff.

Put a big ol' check next to ALL the statements below that you can honestly make about yourself.

_____ I don't always get guys (who does?) but they're not a total mystery to me either.

_____ I realize the amount of attention I get from guys is not a true measure of who I am.

_____ I can have a conversation with a guy without losing track of my personality.

_____ When I see a girl totally throwing herself a boy, I think, "Oh, sister, you're so much better than that."

_____ I can be friendly to a guy without worrying if he'll think I'm flirting.

_____ If I flirt, I still feel like me.

_____ If I want to talk to a guy I like I can do it *without* feeling like my arms are too long or my mouth is too big or my whole face is saying, "You think I'm a total geek right now, don't you?"

_____ I know guys I'd like to be friends with.

_____ I'm good friends with a guy or two. Or three.

_____ I love being in a group where there are fun guys (who don't need water balloons or beer hidden in the bushes to call the evening a success).

_____ One of my best friends is a guy.

_____ I don't date but it isn't because I'm afraid to.

_____ I date for fun.

_____ I know having a boyfriend won't automatically make me okay.

_____ I have a boyfriend because the guy is great and we have a blast together.

_____ I know what "too serious" looks like and I'm not going there.

_____ I don't let myself get into situations where sex is even a remote possibility.

_____ I don't feed my random thoughts about sex.

_____ It isn't easy to totally avoid sex in the media, but I give it my best shot.

_____ I know the signs of potential abuse in a relationship (but I don't suspect every guy of being a closet monster).

_____ I don't judge girls who've made mistakes with guys. I get how hard the whole thing is even if I haven't been there.

_____ I know God forgives me for the mistakes I've made with guys.

_____ I'm letting God help me get past my mistakes with guys and turn me in a new direction.

_____ I'm honest with my parents about where I stand on guy issues.

_____ I honor my parents' rules, whether I agree with them or not.

_____ I know I'm a girl that a guy could enjoy being with — whether any of them actually do yet or not!

By now, I don't think I have to guide you through interpreting your results. You can see how far you've come and where you might want to focus. You can even just take a look at your big picture and let the next brush strokes fill in as you naturally grow as a young woman. Knowing it's happening, though — that's satisfying. That's maturity.

As a matter of fact, that's God.

Making It Real

"My longing is kind of old-fashioned and probably comes from too much Jane Austen. What I would love is for a guy to be chivalrous and honorable. My mom says that I have such high standards for guys that no one will ever be able to meet them."

I know that if I suggested you make a list of the characteristics of the man you see yourself marrying, you'd come up with a list that would have your mom saying the same thing. I've seen those lists, and they include everything from "never gets mad" to "has to know Chinese." As much of a hoot as it may be to describe Mr. Perfect, the fact that he doesn't exist makes it just that: a hoot.

Even if you're more realistic and limit your requirements to "he has to want to be in some kind of ministry" and "he must want children," that doesn't help you much with the guys you're looking at right now. They aren't even close to being who they're going to be when that list even becomes useful. What guy absolutely knows what he's going to do ten years from now? (Do *you*? Really?) And just mention having kids to a guy and watch him panic. He'll cut and run like he's being chased by the SWAT Team. You can look for future husband traits in the guys you know, but you can't expect to find more than a trace or two. They're not *supposed* to look like spouses yet. Nobody has the maturity of a thirty-year-old at age fifteen or sixteen. Not even you. You're not the woman you're going to be either. She's starting to show up in beautiful glimmers, but the real thing hasn't been fully formed.

So as much fun as it is to daydream about the guy who's going to take you to the altar, it makes more sense here to think about the vision of your life as a whole. What glimpses of that is God giving you right now? What kind of *person* do you feel yourself becoming? What passions are starting to stir in you — things you find yourself really caring about in your soul? What gifts and talents are surprising you as they show up in your behavior? What positive direction do you suddenly find yourself moving in?

I suggest that for your last "making it real" exercise — at least in this book! — you consider, with God, where you'd like to be just one year from now. These questions might be a good start, but of course feel free to let your own experience take you farther:

> What challenge do you want to have met by then? What current issue do you hope to have resolved? (In other words, what thing that's driving you crazy do you want to no longer have sending you up the wall?)

What friendships do you want to be significant? Some you already have that could use some growing? People you don't know that well and want to?

What confusion do you want to have untangled? Something about guys? Something you just don't get about parents? Something on a more spiritual level?

What passion or personal gift do you want to have done something with, even on a small scale? How do you want to be able to say, "I don't just *dream* about this anymore — I'm actually *into* it because I ________."

How do you want to be able to fill in this blank: I know I'm more confident because ________.

If you go to God with your answers and pay attention to God's response over time, and you sense that those really are good goals for you, then do this. Figure out one small step you could take in that direction, something that would get you an inch or two closer to where you and God want you to be.

Whether it's breaking the ice with someone you've never talked to or googling organizations that share your passion or biting the bullet and apologizing to your parents for making them want to send you off to a convent — make like a Nike commercial and just do it. It'll be easier if you remember you're not doing it alone.

Keep that written-down vision where you can look at it every time you've taken another baby step. If you forget about it for a while, that's okay. When you remember, go back to it and pick up where you left off. The more progress you see, the more progress you'll make.

And although "feeling more confident with the whole boy thing" may not be one of your goals, doing the above intentionally and prayerfully might just accomplish that anyway. Guys won't know why they're suddenly finding you interesting, but then, when did a guy ever analyze that anyway? If you find yourself enjoying that, then there you go. But more importantly, you're going to be God-confident overall. And it doesn't get much better than that.

Mom, Dad ... Now Don't Freak Out

If you thought they were going to freak before if you approached them with the topics in the previous chapters, that's nothing compared to what their reaction is likely to be when you go to them with what I'm about to suggest. However, this kind of freak-out is the kind every girl longs for from her parents. The kind where they go, "Okay, who are you and what have you done with our daughter?", or at the very least, "Wait, is this maturity that I'm seeing?" Whether they actually voice it or not, your parents will be impressed if you say:

"I've been thinking about some personal goals for this next year and I wondered if I could run them by you and get your opinion."

"I've decided I need to be more intentional about getting to where I want to be a year from now, so would you mind hearing me out and telling me what you think?"

"I didn't like the direction I was going in and I've been praying about how to turn that around. Do you want to see what I've come up with?"

What father isn't going to put down his iPhone and give you his undivided attention? Is there a mother in the world who wouldn't stop folding the laundry or checking her email or driving the *car*, for Pete's sake, to listen to what you have to tell her? Most of them would pull into the nearest Starbucks and buy you a venti anything and say, "Tell me everything. I love this."

If for some reason you don't get that kind of response (you've

> **The Twitter Version**
> Share your personal goals with your parents. They may freak out. That's a good thing.

approached your dad when he's in the middle of doing the taxes or your mom has the mother of all migraines), find out when would be a good time. Or just keeping taking those tiny, shuffling steps and let them see that you're serious. You do have the Ultimate Parent in your corner. Know that God's working on them too. The bottom line is they want you to be your best you. If you're headed there, eventually they're going to get on board. And heaven knows they have wisdom to make your journey even deeper.

If I'm Totally Honest ...

I see a new possibility for me with guys, maybe even just with life, and that is:

____

____

____

____

____

____

[illegible] Writer notes

[illegible]

your [illegible]

[illegible]

those [illegible] and [illegible]

[illegible] you [illegible] confident [illegible] know [illegible]

[illegible] Total [illegible]

[illegible]

My Hope for You

I can't wrap up this conversation with you without making sure you know that *my* life's passion is you. My entire ministry is about giving you every chance to be the person God made you to be—your awesome, authentic self. That goes beyond just writing this book or any of my other titles for young women.

It's there in my prayers that you will embrace what the whole guy thing truly has to offer to your growth. It's there in my commitment to answering every email that arrives in my inbox asking for help with why boys are being stupid. It's very much there in every twice-weekly blog post I write called "In Real Life" and every response to a comment. If you haven't checked out that community, please do. We would love to have you. It's always here in my soul where God quietly whispers, "Tell them I love them. Tell them I have made them worthy. Tell them there's a reason I made boys the way I did and to hang in there with me. Make sure they know that who they truly are was created by me, and I'm here to make sure they flower into that with grace. Tell them. Tell them."

So I'm telling you: you do have the ability to make good, godly choices about guys. You can be wise, not fearful. You can be attractive as your child-of-God self. You can make your parents your allies instead of your opponents. You can do this.

And all God's fearless, beautiful young women said—amen.

To join my blog community, go to
tweenyouandme.typepad.com/in_real_life

Or, email me directly at *nnrue@att.net*

Check out this sample chapter from Nancy Rue's **Motorcycles, Sushi & One Strange Book**, *book one of the Real Life Series*

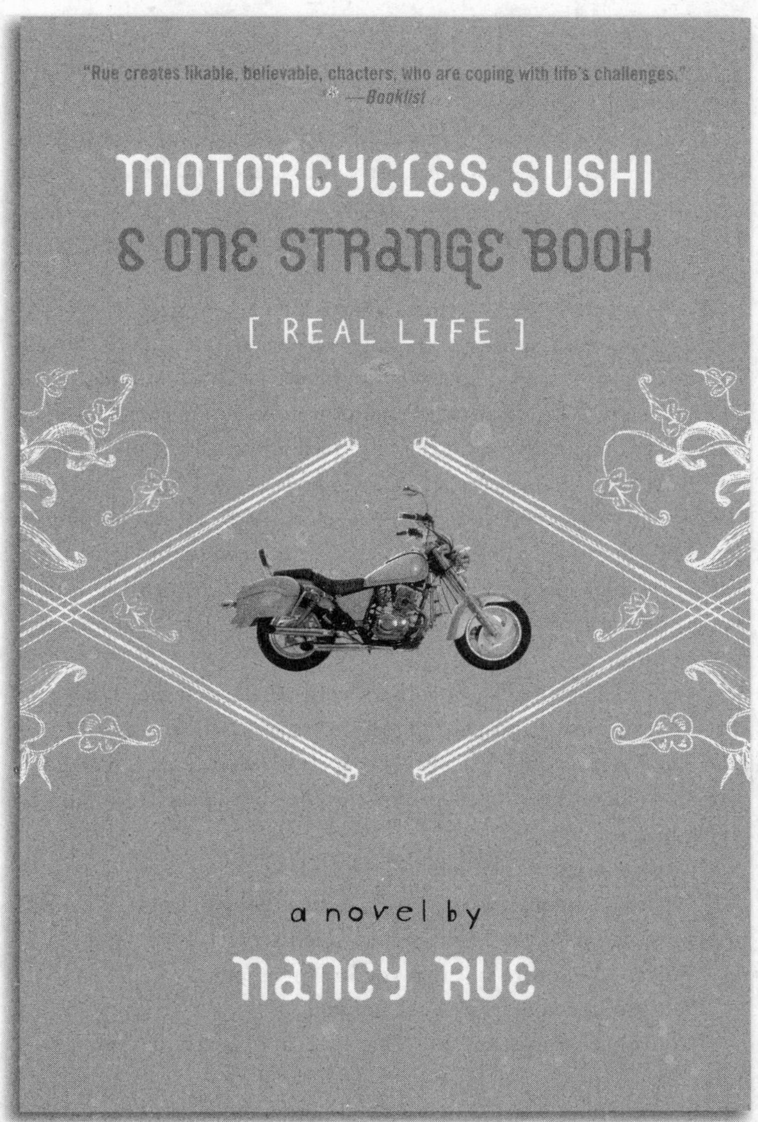
"Rue creates likable, believable, chacters, who are coping with life's challenges."
—Booklist
MOTORCYCLES, SUSHI
& ONE STRANGE BOOK
[REAL LIFE]
a novel by
NANCY RUE

CHAPTER ONE

I guess my life was crazy even before the day it really lost its mind. I just didn't think it was.

I did think my friend Chelsea's life was a little weird. Her parents had been married to each other for twenty years and her family sat down at the table to eat supper together every night. They always had dishes like broccoli-and-cheese casserole or green beans à la mode. Or something.

I *definitely* considered my friend Marcus's life to be strange. His family went on a two-week vacation every single summer to places like Key West and the Grand Canyon. The day my world went insane, he was off with his parents and his little sister in California where they were staying in hotels and eating in restaurants that had tablecloths. Totally off the wall.

Okay, so I need to get to the point, which as you'll see I sometimes have trouble doing. I was like that even before that Saturday morning in late June—or was it early July? Doesn't matter. It was summer, so there was no reason to keep track of what month it was. At least not until August, when it would be time to think about going back to school. I tried not to.

It was going along like any other day in the life of Jessie Hatcher—that would be me. I was cleaning the house, sort of, and watching *"I Love Lucy"* reruns on TV Land—now *there* was a wacko, that Lucy woman—and talking to Chelsea on the phone. And she, as usual, was giving me grief.

"I wish you'd get a cell phone," she said.

"What's wrong with a landline?" I said, although I knew. We'd had this conversation before. I always pretended to forget.

"What's wrong with it is that you can't text on it."

"Why do I need to text? We're talking."

"No, you're whispering. I can hardly hear you. It's like you're in a library."

"Or a bank," I said. "Why do people always whisper in banks? Are they afraid somebody will find out how much money they have? Or don't have?"

"I don't *know*!"

I could imagine Chelsea raking her hand through that ginormous head of butter-blonde hair. She has enough for thirty-seven people. I barely have enough for me, which is probably good because it's bright red. The kind of red that makes people stare at you like you're Raggedy Ann come to life. So the less of it the better.

"Why are you whispering anyway?" Chelsea said.

I shifted the phone to my other shoulder so I could lift the corner of the dining room rug and slide a pile of crumbs under it with my foot. I'd already put the Swiffer away. Not that my mother would have noticed anyway. Those crumbs must have been there awhile, because the last time we ate in the dining room was probably four years ago on my eleventh birthday.

"I'm whispering because my mom's asleep," I said.

"At one in the afternoon? Oh, I forgot she works at night."

That wasn't exactly true. Okay, it wasn't true at all, but I must have led Chelsea to believe it at some point. I tried not to out-and-out lie. Usually.

"See, it would be so much easier to have a conversation if you could text," Chelsea said. "I'm totally getting you a cell phone for your birthday."

"Oh no—the whole thing's overflowing. I knew that was going to happen."

"What's overflowing? What are you doing, anyway?"

"I'm watching Lucy."

"Lucy who?"

I changed which ear was on the phone again and used my forearm to shove all the random stuff on top of the buffet into the drawer and craned my neck again to see the TV in the family room. Lucy and Ethel were knee-deep in suds pouring out of an industrial-sized washing machine. Speaking of which ...

I darted for the laundry room.

"Lucy Ricardo," I said.

"*Who?* Never mind. I need to talk to you about Marcus."

Good. A safe topic. I hated it when Chelsea went off about text messaging. I couldn't have done it if I had an iPhone in my hand at that very moment. Not so anybody could understand it, anyway. Writing of any kind wasn't one of my talents. Actually, I hadn't really discovered any talents—

"Are you serious about him?" she said.

"Who?"

"Marcus."

"Define serious."

"You know what I mean."

Chelsea's voice dipped into that rich place where only the most delicious news can dwell. I knew her huge brown eyes were bubbling like chocolate fudge. My blue ones were so small compared to hers, I always imagined myself looking cross-eyed when I was around her. I looked in the round glass on the front of the washing machine. Okay, not exactly cross-eyed. But definitely too close together. My nose didn't help.

"Did you hear me?"

"What?" I said.

"I just think that for as long as you and Marcus have been together, it's time to either get serious or move on."

"Uh—hello—you know I don't do 'serious.'" I picked up a hunk of clothes out of the dirty clothes hamper and dumped them into the washer. "I want to be able to flirt with whoever I want. Aw, man, we're out of detergent. Can you use dish soap in a washing machine, I wonder?"

"Huh," Chelsea said.

"Is that 'huh, yes' or 'huh, you're an idiot' or 'huh, I don't know'?"

"Okay, could you focus for like ten seconds?"

That would be about it, yeah.

I heard Chelsea sigh like she was practicing to be a parent. "Before Marcus left for California, he told me he was getting ready to ask you to go out seriously. Would your mom let you?"

I stopped with the thing of dish soap in my hand and considered that. Right now Mom might, since she was going through one of her

In-Bed Phases. Actually, she might have let me take her credit cards and go to Acapulco if I'd asked her during an In-Bed Phase. Which I didn't, because I never knew when she'd emerge from her dark-as-a-movie-theater bedroom and go into one of her No-Bed Phases, where she polished the doorknobs and put the spices in alphabetical order. During her last No-Bed Phase, during which she didn't sleep for seventy-two hours, she "housecleaned" my room and found that letter from the school that said I needed to repeat ninth grade English, and the note from Adam Ackerson telling me he wanted to take me out as soon as he got his license in two years, and that other letter addressed to "Jessica Hatcher" that I got in the mail from somebody in Florida but never opened because it looked official and I was sure I wouldn't be able to figure out what it was talking about anyway.

Fortunately, that was all just a few hours before Mom returned to her bedroom. Most of the time I wondered which was better, the In-Bed Phases or the No-Bed Phases—but in situations like that, when she was too busy sleeping to call the school or Adam Ackerson's mother or whoever the stiff-looking letter was from, I had to go with the In-Bed Phase. I might have to clean the house, sort of, and do the laundry when I ran out of underwear, but it was better than having my space invaded and my CD collection arranged by album color.

"So would she?" Chelsea said.

"Would who what?"

"Would your mom let you date Marcus?"

"I don't know!" I said.

"Do you *want* to get serious with him?"

"Do I have to make a commitment this minute?" I squirted some dish soap into the washer.

"No," Chelsea said. I could picture her folding her arms like the guidance counselor who was constantly calling me into her office. "So what are you gonna tell him when he asks you? He's *so* going to when he gets back. Tonight."

I heard a door click down the hall, and I shut the door on the washer and tiptoed through the kitchen to peek. Mom was just crossing into the guest room, half-blonde, half-roots hair falling out of that attempt-at-a-bun thing she did when she was about to spend a week with the covers over her head. She squinted as she shuffled through the doorway. The sun was coming down on the west side of the house, which meant cracks of light were breaking in around the edges of the shades in the bedroom she'd just vacated. She was moving to darker territory.

Which put her closer to where I was. I padded to the back door and stepped out onto the porch, immediately scorching my bare feet on the blinding-white decking. It was hotter than the surface of the sun back there, so I slid down into the only corner where there was shade and let my feet stick out into the Alabama sunlight. My legs were as white as the floorboards, and they kind of reminded me of the skin on the chickens Mom had made two gallons of broth from during her last No-Bed Phase. I'd never figured out what she was going to do with all that juice, so I'd stuck it, pot and all, into the freezer.

"I wish I could get a tan," I said.

"Could we puh-leeze get back to Marcus?" Chelsea said.

"There's nothing to get back to. He's my best guy friend. Period."

"Then what about Adam Ackerson?"

"Why are you all over my love life today?"

"Because."

Silence. Which meant she was about to drop some bomb on me. As long as it wasn't, "You're too weird for me to hang out with anymore," I was okay with a bomb. It was better than discussing my mother and why I didn't text message and why I couldn't stick to one topic of conversation. Chelsea was my best girl friend, but I already knew what happened when somebody else figured out that my normal wasn't the same as their normal.

"Because why?" I said.

"Okay, I wasn't keeping this from you. I was just trying to figure out the best way to tell you."

"Tell me what?" I watched a spider swing on the tiniest thread from one porch rail to the other. I really did try to stay with Chelsea, but—had I taken my medication that morning?

"I'm just going to come out with it," Chelsea said. "Donovan and I are going out."

"Going out where?"

"Going *out*. He's my boyfriend. It's a serious relationship."

"Well—so?"

"Aren't you upset?"

"Why would I be? He's an okay guy. I think his teeth are kinda weird, but who am I to talk? Mine are like Bugs Bunny's." No, I had definitely not taken my meds. Later. Right now I toughed out the hot decking and stretched so I could prop my feet on the porch railing, just a few inches from the spiderweb. It would be cool if she would attach her web to my big toe. Not that I could sit still that long ...

"I like his teeth, but that's not the point," Chelsea said. "The point is, now that we're together, I'm going to be spending a lot of time with *him*."

"And not with me, chasing guys and getting them to chase us," I said. "I get it."

"You're mad."

"No, I'm not."

"Yes, you are, I can tell."

"How?"

"Because you're pretending you're not."

At the risk of waking my mother, I laughed out loud. The spider skittered up the pole and out of sight.

"What's so funny?" Chelsea said.

"Since when did I ever pretend not to be mad?"

Chelsea giggled. "Oh, yeah, huh?"

I didn't add that I pretended a lot of things, but that wasn't one of them. It was one of the curses of being a redhead. So people told me. Mostly the people I went off on.

"So you're really not mad that I won't get to spend as much time with you?" she said. "I know it's bad timing with Marcus being gone too."

The phone beeped its Call Waiting signal, and I could have kissed it. Maybe she'd get off the whole Marcus thing while I found out who it was.

"I'll call you back," I said, and punched the button. "Hello?"

"Is this Jessica?" a man's voice said.

"This is *Jessie*," I said. I got an automatic burst of bad energy up my back. Nobody ever called me Jessica except substitute teachers when they were taking roll. Or people who were about to tell me I was in trouble. Again.

"I'm sorry." The guy took in such a huge breath I wondered if he was locked in a walk-in refrigerator and was running out of air.

The big inhale turned into an even longer exhale. Okay, so maybe he was trying to sell me a yoga course.

"Well, Jessie," he said. "This is your father."

I froze, there in the cooking heat on the porch, and I forgot about spiders and Chelsea and Marcus and Lucy and Ethel. I tried to funnel what focus I had on that voice on the phone.

Because I didn't *have* a father.

Okay, so, weird. Very weird. My father died before I was even born. Were we talking psycho here? The man would have to be to want to be *my* father.

I stood up and shook my feet so the pant legs of my shorts would straighten out. "Sorry," I said. "I think you have the wrong number."

"You're not Jessica—Jessie Hatcher? Brooke Hatcher's daughter?"

"Yeah," I said—and only then remembered that you're not supposed to give out personal information to strangers over the phone. Or was that the Internet?

"Then I have the right number," he said.

It occurred to me that he sounded kind of nervous. Weren't psychos usually pretty jittery? In movies they always showed them sweating and pacing when they were holding people hostage in a bank vault.

"You didn't get a letter from me, Jessie?" he said.

"You sent me a letter?" Did that mean he had my address too? Now *I* was starting to sweat and pace.

"A couple of weeks ago. From St. Augustine."

"Where's St. Augustine?" I said.

"St. Augustine, Florida."

"Oh," I said. "That St. Augustine."

I could feel the perspiration running down between my shoulder blades, but I couldn't seem to get it together to go back into the air-conditioned house. I just stood there in the middle of the frying porch and saw the letter Mom had confiscated from my room wiggling in my memory the way the hot pavement ahead does when you're going down the road.

"Maybe we should start over," the man who claimed to be my father said. "If you didn't get the letter, I could see how this would catch you off guard."

"Ya think?" I said. "I got a letter but I didn't open it."

"That would make sense then."

Uh, no, none of this made sense.

"I'm Lou Kennesaw. Apparently your mom has never talked to you about me."

I added the psycho-pacing to the psycho-sweating. "No," I said. "I mean, yes, she told me about Lou Kennesaw, but you died before you could marry her. You're dead."

There was a silence so long I thought he'd hung up—which was fine with me because I was ready to unzip my skin and jump out of it. I even had my finger on the End button when he said—in a voice like that spider web I was toeing earlier as if I didn't have a problem in the world—"Jessie, I'm so sorry you were told that, but I am very much alive and I thought it was time I met you. If I'd known you thought I was dead, I never would have called you like this."

"Okay, so let's pretend you never did," I said.

I didn't mean to say it, but like most things I haven't meant to say in my life, it just came out. I called that a Blurt.

"I don't think we can do that," he said.

"Maybe you can't, but me, I'm great at pretending. Lou who? A wrong number, you say?"

"I know this is a lot to take in, so I'm going to let you soak it up a little—but I would like to see you."

He was actually sounding fatherly. Not that I'd had much experience with having a father. Okay, I'd had exactly none. Except my grandfather, who I hadn't seen much since he married that woman Mom didn't like, which was before I even started wearing a bra so he didn't count. But I'd heard Chelsea's dad say stuff like, "I would like for you to clean your room," in a way that sounded like she'd better do it or she was going to be placed under house arrest. This Lou person had that sound down. I always wondered why Chelsea went right up and cleaned her room instead of telling the man how stupid it was to tidy up a space you were only going to trash again an hour later. Until now.

But this dude was *not* my parent. I only had one parent, and even she—

Might come in handy at that moment.

"I'd have to ask my mom," I said.

"Well, of course. I didn't mean I was going to come by in the next ten minutes."

"Don't come by," I said. "Call. No, I'll call you. After I ask her. Which could be tomorrow, maybe Monday, depending on— "

I chomped down on my lip. When it came to certain subjects I did have *some* control over my mouth. But it never lasted long, and once again I had my finger on the button that could end this call so I could go back to arguing with Chelsea about Marcus and wondering how I was going to wash clothes without laundry detergent.

"I tell you what let's do," the Lou-person said. "You talk to your mom, and I'll call you later tonight. If you want me to talk to her, we can do that too."

"No," I said. "I'll do it. You can't do it."

"I'll call tonight," he said. And before I could beat him to it, he hung up. That ticked me off more than anything. Well, almost anything.

I went inside and pitched the phone onto a pile of laundry and charged down the hall to the guest room. I was about to break the one and only rule I had never broken before. I was going to wake up my mother.

Check Out These Books by Nancy Rue in the Real Life Series

Four girls are brought together through the power of a mysterious book that helps them sort through the issues of their very real lives.

Motorcycles, Sushi & One Strange Book

Boyfriends, Burritos & an Ocean of Trouble

Tournaments, Cocoa & One Wrong Move

Limos, Lattes & My Life on the Fringe

Also available in ebook and enhanced ebook versions.
Available in stores and online!

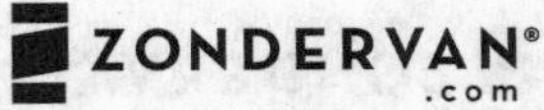

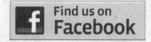

EAT THIS NOT THAT! FOR

Thousands of s[illegible]ple food swaps that can save your child from obesity!

BY DAVID ZINCZENKO
WITH MATT GOULDING

PRAISE FOR *EAT THIS, NOT THAT!*

"**EAT THIS, NOT THAT!** is gonna freak the weight right off of you."
—Ellen DeGeneres

"Another blockbuster"
—*Publisher's Weekly*

"Once you open it, just try to put it down."
—*The Washington Post*

"These are realistic changes people can make to save hundreds of calories."
—Dawn Jackson Blatner, spokesperson for
the American Dietetic Association

"The comparisons are always interesting and often surprising."
—*The New York Times*

"Most people have no idea how many calories are in their favorite foods,
and this book does a wonderful job enlightening them."
—Jennifer Neily, MS, RD,
president of the Texas Dietetic Association

"If you eat out much (and who doesn't) you need to brown-bag it
for a few days and buy **EAT THIS, NOT THAT!**"
—*St. Louis Dispatch*

DEDICATION

To all parents trying their best to make smart choices for their children

Rodale books may be purchased for business or promotional use or for special sales.
For information, please write to:
Special Markets Department, Rodale Inc., 733 Third Avenue, New York, NY 10017

Printed in the United States of America

Rodale Inc. makes every effort to use acid-free ♾, recycled paper ♻

Book design by George Karabotsos

Photographs by Orly Catz (pages 46–47, 50–51, 82–83, 84–85, 94–95, 78–79); Jeff Harris, photographer; Roscoe Betsill, stylist (cover photos, pages 13 -18, 295); Michael LoBiondo, photographer; John Hartley, stylist (pages 62–63, 70–71, 88–89, 102–103, 110–111); all other photos © Mitch Mandel and Tom MacDonald/Rodale Images; Melissa Reiss, stylist

Library of Congress Cataloging-in-Publication Data is on file with the publisher.

ISBN-13 978–1–60529–943–3 paperback
ISBN-10 1–60529–943–X paperback

Distributed to the trade by Macmillan

2 4 6 8 10 9 7 5 3 1 paperback

We inspire and enable people to improve their lives and the world around them

For more of our products visit **rodalestore.com** or call 800-848-4735

CONTENTS

ACKNOWLEDGMENTS

This book is the product of thousands of meals, hundreds of conversations with experts and concerned parents, and the collective smarts, dedication, and raw talent of dozens of individuals. Our undying thanks to all of you who have inspired this project in any way. In particular:

Steve Murphy, who captains the ship called Rodale Inc. with grace, courage, and remarkable vision. Thanks for continuing to make this the best publishing company on the planet.

The Rodale family, whose dedication to improving the lives and well-being of their readers is apparent in every book and magazine they put their name on.

George Karabotsos, whose vision has turned a jumble of words and numbers into something that's impossible to put down.

Stephen Perrine, with whom we've conferred over many a fast-food lunch and who never met an exclamation mark he didn't like.

Clint Carter, whose heroic efforts helped make sense out of a daunting database of numbers and ingredients.

The entire *Men's Health* editorial staff: a smarter, more inspiring group of writers, editors, researchers, designers, and photo directors does not exist, in the magazine world or beyond.

To the Rodale book team: Karen Rinaldi, Chris Krogermeier, Sara Cox, Tara Long, Marc Sirinsky, Mitch Mandel, Susan Eugster, Jennifer Giandomenico, Steve Schirra, and Nancy Bailey. Your extraordinary sacrifices of time and sanity brought another project to reality in record time.

The doctors, researchers, and nutritionists whose expertise helped inform this book: David Katz, MD; Beth Wallace, RD; and Mary Story, PhD, RD, among others.

Special thanks to: Adam Campbell, Mark Michaelson, Willy Gutierrez, John Dixon, Laura White, and Jaclyn Colletti.

And to the people who matter most to us in this world: families, friends, and our lovely partners, Melissa and Lauren.

Sorry for all the talk about calorie counts.

—Dave and Matt

The Choice Is Yours

You have already made a million smart choices for your children.

From the moment you discovered you were an expectant parent, you began to change your life. You thought hard about your finances, setting aside some frivolous expenses in order to save for a new future. You looked at your home, your neighborhood, your life and thought—is this a good place for a child to grow up? And you made some hard choices there, as well.

That's what being a parent is all about—making choices, not on your own behalf, but on behalf of another. It's a difficult job, and you should be proud of what you've already achieved.

But not every choice is clear-cut. Feeding your kids well, and keeping them healthy, is a particular challenge—especially in today's fast-food culture.

Fortunately, being a parent, and making smart choices, has just gotten easier. Because you have in your hands a revolutionary new guide that is going to arm you, and your son or daughter, in the battle against an emerging threat to your children's health and happiness—the threat of obesity. ***EAT THIS, NOT THAT! FOR KIDS!*** is your essential guide to making smart nutritional choices no matter where or when you're faced with them.

The New Challenge for Parents

Being a parent has always been hard, but it seems that here in the early stages of the 21st century, it's gotten harder than ever—and not just because we've traded drive-ins for drive-bys, *Father Knows Best* for *Flavor of Love*, and role models like Joni Mitchell and Joe Montana for Britney Spears and Barry Bonds.

It's gotten harder because America's restaurants and food marketers are putting our children in danger.

Consider this: Since the 1970s, the obesity rate in this country has doubled, with two-thirds of our population now overweight. The health condition most directly tied to obesity—diabetes—eats up one in every five dollars Americans spend on health care, and a recent study at Harvard found that obesity may soon surpass tobacco as the number-one cause of cancer deaths.

And no matter how frightening that may sound, the statistics are even worse for our children. The percentage of overweight youths age 12 to 19 in the United States has nearly quadrupled between 1976 and 2004. Indeed, 17 percent of this country's youth are now overweight or obese.

To put it another way: Do you remember what you and your friends looked like when you were growing up? Think back, and then look around: Do the children you see in your neighborhood look like that?

No. The children are different. Your children may be different. Think about it: No matter what your weight may have been growing up, your child faces four times the risk of obesity as you did.

HOW CAN THIS BE?

You're probably ready to finger the same bad guy that most parents point to: the pop culture boogeyman. When we were kids, we cared more about fishing nets than the Internet, played our tennis games on actual courts instead of virtual ones, and even walked to our friends' homes on the other side of the neighborhood (remember when they used to have sidewalks in neighborhoods?). Sure, the jocks dominated the sports teams, but you didn't have to be a jock to ride a bike or zip around on a skateboard. Even the slackers and the rockers at least got some exercise toting electric guitars and amps around town, instead of doing all their rocking out on Guitar Hero.

Have our kids cut down on their physical exercise? Sure. The Centers for Disease Control found that daily participation in school physical education among adolescents dropped from 42 percent in 1991 to 33 percent in 2005. It also found that a mere 36 percent of kids are currently meeting their recommended levels of activity each week.

But before you blame the rise in childhood obesity on our budding couch potatoes sending roots down into the upholstery, consider this: Only 15 percent of our daily calorie burn comes from exercise. The majority of the calories we burn off each day are eaten up by the simple acts of growing and breathing and maintaining our bodies, and from the digestion of food. That's why you see even kids dedicated to sports having to struggle with their weight.

So what's causing this crisis? And what, exactly, is happening to our children?

Here's the truth: It's not the TV, and it's not the Internet, and it's not the video games or the cell phones or the iPods. It's not the culture that's endangering our children's health.

It's the food.

The Hidden Health Danger

When a child's weight begins to grow out of proportion, so does his risk of disease—both in childhood and in his or her later life. Consider:

- The most common form of diabetes is called Type 2 or "adult-onset" diabetes and is caused primarily by years of poor eating habits. But "adult onset" no longer fits because for the first time in history, we realize that children can come down with it, too. Indeed, doctors have reported seeing children as young as 4 with the disease, and the American Diabetes Association says it is approaching catastrophic proportions in teens. The Centers for Disease Control recently predicted that one in three children born in the year 2000 will develop diabetes at some point in his or her lifetime. The laundry list of diabetes' complications? Blindness. Heart attack. Stroke. Amputation.

- Researchers at the National Institute of Child Health and Human Development found that overweight kids were more likely to suffer bone fractures and 30 percent more likely to suffer from joint or muscle pain than children of normal weight.

- The Centers for Disease Control found that almost 60 percent of overweight children have at least one cardiovascular disease risk, including high cholesterol, high blood pressure, and abnormal glucose tolerance. Twenty-five percent of overweight kids displayed at least two of these risk factors.

- A link between body weight and asthma in children has emerged in recent years. A 2008 study in the *Journal of Asthma* found that a disproportionate percentage of children with asthma were overweight, and that overweight sufferers of asthma had more severe cases than those of normal weight. And according to *Pediatric Respiratory Reviews*, obesity in children is also associated with obstructive sleep apnea syndrome, which can contribute to high blood pressure and cardiovascular disease.

- Indeed, even an old complaint of middle-age curmudgeons, kidney stones, has begun to surface with regularity in children, according to researchers at Johns Hopkins Medical Institutions. The reason: too much salt in their diets and water being replaced with sugary sodas and juice boxes.

Those are some strange and scary statistics, but the reality of our children's obesity epidemic is unavoidable. It's right there in front of us—at the school, in the playground, and too often, in our own homes.

But how is this happening? How are our children being supersized? And why do we seem powerless to stop it?

Attack of the Frankenfoods

Here's an eye-opener: The Centers for Disease Control found that American kids eat more than 150 additional calories *every day* than they did in 1989.

Let's run the math on that one. It takes 3,500 calories to create an extra pound of body weight. That means every 20 days, the average American child eats enough extra calories to weigh a pound more than his 1989 contemporary. Over the course of a year, that's enough to add 18 pounds of extra heft to your child's frame.

How can this be? Are children today simply that much more gluttonous? Are parents that much more lax? Did somebody farm out all our new home construction to Hansel and Gretel Architects, Inc.?

Well, consider this: It's not just our kids who are eating vastly more calories. In 1971, the average American male consumed 2,450 calories a day; the average woman, 1,542. But by the year 2000, American men were averaging about 2,618 daily calories (up 7 percent), while women were eating 1,877 calories (a whopping 18 percent increase, or 335 more calories every day!). The real truth of the matter is this: The food that we consume today is simply different from the food that Americans ate 20 or 30 years ago. And the reasons are as simple as they are sneaky:

✖ **WE'VE ADDED EXTRA CALORIES TO TRADITIONAL FOODS.** In the early 1970s, food manufacturers, looking for a cheaper ingredient to replace sugar, came up with a substance called high-fructose corn syrup (HFCS). Today, HFCS is in an unbelievable array of foods—everything from breakfast cereals to bread, from ketchup to pasta sauce, from juice boxes to iced tea. According to the FDA, the average American consumes 82 grams of added sugars every day, which contribute an empty 317 calories to our diets. HFCS no doubt shares some of the blame; as a cheap by-product with a long shelf life, the food industry is finding all sorts of new foods in which to hide sugar. So Grandma's pasta sauce now comes in a jar, and it's loaded with stuff just perfect for adding meat to your bones—and flab on your belly.

✖ **WE'VE BEEN TRAINED TO SUPERSIZE IT.** It seems like Economics 101: If you can get a lot more food for just a few cents more, then it makes all the sense in the world to upgrade to the "value meal." And because food is so inexpensive for manufacturers to produce on a large scale, your average fast-food emporium makes a hefty profit whenever you supersize your meal—even though you're getting an average of 73 percent more calories for only a 17 percent increase in cost. The problem is the way we look at food—we should be looking at cutting down on our calories, not adding to them. In fact, if we were really smart, fast food shops would be charging us more for the smaller portions!

✖ **WE'VE LACED OUR FOOD WITH TIME BOMBS.** A generation ago it was hard for food manufacturers to create baked goods that would last on store shelves. Most baked goods require oils, and oil leaks at room temperature. But since the 1960s, manufacturers have been baking with—and restaurateurs have been frying with—something called trans fats. Trans fats are cheap and effective: They make potato chips crispier and Oreo cookies tastier, and they let fry cooks make pound after pound of fries without smoking up their kitchens. The downside: Trans fats increase your bad cholesterol, lower your good cholesterol, and greatly increase your risk of heart disease.

✖ **WE'RE DRINKING MORE CALORIES THAN EVER.** A study from the University of North Carolina found that we consume 450 calories a day from beverages, nearly twice as many as 30 years ago. This increase amounts to an extra 23 pounds a year that we're forced to work off—or carry around with us. Many of the calories come from HFCS in our drinks—especially, when it comes to kids, in our "fruit" drinks that are often nothing more than water, food coloring, and sweetener. In fact, anything you have for your kids to drink in your fridge right now—unless it's water, milk, or a diet soda—probably has HFCS in it. Go ahead—read the label.

✖ **WE DON'T KNOW WHAT'S IN OUR FOOD.** More and more, marketers are adding new types of preservatives, fats, sugars, and other "new" food substances to our daily meals. But often, they go unexplained (what is "xanthan gum" anyway?) or, in the case of restaurant food, unmentioned. Unless we're eating it right off the tree, it's hard to know what, exactly, is in that fruity dish.

All of these disturbing trends in our food supply are a lot to chew on—but chew on them we do. Indeed, some of the food that restaurants and packaged-goods manufacturers are marketing to our children are so unbelievably bad for our kids, you have to take a step back and ask, "Do these people have any idea what they're doing?" Consider that the recommended daily calorie intake for a 12-year-old is 2,000, and that his recommended intake of sodium is no more than 2,200 milligrams of sodium. Then, consider this:

AT RUBY TUESDAY'S, the Kid's Turkey Minis & Fries pack 893 calories and 47 grams of fat. Talk about deceptive! Who would have guessed that two tiny turkey burgers could pack as many calories as a Double Whopper? Want dessert with that? The Strawberries and Ice Cream come with 914 calories and 50 grams of fat.

AT COSÍ'S, the Kids Pepperoni Pizza will feed your child 911 calories, 43 grams of fat, and a seemingly heart-stopping 2,731 milligrams of sodium—that's as much salt as you'd find in 15 small bags of potato chips!

AT ON THE BORDER, the Kids Bean & Cheese Nachos comes with a 980-calorie price tag. On top of that, this plate of chips and cheese has a full day's worth of sodium and as much saturated fat as 29 strips of bacon!

Unfortunately, there's no way to tell which Bart Simpson—size meals come with Homer-size loads of calories, sodium, and fat. Unlike packaged-goods manufacturers, who are required to post detailed nutritional information on their boxes, bags, and cans, restaurant chains don't labor under any nutritional disclosure regulations. A handful do list such information on their Web sites—major chains who deserve kudos for helping parents make informed choices include Chili's, Panera Bread, and Uno Chicago Grill. But nutritional information at most sit-down and fast-food restaurants is murkier than a Florida election.

And if you're shocked at how bad much of today's "kids menus" are, you're not alone. Most of us don't labor under the illusion that ice cream snacks and fast-food burgers are healthy—the occasional sinful indulgence is part of living, even for (or especially for) kids. But most parents could never guess how bad many of today's kids' meals really are. In a 2006 study published in the *American Journal of Public Health,* consumers presented with obviously high-calorie restaurant foods still underestimated the nutritional heft of the items by an average of 600 calories.

That's why ***EAT THIS, NOT THAT! FOR KIDS!*** is your secret weapon. We've analyzed kids offerings from all of the major chains, taken a hard look at packaged foods and snacks, and uncovered the real truth about what America is really feeding its children. And the great news: You can have a major impact on your children's health and future simply by making a handful of smart choices.

And as a parent, that's what you're already good at: making choices for your children. All you need is the right information at the right time.

And now you have it.

For more great food swaps, nutritional secrets, weight-loss strategies, and the latest breaking news on how to keep you and your family feeling great, go to ***eatthis.com***

Our Children's Future

A child who's overweight is 15 times more likely to be overweight as an adult. What does that really mean in terms of your child's health? Take a look at the numbers:

Overweight people are:

- **50 percent more likely to develop heart disease** (obese: up to 100 percent)
- **Up to 360 percent more likely to develop diabetes** (obese: up to 1,020 percent)
- **16 percent more likely to die of a first heart attack** (obese: 49 percent)
- **Roughly 50 percent more likely to have total cholesterol above 250** (obese: up to 122 percent)
- **14 percent less attractive to the opposite sex** (obese: 43 percent)
- **Likely to spend 37 percent more a year at the pharmacy** (obese: 105 percent)
- **Likely to stay 19 percent longer in the hospital** (obese: 49 percent)
- **20 percent more likely to have asthma** (obese: 50 percent)
- **Up to 31 percent more likely to die of any cause** (obese: 62 percent)
- **19 percent more likely to die in a car crash** (obese: 37 percent)
- **120 percent more likely to develop stomach cancer** (obese: 330 percent)
- **Up to 90 percent more likely to develop gallstones** (obese: up to 150 percent)
- **590 percent more likely to develop esophageal cancer** (obese: 1,520 percent)
- **35 percent more likely to develop kidney cancer** (obese: 70 percent)
- **14 percent more likely to have osteoarthritis** (obese: 34 percent)
- **70 percent more likely to develop high blood pressure** (obese: up to 170 percent)

We Can Change the Future

Children who struggle with weight issues today can grow up to lead healthy, active lives. How do I know? Because I used to be one of the "fat kids" myself.

As a boy growing up in a small town in Pennsylvania, I, too, struggled with weight issues. I made bad choices—choosing fast food over smart food, then trying to starve myself to get my body in the shape I wanted it in. Sure enough, I'd get hungry again—or sad, or lonely, or just bored—and there I'd be, barking orders into a clown's mouth once again. My brother, Eric, used to invite his friends over to watch my dietary indiscretions: "Don't disturb the big animal," he'd tell his buddies. "It's feeding."

Several things happened that changed my life for the better. I joined the high school wrestling team, which made me cognizant of my weight and my fitness. I paid my way through college by joining the Navy Reserve, where I learned the importance of discipline and the life-or-death impact of staying in shape. And I came to work at *Men's Health* magazine, where I've spent the last 15 years studying nutrition and fitness and learning more than I ever thought possible about the role that our diets play in our overall health.

And then, in 1998, my life changed forever. My father, Bohdan, died of a stroke at the age of 52.

My father struggled with his weight all his life—starting in his teen years. I remember him, even in his 30s, laboring to catch his breath as he climbed a simple flight of stairs.

His death drove it all home for me: If we allow the bad stuff into our diets, if we trust the chain restaurants and mass-food marketers with our health—and if we don't raise questions such as "what's really in this?" and "how is this food affecting my body," we risk so much. We risk being able to do the things we like. To be proud of the way we look and feel. To live to see our children and our grandchildren grow.

EAT THIS, NOT THAT! FOR KIDS! is designed to help you and your children avoid that fate. With the simple photo-driven information and intensively researched nutritional data in these pages, you'll finally have control of your diet, your body, your life. And more important, you'll pass that gift on to your children.

The tough choices won't end here. As a parent, you'll be called upon to give your kids advice, solace, and guidance for the next, oh, 60 years or so. But one aspect of parenthood—making smart nutritional choices for your children—is going to be a whole heck of a lot easier.

So turn the page, and let's get started on building a better future for ourselves and our children.

1

FEEDING THE FUTURE

Feeding the Future

Imagine you and I, and all our friends and relatives, and our children, are on a big boat in the middle of the ocean. And the boat is taking on water. On one side of the boat, you and I and our friends and families and a whole bunch of other folks are bailing as fast as we can. We're working hard, thinking smart, trying to save all of our lives and keep the ship afloat. On the other side of the boat is a smaller group working just as hard, punching holes in the hull. And no matter how much progress the big group makes, it just can't compensate for the damage the smaller group is doing.

Frustrating, right? Well, that's sort of the way I feel when I think about the battle against obesity and what America's food marketers are doing to us, to our children, and to our country.

Like most parents, you probably try hard to get your kids to eat healthy. You play "green bean airplane" with your toddler's spoon. ("Here comes the plane, open the hangar!") You read the labels in the grocery store, always on the lookout for bad stuff. You keep an eye on their snack consumption and do all you can to urge them to try new things. And you worry, too, about your own fitness levels: Every year, Americans spend an estimated $42 billion on diet books; $18.5 billion on health club memberships; and $5.2 billion on diet foods and weight loss programs. We're all trying to exercise, to eat healthy, and to keep ourselves slim, and in doing so, we're trying to set a good example for our children.

But no matter how hard those of us on this side of the boat try, there's a group of folks on the other side of the boat punching holes in our efforts. And those are the food marketers who make money by getting our children to eat junk.

According to media industry estimates, advertisers spend $900 million every year on television shows aimed at children under 12. And more than two-thirds of that advertising is for food products: fast-food meals with action figures and dolls; sugary cereals with cartoon spokespeople; "juice" drinks that have about as much to do with actual fruit as Swedish Fish have to do with mackerel. The average child between 8 and 18 spends 3 hours a day in front of the television, and according to the Federal Trade Commission, kids ages 2 to 11 will see 26,000 TV ads this year—22 percent of them marketing food.

Now think about the messages that your child is receiving about food. Think about the fun and happy lands portrayed on TV advertisements, where cartoon characters come to life and magic carpet rides become a reality as soon as he or she opens a box of Sugary Sweet Mouthrot Cereal, or whatever today's big craze might be. The more advertisers promise this golden land of happiness, and associate it in our children's minds with junk food, the more our children will want to follow those promises—again and again—in hopes of finding themselves there, in Sugary Sweet Mouthrot Paradise Land. The message—that junk food equals instant happiness—is one that sticks with a child for all his life. Our "eat this, feel better" culture just promotes more unhealthy nutritional habits for years to come.

And the worst part of it all may be this: The foods that advertisers are selling to kids, the stuff that supposedly is going to make them happier, has in fact the opposite result. No kid feels happy when he's nodding off in class at the end of a sugar high, getting picked last in gym class because he's too heavy to make basic athletic moves, or skipping social events because he's ashamed of the way his body looks.

In other words, it's a setup: Our society is promising our children one thing and delivering something completely different. As a result, the nonpartisan consumer group Trust for America's Health has warned, "Today's children are likely to be the first generation to live shorter, less-healthy lives than their parents."

It doesn't have to be this way. We can bail all we want, but we can't keep our kids' ship from sinking if fast-food marketers are going to keep punching holes in our hull.

But there is something we can do.

We can teach our children how to swim.

Doggie Paddling Through the Nutritional Ocean

One of the biggest mistakes we make when we think about "watching our weight" is to assume that our first goal is to eat less. In fact, what we really need to concentrate on is eating more—not more food or calories, but more nutrients. Because while our consumption of calories is way up, our consumption of essential nutrients, including vitamins, minerals, and fiber, is actually down. That's right. We're eating more food, but we're eating less nutrition! Refined grains, added fats and sugars, hard-to-pronounce chemical ingredients—all conspire to bloat our waistlines, but add nothing to our nutritional bottom lines. It's like we're filling our piggy banks with pennies and overlooking the $100 bills lying around us.

A parent's first instinct, when she sees her child gaining weight, is to deny him or her those extra snacks and nibbles. But that's a losing strategy, just like any fad diet. One of the reasons diets fail is because nobody likes to feel as though they are denying themselves—in a land of plenty, we don't want to feel left out. And children are no different. Why should some other kid get a snack and our child miss out? Besides, skipping a snack is a guaranteed way to feel hungry, and a child's hunger is a VIP first-class ticket to Candy Aisle Meltdown.

Instead of even thinking about cutting down on your child's food intake, think of expanding his or her palette. Here are some simple rules that will teach your child to swim—no matter how rough the nutritional seas may get.

RULE #1:
NEVER SKIP BREAKFAST. EVER.

Yes, mornings are crazy. But they're also our best hope at regaining our nutritional sanity. A 2005 study synthesized the results of 47 studies that examined the impact of starting the day with a healthy breakfast. Here's what they found.

Children skipped breakfast more than any other meal. Skipping is more prevalent in girls, older children, and adolescents.

People who skip breakfast are more likely to take up smoking or drink-

ing, less likely to exercise, and more likely to follow fad diets or express concerns about body weight. Common reasons cited for skipping were lack of time, lack of hunger, or dieting.

- On the day of the surveys, 8 percent of 1- to 7-year-olds skipped, 12 percent of 8- to 10-year-olds skipped, 20 percent of 11- to 14-year-olds skipped, and 30 percent of 15- to 18-year-olds skipped.

Bad news. And sure, it would seem to make sense that skipping breakfast means eating fewer calories, which means weighing less. But it doesn't work that way. Consider:

- Breakfast eaters tend to have higher total calorie intakes throughout the day, but compared to skippers, they also received significantly more fiber, calcium, and other micronutrients. Breakfast eaters also tended to consume less soda and French fries and more fruits, vegetables, and milk.
- Breakfast eaters were approximately 30 percent less likely to be overweight or obese. (And think about that—kids who eat breakfast eat more food, but weigh less!)

RULE #2: SNACK WITH PURPOSE

There's a big difference between mindless munching and strategic snacking. Snacking with a purpose means reinforcing good habits, keeping the metabolic rate high, and filling the gaps between meals with the nutrients a child's body craves.

- In the 20 years leading up to the 21st century (1977 to 1996), salty snack portions increased by 93 calories, and soft drink portions increased by 49 calories. This data comes from the Nationwide Food Consumption Survey and the Continuing Survey of Food Intake, which together create a sample of 63,380 people ages 2 and older. So when you give your kid an individual bag of chips and a soda—the same snack you might have enjoyed when you were 10—he's ingesting 142 more calories than you did. Feeding him that just twice a week means he'll weigh about a pound more than you did within a year.

Need snack ideas? Try popcorn. The 2005 Dietary Guidelines for Americans lists it as a viable means by which to increase whole-grain consumption. (This doesn't work if the popcorn's saturated with butter and salt.) A study of popcorn consumers published in the *Journal of the American Dietetic Association* found that popcorn eaters had a 22 percent higher intake of fiber and 250 percent higher intake of whole grains than noneaters. Other great choices include not just the low-cal stuff (vegetables and fruit) but more filling fare like unsalted nuts and even dark chocolate, which is packed with antioxidants and even some fiber. The point is not to deny food, but to teach our children to crave foods that are healthy for them. One parent I know has a great rule for her kids: They must always ask permission to have a snack, but they never need permission to reach for a piece of fruit. She says it has helped train her kids to go the easy route—and that just happens to be the healthy route.

RULE #3:
BEWARE OF PORTION DISTORTION

Snacks aren't the only thing that's increased wildly in portion size. Since 1977, hamburgers have increased by 97 calories, French fries by 68 calories, and Mexican foods by 133 calories, according to the Nationwide Food Consumption Survey.

Eat This Pyramid, Not That One

The USDA has their pyramid, of course, but the iconic image young students learn so well in our school system leaves a lot to be desired in terms of specifics. According to the vagaries of the image, a serving of white rice and quinoa both count the same toward the daily recommended six servings, despite the fact that one is packed with fiber, healthy fat, and essential amino acids (quinoa) and the other is a nutritional black hole (rice).

It's time for parental discretion. One-quarter of all vegetables consumed by kids are French fries, and according to a government study of 4,000 kids between the ages of 2 and 19, the overwhelming bulk of their nutrients comes from fruit juice and sugary cereals. While those might have a place in the USDA's pyramid, they have no place in ours. It's still important for your kids to go about constructing their pyramids each day—you just need to be sure they have the right building blocks.

FATS AND OILS

Eat This	*Not That!*
Healthy fats: olive oil, canola oil, monounsaturated fats from nuts, avocado, salmon	Unhealthy fats: Stick margarine, lard, palm oil, anything with partially hydrogenated oil

DAIRY (2 TO 3 1-CUP SERVINGS)

Eat This	*Not That!*
2 percent milk, string cheese, cottage cheese, plain yogurt sweetened with fresh fruit	Chocolate milk, ice cream, hot cheese dip, yogurt with fruit on the bottom

MEAT, POULTRY, FISH, EGGS, AND BEANS (2 TO 3 2-OUNCE SERVINGS)

Eat This	*Not That!*
Grilled chicken breast, roast pork tenderloin, sirloin steak, scrambled, boiled, or poached eggs, stewed black beans, almonds, unsweetened peanut butter	Chicken fingers, crispy chicken sandwiches, cheeseburgers, strip or rib-eye steak, peanut butter with added sugars

VEGETABLES (5 ½-CUP SERVINGS)

Eat This	*Not That!*
Sautéed spinach, steamed broccoli, romaine or mixed green salads, roasted mushrooms, grilled pepper and onion skewers, baby carrots, tomato sauce, salsa, homemade guacamole	French fries, potato chips, onion rings, eggplant parmesan

FRUIT (3 ½-CUP SERVINGS)

Eat This	*Not That!*
Sliced apples or pears, berries, grapes, stone fruit like peaches, plums, and apricots, 100 percent fruit smoothies	More than one 8-ounce glass of juice a day; more than a few tablespoons of dried fruit a day; smoothies made with sherbet, frozen yogurt, or added sugar

GRAINS (6 1-OUNCE SERVINGS)

Eat This	*Not That!*
Brown rice, whole grain bread, quinoa, whole grain pasta, oatmeal	White rice, white bread, pasta, muffins, tortillas, pancakes, waffles, heavily sweetened cereal

- A study published in the *American Journal of Preventive Medicine* looked at 63,380 individuals' drinking habits over a span of 19 years. The results show that for children ages 2 to 18, portions of sweetened beverages increased from 13.1 ounces in 1977 to 18.9 ounces in 1996.

One easy way to short-circuit this growing trend? **Buy smaller bowls and cups.** A recent study at the Children's Nutrition Research Center in Houston, Texas, shows that 5- and 6-year-old children will consume a third more calories when presented with a larger portion. The findings are based on a sample of 53 children who were served either 1- or 2-cup portions of macaroni and cheese.

RULE #4:
DRINK RESPONSIBLY

Too many of us keep in mind the adage "watch what you eat," and we forget another serious threat to our children's health: We don't watch what we drink. One study found that that sweetened beverages constituted more than half (51 percent) of all beverages consumed by fourth through sixth grade students. The students who consumed the most sweetened beverages took on approximately 330 extra calories per day, and on average they ate less than half the amount of real fruit than did their nondrinking or light-drinking peers.

One important strategy is to keep cold, filtered water in a pitcher in the fridge. You might even want to keep some cut-up limes, oranges, or lemons nearby for kids to flavor their own water. A UK study showed that in classrooms with limited access to water, only 29 percent of students met their daily needs; free access to water led to higher intake.

- The *American Journal of Preventive Medicine* looked at four studies that showed 73,345 individuals' drinking habits over a span of 24 years. They found that for children ages 2 to 18, the amount of calories from soft drinks as a percentage of total calories more than doubled from 3 to 6.9 percent. The same is true for fruit drinks, which increased from 1.8 to 3.4 percent. And total calories from sweetened beverages increased from 4.8 to 10.3 percent. The percentage of calories from milk, on the other hand, decreased from 13.2 to 8.3 percent.

- A study using the national survey Continuing Survey of Food Intakes by Individuals found that consumption of real fruit juice is higher than other beverages only for very young children. By the age of 5, the consumption of fruit drinks, -ades, and sodas surpassed that of real fruit juice. As children get older, the gap between soda consumption and real fruit drinks continues to grow until, for the 14- to 18-year-old demographic, children are drinking only one-fifth as much fruit juice as soda (3.7 ounces juice, 18 ounces soda).

As it is with all things, a parent's example is a critical determinant as to whether a child will drown him- or herself in soda. A Minnesota study showed that children were 3 times more likely to drink soda five or more times per week when their parents regularly drank soda.

- A USDA report shows that soft drink availability doubled between 1970 and 1995.

The importance of drinking milk is overrated, right? Nope. In fact, growing boys and girls create at least 40 percent of their adult bone mass during adolescence, and 73 percent of the calcium in the US food supply comes from dairy foods. Children who do not receive adequate amounts of this critical mineral are at an increased risk of bone disease later in life.

RULE #5:
EAT MORE WHOLE FOODS AND FEWER SCIENCE EXPERIMENTS

Here's a rule of healthy eating that will serve you well when picking out foods for your family: The shorter the ingredient list, the healthier the food. (One of the worst foods we've ever found, the Baskin Robbins Heath Shake, has 73 ingredients—and, by the way, a whopping 2,310 calories and more than three days' worth of saturated fat! Whatever happened to the idea that a milkshake was, um, milk and ice cream?) And don't think that you're the only one who's confused: The FDA maintains a list of more than 3,000 ingredients that are considered safe to eat, and any one of them could wind up in your next box of mac 'n' cheese.

- According to USDA reports, most of the sodium in the American's diet comes from packaged and processed foods. Naturally occurring salt accounts for only 12 percent of total intake, while 77 percent is added by food manufacturers.

RULE #6: SET THE TABLE

Children in families with a more structured mealtime exhibit healthier eating habits. Among middle-school and high-school girls, those whose families ate together only one or two times per week were more than twice as likely to exhibit weight control issues compared with those who ate together three or four times per week.

Of course, the notion of 6 PM dinnertime and then everyone into their pjs is a quaint one, but it hardly fits within a society where both Mom and Dad work, where the office may call at any time day or night, and where our kids have such highly scheduled social lives that the delineation between "parent" and "chauffeur" is sometimes difficult to parse. While we can't always bring the family together like Ozzie Nelson's (or, heck, even like Ozzy Osbourne's), we can make some positive steps in that direction. One busy family I know keeps Sunday night dinner sacred—no social plans, no school projects, no extra work brought home from the office. And although it's not ideal, keeping the family ritual just once a week gives parents the opportunity to point out what is and isn't healthy at the dinner table.

Another smart move: **Get your kids involved in cooking.** Make a game of trying to pack the most healthful ingredients into your meals. A Texas study showed that children can be encouraged to eat more fruits and vegetables by giving them goals and allowing them to help in preparation. In a classroom curriculum program called *Squire's Quest!*, 671 fourth-grade students were asked to select a fruit, fruit-juice, or vegetable recipe to prepare at home. Among those who completed the study, the average increase was one serving per day of fruit or vegetables. Those who completed more of the recipes showed the biggest improvements.

RULE# 7: KICK THE SUGAR HABIT

Take a look at the label on your loaf of sliced bread. Then take a look at the label on your ketchup. Now, for the coup de grâce, take a look at the label on a package of Twizzlers, or Jolly Ranchers, or Nerds. As different as they may seem, chances are these foods all contain the same ingredient: high-fructose corn syrup, or HFCS. According to the USDA, high-fructose corn syrup constitutes more than 40 percent of the caloric sweeteners

What Our Kids Need Each Day

	1-3 YEARS	4-8 YEARS	9-13 YEARS	14-18 YEARS
CALORIES	1000–1400	1400–1600	1800–2200 (B)	2200–2400 (B)
			1600–2200 (G)	2000 (G)
FAT	33–54 grams	39–62	62–85	61–95 (B) 55–78 (G)
SATURATED FAT	<12–16 grams	<16–18	<20–24 (B) <18–22 (G)	<24–27 (B) <22 (G)
SODIUM	1000–1500 mg	1200–1900	1500–2200	1500–2300
CARBS	130 grams	130	130	130
FIBER	19 grams	25	31 (B) 26 (G)	38 (B) 26 (G)
PROTEIN	13 grams	19	31 (B) 26 (G)	52 (B) 46 (G)

used in US foods and beverages. Now consider this: In 1970, high-fructose corn syrup accounted for less than 1 percent of all caloric sweeteners.

Why is this so bad? It's not because HFCS is more dangerous for you than sucrose; in fact, most recent data suggests that the body metabolizes HFCS in the same way it does ordinary sugar. No, the major concern is that HFCS—a derivative of corn that's cheaper to produce than sugar and has a longer shelf life—is being added to foods that you'd never imagine would need sugar. But as Americans have been trained to develop a more intense sweet tooth, marketers have begun adding cheap sugar substitutes into everything from tomato sauce to wheat bread. And that pads everything we eat with extra calories. Today, the average American consumes 132 calories' worth of HFCS every day.

To completely avoid HFCS, you'd have to give up eating packaged foods, and that's just not practical for most families. Instead, become a savvy label reader (learn how on page 154) and eliminate foods not just with HFCS, but with any form of sugar at the top of the ingredient list.

RULE# 8:
EAT THE RAINBOW

Kids need a colorful diet. Turn the page to find out why.

Eat the Rainbow

Better nutrition starts not with cutting out the bad, but with adding in the good. Fill your children's meals with healthful, high-quality food and you'll eventually squeeze out the bad stuff.

I'm not going to pretend that getting a child to eat what's good for him isn't sometimes a struggle. "A lot of parents tell me, 'My kids don't like healthy foods,'" says David Katz, MD, an associate clinical professor of epidemiology and public health at Yale Medical School. "'Finicky' is not an excuse. You never hear a parent say, 'My child doesn't like to look both ways before he crosses the street.' They tell him to do it. More kids today will die of complications from bad foods they eat than they will from tobacco, drugs, and alcohol."

So how do you teach the basics of nutrition to a 7-year-old? Even we grownups have trouble understanding which vitamins and minerals we need more of and which complicated chemical ingredients we need to avoid.

Well, here's a simple trick: Just teach your kids to eat as many different colors as they can. And no, I'm not talking about mixing the red, green, and purple Skittles. I'm talking about adding as much of a mix of fruits and vegetables as possible. That's because the colors represented in foods are indicators of nutritional value—and different colors mean different vitamins and minerals.

Not everything on this list is going to appeal to your child's appetite. But there's enough variation here that he or she can squeeze one food from each category into a day's worth of eating. For a fun project, make a multicolor checklist, and have your kid check off each color as he or she eats it throughout the day.

Or do what our parents did and sell them on the kid-friendly benefits trapped inside of spinach, carrots, and the like. Each group of produce offers seriously cool "superpowers" that appeal to kids' deepest desires to dominate math quizzes and monkey bars alike. Feel free to sell these as hard as you want. Hey, even if it didn't end up making you as strong as Popeye, you still ate your spinach, right?

TOMATO

This queen of lycopene is also packed with antioxidant-rich vitamins A and C, as well as vitamin K, which is important for maintaining healthy bones. Good news for finicky eaters: Canned and cooked tomatoes have been shown to contain more lycopene than fresh, so go crazy with the ketchup, salsa, and marinara sauce. When possible, buy organic: USDA researchers found that organic ketchup has three times the lycopene as nonorganic ketchup.

PINK GRAPEFRUIT

This contains one of the highest concentrations of antioxidants in the produce aisle. Mix segments into yogurt and granola in the morning for breakfast, slip them into salads, or just swap out the OJ for the occasional glass of ruby red grapefruit juice.

WATERMELON

This summertime favorite is also a big provider of vitamins A and C, which help to neutralize cancer-causing free radicals. Spike a fruit salad with big hunks of watermelon, blend with yogurt, ice, and OJ for a refreshing smoothie, or just hand over a big hunk to the little ones next time you fire up the grill.

RED BELL PEPPER

The reds pack twice the vitamin C and nine times as much vitamin A as their green relatives. They've been shown to aid in the fight against everything from asthma to cancer to cataracts. Slice them up raw and serve with hummus for an after-school snack or buy jarred roasted peppers and puree them into a soup (it tastes just like tomato soup).

GUAVA

Like most lycopene vessels, guava is packed with vitamins A and C. It also contains heart-healthy omega-3 fatty acids and belly-filling fiber. Get your hands on these in the produce aisle of larger supermarkets or Latin grocers, or simply stock a bottle of guava nectar in the fridge.

RED

Rosy-hued fruits and vegetables offer a payload of an important antioxidant called *lycopene*. Lycopene is a carotenoid that is associated with a cache of health benefits, including protecting the skin from sun damage and decreasing the risk of heart disease and certain forms of cancer. Lycopene is most strongly concentrated in the most red of all red fruits: the tomato. What is surprising, though, is that cooked and processed tomatoes have higher lycopene concentrations, so don't shy away from the salsa or marinara sauce. **SUPERPOWER:** Red food makes you dash like the Flash! There's a reason he wore red: Lycopene-rich foods have been shown to decrease symptoms of wheezing, asthma, and shortness of breath in people when they exercise.

ORANGE Beta-carotene is the nutrient responsible for fruits and vegetables' dramatic orange color, and although the carotenoid is present in a host of other vegetables (spinach, kale, and broccoli, for instance), the orange ones have the highest concentration. But the conspicuous hue of this carotenoid does more than just attract your attention; once inside the body, it is converted into vitamin A, a powerful antioxidant that contributes to immune health, improves communication between cells, and helps fight off cell-damaging free radicals. **SUPERPOWER:** Orange foods give you night vision! That's because vitamin A is vital for creating the pigment in the retina responsible for vision in low-light situations. Just think of the benefits: perfect for beating their friends at hide-and-seek, spying on their brothers or sisters, and spotting bogeymen before they can hide under their beds.

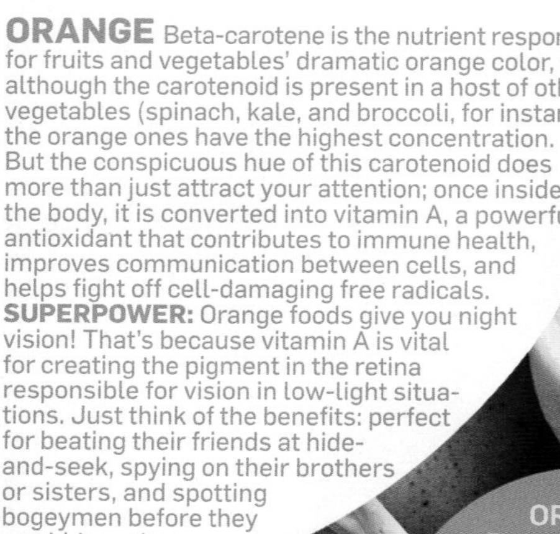

WINTER SQUASH
A true party bag of nutrients, winter squash is a great source of a dozen different vitamins, including a host of B vitamins, folate, manganese, and fiber. What does that all mean? It means feed it to your kid! And lots of it! The best way is to cut the squash into 1-inch wedges and bake at 375°F for 40 minutes, until soft and caramelized.

ORANGE
The vaunted vitamin C monster has a cadre of critical phytonutrients known to lower blood pressure and contain strong anti-inflammatory properties. Juice is fine, but the real fruit is even better. The secret, though, is that the orange's most powerful healing properties are found in the peel; use a zester to grate the peel over bowls of yogurt, salads, or directly into smoothies.

CANTALOUPE
The surge of vitamin A is important not just for the eyes, but also for healthy lungs, and the megadose of vitamin C helps white blood cells ward off infection. Sliced cantaloupe and yogurt make a killer breakfast, or combine the two in a food processor with a touch of honey and lemon and puree into a soup, which makes a great low-cal dessert.

SWEET POTATO
The best part about sweet potatoes, outside of the beta-carotene, is that they're loaded with fiber. That means they have a gentler effect on your kid's blood sugar levels than regular potatoes. Substitute baked sweet potatoes for baked potatoes, mash them up like you would an Idaho, or make fries out of them by tossing spears with olive oil and roasting in a 400°F oven for 30 minutes.

CARROT
The snack of choice for Bugs Bunny happens to be the richest carotene source of all. Baby carrots are perfect plain for dipping or snacking on, of course, but also try shredding carrots into a salad or marinara for a hit of natural sweetness, or roasting them slowly in the oven with olive oil and salt.

CORN

This king of the summer barbecue is loaded with thiamin, which plays a central role in energy production and cognitive function. Boost their brains and their energy levels by carefully removing the kernels from the cob with a kitchen knife and sautéing with a bit of olive oil. Eat as is, or sprinkle the toasty corn niblets on top of soups and salads.

YELLOW BELL PEPPER

Yellow bells are vitamin C treasure troves, providing two and a half times the amount you'd get from an orange. Their sweet, mellow flavor is perfect for kids, making them a good addition to stir-fries, sandwiches, or cooked on the grill as a side to chicken.

YELLOW SQUASH

With huge doses of fiber, manganese, magnesium, and folate, summer squash proves to be a serious nutritional player. Drizzle grilled slices with a bit of basil pesto.

PINEAPPLE

This fruit might be high on the list of carotenoid-containing fruits, but it does have other benefits—notably an abundance of bromelain, which has strong digestive benefits. Skewer chunks and cook on a hot grill for a killer dessert.

YELLOW

Yellow foods are close relatives to orange foods, and likewise, they are rich in carotenoids. The more common yellow carotenoid is beta-cryptoxanthin, which supplies about half the vitamin A as beta-carotene. Studies show it decreases the likelihood for such diseases as lung cancer and arthritis, but since youngsters have more important things to worry about, you're better off selling yellow foods on their superpowers. **SUPERPOWER:** Yellow foods make you jump higher and play harder! Research shows that foods rich in beta-cryptoxanthin help decrease inflammation in the joints, ensuring a springy step in kids for years to come. Studies also show that this potent carotenoid may improve the functioning of the respiratory system, making beating their classmates in dodgeball and relay races just that much easier.

BANANA

Bananas are loaded with potassium, which will help your kids grow strong, durable bones. They also contain a compound called a prebiotic, making it easier for eaters to absorb nutrients of all kinds. Shopping tip: Not all bananas are equally rich in carotenoids. Search for those with a deeper gold to their edible flesh.

GREEN Not just potent vitamin vessels capable of strengthening bones, muscles, and brains, green foods are also among the most abundant sources of lutein and zeaxanthin, an antioxidant tag team that, among other things, promotes healthy vision. **SUPERPOWER:** Green foods give you sharp vision and superhuman healing abilities! Beyond the peeper protection kids get from lutein and zeaxanthin, green fruits and vegetables get their color from chlorophyll, which studies show helps play an important role in stimulating the growth of new tissue and hindering the growth of bacteria. As a topical treatment, it can speed healing time by 25 percent.

AVOCADO

This creamy fruit is bursting with monounsaturated fats, the kind that are proven to be great for your heart. Tossing avocado slices in sandwiches and soups is one way to add some healthy fat, but your best bet for slipping them into your kid's diet is to mash 'em up with garlic, onion, and lemon juice for a tasty homemade guacamole.

ZUCCHINI

A dense and diverse source of nutrients, this summer squash comes with everything from omega-3s to copper. Toss sautéed zucchini with a drizzle of balsamic vinegar, or add grated zucchini to your favorite bread or muffin recipe.

ASPARAGUS

These potent spears contain a special kind of carbohydrate called *inulin*, which promotes the growth of healthy bacteria in our large intestines, forcing out the more mischievous kind. Wrap spears in thin slices of ham and bake in a 400°F oven until the ham is crispy.

BRUSSELS SPROUTS

One of the strongest natural cancer-fighters on the planet, brussels sprouts too often get a bad rap for being boring. Combat the boredom by roasting in a hot oven until crispy and caramelized.

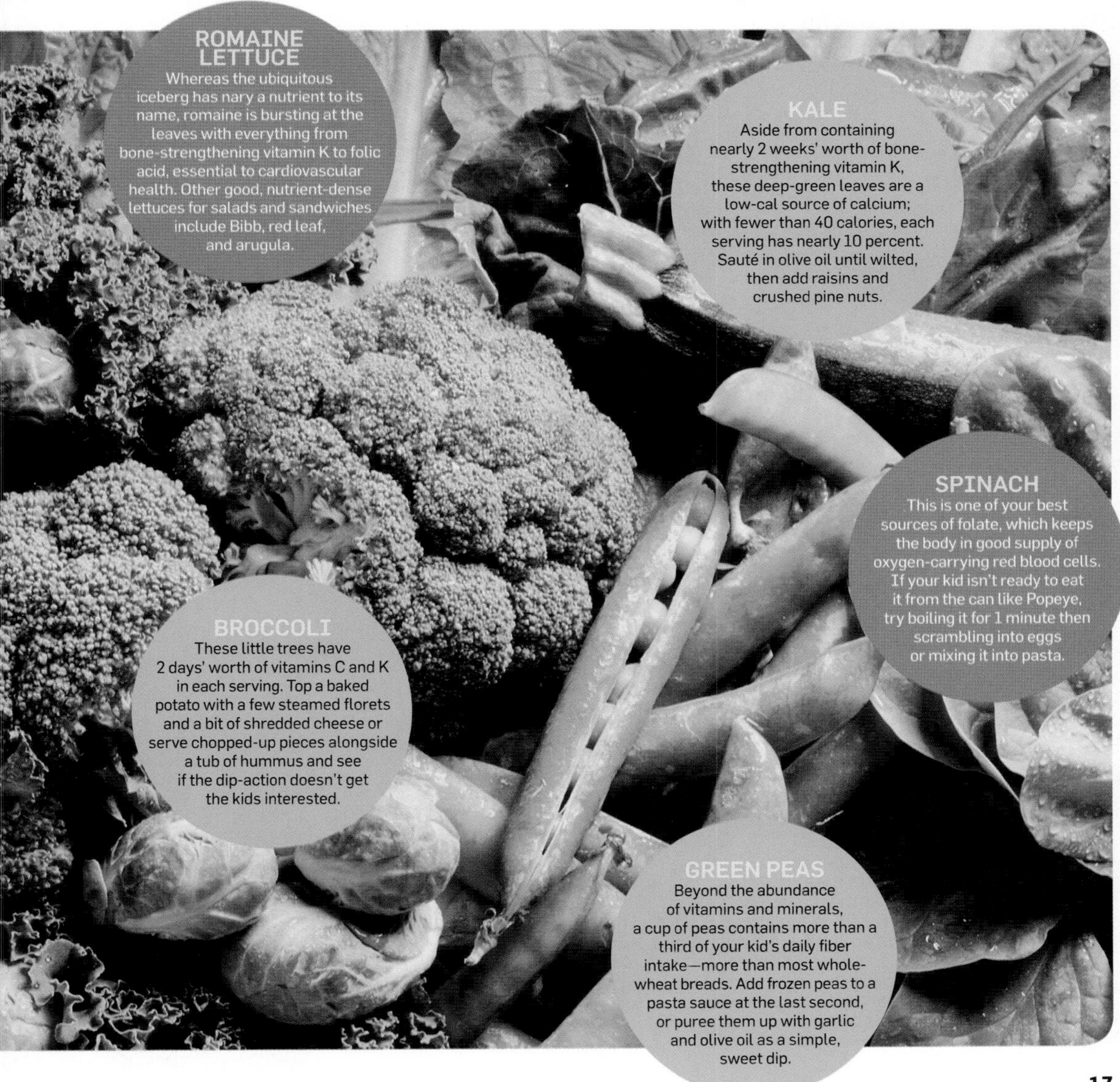
ROMAINE LETTUCE
Whereas the ubiquitous iceberg has nary a nutrient to its name, romaine is bursting at the leaves with everything from bone-strengthening vitamin K to folic acid, essential to cardiovascular health. Other good, nutrient-dense lettuces for salads and sandwiches include Bibb, red leaf, and arugula.
KALE
Aside from containing nearly 2 weeks' worth of bone-strengthening vitamin K, these deep-green leaves are a low-cal source of calcium; with fewer than 40 calories, each serving has nearly 10 percent. Sauté in olive oil until wilted, then add raisins and crushed pine nuts.
SPINACH
This is one of your best sources of folate, which keeps the body in good supply of oxygen-carrying red blood cells. If your kid isn't ready to eat it from the can like Popeye, try boiling it for 1 minute then scrambling into eggs or mixing it into pasta.
BROCCOLI
These little trees have 2 days' worth of vitamins C and K in each serving. Top a baked potato with a few steamed florets and a bit of shredded cheese or serve chopped-up pieces alongside a tub of hummus and see if the dip-action doesn't get the kids interested.
GREEN PEAS
Beyond the abundance of vitamins and minerals, a cup of peas contains more than a third of your kid's daily fiber intake—more than most whole-wheat breads. Add frozen peas to a pasta sauce at the last second, or puree them up with garlic and olive oil as a simple, sweet dip.

BLUE/PURPLE

Blue and purple foods get their colors from the presence of a unique set of flavonoids called *anthocyanins*. Flavonoids in general are known to improve cardiovascular health and prevent short-term memory loss, but the deeply pigmented anthocyanins go even further. Researchers at Tufts University have found that blueberries may make brain cells respond better to incoming messages and might even spur the growth of new nerve cells, providing a new meaning to smart eating. **SUPERPOWER:** Blue foods make you the smartest kid in the class!

EGGPLANT

A pigment called *nasunin* is concentrated in the peel of the eggplant, and studies have shown it has powerful disease-fighting properties. Simplify eggplant parmesan by baking 1/2-inch-thick slices and layering them with marinara and cheese.

BLACKBERRY

One cup of berries contains 5 percent of your child's daily folate and half the day's vitamin C. Try pureeing blackberries, then combining with olive oil and balsamic vinegar for a super healthy salad dressing.

BEET

This candy-sweet vegetable derives most of its color from a cancer-fighting pigment called *betacyanin*. The edible root is replete with fiber, potassium, and manganese. Toss roasted beet chunks with toasted walnuts and orange segments, or grate them raw into salads.

RADISH

Nutritional benefits vary among the many varieties of radishes, but they share an abundance of vitamin C and a tendency to facilitate the digestive process. Try serving thinly sliced radishes on a bagel with low-fat cream cheese and black pepper.

BLUEBERRY

The most abundant source of anthocyanins has more antioxidant punch than red wine, and it helps the body's vitamin C do its job better. Sprinkle blueberries into oatmeal, cereal, or yogurt, or mix with almonds and a few chocolate chips for a quick trail mix.

PURPLE GRAPE

Some researchers believe that, despite their high-fat diets, the French are protected from heart disease by their mass consumption of grapes and wine. Look for a deeper shade of purple—that's an indication of a high flavonoid concentration. Try freezing grapes in the dead of summer for a cool, healthy treat.

PLUM

Another rich source of antioxidants, plums have also been shown to help the body better absorb iron. Roast chunks in the oven and serve warm over a small scoop of vanilla ice cream.

What Our Kids Aren't Eating

In the grips of an obesity crisis, it might be counterintuitive to talk about encouraging our children to eat more. But according to the *Journal of the American College of Nutrition*, only 25 percent of kids met the daily recommendations for fruit and vegetable intake, which in turn creates an array of nutrient deficiencies that can have lasting health implications. Combat the problem by turning the missing nutrients into a treasure hunt with your kids.

WHAT'S MISSING	WHO'S MISSING IT	WHERE TO FIND IT
CALCIUM Vital for building strong, dense bones. Also important in many cell and muscle functions	Calcium's a concern for children of all ages, but especially among young children and girls between 9 and 13	Green leafy vegetables, broccoli, oranges, milk and other dairy products
IRON Helps our bodies produce energy, as well as maintain a healthy immune system	Infants and adolescent girls	Lean red meat, legumes, tofu, green vegetables, mushrooms, and tomatoes
VITAMIN D Builds strong bones and teeth, fights inflammation, and protects against diabetes, heart disease, and cancer	More than half of all children have inadequate levels of vitamin D in their blood.	Milk, eggs, salmon, and shrimp. For infants, the American Academy of Pediatrics recommends providing vitamin D supplements.
VITAMIN E Promotes healthy cell communication, fights off free radicals, and guards our skin against ultraviolet light	For children ages 1 to 8, only 48 percent meet their daily requirements.	Sunflower seeds, almonds, olives, papaya, spinach, and blueberries
FIBER Normalizes blood sugar levels to fight against diabetes, maintains cholesterol levels, and aids satiety	According to a USDA report, only 3 percent of children eat an adequate amount of fiber.	Whole fruits (not juice), whole grains, beans, lentils, peas, berries, cauliflower, spinach, and carrots

AT THEIR FAVORITE RESTAURANTS

Eat Out, Eat Right

Being a parent is hard. Being a parent who's trying to feed her kids healthy fare is even harder.

But being a parent who wants to feed her kids healthy fare at today's restaurants? Nearly impossible.

First, there's the simple logistical challenge of keeping kids—especially little ones—fed and happy on the road. They don't adhere to scheduled mealtimes. They don't adhere to accepted standards of polite behavior. Traveling with little children is like being the road manager for a gaggle of crazed rock stars—they won't listen to reason, their demands are impossible, and when they've worked up an appetite, they want it satisfied now.

And let's face it—a kid's palate is not what you'd call sophisticated. Most young kids have two major food groups: stuff that's beige (fries, chicken fingers, crackers, and bananas), and stuff that has cartoon characters on the box.

Kids don't make mealtimes easy for their parents.

But neither do today's restaurants. Oh sure, most offer "kids' menus," which almost always include the same five choices—pasta, grilled cheese, burgers, mac and cheese. Nothing that's going to set the nutritional world on fire there, but it's not much different than what we ate as kids, right? How bad could such fare be?

The answer is: really, really bad. In fact, even though we try to feed our kids the same type of stuff we remember eating when we were growing up, in reality, today's food is just plain different. According to the New York City Department of Health and Mental Hygiene, fast food and other chain restaurants have allowed their portion sizes and calorie counts to grow faster than Lindsay Lohan's arrest record.

Consider the average fast-food dinner of burger, fries, and a soda—just what Fonzie and Richie ate at Arnold's Drive-In in the '50s and '60s, just what you and I ate when we were kids in the '70s and '80s. But since the 1970s, that simple meal has morphed into something grotesque: The typical serving size for soft drinks has increased by 49 calories; for French fries by 68 calories; and for hamburgers by 97 calories. Eating this standard fast-food meal once a week will give you 11,128 more calories a year—or 3 pounds of extra body weight—than the same meal did when we were kids.

The reasons for this caloric bonanza are complex, but they come down to sheer numbers: Restaurants in general, and chain restaurants in particular, want to create the largest foods they can for the lowest cost. Then they pass those giant portions and low prices on to their customers, and the meals seem like a bargain. And chain restaurants are a bargain—if you're shopping for flab. That's because the cheapest cost comes from the cheapest ingredients: starch, sugar (especially high-fructose corn syrup), salt, and grease (especially trans fats). Because big farms grow high-yield crops (read: soy, corn, and wheat; cows, pigs, and chickens) and don't bother with crops that are hard to grow (read: vegetables and fruit), the cheapest ingredients are also the most calorie-dense and nutrition-thin. That's why—against what would seem to be all logic—you can buy a Big Mac for half the cost of a fresh cantaloupe.

It's also why, even though only one in four meals is prepared in restaurants, a whopping 35 percent of our weekly caloric intake is consumed there—up from 23 percent in the 1970s. Sure, we eat out more, and take out more, than we did when you and I were kids—it's a by-product of our crazy, two-income, 24/7 lifestyle, which happens to be the same lifestyle that's made cooking at home much more of a rarity than it once was. But the number of calories being pumped into us by restaurants is out of proportion with the actual number of meals we eat there. To put it another way: Restaurants make up only one-quarter of our meals, but account for more than one-third of our calories. (And, incredibly, eating out now sucks up 47 percent of Americans' food dollars.)

And the drive-through calories are piling up even faster for those of us not yet old enough to drive. According to researchers from Harvard Medical School, consumption of fast food by children 4 to 19 years old increased by a remarkable fivefold in

2 decades, from 2 percent of their total calorie intake in the late 1970s to 10 percent by the mid 1990s. (If you are what you eat, the typical American adolescent is 10 percent McNugget.) According to a study in the Journal of Pediatrics, children who eat fast food not only consume more calories, fat, carbohydrates, and added sugar, they also drink more soda, consume less milk, and eat fewer fruits and vegetables than kids who lay off the Unhappy Meal. Sadly, not many of our kids are ignoring the clown: In a study of 1,474 middle school students by the Harvard School of Public Health, 66 percent had eaten fast food in just the past 7 days!

Now, we all know that fast food is often bad for us. And, interestingly enough, American dining trends aren't pointing to the big burger pusher with the crown. More and more, we're turning to the big chain sit-down restaurants: Olive Garden, Don Pablo's, T.G.I. Friday's, and the like. Indeed, some economists forecast that between 2000 and 2020, spending at sit-down, or full-service, restaurants will grow three times as fast as spending at fast-food restaurants.

You'd think that would be a good thing. Waiters, tablecloths, and salad forks ought to indicate that we're eating healthier than if we're scarfing down dinner with one hand on the steering wheel, no?

Well, no. See, we've all come to the conclusion that fast food is bad for us. But few of us realize that sit-down restaurants are just as culpable in the supersizing of American children.

Part of the problem is that sit-down meals just feel healthier—and they aren't. In fact, we conducted a survey of over 40 chain restaurants and found that the average entree at a sit-down restaurant has 345 more calories than a fast-food entree. And worse, there's no way for the typical American to tell just how unhealthy these choices are. Unlike packaged-goods manufacturers, whose supermarket wares are required by law to contain detailed nutritional information on their labels, restaurant chains don't labor under any nutritional disclosure regulations. Some of them do list nutritional information on their Web sites—major chains who trust their customers to make informed choices include Burger King, Quizno's, and Romano's Macaroni Grill. But if you can decipher the nutritional makeup of a typical chicken nugget, then please, feel free to also explain to me how, exactly, the electoral college works.

In fact, many restaurants' foods are so bad for us that, even when we know they're unhealthy, we still don't understand just how belly-bloating, artery-choking, and energy-sucking they really are. As mentioned before—and it certainly bears repeating—consumers presented with obviously high-calorie restaurant foods still underestimated the nutritional heft of the items by an average of 600 calories. (Eating 600 unexpected calories just once a week would add an extra 30,000 calories annually to one's diet—enough to add 9 pounds to your weight every year!)

Don't believe me? Let's test the theory. Come with me to a restaurant that's probably somewhere in your neighborhood: Chili's Grill & Bar. You know it? It's a national, family-friendly chain that caters to fajita and burger lovers. Now settle in and take a look at the menu. No, not the grown-ups' menu—the kids' menu. Let's try, hmmm . . . how about the Pepper Pals Country-Fried Chicken Crispers?

Chicken fingers are a staple of the harried parent's food artillery, right up there with Goldfish crackers and Cheerios. It's hardly a health food, but how bad can it be? For example, an entire bag of breaded Chicken Breast Tenders from Tyson has 880 calories, 48 grams of fat, and 1400 milligrams of sodium. Not great, but that's 20 tenders.

So how many calories, and how much sodium and fat, does a single serving of chicken fingers at Chili's have? The same? Double? More?

Turns out just three Crispers have a mind-boggling 610 calories and 41 grams of fat. Factor in the fries and ranch dipping sauce that's offered with this meal and suddenly your kid is taking in 1,100 calories, 1,980 milligrams of sodium, and more fat (82 grams) than you'd find in seven Krispy Kreme glazed doughnuts. I'm not making this stuff up.

In the following pages, you're going to find dozens more shocking revelations about what restaurateurs are shilling to America's children. But you're also going to find hundreds of smart swaps you can make to keep your own kids safe from these dietary time bombs.

More and more, the local family restaurant is where your child's future health will be determined. Stay vigilant, stay savvy, stay smart.

You can make a difference.

600
CALORIES

Romano's Macaroni Grill's Mac 'n' Cheese has as much saturated fat as 20 strips of bacon.

The 20 Worst Kids' Foods in America

The restaurant industry has declared war on our kids' waistlines. It's time for parents to fight back.

WORST BREAKFAST CEREAL

20 Cap'n Crunch® (1 cup)

146 calories
2 g fat (1 g saturated)
16 g sugars
1 g fiber

The Cap'n's cereal didn't make the list because it's loaded with fat or calories; it made the list by being among the most dominant sources of empty calories in a child's diet. Aside from the small amount of added vitamins, which are mandated by the government, this cereal is an amalgam of worthless food particles and chemicals. Buyer beware: Most cereals marketed to kids suffer similar problems.

Eat This Instead!

Cascadian Farm® Clifford Crunch (1 cup)

100 calories
1 g fat (0 g saturated)
6 g sugars
5 g fiber

WORST SIDE

19 Bob Evans® Smiley Face Potatoes

524 calories
31 g fat (6 g saturated)
646 mg sodium
57 g carbohydrates

Not even an extended bath in hot oil could wipe the grins from the faces of these creepy-looking potatoes. When eating out, side dishes make or break a meal, and with more fat and calories than Bob's Sirloin Steak, this side falls woefully into the latter category. Let this be a lesson to all the kids out there: Just because they're smiling doesn't mean they're nice.

Eat This Instead!

Home Fries

186 calories
7 g fat (1 g saturated)
547 mg sodium
27 g carbohydrates

WORST PB&J

18 Così's® Kids Peanut Butter and Jelly

560 calories
26 g fat (5 g saturated)*
*65 g carbohydrates**

Normally a nutritional safe haven, the American classic enters the danger zone at Cosí. Somehow, the sandwich chain manages to create a PB&J with 60 percent more calories than their own Gooey Grilled Cheese. Add in the chips that come with this meal and you're at 700 calories—before the drink.

**Numbers based on estimates. Cosí will not provide fat and carbohydrate counts for this sandwich.*

Eat This Instead!

Kids Turkey Sandwich

289 calories
7 g fat (1 g saturated)
48 g carbohydrates

WORST PASTA MEAL

17 Romano's Macaroni Grill® Kids Macaroni 'n' Cheese

600 calories
31 g fat (20 g saturated)
1,720 mg sodium

This dish used to be double the size and caloric impact, but after we attacked it in the first *Eat This, Not That!*, they finally cut the massive portion size down. Thanks, Macaroni Grill. (P.S. It's still a disaster.)

Eat This Instead!

Spaghetti & Meatballs with Tomato Sauce

500 calories
20 g fat (8 g saturated)
1,520 mg sodium

WORST HOME-STYLE MEAL

16 Boston Market's™ Kids' Meatloaf with Sweet Potato Casserole and Cornbread

650 calories
30 g fat (11 g saturated)
910 mg sodium

This slab-o-meat begins as beef and ends as a science project, with 55 ingredients that include the understandable (cheese cultures), the detestable (partially hydrogenated cottonseed oil), and the unpronounceable (azodicarbonamide). Don't let your kid be the lab rat.

Eat This Instead!

Kids' Roasted Turkey with Green Bean Casserole and Cornbread

300 calories
7.5 g fat (2.5 g saturated)
948 mg sodium

WORST SANDWICH

15 Au Bon Pain® Kids' Grilled Cheese

670 calories
41 g fat (25 g saturated)
1,060 mg sodium

Au Bon Pain turns a simple sandwich into a complicated mess, with as much saturated fat as 25 strips of bacon. As a rule of thumb, avoid all of Au Bon Pain's kids' sandwiches, as every one of them contains more than 500 calories.

Eat This Instead!

Kids' Macaroni and Cheese

220 calories
14 g fat (9 g saturated)
650 mg sodium

WORST PREPARED LUNCH

14 Oscar Mayer® Maxed Out Turkey & Cheddar Cracker Combo Lunchables

680 calories
22 g fat (9 g saturated)
1,440 mg sodium

The Maxed Out line is the worst of the lackluster Lunchables, with a back label that looks like a chemistry textbook index. Oscar even crams in 61 grams of sugar—more than you'll find in two packs of Reese's Peanut Butter Cups!

Eat This Instead!

Hillshire Farm® Deli Wrap Smokehouse Ham & Swiss Wrap Kit

260 calories
11 g fat (4 g saturated)
960 mg sodium

WORST FAST-FOOD MEAL

13 Burger King's® Kids Double Cheeseburger and Kids Fries

740 calories
42 g fat (17 g saturated, 4.5 g trans)
1,410 mg sodium

BK's dubious double burger earns the distinction of being the fattiest meal for an on-the-go kid, with nearly a day's worth of saturated fat for the average 8-year-old.

Eat This Instead!

4-piece Chicken Tenders® with Strawberry-Flavored Applesauce

280 calories
11 g fat (3 g saturated)
440 mg sodium

WORST BREAKFAST

12 Denny's® Big Dipper French Toastix™ with whipped margarine and syrup

770 calories
71 g fat (13 g saturated)
107 g carbohydrates

It's hard to deny that breakfast is the most important meal of the day, but that doesn't mean you should make your kids eat it twice in one sitting. At this size, four French Toastix is three too many.

Eat This Instead!

Smiley-Alien Hotcakes with sugar-free syrup and Anti-Gravity Grapes

313 calories
3 g fat (0.5 g saturated)
71 g carbohydrates

911 CALORIES

Così's Kids' Pepperoni Pizza could feed a small family.

650
CALORIES
Boston Market's Kids' Meatloaf is a science experiment gone awry.
TROPICAL PUNCH
Cherry
680
CALORIES
Kids construct their own calorie bombs with Lunchables' line of Maxed Out meals.

WORST FROZEN SUPERMARKET MEAL

11 DiGiorno® For One Garlic Bread Crust Pepperoni Pizza

840 calories
44 g fat (16 g saturated, 3.5 g trans)
1,450 mg sodium

This is why parents need to spend the time reading nutrition labels. The name says it's made to satisfy a single appetite, yet it contains a child's full day of saturated fat and a giant glob of trans fat baked into the crust. Whether fresh or frozen, keep your pizza thin crust and pepperoni-free.

Eat This Instead!

Red Baron® Thin & Crispy Four Cheese Pizza

300 calories
14 g fat (8 g saturated)
600 mg sodium

WORST DESSERT

10 Uno Chicago Grill's® Kid's Sundae

840 calories
36 g fat (18 g saturated)
98 g sugars

You wouldn't let your kid finish dinner at home with three Baby Ruth® candy bars, would you? Then don't let him tackle this caloric equivalent after dinner at Uno. Weighing in at a hulking three-quarters of a pound, this abominable sundae is twice as big as the Kid's Pasta, and twice as caloric as his entire meal should be.

Eat This Instead!

Kid's Slush

140 calories
0 g fat
32 g sugars

WORST MEXICAN MEAL

9 On the Border's® Kids' Beef Soft Taco Mexican Dinner with Rice and Refried Beans

840 calories
35 g fat (14 g saturated)
2,760 mg sodium
91 g carbohydrates

The taco (yes, this scale-tipping meal has just one taco) alone has 19 grams of fat, and there are 11 grams more stowed in the beans. Taken together, the taco, beans, and rice provide enough calories for two kids' meals and enough sodium to preserve a small city.

Eat This Instead!

Kids' Grilled Chicken with Black Beans

310 calories
9 g fat (3 g saturated)
1,230 mg sodium
20 g carbohydrates

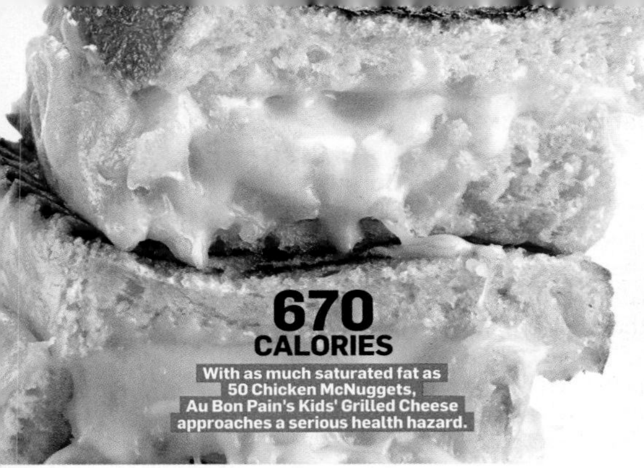

670
CALORIES
With as much saturated fat as
50 Chicken McNuggets,
Au Bon Pain's Kids' Grilled Cheese
approaches a serious health hazard.

893
CALORIES
Ruby Tuesday's Turkey Minis
have a major impact on your
kid's waistline.

WORST FINGER FOOD

8 Denny's® Little Dippers with Marinara and Fries

860 calories
43 g fat (17 g saturated)
1,679 mg sodium
80 g carbohydrates

Dippable foods are usually dangerous, and this one meal combines three of the worst of them: nuggets, mozzarella sticks, and fries. The treacherous trio packs a punishing wallop of calories, fat, carbs, and sodium. For a meal that doesn't require a fork to eat, this option, containing half of a kid's daily calories, is toxic.

Eat This Instead!

Moons & Stars Chicken Nuggets with Moon Crater Mashed™ Potatoes and Gravy

335 calories
19 g fat (6 g saturated)
897 mg sodium
29 g carbohydrates

WORST BURGER

7 Ruby Tuesday's® Kids Turkey Minis & Fries

893 calories
47 g fat
88 g carbohydrates

In a perfect world, ground turkey is leaner than ground beef and a turkey burger is a decent thing to feed your kid. But Ruby Tuesday finds a way to confound all expectations by cramming half a day's worth of calories into these tiny burgers. We chose the turkey version because it presents itself as a healthier alternative to the beef burgers, but in reality it has just 14 fewer calories.

Eat This Instead!

Petite Sirloin (7 oz) with Mashed Potatoes

460 calories
20 g fat
31 g carbohydrates

WORST PIZZA

6 Così's® Kids' Pepperoni Pizza

911 calories
43 g fat
2,731 mg sodium
112 g carbohydrates

Before your child eats this doughy, oversized pizza, consider strapping two boxes of mozzarella Bagel Bites® to her stomach to see if she likes the added bulk, because that's how many calories she stands to absorb. You're better off ordering in—even two slices of a 12-inch pepperoni pizza from Papa John's® is only 440 calories.

Eat This Instead!

Gooey Grilled Cheese

357 calories
21 g fat
759 mg sodium
26 g carbohydrates

WORST NACHOS

5 On the Border's® Kids Bean & Cheese Nachos

980 calories
57 g fat (29 g saturated)
1,850 mg sodium

The kids' portion is a scaled-down version of the massive, 1,900-calorie appetizer, but it still contains enough saturated fat to make a cardiologist shudder. By the time your kid makes it through the complimentary sundae, he'll have taken in 1,300 calories and 70 grams of fat.

Eat This Instead!

Crispy Chicken Tacos (2)

480 calories
24 g fat (10 g saturated)
1,240 mg sodium

WORST DRINK

4 Baskin-Robbins® Heath® Shake (small)

990 calories
46 g fat (28 g saturated)
113 g sugars

It's a marvel of modern food science that Baskin-Robbins can fit this much fat and sugar into a 16-ounce cup. It took 73 ingredients and a reckless sense of abandon to do so. All told, it has almost as many calories as five actual Heath bars.

Drink This Instead!

Strawberry Citrus Fruit Blast (small)

350 calories
1 g fat (0 g saturated)
85 g sugars

WORST CHINESE ENTRÉE

3 P.F. Chang's® Chicken Lo Mein

1,198 calories
67 g fat (11 g saturated)

P.F. Chang's doesn't offer a kids' menu, but for many parents, this traditional Chinese dish meets the criteria: thin noodles stir-fried and served with chicken. Problem is, Chang's take on this seemingly innocent Chinese staple packs more fat than five chocolate Krispy Kreme® doughnuts.

Eat This Instead!

Buddha's Feast Lunch Bowl with brown rice

541 calories
8 g fat (1 g saturated)

WORST APPETIZER

2 T.G.I. Friday's® Potato Skins (½ order)

*1,430 calories**

What happened to the appetizer that simply roused the appetite? This monstrosity contains 80 percent of a 9-year-old child's daily caloric intake. Splitting a full order of skins among a family of four would still saddle each member with over 550 calories.

Eat This Instead!

Zen Chicken Pot Stickers

*370 calories**

**T.G.I. Friday's will not provide nutritional information on anything other than calories.*

THE WORST KIDS' MEAL IN AMERICA

1 Chili's® Pepper Pals® Country-Fried Chicken Crispers with Ranch Dressing and Homestyle Fries

1,110 calories
82 g fat (15 g saturated)
1,980 mg sodium
56 g carbohydrates

Most kids, if given the choice, would live on chicken fingers for the duration of their adolescent lives. If those chicken fingers happened to come from Chili's, it might be a pretty short life. A moderately active 8-year-old boy should eat around 1,600 calories a day. This single meal plows through 75 percent of that allotment. So unless he plans to eat carrots and celery sticks for the rest of the day (and we know he doesn't), find a healthier chicken alternative. Chili's Pepper Pals menu has one of the most extensive collection of kids' entrées and side dishes in America, all of which prove considerably healthier than this country-fried disaster.

Eat This Instead!

Pepper Pals® Grilled Chicken Platter with Cinnamon Apples

350 calories
11 g fat (3 g saturated)
870 mg sodium
38 g carbohydrates

524
CALORIES

As America's worst side dish for kids, Bob Evans Smiley Face Potatoes are no laughing matter.

Applebee's

REPORT CARD F

Applebee's is one of a handful of restaurant-industry titans that refuses to give up the goods on their nutritional information. Until they tell diners what they're putting in their bodies, we'll be forced to fail them.

SURVIVAL STRATEGY
The 10-item menu in partnership with Weight Watchers® provides a smattering of nutritional analysis for each dish. It's a small step, but until Applebee's coughs up all the info, stick with these 10 dishes, or find another restaurant.

GREAT GROWN-UP GRUB

Italian Chicken & Portobello Sandwich

360 calories,
6 g fat
11 g fiber

This wheat-bun sandwich is spread with chunky marinara instead of fattening mayonnaise. Between the mushroom stack, rich in B vitamins, and the side of fresh fruit, you'll knock out a couple of servings of fruits and vegetables for the kids without breaking a sweat.

Eat This

Grilled Chicken Sandwich

with broccoli

340 calories
10 g fat
(4 g saturated)
820 mg sodium

Because Applebee's doesn't offer nutritional information to its customers, many of the numbers on this page are estimates drawn from independent research and consultation with nutritionists in order to help you determine what the restaurant is feeding your child.

As simple and healthy as it gets, this meal provides nearly two servings of vegetables for nutrition-starved children. If your kid tops this with anything, make sure it's not ranch or mayo.

Other Picks

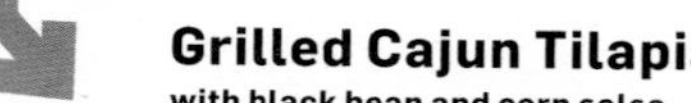

Grilled Cajun Tilapia
with black bean and corn salsa

310 calories
6 g fat (0 g saturated)
1,025 mg sodium

Tortilla Chicken Melt

480 calories
13 g fat (4 g saturated)
935 mg sodium

Hot Fudge Sundae Dessert Shooter

310 calories
10 g fat (4 g saturated)
22 g sugars

690 calories
32 g fat
(9 g saturated)
950 mg sodium

Not That!

Chicken Fingers

with celery with ranch dressing

On nearly every kids' menu in America, chicken fingers generally cost about 140 calories a piece, and that's before dunking.

UNHAPPY MEALS

Chicken Fajita Rollup

with Mexi-ranch dipping sauce and fries

1,480 calories
85 g fat
(37 g saturated)
2,661 mg sodium
112 g carbohydrates

How bad can chicken be? When it's rolled into a massive tortilla, suffocated by a tide of melted cheese, and dipped into a vat of ranch dressing, it picks up more calories than four Crispy Chicken Sandwiches from Wendy's. Avoid all of the disastrous Applebee's rollups—not a single one contains under 1,100 calories.

Other Passes

1,330 calories
62 g fat (23 g saturated)
1,890 mg sodium

Double Crunch Shrimp
with fries, cole slaw, and cocktail sauce

1,280 calories
58 g fat (21 g saturated)
1,970 mg sodium

Honey Barbecue Chicken Sandwich

1,290 calories
58 g fat (23 g saturated)
95 g sugars

Blue Ribon Brownie

11

The number of hours a kid would have to spend raking leaves in order to burn off the 2,027 calories in Applebee's Riblet meal with beans, coleslaw, and fries.

Arby's

REPORT CARD B

Although the choices for kids are few, no entrée contains more than 275 calories, and the fruit-cup side earns the sandwich shop extra points. Too bad the rest of the menu is so lousy—most sandwiches suffer from spread overload or big-bread syndrome. And breakfast should be avoided altogether.

SURVIVAL STRATEGY
Lean roast beef is what they're known for, and it's never a bad way to go.

FOOD MYTH #1

Wheat bread is always healthier than white bread.

Not all wheat bread is 100 percent whole grain, which means your kid may not be getting the fiber benefits of true wheat breads. On top of that, manufacturers tend to add extra sugar to wheat bread to make it more appealing to eaters. The honey wheat bread on Arby's Market Fresh™ sandwiches contains vegetable shortening, high-fructose corn syrup, and 361 calories.

Eat This

Arby's Melt

303 calories
12 g fat (5 g saturated)
921 mg sodium

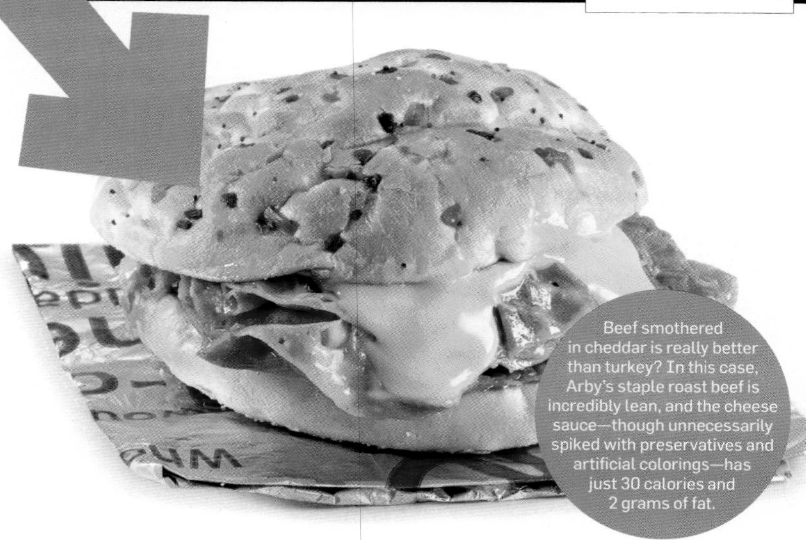

Beef smothered in cheddar is really better than turkey? In this case, Arby's staple roast beef is incredibly lean, and the cheese sauce—though unnecessarily spiked with preservatives and artificial colorings—has just 30 calories and 2 grams of fat.

Other Picks

Ham and Swiss Melt Sandwich
268 calories
5 g fat (2 g saturated)
1,042 mg sodium

Market Fresh™ Mini Turkey and Cheese Sandwich
244 calories
5 g fat (1 g saturated)
854 mg sodium

T.J. Cinnamons® Chocolate Twist
250 calories
12 g fat (4 g saturated)
12 g sugars

708 calories
30 g fat
(8 g saturated)
1,677 mg sodium

Not That!

Roasted Turkey and Swiss Sandwich

True, turkey on its own is a safe bet as a lean deli meat. Problem is, the bread it's served on packs 361 calories on its own. Switch to a sesame bun and hold the mayo and the sandwich sheds 284 calories instantly.

Other Passes

395 calories
17 g fat (3 g saturated)
1,002 mg sodium

Grilled Chicken Fillet Sandwich

272 calories
12 g fat (2 g saturated)
698 mg sodium

Kids Popcorn Chicken

377 calories
16 g fat (5 g saturated)
41 g sugars

Apple Turnover

HIDDEN DANGER
Chicken Club Salad with Buttermilk Ranch

Just in case you were tempted to encourage your child to eat a "healthy" salad. Yes, there's popcorn chicken, bacon, and cheese polluting the innocent lettuce leaves, but the real damage comes from the ranch, which packs a whopping 34 grams of fat.

750 calories,
56 g fat
(12 g saturated)
1,551 mg sodium

UNHAPPY MEALS
Regular Jalapeño Bites® with Bronco Berry Dipping Sauce™

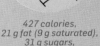

427 calories,
21 g fat (9 g saturated),
31 g sugars,
526 mg sodium

There's not one berry in the Bronco Berry sauce—but lots of added sugar. The fat comes from the jalapeños' fried breading and cream-cheese filling. If your kid has a taste for spicy foods, go for Arby's Spicy Three Pepper Sauce®.

Au Bon Pain

REPORT CARD
C

The virtues of Au Bon Pain's nutritional transparency, which include on-location kiosks that provide the calorie counts, are unfortunately outweighed by the pitfalls of calorie-laden baked goods and a kids' sandwich lineup that doesn't include a single selection that comes in under 500 calories. Au Bon Pain Portions are, however, a beacon of health for kids and parents alike.

SURVIVAL STRATEGY
Skip over sandwiches and nudge your kids toward a hearty soup, or help them mix and match 200-calorie Portion plates.

SMART SIDES

Hummus and Cucumber
130 calories, 8 g fat (0 g saturated) 460 mg sodium

The base of hummus is made from chickpeas, which has fiber that helps prevent your child's blood sugar level from rising too quickly after a meal. And don't fear the fat—it's the good kind.

Eat This

Honey Mustard Chicken

and cheddar, fruit, and crackers portions

360 calories
13 g fat (5 g saturated)
530 mg sodium

Go for the mac and cheese listed below, or one of these portion-controlled snacks. You can pair cheese and crackers with a variety of chicken options and still keep the calorie count under 400.

Other Picks

Kids Macaroni and Cheese
220 calories
14 g fat (9 g saturated)
650 mg sodium

Au Bon Pain Portions BBQ Chicken
170 calories
2 g fat (0 g saturated)
340 mg sodium

Bacon and Bagel
340 calories
6 g fat (2 g saturated)
630 mg sodium

670 calories
41 g fat
(25 g saturated)
1,060 mg sodium

Not That!

Kids Grilled Cheese Sandwich

If the kids are going to order grilled cheese, you're better off staying in: The average homemade grilled cheese runs a reasonable 300 calories, with about 6 grams of saturated fat.

Other Passes

310 calories
21 g fat (10 g saturated)
1,000 mg sodium

Broccoli and Cheddar Soup

550 calories
27 g fat (5 g saturated)
1,330 mg sodium

Kids Smoked Turkey Sandwich

510 calories
19 g fat (2 g saturated)
550 mg sodium

Blueberry Muffin

Genius PARENT TRICK

Think soup. Most of them here are low in fat and filled with vegetables, which help satisfy and nourish better than most entrées. Stay away from cream-based bowls and you'll land a lunch under 200 calories.

STEALTH HEALTH FOOD

Turkish Apricots

120 calories,
0 g fat,
4 g fiber

This exotic dried-fruit snack benefits from a ton of fiber and a rich reserve of beta-carotene. Plus, they're sweet enough to win any picky eater over.

SUGAR SPIKES

Low-Fat Blueberry Yogurt with Fruit (small)

The Impact:
37 g sugars

The bulk of the sugar isn't from blueberries, but a mix of cane sugar and corn syrup sweeteners.

Baja Fresh

REPORT CARD

D

Baja's bad grade stems from an inability to serve a single kids' entrée with fewer than 500 calories and 900 milligrams of sodium. Add to that an array of appealing, cheesy entrées and sides likely to catch a kid's attention, and you see how hard it is to feed your kids well at this Cali-Mex chain.

SURVIVAL STRATEGY
Unless you can convince the tots to tackle a bowl of fiber-rich beans and salsa, then the only viable option (for them and you) is tacos.

SMART SIDES

Guacamole
110 calories, 9 g fat (2 g saturated), 280 mg sodium

Scoop some guac into a taco or mix it with rice and beans. Aside from being one of the world's best condiments, the mashed avocados are packed with fiber, vitamin C, and healthy monounsaturated fats, which help the body regulate weight and metabolism.

Eat This

Original Baja Chicken Tacos

(2)

420 calories
10 g fat (2 g saturated)
460 mg sodium

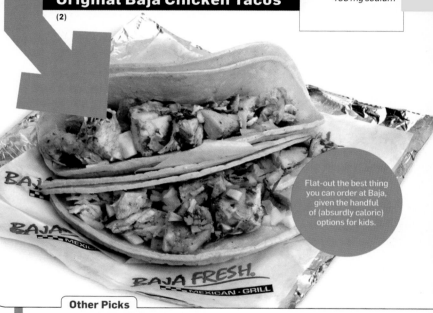

Flat-out the best thing you can order at Baja, given the handful of (absurdly caloric) options for kids.

Other Picks

Kids Mini Bean and Cheese Burrito with Chicken

590 calories
15 g fat (7 g saturated)
1,200 mg sodium

Steak Original Baja Tacos
(2)

460 calories
16 g fat (4 g saturated)
520 mg sodium

Rice and Beans Plate
with tortilla chips

630 calories
14 g fat (2.5 g saturated)
1,375 mg sodium

630 calories
33 g fat
(7 g saturated)
990 mg sodium

Not That!

Kids Chicken Taquitos

(served with ranch dressing)

Why Baja abandons their healthy homemade salsas for ranch dressing here is beyond us. If your kids must have taquitos, save them a few hundred calories and a boatload of fat by switching back over to the salsa.

Other Passes

1,200 calories
78 g fat (37 g saturated)
2,140 mg sodium

Cheese Quesadilla

520 calories
26 g fat (12 g saturated)
1,280 mg sodium

Steak Americano Soft Tacos (2)

1,890 calories
108 g fat (40 g saturated)
2,530 mg sodium

Cheese Nachos

Genius PARENT TRICK

Get your kids hooked on beans. Rice may have 40 fewer calories than beans at Baja, but calories from rice are driven by quick-burning carbohydrates, whereas a side order of pinto beans has an astounding 21 grams of fiber—enough to keep the young ones full and content until dinnertime.

HIDDEN DANGER
Steak Nachos

How bad can a plate of chips and cheese really be? Bad enough to be the caloric equivalent of four Big Macs®, with 2 full days' worth of saturated fat tangled in the heap. Even split among a family of four, this dish would still have a punishing impact.

2,120 calories, 118 g fat (44 g saturated, 4.5 g trans), 2,990 mg sodium

Baskin-Robbins

It's hard to serve just ice cream and still make the grade, but Baskin-Robbins does nothing to help its case by serving up some of the fattiest scoops in the industry, plus 900-calorie soft serve concoctions, smoothies with more sugar than fruit, and, as of publication, the worst drink on the planet, a Heath® Premium Shake with 2,310 calories in a large serving!

SURVIVAL STRATEGY
Seek solace in Baskin's lighter side, where sherbets, sorbets, and low-sugar treats offer ample opportunity to feel indulgent without really being so.

CONE DECODER

● **WAFFLE:** 160 calories, 4 g fat (1 g saturated), 13 g sugars

● **SUGAR:** 45 calories, 0.5 g fat (0 g saturated fat), 3 g sugars

● **CAKE:** 25 calories, 0 g fat, 0 g sugars

Eat This

No Sugar Added Chocolate Chocolate Chip Ice Cream

in a waffle cone (1 scoop)

310 calories
9 g fat (4.5 g saturated)
20 g sugars

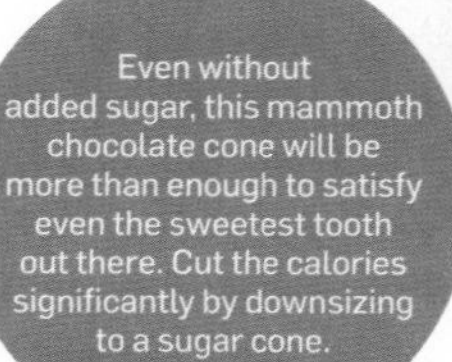

Even without added sugar, this mammoth chocolate cone will be more than enough to satisfy even the sweetest tooth out there. Cut the calories significantly by downsizing to a sugar cone.

Other Picks

Chocolate Ice Cream in a sugar cone **(1 scoop)**

305 calories
14.5 g fat (9 g saturated)
34 g sugars

Strawberry Sorbet in a cup **(1 scoop)**

130 calories
0 g fat
34 g sugars

Wild Mango Fruit Blast **(small)**

340 calories
1 g fat (0 g saturated)
82 g sugars

480 calories
24 g fat (10 g saturated)
41 g sugars

Not That!

Peanut Butter 'n Chocolate Ice Cream

in a waffle cone (1 scoop)

The worst ice cream you can order at Baskin-Robbins. Two scoops on this calamitous cone will saddle you with an entire day's worth of saturated fat.

Other Passes

620 calories
30 g fat (18 g saturated)
77 g sugars

Chocolate Shake **(small)**

240 calories
12 g fat (7 g saturated)
26 g sugars

Cherries Jubilee Ice Cream in a cup (1 scoop)

440 calories
1.5 g fat (0 g saturated)
101 g sugars

Mango Fruit Blast Smoothie **(small)**

Ordering an ice cream cake for the next birthday bash? Make it one of Baskin-Robbins's roll cakes, which provide slices that are neither as dense nor as giant as those cut from the more popular round and sheet cakes. The proof is in the numbers: A slice of chocolate chip from a round cake weighs in at 410 calories, while a slice of the same flavor from a roll cake has only 290 calories.

SUGAR SPIKES

Strawberry Banana Fruit Blast Smoothie (small)

The Impact: 110 g sugars

This smoothie contains the combined sugars of one scoop each of Rocky Road, French Vanilla, Chocolate Chip, and Very Berry Strawberry Ice Cream. We say skip the smoothie, pick one scoop, and count your savings.

Ben & Jerry's

REPORT CARD

C+

The hippy-hued company's commitment to hormone-free Vermont milk and Fair Trade vanilla, cocoa, and coffee—ingredients that quell the sweet tooth while calming the conscience—is good news for your family. So is the fact that many single scoops fall below 250 calories. But at the end of the day, it's still just an ice cream shop.

SURVIVAL STRATEGY

Sorbet and frozen yogurt always trump the cream-and-candy scoops that Ben and Jerry's is known for. Rule of thumb: The more complicated an ice cream sounds, the worse it is for you.

GUILTY PLEASURES

Cherry Garcia® Low-Fat Frozen Yogurt (1/2 c)

170 calories, 3 g fat (2 g saturated), 20 g sugars

There's a reason this is on Ben & Jerry's top-selling flavors list. Bring home some of Jerry's cherry flavor, and it will keep you satiated without busting your belt.

Eat This

Strawberry Original Ice Cream

in a sugar cone (1/2 c)

215 calories
9.5 g fat (6 g saturated)
22 g sugars

The "healthiest" of all of Ben & Jerry's regular scoops, with the lowest levels of fat and calories, plus the addition of real fruit—not just artificial flavoring and red dye, which many other major producers rely on.

Other Picks

Chocolate Chip Cookie Dough Original Ice Cream (1/2 c)

270 calories
14 g fat (9 g saturated)
24 g sugars

Chocolate Fudge Brownie Frozen Yogurt (1/2 c)

170 calories
2.5 g fat (0.5 g saturated)
23 g sugars

Berry Berry Extraordinary Sorbet (1/2 c)

100 calories
0 g fat
23 g sugars

295 calories
15.5 g fat (11 g saturated)
25 g sugars

Not That!

Chocolate Original Ice Cream

in a sugar cone (1/2 c)

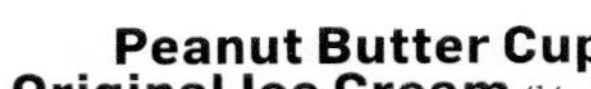

In the classic showdown of chocolate versus strawberry, chocolate loses out with more of everything that hurts—calories, fat, sugar—and less of the one ingredient that helps: real fruit.

Other Passes

340 calories
24 g fat (12 g saturated)
24 g sugars

Peanut Butter Cup Original Ice Cream (1/2 c)

250 calories
12 g fat (8 g saturated)
25 g sugars

Chocolate Fudge Brownie Original Ice Cream (1/2 c)

140 calories
1.5 g fat (1 g saturated)
20 g sugars

Black Raspberry Frozen Yogurt (1/2 c)

SUGAR SPIKES

Jamaican Me Crazy Sorbet (1/2 c)

The Impact: 29 g sugars

The sorbet is fat-free, but the sugar is sky-high. Try to keep your intake of added sugars to fewer than 65 grams a day. A 2004 study linked irregular blood-sugar levels with brain decay. Over a 4-year span, women who had diabetes were twice as likely as women with normal blood sugar to develop the signs of dementia.

Ben & Jerry's uses real fruit in their smoothies, and if you ask, they'll let you create your own recipe. Ask them to start with sorbet and then have your child pick the fruit. The result will be relatively healthy and totally delicious, and the experience will teach your child to make good nutritional decisions.

Bob Evans

REPORT CARD **B-**

Bob Evans provides kids' meals with modest portions and a bounty of wholesome sides. You can run up a dangerously high calorie count, though, by matching the wrong entrées—chicken strips, mini cheeseburgers—with the wrong sides, namely the creepy Smiley Face Potatoes.

SURVIVAL STRATEGY: Opt for fruit, yogurt, and eggs over pancakes and French toast in the morning. At night, pair a few vegetable sides with lean turkey, chicken breast, or even pasta.

Genius PARENT TRICK

Get your kids hooked on turkey sausage early. The Bob Evans turkey links are one-third bigger and have two-thirds less fat and calories than the pork sausage.

Eat This

Turkey Lurkey

with glazed carrots, mashed potatoes, and gravy

429 calories
16 g fat (8 g saturated)
1,355 mg sodium

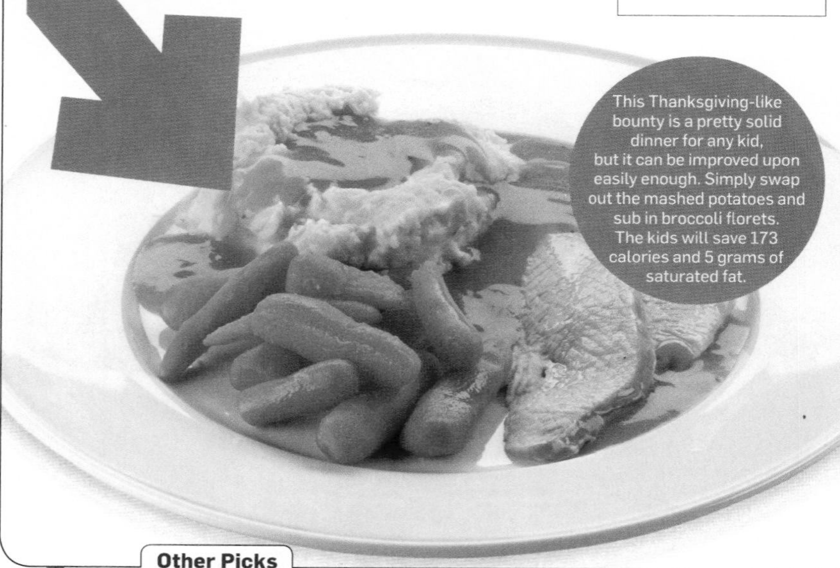

This Thanksgiving-like bounty is a pretty solid dinner for any kid, but it can be improved upon easily enough. Simply swap out the mashed potatoes and sub in broccoli florets. The kids will save 173 calories and 5 grams of saturated fat.

Other Picks

Kids Marinara Pasta

206 calories
5 g fat (1 g saturated)
858 mg sodium

Fit from the Farm Breakfast
with parfait

359 calories
12 g fat (3 g saturated)
707 mg sodium
33 g sugars

Fried Chicken Breast
with home fries and broccoli florets

503 calories
20 g fat (4 g saturated)
1,334 mg sodium

495 calories
38 g fat (8 g saturated)
1,165 mg sodium

Not That!

Grilled Chicken Strips

with side salad with ranch

The problem here isn't the chicken strips—after all, they're a major improvement on the fried chicken fingers also on the kids' menu. Nor is it the salad itself, which carries a meager 60-calorie price tag. No, the real culprit is the ranch, which on its own packs as many calories and more fat than the turkey and gravy do.

Other Passes

320 calories
11 g fat (3 g saturated)
778 mg sodium

Kids Macaroni and Cheese

750 calories
21 g fat (2 g saturated)
1,226 mg sodium
70 g sugars

Kids Plenty-o-Pancakes
with syrup

830 calories
50 g fat (13 g saturated)
1,171 mg sodium

Kids Mini Cheeseburgers
with Smiley Face Potatoes

UNHAPPY MEALS

Slow-Roasted Chicken Pot Pie

908 calories, 60 g fat (16 g saturated), 2,847 mg sodium

Pot pies are scary stuff. The lean chicken and smattering of vegetables are overwhelmed by the buttery crust and viscous, creamy sauce.

GREAT GROWN-UP GRUB

Slow-Roasted Chicken-N-Noodles

296 calories, 16 g fat (3 g saturated), 846 mg sodium, 13 g protein

We've never met a kid who didn't appreciate a good bowl of chicken-noodle soup. This one's especially tasty, with a healthy mix of carrots, celery, and onions.

SMART SIDES

Cottage Cheese

115 calories, 5 g fat (3 g saturated), 14 g protein

Turn your kids into cottage converts. The protein contains all of the essential amino acids, so your child's body will be less likely to metabolize it into fat.

Boston Market

REPORT CARD B

With more than a dozen healthy vegetable sides and lean meats like turkey and roast sirloin on the menu, the low-cal, high-nutrient possibilities at Boston Market are endless. But with nearly a dozen calorie-packed sides and fatty meats like dark meat chicken and meat loaf, it's almost as easy to construct a lousy meal.

SURVIVAL STRATEGY

There are three simple steps to nutritional salvation: 1) Start with turkey, sirloin, or rotisserie chicken. 2) Add two noncreamy, nonstarchy vegetable sides. 3) Ignore all special items, such as potpie and nearly all of the sandwiches.

SUGAR SPIKES

Sweet-Potato Casserole

The Impact:
39 g sugars

Sweet potatoes are one of nature's most nutritional treats, so why ruin them with boatloads of sugar, oil, and butter? This side dish has almost twice as much sugar as Boston Market's Apple Pie.

Eat This

Roasted Sirloin

with garlic dill new potatoes

430 calories
18 g fat
(7 g saturated)
560 mg sodium

No mystery meat here, just top sirloin and spices. Sirloin is the leanest cut of beef out there, which is why a substantial portion like they serve up at Boston Market has just 290 calories.

Other Picks

Rotisserie Chicken Open Face Sandwich

330 calories
9 g fat (2 g saturated)
1,540 mg sodium

Individual Roasted Turkey Meal

180 calories
3 g fat (1 g saturated)
635 mg sodium

Chicken Noodle Soup

170 calories
5 g fat (1.5 g saturated)
930 mg sodium

765 calories
49 g fat
(20.5 g saturated)
2,350 mg sodium

Not That!

Meatloaf

with mashed potatoes and gravy

Mom's meat loaf this ain't, unless mom makes hers with azodicarbonamide calcium peroxide, partially hydrogenated cottonseed oil, ammonium chloride, and 57 other hard-to-pronounce fillers, preservatives, and artificial flavorings.

Other Passes

1,190 calories
77 g fat (18 g saturated)
2,110 mg sodium

Tuscan Herb Chicken Salad Sandwich

470 calories
28 g fat (15 g saturated)
690 mg sodium

Baked Whitefish

400 calories
40 g fat (8 g saturated)
980 mg sodium

Caesar Side Salad

UNHAPPY MEALS

Boston Sirloin Dip Carver®

1,000 calories, 51 g fat (15 g saturated), 1,690 mg sodium, 70 g carbohydrates

Boston Market's Carvers are a precarious lot. If you must, go for a half Carver, and then stick to chicken or turkey—not sirloin.

Excluding the sandwiches, all Boston Market meals get a complimentary hunk of cornbread. Ask them to leave it off when you order; you'll save your child 180 calories and 12 grams of sugar, and she'll never even know it's missing.

Burger King

REPORT CARD **C-**

Burger King has only three legitimate kids' entrées on the menu, and none of them—French Toast Sticks, hamburger, chicken tenders—are particularly healthy. A menu sullied with trans fats is another major reason for concern. BK has pledged to follow in the wake of nearly every other chain restaurant and remove trans fats from the menu by the end of 2008, but so far, we've seen little action.

SURVIVAL STRATEGY
The best kids' meal? A 4-piece Chicken Tenders®, applesauce, and water or milk. Beyond that, there is little hope of escaping unscathed.

7

The number of hours a child would have to sit in detention in order to burn off a large order of French fries.

Eat This

Whopper Jr.®

no mayo, with onion rings (small)

430 calories
19 g fat (6 g saturated, 1.5 g trans)
700 mg sodium
4 g fiber

Hold the mayo, and the Whopper Jr. becomes one of the better burgers in the fast-food world, offering a substantial patty and a heap of produce for under 300 calories.

Other Picks

Chicken Tenders®
(5 pieces)
210 calories
12 g fat (3 g saturated, 2 g trans)
600 mg sodium

Ham Omelet Sandwich
290 calories
13 g fat (4.5 g saturated)
870 mg sodium

Vanilla Milk Shake
(Value Size: 12 fl oz)
310 calories
11 g fat (7 g saturated)
43 g sugars

560 calories
29 g fat
(10 g saturated, 3.5 g trans)
1,160 mg sodium
3 g fiber

Not That!

Cheeseburger

with French fries (small)

Burger King bucks all established fast food rules by serving onion rings that actually have fewer calories than fries. In this case, a small order of rings will save you 90 calories and 2 grams of trans fats over the small fry.

Genius PARENT TRICK

Replace mayo with barbecue sauce on all burgers and sandwiches. BK loads on the fatty stuff thick, adding as much as 160 calories and 17 grams of fat to burgers and sandwiches.

Other Passes

510 calories
19 g fat (3.5 g saturated, 0.5 g trans)
1,180 mg sodium

Tendergrill® Chicken Sandwich

680 calories
24 g fat (6 g saturated, 3 g trans)
590 mg sodium

French Toast Sticks Kids Meal with syrup

610 calories
24 g fat (16 g saturated)
78 g sugars

Vanilla Oreo® Sundae Shake (small: 16 fl oz)

DIPPING SAUCE DECODER (1 OZ EACH)

- **ZESTY ONION:** 150 calories, 15 g fat (2.5 g saturated)
- **RANCH:** 140 calories, 15 g fat (2.5 g saturated)
- **HONEY MUSTARD:** 90 calories, 6 g fat (1 g saturated)
- **BUFFALO:** 80 calories, 8 g fat (1.5 g saturated)
- **SWEET & SOUR:** 45 calories, 0 g fat
- **BARBECUE:** 40 calories, 0 g fat

Chick-fil-A

No kids' menu? No problem. With every single sandwich below 500 calories, a variety of healthy sides like fresh fruit that can be substituted into any meal, and nutritional brochures readily available for perusing at each location, Chick-fil-A earns the award for America's Healthiest Chain Restaurant for Kids.

SURVIVAL STRATEGY
Even the smartest kid in the class can still fail a test, so be on your toes at all times. Skip salads with ranch or Caesar dressings, any sandwich with bacon, and all milkshakes.

SUGAR SPIKES

Chocolate Hand-Spun Milkshake (20 oz)

The Impact:
107 g sugars

One of these hand-spun choco-bombs is the equivalent of 75 Milk Duds®. The chocolate syrup consists primarily of high-fructose corn syrup, corn syrup, and sugar.

Chicken Nuggets

with Barbecue Sauce (8 pieces)

305 calories
13 g fat (2.5 g saturated)
1,020 mg sodium

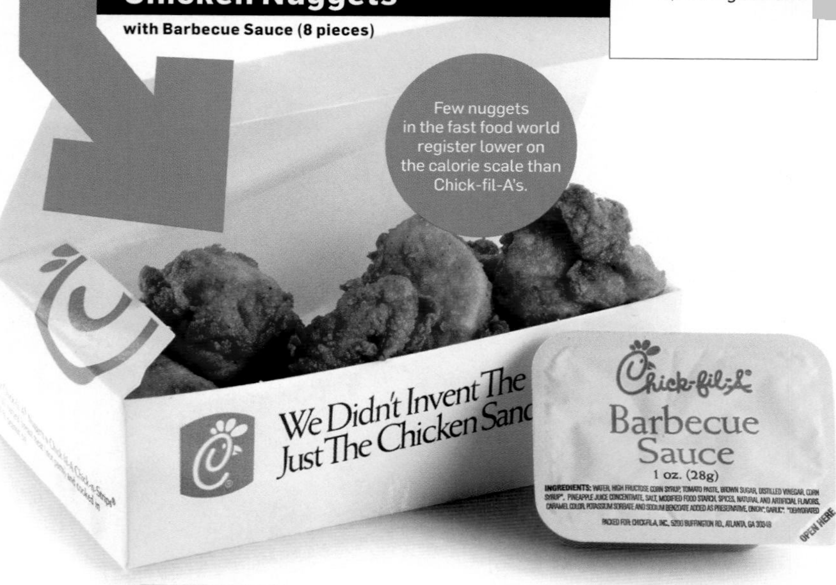

We Didn't Invent The
Just The Chicken Sand
Chick-fil-A
Barbecue Sauce
1 oz. (28g)
OPEN HERE

Few nuggets in the fast food world register lower on the calorie scale than Chick-fil-A's.

Other Picks

Chargrilled Chicken Club Sandwich

380 calories
11 g fat (5 g saturated)
1,240 mg sodium

Chick-n-Minis™

280 calories
11 g fat (3.5 g saturated)
580 mg sodium

Icedream®

240 calories
6 g fat (3.5 g saturated)
42 g sugars

480 calories
16 g fat
(6 g saturated)
1,640 mg sodium

Not That!

Chicken Caesar Cool Wrap®

Wraps got a good rap a while back, but the truth is, they are almost always worse than normal sandwiches. The reason? Tortillas are massive vessels that add more calories than buns do, plus they have the structural integrity to hold a lot of goopy filling.

Other Passes

410 calories
16 g fat (3.5 g saturated)
1,300 mg sodium

Chicken Sandwich

490 calories
32 g fat (10 g saturated)
1,060 mg sodium

Sausage Biscuit

660 calories
27 g fat (16 g saturated)
89 g sugars

Vanilla Milkshake

SMART SIDES

Fruit Cup (medium)

70 calories, 0 g fat, 0 mg sodium, 17 g carbohydrates

Out of every five Americans, only one consumes the recommended daily amount of fruit. With progressive side options like this, you can help your child be a part of that healthy minority. These cups are prepared fresh on location, and they include apple slices, grapes, strawberries, and mandarin oranges—a bounty of natural energy for your child's body.

GREAT GROWN-UP GRUB

Chargrilled Chicken Sandwich

270 calories, 3 g fat (1 g saturated), 28 g protein, 37 g carbohydrates

Good luck finding a better chicken sandwich. This one has less than one-fifth of the fat in the McDonald's® Premium Grilled Chicken Club.

STEALTH HEALTH FOOD

Carrot & Raisin Salad

260 calories, 12 g fat (1.5 g saturated), 160 mg sodium

This salad will smack your kid's cellular and immune systems with a nutritious wallop of vitamin A.

Chili's

REPORT CARD C- Chili's gets the award for the longest, most diverse kids' menu we've seen, and many of the items on it represent reasonable nutritional options. Unfortunately, sodium is a major problem. And the adult menu, where older kids might be tempted to wander, is an abomination.

SURVIVAL STRATEGY
Choose wisely, as the difference between good (corn dog) and bad (chicken strips) can be 700 calories. On the adult menu, the Chicken Fajita pita is a solid choice.

Think marinara. Not just for pasta, but also as a dip or a sandwich spread. Marinara is nearly fat-free and packed full of lycopene, an antioxidant that helps skin fight the sun's UV rays.

Eat This

Pepper Pals® Corn Dog

with mashed potatoes

440 calories
28 g fat (6 g saturated)
620 mg sodium

Surprisingly enough, Chili's corn dog is one of the healthiest options on the entire Pepper Pals menu, beating out the mac and cheese by 210 calories.

Other Picks

Pepper Pals® Little Mouth Burger

280 calories
15 g fat (5 g saturated)
300 mg sodium

6 Spicy Garlic & Lime Grilled Shrimp **with black beans**

295 calories
10 g fat (1.5 g saturated)
1,250 mg sodium

Dutch Apple Caramel Cheesecake Sweet Shot

230 calories
6 g fat (3 g saturated)
41 g carbohydrates

1,110 calories
82 g fat (15 g saturated)
1,980 mg sodium

Not That!

Pepper Pals® Country-Fried Chicken Crispers

with ranch and Homestyle Fries

Chili's interpretation of the kids' classic involves three substantial fingers encased in a thick bread coating and piled next to a heap of fries and a 240-calorie saucer of ranch dressing. With half a day's calories and more than a full day's worth of fat trapped on the plate, this qualifies as one of the worst kids' meals in America.

Other Passes

420 calories
27 g fat (16 g saturated)
1,200 mg sodium

Pepper Pals® Grilled Cheese Sandwich

620 calories
26 g fat (13 g saturated)
1,720 mg sodium

Pepper Pals® Cheese Quesadilla
with rice

640 calories
27 g fat (16 g saturated)
92 g carbohydrates

Frosty Choc-A-Lot Shake
with chocolate sprinkles

UNHAPPY MEALS

Honey BBQ Ribs
with Honey BBQ Sauce

1,060 calories, 65 g fat (24 g saturated), 4,460 mg sodium

Kids might be attracted to these sickly sweet, fatty ribs, but if you let them indulge, they'll be eating the fat equivalent of 22 strips of bacon and the sodium equivalent of 13 large orders of McDonald's® French fries.

SMART SIDES

Black Beans with Pico de Gallo

120 calories, 0 g fat, 660 mg sodium

Black beans are rich in protein and fiber, and they have a high concentration of omega-3 fats. They're even better with a scoop of salsa.

STEALTH HEALTH FOOD

Guiltless Salmon

480 calories, 14 g fat (3 g saturated)

Salmon is one of the best sources of omega-3 fats, which are vital brain builders. One study found that children who took omega-3s for just 3 months showed big improvements in reading, spelling, and behavior.

Chipotle

REPORT CARD

D

We noticed a sudden drop in calories on Chipotle's nutritional accounting right around the time New York City law forced chain restaurants to display calorie counts on their menu boards. Did they just suddenly downsize their mammoth portions? Not likely. It doesn't much matter, though, because the lack of options for kids means young eaters are forced to tussle with one of Chipotle's massive burritos or taco platters, which can easily top 1,000 calories.

SURVIVAL STRATEGY
Stick to the crispy tacos or burrito bowls, or saw a burrito in half.

570

The number of calories you'll save if you skip the chips. You'll also cut 27 grams of fat.

Eat This

Crispy Steak Tacos

with tomato salsa and romaine lettuce (3)

395 calories
14 g fat (3.5 g saturated)
940 mg sodium

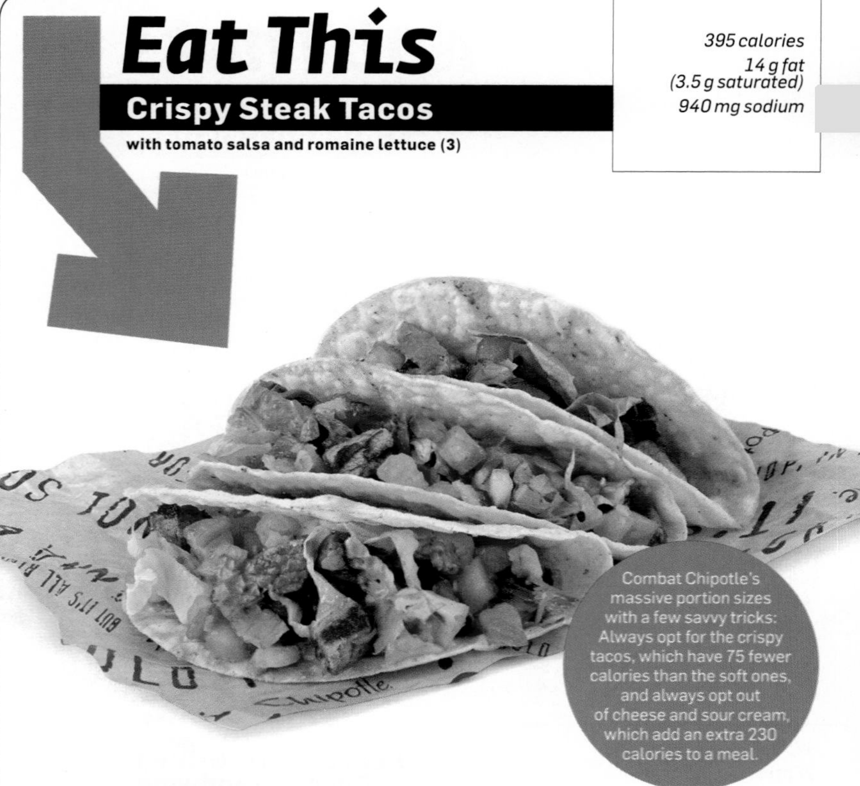

Combat Chipotle's massive portion sizes with a few savvy tricks: Always opt for the crispy tacos, which have 75 fewer calories than the soft ones, and always opt out of cheese and sour cream, which add an extra 230 calories to a meal.

Other Picks

Chicken Burrito **with black beans, salsa verde, cheese, and romaine lettuce (1/2 burrito)**

380 calories
13 g fat (5 g saturated)
913 mg sodium

Burrito Bowl
with pinto beans, carnitas, green salsa, and lettuce

368 calories
16 g fat (3 g saturated)
1,884 mg sodium

670 calories
25 g fat
(10.5 g saturated)
1,735 mg sodium

Not That!

Chicken Soft Tacos

with corn salsa, cheese, and romaine lettuce (3)

Most people automatically assume steak is worse for you than chicken, but that's not always the case. At Chipotle, the chicken actually has 10 more calories than the steak. It's not much, but it's a good reminder that it's never safe to assume—especially with nutrition.

Other Passes

755 calories
36 g fat (12 g saturated)
2,453 mg sodium

Vegetarian Soft Tacos
with black beans, tomato salsa, guacamole, and cheese

775 calories
48 g fat (12 g saturated)
1,888 mg sodium

Chicken Salad
with black beans, cheese, and dressing

HIDDEN DANGER
Rice

This sorry excuse for a grain will spike your kid's blood sugar to the moon; there's not a single gram of fiber in a whole serving. Go riceless and rest easy.

160 calories, 4 g fat (0 g saturated) 330 mg sodium, 30 g carbohydrates

Teach your kids about the benefits of bowling—eating a burrito from a bowl instead of a tortilla. The white-flour tortilla adds 42 grams of carbohydrates, 670 milligrams of sodium, and 290 calories to your burrito. It's the nutritional equivalent of a gutter ball.

Chuck E. Cheese's

REPORT CARD

C-

Unlike most big pizza chains, Chuck E. Cheese's has no thin crust option, which leaves you with the standard calorie- and carb-heavy slices. It redeems itself slightly by offering a handful of nonsoda drink options, as well as a salad bar. But beware: A kid left to run wild in a salad bar can do more harm than good.

SURVIVAL STRATEGY
Stick to the cheese, vegetable, and Hawaiian pizzas, and cap the slice consumption at two a kid. If they're still hungry, help them construct a salad from the bar.

Eat This

Canadian Bacon and Pineapple Pizza

with 3 Buffalo wings (1 medium slice)

410 calories
18 g fat
(5.5 g saturated)
1,028 mg sodium

Outside of the vegetable combo, you won't find a better slice at Chuck E. Cheese's. That being said, you're still better off (by 80 calories) giving them three wings apiece with celery (sans blue cheese) than you are handing out second slices.

Other Picks

BBQ Chicken Pizza
(2 small slices)

428 calories
12 g fat (4 g saturated)
992 mg sodium

Hot Dog

170 calories
17 g fat (6 g saturated)
830 mg sodium

Apple Pie Pizza
(1 slice)

194 calories
2 g fat (0 g saturated)
24 g sugars

HIDDEN DANGER
Hi-C
(12 oz)

Hi-C® is not juice. In fact, it has more sugar per ounce than Coke®. And with Chuck's free refills flowing, the calories add up fast.

156 calories
42 g sugars

667 calories
27 g fat
(6 g saturated)
1,426 mg sodium

Not That!

Pepperoni and Sausage Pizza

with 2 Italian bread sticks (1 medium slice)

They've already got one oily bread product on their plate, why would they need another? Especially when each dense stick adds 193 calories and 11 grams of fat to your kid's meal.

Other Passes

454 calories
18 g fat (6 g saturated)
1,090 mg sodium

All Meat Combo Pizza
(2 small slices)

622 calories
28 g fat (7 g saturated)
2,296 mg sodium

Ham and Cheese

310 calories
13 g fat (4 g saturated)
29 g sugars

White Birthday Cake
(1 slice)

"Where a kid can be a kid" is a motto you should follow. Load them up with tokens before the pizzas arrive and watch as the games keep them too distracted to overeat. It might cost you a couple of bucks, but you'll make it back on the extra pizza you don't have to buy.

UNHAPPY MEALS
Roasted Chicken Ciabatta

652 calories,
31 g fat (9 g saturated),
1,936 mg sodium

Roasted chicken anything seems like a universally safe bet, but Chuck sabotages this sandwich with a blanket of cheese and a thick coat of mayo. Beyond the high calorie and fat counts, this chicken sandwich sucks up your sodium allowance for an entire day.

Cold Stone Creamery

REPORT CARD C

The average regular shake is nearly 900 calories, but the regular Like It™ size ice creams are almost all within the 300-calorie range. Factor that in with the creamery's real fruit toppings, light ice cream, and sorbet, and Cold Stone starts to compensate for its dangerous shakes and its more dubious ice cream add-ons.

SURVIVAL STRATEGY
Lace a Like It™ cup with light ice cream, fresh fruit, and maybe a touch of chocolate shavings or whipped cream for good measure.

SUGAR SPIKES

Dew Iced™ Smoothie (Like It™ size)

The Impact: 141 g sugars

Cold Stone likes to wave the healthy flag in celebration of its fruit smoothies, but then they tack this Mountain Dew® slush onto the menu. Instead of supercharging your child with sucrose, order a smoothie that sticks to the fruit-and-yogurt formula.

Eat This

Chocolate Light Ice Cream

with bananas, maraschino cherries, and Reddi Wip® (Like It™ size)

320 calories
8.5 g fat (5 g saturated)
40 g sugars

This version of a banana split gets the job done in spectacular fashion for one-third of the calories and one-fifth of the fat that normally goes into America's favorite sundae. Besides, if you're going to feed them ice cream, you may as well sneak some fruit in there, right?

Other Picks

Raspberry Sorbet™
with raspberries and Nilla Wafers (Like It™ size)

255 calories
2.5 g fat (0 g saturated)
44 g sugars

Cake Batter Confetti™ Cake
6" round (1 slice)

350 calories
17 g fat (10 g saturated)
34 g sugars

Man-Go Bananas™ Yogurt Smoothie (Like It™ size)

360 calories
0 g fat
67 g sugars

520 calories
31 g fat
(17 g saturated)
47 g sugars

Not That!

Chocolate Ice Cream

with Reese's® Peanut Butter Cup (Like It™ size)

Reese's qualify as the worst mix-in on the menu, beating out brownies and Oreo pie crust for the title. Get the same effect for fewer calories, less sugar, and more healthy fat by mixing chocolate ice cream with real peanut butter.

Other Passes

460 calories
25 g fat (14.5 g saturated)
38 g sugars

Raspberry Ice Cream
with graham cracker pie crust (Like It™ size)

510 calories
28 g fat (12 g saturated)
46 g sugars

Midnight Delight™ Cake
6" round (1 slice)

910 calories
42 g fat (30 g saturated)
96 g sugars

Very Vanilla™ Shake
(Like It™ size)

5,640

The jumping jacks a kid would have to do to burn off the 540 calories in a Love It™-size Oatmeal Cookie Batter Ice Cream.

Top your child's ice-cream cup with a big dash of ground cinnamon. By preventing the ice cream's sugar from passing through the stomach too quickly, cinnamon helps suppress the blood-sugar spike that follows a sweet dessert. Caloric cost: zero.

Così

Half of Così's kids' offerings cross the 500-calorie threshold, with the pepperoni pizza being one of the country's worst offenders with 911 calories. The adult sandwich section won't provide much relief, either, considering that almost everything Così squeezes between two loaves soars into the 600 to 900 calorie range.

SURVIVAL STRATEGY
Stick with the kids' turkey and tuna sandwiches and leave calorie-laden desserts and drinks behind the counter.

HIDDEN DANGER
Etruscan Whole Grain (1 slice)

Wonder why many Così sandwiches top 700 calories? Maybe because two slices of its whole grain bread have as many calories as a Big Mac.

270 calories
740 mg sodium
49 g carbohydrates

Eat This

Granola Peach Parfait

389 g calories
*6 g fat **
257 mg sodium

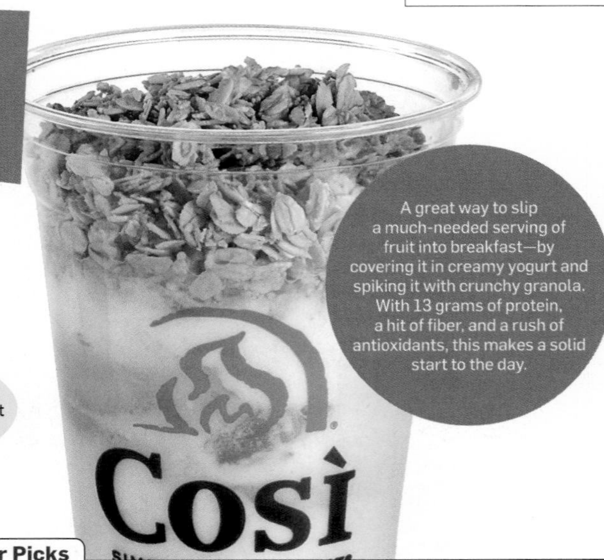

A great way to slip a much-needed serving of fruit into breakfast—by covering it in creamy yogurt and spiking it with crunchy granola. With 13 grams of protein, a hit of fiber, and a rush of antioxidants, this makes a solid start to the day.

*Cosi does not disclose saturated fat content

Other Picks

Kids Gooey Grilled Cheese Sandwich
357 calories
*21 g fat**
759 mg sodium

Chocolate Croissant
370 calories
*18 g fat**
300 mg sodium

Three Bean Chili
(cup)
159 calories
*1 g fat**
919 mg sodium

564 calories
*12 g fat**
371 mg sodium

Not That!

Granola Cereal

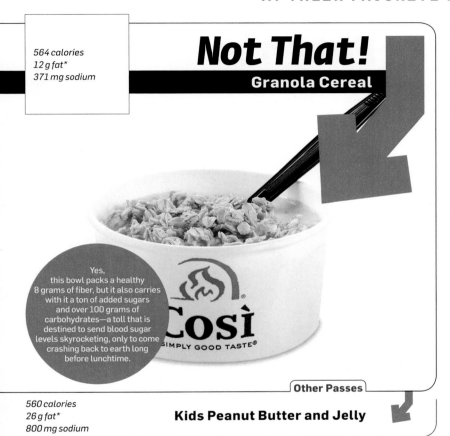

Yes, this bowl packs a healthy 8 grams of fiber, but it also carries with it a ton of added sugars and over 100 grams of carbohydrates—a toll that is destined to send blood sugar levels skyrocketing, only to come crashing back to earth long before lunchtime.

Other Passes

560 calories
*26 g fat**
800 mg sodium

Kids Peanut Butter and Jelly

440 calories
*19 g fat**
490 mg sodium

Blueberry Muffin

374 calories
*34 g fat**
987 mg sodium

Tomato Basil Aurora Soup
(10 oz cup)

STEALTH HEALTH FOOD

Moroccan Lentil Soup (10 oz cup)

199 calories,
3 g fat
1,159 mg sodium

Lentils ought to be a regular food in every child's diet. They're lean and packed with protein and fiber, so your children will grow up tall with full bellies.

1,910

The average amount of sodium, in milligrams, that comes in each melt sandwich on Così's menu.

FOOD MYTH #2

Vegetarian meals are always healthy.

Many vegetarian meals are deceptively full of fattening oils and cheeses. With 824 calories, 51 grams of fat, and 2,929 milligrams of sodium, Così's Vegi Muffa-letta is the third most fattening sandwich on the menu, and it has 133 percent of your recommended daily sodium. For a *truly* healthy vegetarian option, try the Hummus and Fresh Veggies sandwich. It has just 8 grams of fat.

Dairy Queen

REPORT CARD

D+

The lack of decent sides kills DQ's chances of serving a healthy kids' meal. Trans-fatty fries and onion rings are the only options, and you'll be lucky to get out of the building without a cold treat to take along for the ride. The child-size ice cream cone is a nice touch, but DQ's holy grail is the ubiquitous and often-mimicked Blizzard, which ought to be renamed the Avalanche.

SURVIVAL STRATEGY
Play solid defense: Skip sides entirely and offer your kid the choice between a soda or a child-size cone.

95

The number of minutes a child would have to spend jumping rope to burn off the 690 calories in a Chili & Cheese Foot Long Dog.

Eat This

Strawberry DQ® Sundae

(small)

260 calories
7 g fat (4.5 g saturated)
36 g sugars

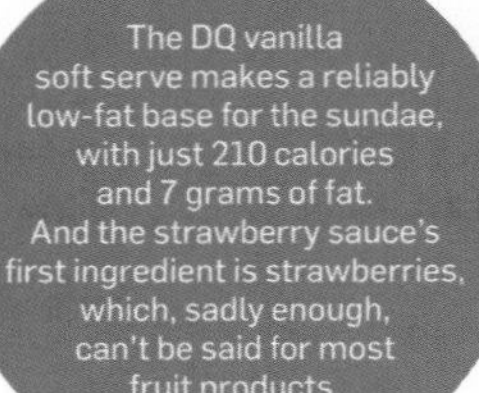

The DQ vanilla soft serve makes a reliably low-fat base for the sundae, with just 210 calories and 7 grams of fat. And the strawberry sauce's first ingredient is strawberries, which, sadly enough, can't be said for most fruit products.

Other Picks

Kid's Quesadilla Meal

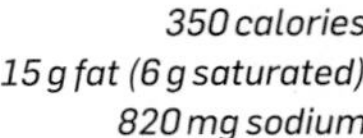

350 calories
15 g fat (6 g saturated)
820 mg sodium

All-Beef Hot Dog

250 calories
14 g fat (5 g saturated)
770 mg sodium

DQ Sandwich

190 calories
5 g fat (2.5 g saturated)
18 g sugars

470 calories
14 g fat
(9 g saturated)
62 g sugars

Not That!

Strawberry Shake
(small)

Milkshakes take a lot of ice cream to make (usually 8 to 10 ounces, compared to the 4 ounces you normally get in an ice cream scoop), so even a small shake is likely to contain more calories than a large sundae at most dessert spots.

Other Passes

580 calories
26 g fat (10 g saturated)
1,300 mg sodium

Kid's Cheeseburger Meal

530 calories
29 g fat (4.5 g saturated, 3 g trans)
1,020 mg sodium

Crispy Chicken Sandwich

550 calories
22 g fat (10 g saturated, 2.5 g trans fat)
59 g sugars

Chocolate Coated Waffle Cone with vanilla soft serve

UNHAPPY MEALS
Wild Buffalo Chicken Strip Basket
(4 pieces)

1,340 calories,
96 g fat
(18 g saturated, 11 g trans),
4,820 mg sodium,
120 g carbohydrates

This is what you call an abused chicken. The Wild Buffalo dipping sauce is a dubious combo of partially hydrogenated oil and hot sauce, and the fries that come in the basket are just as bad: Partially hydrogenated shortening is the most abundant ingredient besides potatoes.

HIDDEN DANGER
Trans Fats

Few chains can compete with the torrent of trans fats that soak the DQ menu board. Every year more than 500,000 people die of heart disease, and trans fats are among the leading causes. Since DQ is one of the few restaurants still frying in partially hydrogenated oil, anything that's touched the grease could be carrying a dangerous dose.

Denny's

REPORT CARD **B-**

Aside from a couple unhealthy invaders like the Little Dippers and the French Toastix™, Denny's asteroid inspired kids' menu is properly portioned for children. Its most impressive feat, however, is its choice offering of sides, which includes fruit medley, grapes, mashed potatoes, and applesauce. It's nice to see a variety of nonfried sides, especially when children so desperately need to increase their intakes of fruits and vegetables.

SURVIVAL STRATEGY

Pair a burger or pizza with a fruit side for an easy, kid-approved 400-calorie dinner.

SMART SIDES

Quaker Oatmeal (4 oz)

100 calories, 2 g fat (0 g saturated), 3 g fiber

The extra fiber in a little oatmeal will slow the kids' digestion to keep them feeling fuller, longer.

Eat This

Kid's D-Zone Smiley Alien Hotcakes

with meat

340 calories
12 g fat (5 g saturated)
1,060 mg sodium

Friendly shaped foods can distract parents and kids from suspect nutrition, but these hotcakes are surprisingly decent. Choose bacon over sausage for the meat and save 96 calories and 7 grams of fat per meal.

Other Picks

Kid's D-Zone Cosmic Cheeseburger™

341 calories
20 g fat (6 g saturated, 1 g trans)
580 mg sodium

Sirloin Steak Dinner
with mashed potatoes and vegetable blend

450 calories
16.5 g fat (5.5 g saturated)
1,150 mg sodium

Root Beer Float

280 calories
10 g fat (6 g saturated)
47 g carbohydrates

770 calories
71 g fat (13 g saturated)
1,094 mg sodium

Not That!

Kid's D-Zone Big Dipper French Toastix™

with syrup

Normally there isn't a huge nutritional discrepancy between pancakes and French toast, but clearly that doesn't hold true at Denny's. We suspect it's the heavy batter job they do on the bread and the amount of oil they use to fry up the toast that push these stix over the edge.

566 calories
27 g fat (13 g saturated)
1,504 mg sodium

Kid's D-Zone Little Dipper Sampler
with applesauce and marinara sauce

983 calories
51 g fat (12 g saturated)
4,323 mg sodium

Lemon Pepper Tilapia
with vegetable rice pilaf

580 calories
29 g fat (15 g saturated)
72 g carbohydrates

Kids Oreo® Blender Blast Off

UNHAPPY MEALS

Western Burger with Fries

1,580 calories, 95 g fat (33 g saturated, 6 g trans), 2,780 mg sodium, 112 g carbohydrates

This meal might be a dream to your taste buds, but it's a nutritional nightmare to your belly. The beef is buried under a pile of onion rings, Swiss cheese, and sweetened steak sauce, and then it's dropped next to a heaping mound of French-fried potatoes. Our arteries are hardening at the thought.

Denny's will substitute Egg Beaters® for eggs at no extra charge. Just ask. Each one of these egg substitutes adds an additional 5 grams of protein while taking off 10 grams of fat.

Domino's Pizza

REPORT CARD C+

Domino's suffers the same pitfalls of any other pizza purveyor: too much cheese, bread, and greasy toppings. If you don't know the pitfalls, you might bag your child a pizza with more than 350 calories per slice. To its credit, Domino's does keep the trans fat off the pizza and it also offers the lowest-calorie thin crust option out there.

SURVIVAL STRATEGY
Stick with the Crunchy Thin Crust pizzas sans sausage and pepperoni. Whenever possible, try to sneak on a vegetable or two per pie.

SMART SIDES

Buffalo Chicken Kickers™ (2)

90 calories, 4 g fat (0 g saturated), 320 mg sodium

Breadsticks are not the end-all of pizza sides. Two Kickers have about half the fat of a single breadstick and provide 8 grams of protein, making it a solid, belly-filling sidekick for a veggie pizza. Just be sure to keep the blue cheese out of dunking distance.

Eat This

Crunchy Thin Crust Cheese Pizza
12" (2 slices)

260 calories
17 g fat (5 g saturated)
480 mg sodium

This is the lowest calorie slice we've found at any pizza chain in America. The only way to make this any better would be to heap a pile of vegetables on top—if you think the kids would go for it, that is.

Other Picks

Crunchy Thin Crust Philly Cheese Steak Pizza 12" (1 slice)

180 calories
10.5 g fat (5 g saturated)
375 mg sodium

Cheesy Bread Sticks
(2) with Marinara Dipping Sauce (1)

305 calories
14 g fat (5.5 g saturated)
540 mg sodium

Chicken Kickers™
(4)

180 calories
8 g fat (0 g saturated)
640 mg sodium

420 calories
16 g fat
(6 g saturated)
670 mg sodium

Not That!

Classic Hand-Tossed Cheese Pizza

12" (2 slices)

The only difference in these two slices is the crust: By making the switch from Domino's standard to their thin crust, you save 80 calories and 16 grams of carbohydrates a slice. It might not seem like much until you really consider how much pizza your family eats each year.

Other Passes

300 calories
14 g fat (6 g saturated)
500 mg sodium

Hand-Tossed Crust Bacon Cheeseburger® Pizza 12" (1 slice)

700 calories
64 g fat (13 g saturated, 7 g trans)
570 mg sodium

Breadsticks
(2) with Garlic Dipping Sauce (1)

340 calories
18 g fat (6 g saturated)
1,000 mg sodium

Hot Buffalo Wings
(4)

FOOD MYTH #3

Blotting grease off of pizza is the best way to make it healthy.

Obsessive blotting of a greasy pie may remove 3 or 4 grams of fat, but the decision to blot or not pales in comparison to the decisions concerning crust type and toppings. The best way to make a healthier pizza is to skip the thick crust, sausage, and pepperoni in favor of thin crusts strewn with vegetables and lean meats like ham and chicken.

DIPPING SAUCE DECODER (PER CONTAINER)

- **GARLIC:** 440 calories, 50 g fat (10 g saturated, 7 g trans)
- **SWEET ICING:** 250 calories, 3 g fat (2.5 g saturated), 55 g sugars
- **BLUE CHEESE:** 230 calories, 24 g fat (5 g saturated)
- **RANCH:** 200 calories, 21 g fat (3 g saturated)
- **HOT:** 120 calories, 12 g fat (2 g saturated)
- **MARINARA:** 25 calories, 0 g fat

Dunkin' Donuts

REPORT CARD

C-

After years as a major trans-fat transgressor, Dunkin' has cleaned up its act and cut them almost entirely from the menu. Unfortunately, between deleterious donuts and bloated bagels, you're still left with a lesser-of-all-evils proposition.

SURVIVAL STRATEGY
Go for sandwiches made on English muffins for breakfast, flatbread sandwiches (preferably the Ham and Swiss) at all other times.

UNHAPPY MEALS

Sausage, Egg & Cheese Sandwich

800 calories, 52 g fat (24 g saturated), 1,960 mg sodium

This biscuit will make even the scrawniest kid's belly jiggle. With over 50 ingredients, including partially hydrogenated vegetable oil, this breakfast sandwich brings a host of unhealthy fats and nearly a day's worth of sodium to the start of the day.

Eat This

Ham, Egg and Cheese English Muffin Sandwich

310 calories
10 g fat (5 g saturated)
1,270 mg sodium

The sodium count may be a bit high, but this is otherwise a great start to the day, with a good balance of calories, fats, and carbohydrates, plus a 21-gram surge of protein and 30 percent of your daily iron.

Other Picks

Sugar Raised Donut and French Cruller (1 of each)

360 calories
15 g fat (9.5 saturated fat)
425 mg sodium

Marble Frosted Donut

230 calories
11 g fat (4.5 g saturated)
13 g sugars

Ham and Swiss Flatbread Sandwich

350 calories
12 g fat (5 g saturated)
1,040 mg sodium

540 calories
25 g fat
(3.5 g saturated)
520 mg sodium

Not That!

Banana Walnut Muffin

Sounds healthy, right? Not quite. Neither bananas nor walnuts can save the misunderstood muffin from itself. All told, you end up with 31 grams of sugar and just 3 grams of fiber.

Other Passes

600 calories
25 g fat (11.5 g saturated)
760 mg sodium

Multigrain Bagel with Strawberry Cream Cheese (2 oz)

330 calories
18 g fat (9 g saturated)
18 g sugars

Glazed Cake Donut

460 calories
24 g fat (12 g saturated)
1,000 mg sodium

Three Cheese Flatbread Sandwich

77

The number of beds a kid would have to make to burn off the 270 calories from a Glazed Cake Donut.

FOOD MYTH #4

Smoothies are a reliable source of fruit for children.

With 104 grams, the average smoothie at Dunkin' Donuts is about 75 percent sugar. The ensuing blood-sugar spike activates fat-storing mechanisms.

HIDDEN DANGER

Multigrain Bagel

It sounds pretty healthy, right? It's actually the most caloric of all of Dunkin's bagels and when spread with cream cheese, contains more calories than a Big Mac.

380 calories
650 mg sodium
68 g carbohydrates

Fazoli's

As long as you can keep the kids from ravishing the breadstick basket, this Italian-on-the-go chain is a sound choice. Most meals on the kids' menu fall below 300 calories, and the pasta toppers provide an additional nutritional boost. If only they added a whole-wheat noodle option, Fazoli's might take home an A.

SURVIVAL STRATEGY
Kids' pastas of any invention are fine, as long as they steer clear of fatty topping like meatballs and sausage.

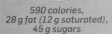

UNHAPPY MEALS
Chocolate Chunk Cookie

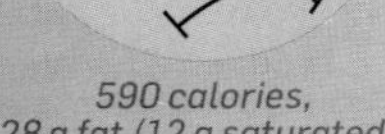

590 calories, 28 g fat (12 g saturated), 45 g sugars

The most caloric cookie we've ever encountered, with more fat and calories than a Quarter Pounder® with Cheese at McDonald's® and as much sugar as two chocolate ice cream bars.

Eat This

Kid's Fettuccine Alfredo
with peppery chicken

360 calories
6 g fat
(1.5 g saturated)
750 mg sodium

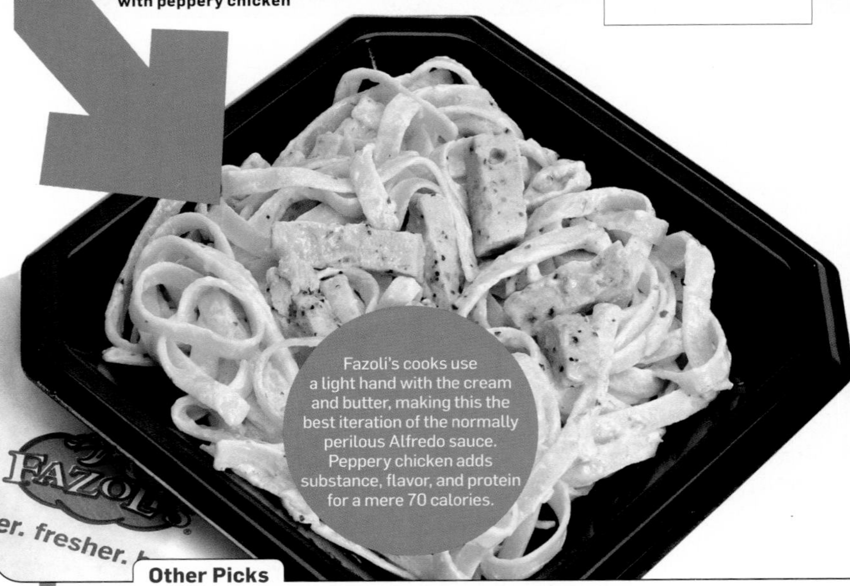

Fazoli's cooks use a light hand with the cream and butter, making this the best iteration of the normally perilous Alfredo sauce. Peppery chicken adds substance, flavor, and protein for a mere 70 calories.

Other Picks

Kids Ziti with Meat Sauce

190 calories
6 g fat (2.5 g saturated)
710 mg sodium

Penne with Meat Sauce
(small)

500 calories
7 g fat (1.5 g saturated)
1,020 mg sodium

Original Lemon Ice
(regular)

180 calories
45 g sugars

430 calories
13.5 g fat
(2.5 g saturated)
830 mg sodium

Not That!

Kids' Spaghetti

with marinara and garlic shrimp

This is one of the only times you'll see a white pasta sauce trumping a red pasta sauce. The blame, however, doesn't rest on the relatively innocent marinara, but rather on the oily garlic shrimp, which add 12 grams of fat and 160 calories. Still, you could do worse—both the meatballs and the Italian sausage carry a much steeper penalty.

There's no better way to coax a little green onto the plate than by mixing it in with noodles and marinara, so it's perfect that Fazoli's gives you the option to upgrade each dish with a helping of folate-rich broccoli. Broccoli's vitamin C will keep the kids' immune systems strong, and the extra fiber will compensate for the pasta's carbohydrates and help keep their bellies feeling full.

Other Passes

Kids Meat Lasagna

260 calories
13 g fat (6 g saturated)
880 mg sodium

Pepperoni Pizza (2 slices)

620 calories
28 g fat (10 g saturated)
1,700 mg sodium

Pomegranate Lemon Ice

360 calories
90 g sugars

SUGAR SPIKES

Triple Berry Lemon Ice

The Impact: 91 g sugars

There's more than a brain freeze at stake here; it's nearly 100 percent sugar, with nary a trace of real fruit in this obscenely sweet slush. Let the kids' insulin rest and make some real lemonade when you get home.

IHOP

REPORT CARD **F**

IHOP refuses to serve up nutritional information, but thanks to the New York City Board of Health, they were forced to publish calorie counts on their menus in April 2008. The big reveal shocked New York diners: 1,700-calorie cheeseburgers, 1,300-calorie omelets, and four salads with more than 1,000 calories. Because IHOP doesn't provide those numbers to the rest of the country, they still receive an automatic F.

SURVIVAL STRATEGY

Write letters, make phone calls, beg, scream, and plead for IHOP to provide nutritional information on all of their products.

SMART SIDES

Fresh Fruit Bowl

100 calories

Don't let the smell of sizzling butter and sausage patties lure you away from healthier side options. Set this bowl of cantaloupe, honeydew, watermelon, and grapes in the middle of your table to supplement a small order of flapjacks.

Eat This

Kid's Silver Five

480 calories
10 g fat
415 mg sodium

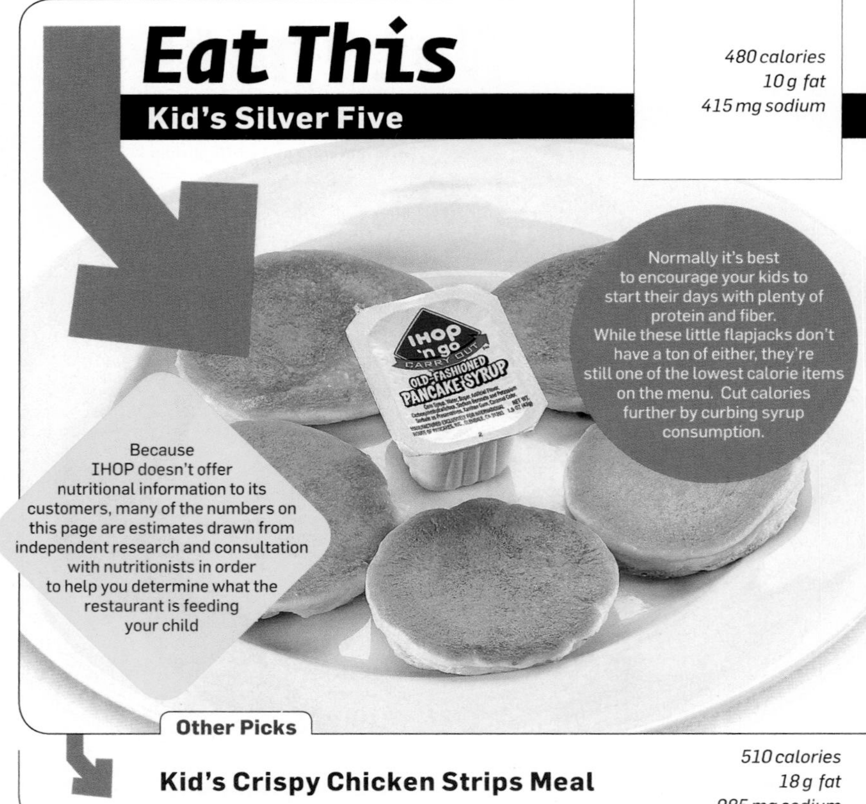

Normally it's best to encourage your kids to start their days with plenty of protein and fiber. While these little flapjacks don't have a ton of either, they're still one of the lowest calorie items on the menu. Cut calories further by curbing syrup consumption.

Because IHOP doesn't offer nutritional information to its customers, many of the numbers on this page are estimates drawn from independent research and consultation with nutritionists in order to help you determine what the restaurant is feeding your child

Other Picks

Kid's Crispy Chicken Strips Meal — *510 calories*, *18 g fat*, *985 mg sodium*

Chocolate Chip Pancakes — *630 calories*, *15 g fat*, *680 mg sodium*

Grilled Ham — *120 calories*, *8 g fat*, *510 mg sodium*

790 calories
40 g fat
1,175 mg sodium

Not That!

Kid's Cheese Omelet

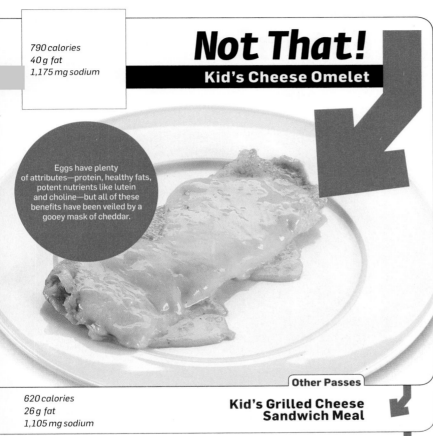

Eggs have plenty of attributes—protein, healthy fats, potent nutrients like lutein and choline—but all of these benefits have been veiled by a gooey mask of cheddar.

Other Passes

620 calories
26 g fat
1,105 mg sodium

Kid's Grilled Cheese Sandwich Meal

790 calories
36 g fat (18 g saturated)
1,240 mg sodium

Harvest Grain 'N Nut® Pancakes

520 calories
22 g fat
525 mg sodium

Beef Sausage Links

83,000

The approximate number of pancakes that IHOP serves every day of the year.

GUILTY PLEASURES

Belgian Waffle

390 calories,
19 g fat
48 g carbs

It doesn't qualify as light fare, but with just 400 calories, it is significantly better than most IHOP breakfast options.

FOOD MYTH #5

Fruit condiments are healthy

Sure, pure fruit preserves have a place on the breakfast table, but IHOP's fruit compote does not. Like so many other foods that invoke fruit in their names, this compote is sunk in a slurry of sugar and sweetened syrup. Ask for fresh strawberries instead.

Jack in the Box

REPORT CARD

C-

No kid's entrée eclipses the 400-calorie mark, a rare feat among fast-food and sit-down purveyors. Stray far from the kids' menu, though, and you'll find trouble fast—particularly with the burgers, which can contain more than 1,100 calories. But the biggest reason Jack is stuck in the middle of the pack is trans fat. From the Curly Fries to the Chicken Strips, Jack's has the trans-fattiest menu in America.

SURVIVAL STRATEGY
Allow free rein of the kids' menu, but insist on a smart side like applesauce and a zero-calorie beverage.

GUILTY PLEASURES

Regular Beef Taco

160 calories, 8 g fat (3 g saturated, 1 g trans), 270 mg sodium

Tacos from Jack's sounds like a bad idea, but two of these will weigh in under most of the burger and chicken options on the menu.

Eat This

Chicken Fajita Pita

300 calories
9 g fat (3.5 g saturated)
1,090 mg sodium

The healthiest item for kids is this rare bright spot on Jack in the Box's grown-up menu. The pita is made with whole grains, so kids get a blast of fiber, plus plenty of fresh produce.

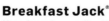

Other Picks

Breakfast Jack®
(American cheese, sliced ham, and grilled egg on a bun)

290 calories
12 g fat (4.5 g saturated)
760 mg sodium

Grilled Chicken Strips
(4)

180 calories
2 g fat (0.5 g saturated)
700 mg sodium

Mozzarella Cheese Sticks
(3)

240 calories
12 g fat (5 g saturated, 2 g trans)
420 mg sodium

330 calories
15 g fat (7 g saturated, 1 g trans)
770 mg sodium

Not That!
Kids Cheeseburger

Ounce for ounce, the burgers here are some of the worst in America. Even this tiny patty packs nearly half a day's worth of saturated fat between the buns. Add a small curly fries and you'll have a 600-calorie meal with 6 grams of trans fat—about three times the amount doctors say is safe to take in daily.

Other Passes

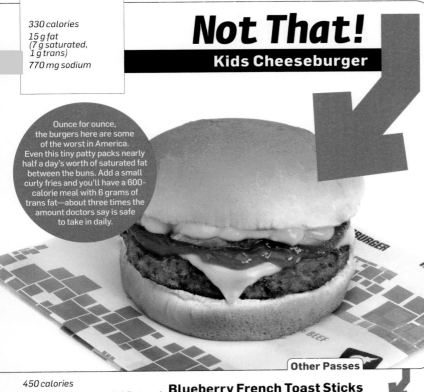

450 calories
20 g fat (4.5 g saturated, 4.5 g trans)
550 mg sodium

Blueberry French Toast Sticks (4)

250 calories
12 g fat (3 g saturated, 3 g trans)
630 mg sodium

Kids Chicken Breast Strips (2)

400 calories
19 g fat (6 g saturated, 3 g trans)
920 mg sodium

Egg Rolls (3)

UNHAPPY MEALS
Bacon Cheddar Potato Wedges

720 calories,
48 g fat (15 g saturated, 12 g trans),
1,360 mg sodium,
48 g carbohydrates

For the record: bacon, cheese, and fried potatoes are not a healthful trio. What's worse, though, is that Jack in the Box cooks in trans-fatty vegetable shortening. The American Heart Association recommends limiting these fats to less than 1 percent of your diet—an allowance your child will surpass with just a couple bites of this side.

SUGAR SPIKES
Strawberry Ice Cream Shake (small)

The Impact:
77 g sugars

The shakes at Jack in the Box are loaded with sugar and cream, which contributes 35 grams of fat to this 730-calorie monster. If your kid simply must have something sweet, cheesecake is a surprisingly good choice. The swap will knock off 54 grams of sugar.

Jamba Juice

REPORT CARD B+

The lack of fresh fruit in kids' diets is a serious concern, and Jamba Juice offers a viable and tasty solution: Stick it all in a blender and let them slurp it up. Still, there are more than a few concoctions with concerning amounts of sugar and calories.

SURVIVAL STRATEGY
Stick with 16-ounce servings of the All Fruit selections and you can pack an extra few servings of fruit into your kid's diet. Skip over the Classics and the Creamy Indulgences—often built with sherbet and frozen yogurt.

STEALTH HEALTH FOOD

Omega-3 Oatmeal Cookie

150 calories, 6 g fat (1.5 g saturated), 15 g sugars

As nutritious as cookies can be. It's made with fiber-rich rolled oats, oat fiber, and ground flaxseed, the source of the heart-healthy omega-3s. And since it's seasoned with cinnamon, it creates a smoother ride for your kid's blood sugar.

Eat This

Strawberry Whirl™
(16 oz)

200 calories
0 g fat
42 g sugars

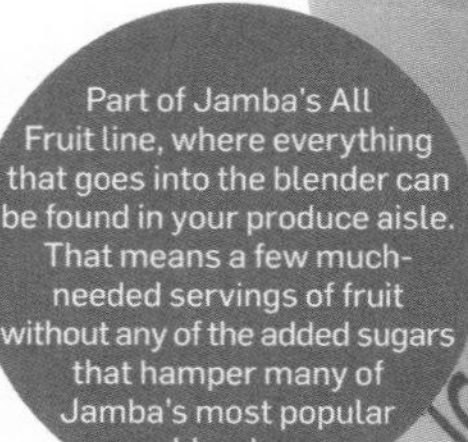

Part of Jamba's All Fruit line, where everything that goes into the blender can be found in your produce aisle. That means a few much-needed servings of fruit without any of the added sugars that hamper many of Jamba's most popular blends.

Other Picks

Mega Mango™
(16 oz)

220 calories
0.5 g fat
50 g sugars

Orange Mango Passion Juicies™
(24 oz)

280 calories
1 g fat
62 g sugars

Omega-3 Chocolate Brownie Cookie

150 calories
3.5 g fat
15 g sugars

340 calories
1.5 g fat
69 g sugars

Not That!

Orange Dream Machine®

(16 oz)

The second ingredient is frozen yogurt, the fourth is orange sherbet. Need another reason not to drink it? No whole fruit goes into this "smoothie"—just a sugary splash of OJ.

Other Passes

300 calories
1.5 g fat
64 g sugars

Mango-a-go-go™
(16 oz)

330 calories
1.5 g fat
76 g sugars

Orange Juice
(24 oz)

380 calories
4 g fat
14 g sugars

Apple Cinnamon Pretzel

If your kid isn't a big milk drinker, add a Calcium Boost to a Jamba smoothie. The supplement provides a full day's worth of calcium and vitamin D.

SUGAR SPIKES

Peanut Butter Moo'd® (30 oz)

The Impact:
169 g sugars

Peanut Butter Moo'd hardly qualifies as a smoothie. The mix of frozen yogurt, chocolate, banana, and peanut butter has more sugar than two pints of Ben & Jerry's® Butter Pecan™ Ice Cream.

132

The percentage by which Americans need to increase their fruit consumption in order to meet the recommended four ½-cup servings per day.

KFC

For a place with the word "fried" in its acronymic title, KFC manages to downplay the damage of their namesake goods by offering low-calorie Snacker sandwiches and a variety of relatively healthy vegetable sides.

SURVIVAL STRATEGY Skip over the fried chicken—unless your family likes it skinless, in which case, have at it—and look instead to the Snackers and the Crispy Strips. Don't miss the opportunity to sneak a serving or two of vegetables into your kid's diet, assuming they don't come out of the fryer.

SUGAR SPIKES

Teriyaki Wings (5)

The Impact: 30 g sugars

You probably wouldn't guess that the Teriyaki Wings have nearly three times as much sugar as the Sweet and Spicy Wings. You also probably wouldn't guess that they have more sugar than KFC's own Double Chocolate Chip Cake.

Eat This

Crispy Strips

(2) with mashed potatoes and gravy

380 calories
18 g fat (3.5 g saturated)
1,360 mg sodium

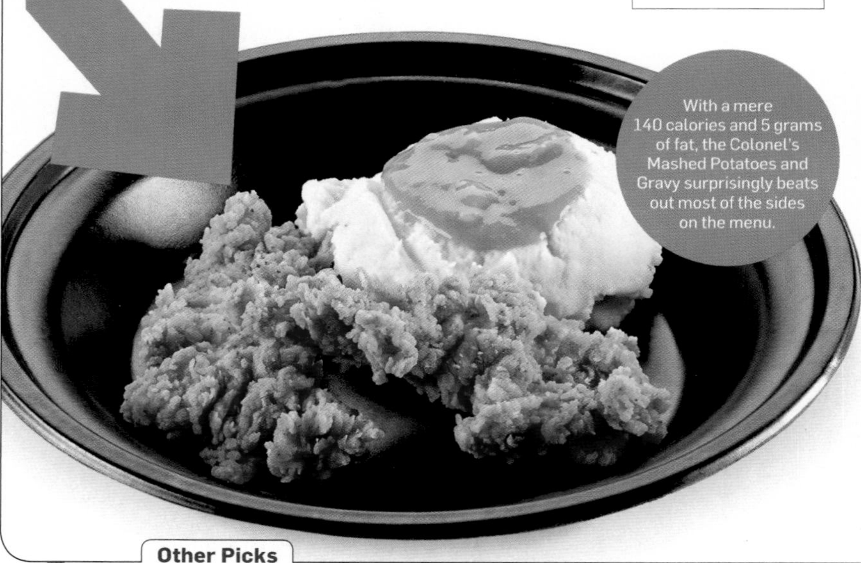

With a mere 140 calories and 5 grams of fat, the Colonel's Mashed Potatoes and Gravy surprisingly beats out most of the sides on the menu.

Other Picks

Original Recipe Skinless Breast (2)

280 calories
4 g fat (0 g saturated)
1,040 mg sodium

KFC Buffalo Snacker®

260 calories
8 g fat (1.5 g saturated)
860 mg sodium

Lil' Bucket™ Strawberry Short Cake

210 calories
7 g fat (5 g saturated)
25 g sugars

Not That!

Kids Popcorn Chicken

with potato wedges

550 calories
32 g fat (6 g saturated)
1,590 mg sodium

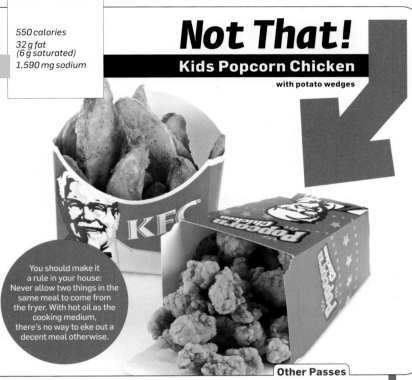

You should make it a rule in your house: Never allow two things in the same meal to come from the fryer. With hot oil as the cooking medium, there's no way to eke out a decent meal otherwise.

Other Passes

Extra Crispy Chicken Breast
and extra crispy thigh

810 calories
55 g fat (12 g saturated)
1,820 mg sodium

KFC Fish Snacker®

330 calories
15 g fat (3 g saturated)
710 mg sodium

Lil' Bucket™ Lemon Crème

410 calories
15 g fat (7 g saturated, 1.5 g trans)
53 g sugars

UNHAPPY MEALS

Chicken Pot Pie

770 calories, 40 grams fat (15 grams saturated, 14 grams trans), 1,680 mg sodium, 70 g carbohydrates

Despite KFC's 2007 commitment to stop using trans fats in their cooking oil, the restaurant still allows this seriously hazardous meal to sneak onto the menu. In fact, every one of the (in)Famous Bowls™ still contains trans fats.

1,576

The number of stairs to the top of the Empire State Building. You'd have to make two trips to the top and back in order to burn off the calories in two pieces of Extra Crispy chicken.

Krispy Kreme

REPORT CARD

D

What do you expect from a place that serves only doughnuts and corn-syrup–spiked drinks? The problem with Krispy Kreme isn't so much the fat and the calories of its staples (though they have plenty of both!), but rather the utter lack of any real nutritional take-away to be found anywhere on its menu. There is but one bright spot for doughnut devotees: Krispy Kreme finally switched over to trans-fat–free frying oils in January 2008. (Collective sigh of relief.)

SURVIVAL STRATEGY

Unless they're running a marathon, stick to a single order of doughnut holes.

GUILTY PLEASURES

Sugar Doughnut

200 calories, 12 g fat (6 g saturated), 10 g sugars

Another sign that the food industry is utterly unpredictable: Krispy Kreme's sugar doughnut has *less* sugar than almost any other doughnut on the menu.

Eat This

Original Glazed Doughnut Holes (4)

200 calories
11 g fat (5 g saturated)
15 g sugars

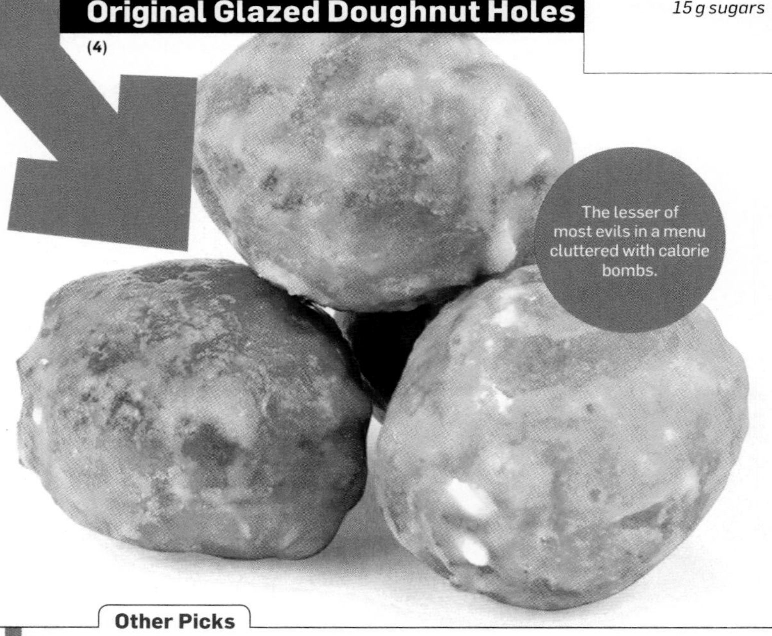

The lesser of most evils in a menu cluttered with calorie bombs.

Other Picks

Glazed Cinnamon Doughnut

210 calories
12 g fat (6 g saturated)
12 g sugars

Glazed Chocolate Cake Doughnut Holes (4)

210 calories
10 g fat (4.5 g saturated)
17 g sugars

Very Berry Chiller (12 oz)

170 calories
0 g fat
43 g sugars

290 calories
14 g fat (6 g saturated)
19 g sugars

Not That!

Powdered Cake Doughnut

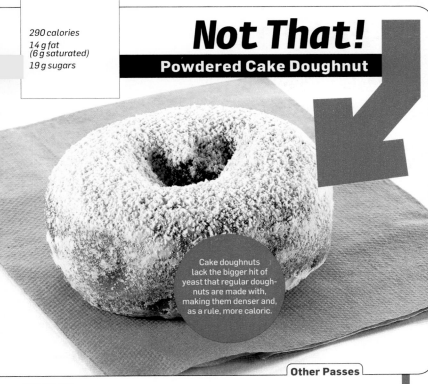

Cake doughnuts lack the bigger hit of yeast that regular doughnuts are made with, making them denser and, as a rule, more caloric.

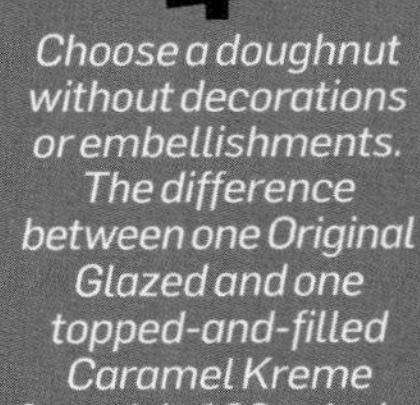

Choose a doughnut without decorations or embellishments. The difference between one Original Glazed and one topped-and-filled Caramel Kreme Crunch is 180 calories and 20 grams of sugar.

Other Passes

380 calories
20 g fat (10 g saturated)
24 g sugars

Apple Fritter

380 calories
19 g fat (9 g saturated)
30 g sugars

Caramel Kreme Crunch

620 calories
28 g fat (24 g saturated)
71 g sugars

Berries & Kreme Chiller (12 oz)

SUGAR SPIKES

Oranges & Kreme Chiller (small)

The Impact:
71 g sugars

Let your kid wash down a couple of doughnuts with this cloying beverage and you can expect a tantrum-inducing sugar crash in your near future. This is a dangerous amount of sugar, but the real *chiller* is the drink's 630 calories and 24 grams of saturated fat.

5,200

The number of donuts Krispy Kreme makes every minute in North America.

McDonald's

REPORT CARD

B

Though not blessed with an abundance of healthy options for kids, Mickey D's isn't burdened with any major calorie bombs, either. Kid standards like McNuggets and cheeseburgers are both in the 300-calorie range.

SURVIVAL STRATEGY
Apple Dippers and 2% milk with a small entrée makes for a pretty decent meal-on-the-go. McDonald's quintessential Happy Meal® makes this possible—just beware the usual French fries and soda pitfalls.

Eat This

Chicken McNuggets®

with Apple Dippers and Caramel Dip (6 nuggets)

355 calories
15.5 g fat (3 g saturated, 1.5 g trans)
705 mg sodium

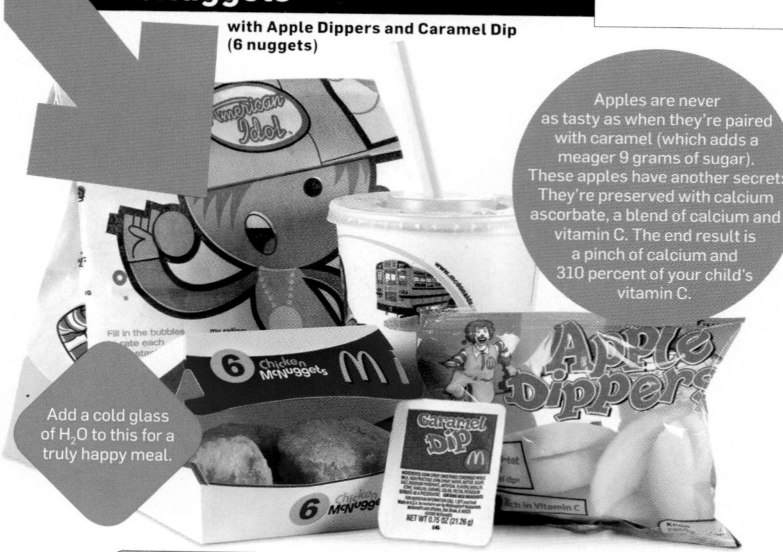

Apples are never as tasty as when they're paired with caramel (which adds a meager 9 grams of sugar). These apples have another secret: They're preserved with calcium ascorbate, a blend of calcium and vitamin C. The end result is a pinch of calcium and 310 percent of your child's vitamin C.

Add a cold glass of H_2O to this for a truly happy meal.

UNHAPPY MEALS
Cheeseburger
with French fries (small) and a Coca-Cola® (small)

700 calories, 25 g fat (8.5 g saturated fat), 915 mg sodium

The classic Happy Meal® is a punishing blow to your kid's diet, with more fat and calories than an active adult man, let alone a kid, should take in from a single meal.

Other Picks

Honey Mustard Snack Wrap®
grilled

260 calories
9 g fat (3.5 g saturated)
800 mg sodium

Egg McMuffin®

300 calories
12 g fat (5 g saturated)
820 mg sodium

Kiddie Cone

45 calories
1 g fat (0.5 g saturated)
6 g sugars

400 calories
23 g fat (4 g saturated, 2 g trans)
1,000 mg sodium

Not That!

Chicken Selects Premium Breast Strips

(3)

The only thing premium about these strips is the caloric price you pay to eat them. A thicker layer of crunchy breading puts each strip at 133 calories, compared to just 45 per McNugget.

Other Passes

300 calories
12 g fat (6 g saturated, 0.5 g trans)
750 mg sodium

Cheeseburger

570 calories
13.5 g fat (3.5 g saturated)
665 mg sodium

Hotcakes
with syrup and margarine

250 calories
8 g fat (2 g saturated)
13 g sugars

McDonaldland® Cookies
(2 oz)

DIP DECODER

(PER PACKAGE)

- **CREAMY RANCH:** 200 calories, 22 g fat (3.5 g saturated), 1 g sugars
- **TANGY HONEY MUSTARD:** 70 calories, 2.5 g fat (0 g saturated), 9 g sugars
- **SPICY BUFFALO:** 70 calories, 7 g fat (1 g saturated), 0 g sugars
- **HONEY:** 50 calories, 0 g fat, 11 g sugars
- **BARBEQUE:** 50 calories, 0 g fat, 10 g sugars
- **SWEET 'N SOUR:** 50 calories, 0 g fat, 10 g sugars

HIDDEN DANGER
Baked Apple Pie

This fruit pocket has more trans fats than anything else on the menu.

270 calories, 12 g fat (3.5 g saturated, 5 g trans)

Olive Garden

REPORT CARD F

There may be some pretty decent stuff on Olive Garden's menu, but you'll never know it—not as long as the country's largest sit-down Italian chain continues to make nutritional nondisclosure a policy.

SURVIVAL STRATEGY

The low-fat options on the Garden Fare® menu provide only sporadic chunks of information, and only a single option for kids: the 349-calorie Grilled Chicken entrée. Until they offer comprehensive data on all their dishes, as competitors Macaroni Grill and Fazoli's gladly do, proceed at your own risk.

GUILTY PLEASURES

Shrimp Primavera (lunch portion)

483 calories, 11 g fat

This penne-pasta dish is teeming with antioxidant-rich shrimp and basting in rich, tomato-based arrabbiata sauce.

Eat This

Kid's Spaghetti & Tomato Sauce

310 calories
6 g fat
770 sodium

Because Olive Garden doesn't offer nutritional information to its customers, many of the numbers on this page are estimates drawn from independent research and consultation with nutritionists in order to help you determine what the restaurant is feeding your child.

It's hard to go wrong with this classic. The pasta itself offers little in the way of nutrition, so look for substance with the sauce. Classic marinara, loaded with lycopene, provides just that.

Other Picks

Kids's Grilled Chicken with Pasta and Broccoli

350 calories
11 fat
485 mg sodium

Kid's Cheese Pizza

420 calories
18 fat
900 mg sodium

Torta di Chocolate

235 calories
7 g fat
20 g sugars

510 calories
18 g fat
940 sodium

Not That!

Macaroni & Cheese

A sauce based on cheese and cream could never compete with one made from simmered tomatoes.

Olive Garden will let you sub whole wheat linguine in place of regular white pasta. The exchange will add an extra 6 grams of fiber to your plate, making sure the meal's energy burns at a slow and steady pace.

UNHAPPY MEALS

Lasagna Classico

858 calories,
47 g fat,
1,403 mg sodium,
49 g carbohydrates

The combined power of four cheeses glosses these noodles with 75 percent of the day's fat allotment. Stick to cheese pizza if your kids want something gooey and saucy.

Other Passes

560 calories
32 fat
500 mg sodium

Kid's Fettuccine Alfredo

520 calories
25 fat
1,100 mg sodium

Kid's Chicken Fingers with Fries

450 calories
22 fat
45 g sugars

Kid's Sundae

On The Border

REPORT CARD
D-

On the Border's eagerness to please might be detrimental to your child's health. Each kids' meal entrée includes a drink, side, and kiddie sundae. Added together, most meals top 1,000 calories. The regular adult menu, with its 1,900-calorie fish tacos and quesadillas, offers little refuge.

SURVIVAL STRATEGY
As funny as it might sound, avoid all Mexican entrées on the kids' menu—every one is disastrous. Go with a burger or a corn dog, or carefully construct a Combo meal.

Order your child's meals with corn tortillas instead of flour. It will cut 130 calories, 4 grams of saturated fat, and 710 mg sodium per order.

Eat This

Kids Grilled Chicken

with black beans and sautéed vegetables

380 calories
13 g fat (4 g saturated)
1,440 mg sodium

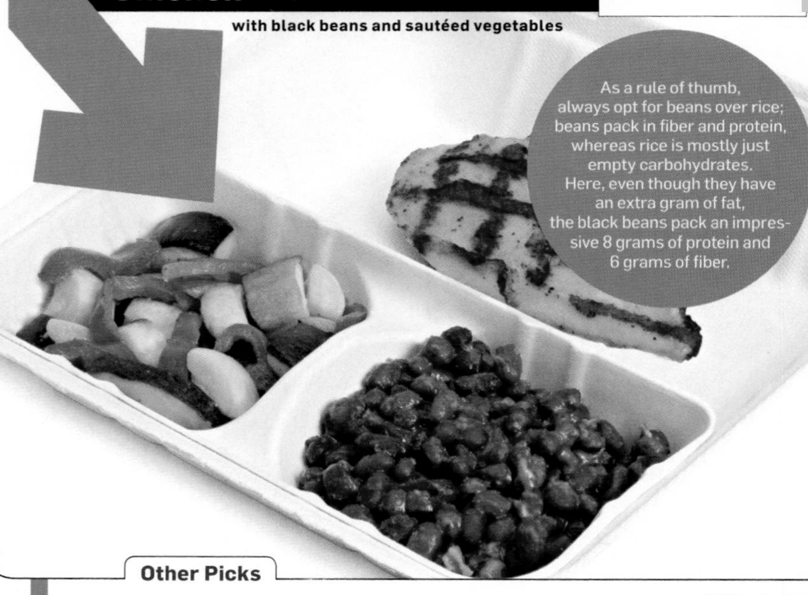

As a rule of thumb, always opt for beans over rice; beans pack in fiber and protein, whereas rice is mostly just empty carbohydrates. Here, even though they have an extra gram of fat, the black beans pack an impressive 8 grams of protein and 6 grams of fiber.

Other Picks

Hamburger
390 calories
23 g fat (7 g saturated)
290 mg sodium

Chicken Tortilla Soup
350 calories
22 g fat (9 g saturated)
1,540 mg sodium

Kids Corn Dog
320 calories
21 g fat (5 g saturated)
760 mg sodium

1,210 calories
56 g fat
(16 g saturated)
3,690 mg sodium

Not That!

Kids Chicken Crispy Taco Mexican Dinner

with Mexican rice and salad with chipotle honey mustard dressing

This is one of America's worst kids' meals. For taco lovers, the only tenable route is to order one or two chicken tacos off the Create Your Own Combo menu. Even then, you'll still have a meal with 500 calories and more than 20 grams of fat, so be extra careful when selecting sides.

Other Passes

710 calories
48 g fat (26 g saturated)
1,230 mg sodium

Kids Quesadilla

980 calories
57 g fat (29 g saturated)
1,850 mg sodium

Kids Bean & Cheese Nachos

630 calories
21 g fat (9 g saturated)
1,490 mg sodium

Kids Grilled Chicken Sandwich

900

The average number of calories in an On The Border salad without dressing. The average sodium content is 1,769 milligrams.

SMART SIDES

Sautéed Shrimp (4)

170 calories, 10 g fat (4 g saturated), 380 mg sodium

These crustaceans are supercharged with tryptophan, an amino acid that has the ability to increase serotonin levels in the brain. The payoff for child and parent alike is in regular sleeping patterns, appetite control, and improved mood.

GREAT GROWN-UP GRUB

Jalapeño-BBQ Salmon

590 calories, 21 g fat (6 g saturated), 1,220 mg sodium

This meal boasts 54 grams of protein, an astonishing 24 grams of fiber, and tons of healthy omega-3s.

Outback Steakhouse

For years we've pestered Outback to provide us with nutritional information. A spokesperson once told us: "Ninety percent of our meals are prepared by hand. Any analysis would be difficult to measure consistently." Yet no fewer than 50 national chain restaurants do just that.

SURVIVAL STRATEGY
Until they do what so many others are doing, we'll be forced to fail them and you'll be forced to trust that their food isn't too nutritionally deficient—which is quite a leap of faith.

SMART SIDES

Sautéed Mushrooms

150 calories, 11 g fat, 12 g carbs

Mushrooms are a powerful force for bodily health, due largely to the sizeable dose of selenium. One serving of the fancy fungus contains half a day's value of this important mineral, which has antioxidant characteristics that have been shown to help ward off cancers, repair DNA, and decrease asthma and arthritis symptoms.

Eat This

Joey Sirloin

with fresh steamed vegetables

510 calories
20 g fat
900 mg sodium

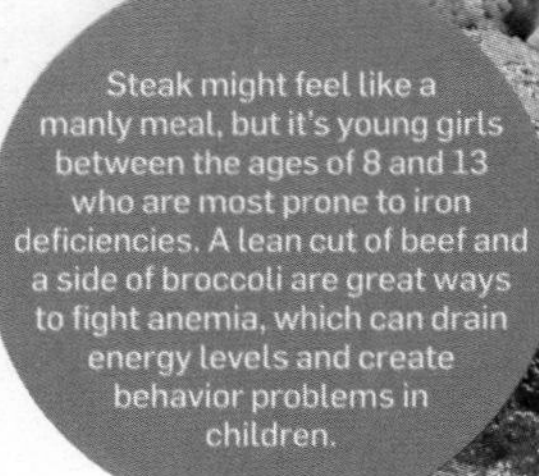

Steak might feel like a manly meal, but it's young girls between the ages of 8 and 13 who are most prone to iron deficiencies. A lean cut of beef and a side of broccoli are great ways to fight anemia, which can drain energy levels and create behavior problems in children.

Because Outback Steakhouse doesn't offer nutritional information to its customers, many of the numbers on this page are estimates drawn from independent research and consultation with nutritionists in order to help you determine what the restaurant is feeding your child.

Other Picks

Kid's Grilled Chicken on the Barbie
with roasted garlic mashed potatoes

420 calories
18 g fat
825 mg sodium

Grilled Cheese
with fresh steamed green beans

500 calories
22 g fat
825 mg sodium

620 calories
26 g fat
1,025 mg sodium

Not That!

Kookaburra Chicken Fingers

with whole grain wild rice

While wild rice is certainly an improvement over a loaded baked potato or French fries, don't be fooled into thinking it's a paradigm of healthy side selections. The fact is, it's high in fast-burning carbohydrates with very little fiber to offset the spike in blood sugar.

Other Passes

850 calories
45 g fat
1,250 mg sodium

Boomerang Cheese Burger with Aussie Chips

910 calories
48 g fat
1,005 mg sodium

Mac-A-Roo 'N Cheese
with dressed baked potato

93

The average amount of fat, in grams, ordered by kids at Outback, the worst-faring restaurant in a study that included 104 adolescents and 10 restaurants. At McDonald's, the meals ordered had 45 grams; at Wendy's and Taco Bell, the results were 34 and 32 grams, respectively.

"SOS" is restaurant speak for "sauce on the side," which is important at Outback, where cooks have a heavy hand with the fatty stuff. Try it out on your server and your kid won't even know.

Panera Bread

REPORT CARD **B**

The kid-size sandwiches at Panera are appropriately portioned so that none tops 400 calories, but everything outside that safety zone is eligible for a red-flag warning, including adult sandwiches, Crispani® pizzas, and most breakfast offerings. Some of the more egregious selections sit close to 1,000 calories—enough to ruin an otherwise disciplined day of eating.

SURVIVAL STRATEGY
Push for a soup and half-sandwich combo. Most combinations will keep your kid under 500 calories and will provide a decent dose of nutrients.

MENU DECODER

● **WHITE WHOLE GRAIN WHEAT BREAD:** Made with flour milled from white whole wheat and malted barley, this loaf has all the fiber and nutritional breakdown of regular whole wheat bread, but with a milder taste.

Eat This

Half Chicken Salad Sandwich on Whole Wheat

with small fruit cup

360 calories
13 g fat (2.5 g saturated)
805 mg sodium

Sometimes the best kids' options are found on the adult menu. Not only is this combo lower in calories and fat, but it also offers your kid a solid source of whole grains and a mix of nutrients and phytochemicals from the fruit.

Other Picks

Egg & Cheese Breakfast Sandwich
380 calories
14 g fat (6 g saturated)
620 mg sodium

Turkey Chickpea Chili Soup
180 calories
5 g fat (1.5 g saturated)
800 mg sodium

Nutty Oatmeal Raisin Cookie
340 calories
14 g fat (6 g saturated)
21 g sugars

470 calories
17 g fat (2 g saturated)
400 mg sodium

Not That!

Panera Kids™ PB&J

with strawberry yogurt tube

This perennial favorite takes a turn for the worse in Panera's hands. They manage to cram 19 grams of sugar into the tiny sandwich, and paired with the sweetened yogurt, it makes for a sucrose-saturated meal for your kid.

Other Passes

560 calories
21 g fat (14 g saturated)
740 mg sodium

Cinnamon Crunch Bagel
with reduced fat cream cheese

230 calories
14 g fat (9 g saturated)
720 mg sodium

Baked Potato Soup

430 calories
24 g fat (10 g saturated)
27 g sugars

Nutty Chocolate Chipper Cookie

HIDDEN DANGER
Hot Chocolate

Despite being a mere 11.5 ounces, this dubious beverage has more fat than any Panera Kids™ Deli Sandwich and more sugar than any of its saucer-size cookies.

410 calories, 17 g fat (12 g saturated), 44 g sugars

GUILTY PLEASURES

Crispani Tomato and Fresh Basil Pizza (2 slices)

330 calories, 16 g fat (6 g saturated), 560 mg sodium

The antioxidant-rich tomatoes and the cracker-thin crust form the basis of a very reasonable pizza, but the often-overlooked basil is what takes it over the top. Like turmeric and cinnamon, basil is a natural anti-inflammatory, so it provides an all-around boost to your child's health.

Papa John's

REPORT CARD

C

Pizza joints suffer the curse of bad report cards because of their thick crusts, fat-speckled meats, and blankets of cheese. That said, Papa John's does have a few advantages over the competition: the absence of trans fats, the assortment of nonsoda beverage options, and the first whole wheat crust offered by a big US pizza chain.

SURVIVAL STRATEGY
Order Chicken Strips with Pizza Sauce to blunt the family's collective hunger. Follow with a slice of thin or wheat crust cheese or Spinach Alfredo.

13.4

Manhattan length, in miles. Johnny would have to walk it to burn off the 1,090 calories in two slices of Spicy Italian Pan Crust Pizza and small Coke®.

Eat This

Original Crust Spinach Alfredo Pizza

12" (2 slices)

400 calories
16 g fat (6 g saturated)
900 mg sodium

Surprisingly enough, this sinful-sounding slice is one of the best on the menu, with the same amount of calories as the plain cheese and veggie pies, but with less sodium. If your kids like fettuccine Alfredo, their taste buds will take well to this pie.

Other Picks

Whole Wheat Crust Garden Fresh Pizza 14" (1 slice)

270 calories
9 g fat (2.5 g saturated)
660 mg sodium

Chickenstrips
with pizza sauce (2 strips)

180 calories
8 g fat (2 g saturated)
490 mg sodium

Apple Twist Sweetreat
($^1/_2$ pie)

380 calories
16 g fat (4 g saturated)
23 g sugars

760 calories
44 g fat
(16 g saturated)
1,220 mg sodium

Not That!

Pan Crust Spinach Alfredo Pizza

12" (2 slices)

The dense, buttery pan crust adds to the overall calorie, fat, and sodium count, but doubles the damage by possessing the structural integrity to withstand unreasonable amounts of sauce, cheese, and toppings.

Other Passes

300 calories
11 g fat (3.5 g saturated)
750 mg sodium

Original Crust Cheese Pizza
14" (1 slice)

520 calories
33 g fat (7.5 g saturated)
1,140 mg sodium

Cheesesticks
with Special Garlic Dip (2 sticks)

570 calories
15 g fat (3 g saturated)
33 g sugars

Cinnamon Sweetsticks
(4)

Genius PARENT TRICK

Don't get too fancy with the dipping sauce. Papa John's includes one of eight different sauces with each order, but some carry a hefty load of sodium, sugar, or fat. At only 20 calories per ounce, the standard Pizza Dipping Sauce is the safest bet.

UNHAPPY MEALS

Full Order of Wings (10)

1,000 calories, 70 g fat (20 g saturated), 4,200 mg sodium

As a meal, these wings gobble up nearly 2 days' worth of sodium and saturated fat. A side of blue cheese tacks on another 170 calories and 18 grams of fat.

P.F. Chang's China Bistro

REPORT CARD
D+

Give Chang's credit for offering options like "stock velveted" (which replaces oil with vegetable stock in the cooking process) and being flexible with substitutions. But without a designated Kids' Menu, young eaters are forced to fly blind with the grown-ups, where massive, 1,000-calorie entrées are hard to avoid.

SURVIVAL STRATEGY
Turn appetizers into entrées. Dumplings, lettuce wraps, and spring rolls are all healthy eats.

GREAT GROWN-UP GRUB

Oolong Marinated Sea Bass

521 calories, 12 g fat (3 g saturated), 37 g carbohydrates

This meal deserves a nutritional gold star. The sea bass is rich with omega-3s and contains 64 grams of protein, and the oolong-tea marinade is packed with antioxidants. The fish dish comes with spinach, one of the most nutrient-rich foods on the planet, and ginger-infused soy, which promotes digestive health.

Eat This

Chang's Chicken Lettuce Wraps

with special sauce

432 calories
13 g fat (3 g saturated)
44 g carbohydrates

It may be found on the appetizer menu, but it makes a great entrée option, especially for kids who like to play with their food.

P.F. Chang's does not disclose sodium values.

Other Picks

Singapore Street Noodles

572 calories
16 g fat (3 g saturated)
81 g carbohydrates

Cantonese Shrimp

330 calories
12 g fat (2 g saturated)
21 g carbohydrates

Apple Pie Mini Dessert

170 calories
4 g fat (2 g saturated)
34 g carbohydrates

Not That!

Orange Peel Chicken

1,151 calories
46 g fat (8 g saturated)
127 g carbohydrates

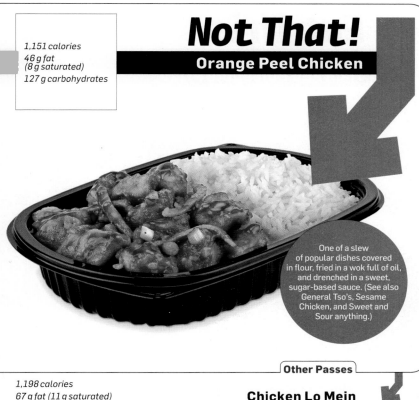

One of a slew of popular dishes covered in flour, fried in a wok full of oil, and drenched in a sweet, sugar-based sauce. (See also General Tso's, Sesame Chicken, and Sweet and Sour anything.)

Other Passes

Chicken Lo Mein
1,198 calories
67 g fat (11 g saturated)
97 g carbohydrates

Kung Pao Shrimp
977 calories
58 g fat (8 g saturated)
58 g carbohydrates

S'Mores Mini Dessert
323 calories
12 g fat (7 g saturated)
50 g carbohydrates

UNHAPPY MEALS

Tam's Noodle with Savory Beef and Shrimp

1,678 calories, 93 g fat (17 g saturated), 138 g carbohydrates

If only the body had a warning system to protect us from unknowingly consuming massive doses of fat and carbohydrates. Even if you take half of this meal home in a to-go box, your child will still have eaten three-fourths of his or her daily fat.

Because diners are encouraged to order "family style" and pass dishes around the table, take charge of the ordering by telling your crew, "I know what's good here." Load up on the picks on this page and skip the passes and your family will be forced to eat healthy without ever knowing it.

Pizza Hut

REPORT CARD

D

Expect no surprises from this quintessential pizza parlor. The chain offers no kid-friendly beverage or side options, and with nothing else to choose from, a couple breadsticks and a soda tack hundreds of calories onto a pizza dinner. A thin-crust delivery can be a lifesaver in a pinch, but as for a buffet of nourishing options, Pizza Hut is an empty shack.

SURVIVAL STRATEGY
Avoid pepperoni at all costs. If the kids want meat, stick to ham and chicken, but try to add veggies whenever possible. The best possible scenario? Fit 'N Delicious Pizzas™. Any of them.

Eat This

Thin 'N Crispy Quartered Ham and Pineapple Pizza

12" (2 slices)

360 calories
12 g fat
(6 g saturated)
1,140 mg sodium

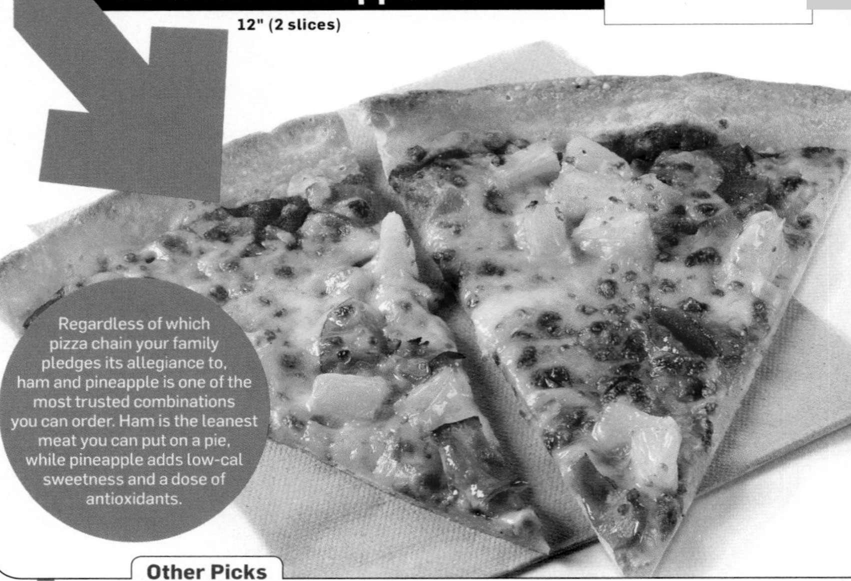

Regardless of which pizza chain your family pledges its allegiance to, ham and pineapple is one of the most trusted combinations you can order. Ham is the leanest meat you can put on a pie, while pineapple adds low-cal sweetness and a dose of antioxidants.

Other Picks

Thin 'N Crispy Pepperoni and Mushroom Pizza 12" (1 slice)

190 calories
8 g fat (3.5 g saturated)
560 mg sodium

Hand-Tossed Veggie Lover's Pizza 12" (1 slice)

210 calories
8 g fat (3.5 g saturated)
580 mg sodium

Fit 'N Delicious Diced Chicken, Red Onion & Green Pepper Pizza 12" (2 slices)

340 calories
9 g fat (4 g saturated)
1,040 mg sodium

SUGAR SPIKES

White Icing Dipping Cup (2 oz)

The Impact:
40 g sugars

The white icing is basically pure sugar, and as a dip for already-sugar-coated cinnamon sticks, it will no doubt sugar buzz your kid.

400 calories
16 g fat (9 g saturated)
1,140 mg sodium

Not That!

Thin 'N Crispy Cheese Pizza

12" (2 slices)

All in all, not a bad slice, but by adding a few healthy toppings, you can displace some of the extra cheese that fills this plain pizza out, which would give it a surprising caloric and fat advantage over the Hawaiian-style pie.

A thin-and-crispy crust will save your pizza 100 calories per large slice. At two slices per week, the switch will cut 10,400 calories in a year's time. Let the little pizza lovers help pick the toppings, but make a thin crust the requisite pizza foundation.

Other Passes

230 calories
11 g fat (4.5 g saturated)
620 mg sodium

Thin 'N Crispy Italian Sausage and Red Onion Pizza 12" (1 slice)

230 calories
10 g fat (4.5 g saturated)
620 mg sodium

Hand-Tossed Cheese Pizza 12" (1 slice)

420 calories
16 g fat (7 g saturated)
1,160 mg sodium

Hand-Tossed Veggie Lovers® Pizza 12" (2 slices)

UNHAPPY MEALS

3-Cheese Penne Bake

980 calories, 61 g fat (29 g saturated, 1.5 g trans), 1,960 mg sodium

This poor penne is drowning in cream and butter. It might induce a growth spurt in your kids—but not the kind you're looking for.

Quizno's

REPORT CARD
C+

Toasty or not, Quizno's offers some of America's worst sandwiches, including the 2,090-calorie large Tuna Melt. Cookies and fatty salads don't make matters any better. What does improve matters is Quizno's line of kid-size Sammies—the rare bright spot in an otherwise dark menu.

SURVIVAL STRATEGY
With a handful of Sammies at 200 calories, they make perfect meals for younger kids. You can double-up for the older eaters—even two of the healthier Sammies will be better than most small sandwiches.

GUILTY PLEASURES

Black Angus and Cheddar Breakfast Sandwich

390 calories, 17.5 g fat (9 g saturated), 1,040 mg sodium

Nothing beats Black Angus steak in the morning, and the 30-gram protein punch will help regulate blood sugar and keep your kid feeling strong through lunchtime.

Eat This

Roadhouse Steak Sammie

with dressing

205 calories
4 g fat (1 g saturated)
565 mg sodium

Don't assume steak is worse than turkey. It's less about the type of meat and more about the condiments. Onions and mushrooms flavor the steak, while cheese and mayo smother the turkey.

Other Picks

Small Honey Bourbon Chicken Sub
310 calories
4 g fat (1 g saturated)
850 mg sodium

Cantina Chicken Sammies
(2)
410 calories
8 g fat (1 g saturated)
890 mg sodium

Toasty® Turkey & Cheese with a Cup of Chili
320 calories
11.5 g fat (3.5 g saturated)
1,235 mg sodium

Not That!

Sonoma Turkey Flatbread Sammie

with cheese and dressing

300 calories
18 g fat (4.5 g saturated)
815 mg sodium

Sammies are billed as low-price, low-calorie alternatives to Quizno's often disastrously caloric regular sandwiches, but clearly this little guy doesn't fit the bill.

Other Passes

Honey Mustard Chicken with Bacon Sub (small)

500 calories
25 g fat (5 g saturated)
1,100 mg sodium

Alpine Chicken Sammies (2)

620 calories
32 g fat (6 g saturated)
1,230 mg sodium

Chili Bread Bowl

730 calories
22 g fat (7 g saturated)
1,680 mg sodium

UNHAPPY MEALS

Country French Chicken Bread Bowl

720 calories, 23 g fat (9 g saturated), 1,730 mg sodium, 100 g carbohydrates

Soup is normally a safe route to go, but not when it comes served in a big pillowy bread bowl—which adds a totally unnecessary 400 calories to the meal. Need something to dunk? Try crackers.

FOOD MYTH #6

Salads are a low-fat, no-fail way to bring extra nutrition to your kid's diet.

Lettuce is healthy. Unfortunately, it's often relegated by restaurants to being a mere vehicle for a flurry of cheese, croutons, crumbled bacon, and fatty meats, making entrée-size salads consistently one of the worst things you can order from a menu. At Quizno's, the average salad with regular dressing and flatbread has 924 calories and 51 grams of fat. Nix the flatbread and sub in the balsamic vinaigrette to save up to 440 calories.

Red Lobster

Too bad Red Lobster makes it a policy not to disclose nutritional information—because we have a sneaking suspicion that they have some decent items on offer. But until they decide to show up to class and take the test, we'll be forced to fail them.

SURVIVAL STRATEGY
When it comes to seafood, the rule is pretty simple: Avoid anything that's been fried or covered in sauce.

SMART SIDES

Baked Potato with Pico de Gallo

185 calories, 2 g fat, 37 carbohydrates

Let your child enjoy the tasty health benefits of vitamin C and fiber found in potatoes—without decorating them with slabs and dollops of extra fat. The pico is made from carotenoid-rich tomatoes, and it only adds a measly 6 calories to the potato. That beats butter and sour cream any day.

Eat This

Snow Crab Legs

with seasoned broccoli and cocktail sauce

318 calories
4.5 g fat
875 mg sodium

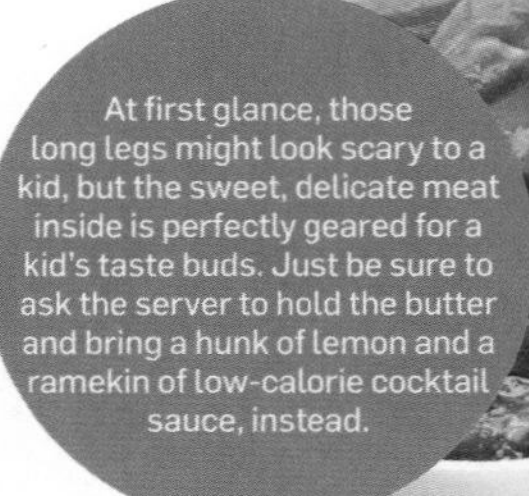

At first glance, those long legs might look scary to a kid, but the sweet, delicate meat inside is perfectly geared for a kid's taste buds. Just be sure to ask the server to hold the butter and bring a hunk of lemon and a ramekin of low-calorie cocktail sauce, instead.

Because Red Lobster doesn't offer nutritional information to its customers, many of the numbers on this page are estimates drawn from independent research and consultation with nutritionists in order to help you determine what the restaurant is feeding your child

Other Picks

Garlic Grilled Jumbo Shrimp
and a baked potato with pico de gallo

329 calories
5 g fat
670 mg sodium

Kid's Popcorn Shrimp & Fries
with applesauce

500 calories
22 g fat
970 mg sodium

520 calories
28 g fat
1,110 mg sodium

Not That!

Grilled Chicken

with Caesar salad

It's not enough for the star of your plate to put on a good performance—you need some help from the supporting cast, too. Unfortunately, few players can muck up an otherwise worthy meal quite as quickly and thoroughly as a Caesar salad.

Other Passes

600 calories
35 g fat
985 mg sodium

Shrimp Linguine Alfredo
(half portion)

650 calories
38 g fat
1,560 mg sodium

Chicken Fingers & Fries
with veggies & ranch dip

Pull your server aside quietly and ask him or her to limit your table to one round of biscuits. Seriously, each infamous Cheddar Bay Biscuit™ has 160 calories and 9 grams of fat.

DIP DECODER

- **LEMON JUICE:** 2 calories, 0 g fat
- **COCKTAIL SAUCE (large, 1/4 cup):** 87 calories, 2 g fat
- **TARTAR SAUCE (1 oz.):** 100 calories, 10 g fat
- **MELTED BUTTER (1 oz.):** 189 calories, 21 g fat

STEALTH HEALTH FOOD

Jumbo Shrimp Cocktail (10 shrimp)

228 calories,
4 g fat,
46 g protein

Aside from being a great source of lean protein, shrimp is packed with bone-strengthening vitamin D.

Romano's Macaroni Grill

Romano's Macaroni Grill is home to a few of the worst kids' dishes in America and a menu that is more sodium-saturated than any we've ever come across. The only redeeming quality is that they allow diners to create their own pastas—which you should absolutely do.

SURVIVAL STRATEGY
Stick to kids' grilled chicken and spaghetti and meatballs, or an invented pasta made with wheat pasta with lots of veggies and red sauce.

HIDDEN DANGER
Roasted Chicken and Cheese Sandwich

This seemingly light lunch sandwich has more calories than a Burger King Triple Whopper® with cheese, mayonnaise, and medium fries.

1,630 calories, 91 g fat (23 g saturated), 2,520 mg sodium, 128 g carbohydrates

Eat This

Kids Spaghetti & Meatballs

with tomato sauce

500 calories
20 g fat (8 g saturated)
1,520 mg sodium
22 g protein

Request tomato sauce instead of meat sauce for this massive plate of pasta—it'll cut 50 calories and a few grams of totally unnecessary saturated fat. After all, who needs a meat sauce when you already have fist-size meatballs on the plate?

Other Picks

Kids Grilled Chicken & Broccoli

390 calories
5 g fat (2 g saturated)
560 mg sodium

BBQ Chicken Pizza
(½ adult pizza)

485 calories
12 g fat (7 g saturated)
1,350 mg sodium

Italian Sorbetto with Biscotti

330 calories
4 g fat (2 g saturated)
80 mg sodium

Not That!

Kids Macaroni 'n' Cheese

600 calories
31 g fat (20 g saturated)
1,720 mg sodium

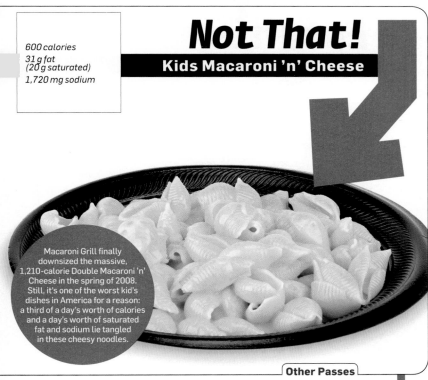

Macaroni Grill finally downsized the massive, 1,210-calorie Double Macaroni 'n' Cheese in the spring of 2008. Still, it's one of the worst kid's dishes in America for a reason: a third of a day's worth of calories and a day's worth of saturated fat and sodium lie tangled in these cheesy noodles.

Other Passes

Kids Chicken Fingerias and Grilled Broccoli

730 calories
48 g fat (7 g saturated)
2,110 mg sodium

Kids Mona Lisa's Pepperoni Masterpizza

920 calories
27 g fat (16 g saturated)
2,140 mg sodium

Kid's Vanilla Ice Cream
with chocolate sauce

400 calories
23 g fat (14 g saturated)
100 mg sodium

UNHAPPY MEALS

Twice Baked Lasagna with Meatballs

1,470 calories, 83 g fat (41 g saturated), 4,420 mg sodium, 75 g carbohydrates

Garfield would really enjoy this lasagna meal, but that doesn't mean your kid should, and lucky for him, cartoons aren't real. In real life this meal would be better suited for four people. It provides the vast majority of the day's calories.

SMART SIDES

Grilled Asparagus

40 calories, 2 g fat (0 g saturated), 590 mg sodium

Asparagus can be a tough sell to a child, but you'll be the envy of every parent in the restaurant if you can pull it off. Asparagus is rich in inulin, a carbohydrate that humans don't digest. Instead, this carb fuels the growth of healthy, gut-protecting bacteria. Tell the kids they better feed the armies and fuel their war on evil bacteria.

Ruby Tuesday

REPORT CARD

C-

No kids' menu is more polarized than Ruby Tuesday's, which serves up everything from a 276-calorie chicken breast to a 907-calorie plate of mini cheeseburgers. Ultimately, the few low-calorie options can't offset the fat bombs that lie scattered like landmines among Ruby Tuesday's kids' meals, but the numerous options for healthy sides help dampen the blow.

SURVIVAL STRATEGY
Stick to the Chicken Breast and Broccoli or Pasta with Marinara and your child can walk out unscathed.

STEALTH HEALTH FOOD

White Bean Chicken Chili

228 calories,
8 g fat,
26 g carbohydrates

This chili is filled with navy beans and chicken, two low-fat foods with a protein punch. Add to that the fiber from the beans, and a cup of chili is likely to fill up a hungry kid better than a burger or a plate of French fries.

Eat This

Kid's Fried Shrimp & Fries

571 calories
*21 g fat**
71 g carbohydrates

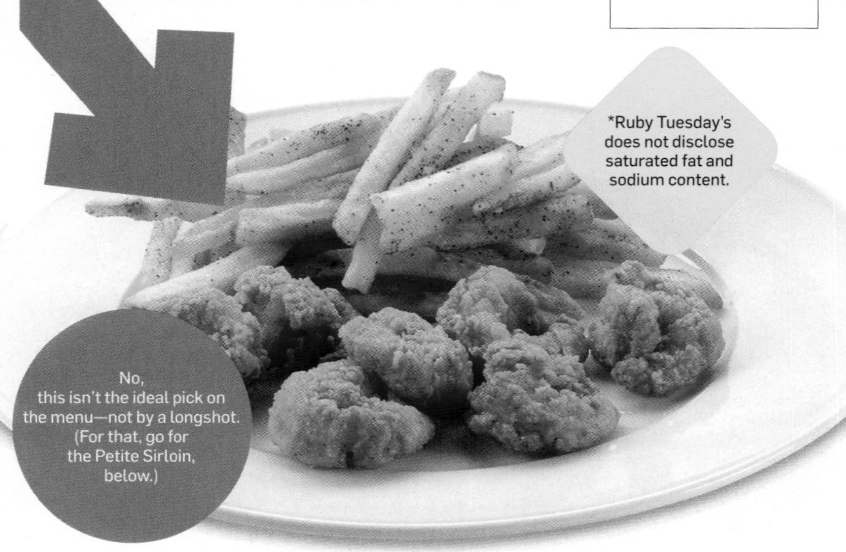

*Ruby Tuesday's does not disclose saturated fat and sodium content.

No, this isn't the ideal pick on the menu—not by a longshot. (For that, go for the Petite Sirloin, below.)

Other Picks

Chicken Oscar

469 calories
*22 g fat**
7 g carbohydrates

Petite Sirloin
(7 oz) with creamy mashed cauliflower

359 calories
*15 g fat**
16 g carbohydrates

Kids Pasta
with marinara

314 calories
*4 g fat**
60 g carbohydrates

893 calories
*47 g fat**
87 g carbohydrates

Not That!

Kids Turkey Minis & Fries

"Turkey Minis" sound like a light approach to the normally bloated burger, right? Not at Ruby Tuesday, which has a reputation for making obscenely caloric burgers out of traditionally healthy components. (See the 1,065-calorie Bella Turkey Burger and the 953-calorie Veggie Burger.) No burger is safe to eat on this menu.

SMART SIDES

Creamy Mashed Cauliflower

153 calories, 10 g fat, 14 g carbohydrates

This Southern recipe might be just what your children need to help them acquire a taste for cauliflower. The brainlike vegetable belongs to a family of vegetables called cruciferous vegetables. These vegetables—broccoli, cabbage, and Brussels sprouts, among others—might play a significant role in preventing cancer later in life.

Other Passes

1,649 calories
*95 g fat**
127 g carbohydrates

Parmesan Chicken Pasta

497 calories
*35 g fat**
33 g carbohydrates

Kids Chop Steak & Mashed Potatoes

448 calories
*24 g fat**
48 g carbohydrates

Kids Pasta with butter

HIDDEN DANGER

Parmesan Shrimp Pasta

Ordinarily you should nudge your kids toward the ocean waters, but not with this dish. The shrimp's leaner side is drowned out by 64 grams of cream-sauce fat.

1,216 calories, 64 g fat, 98 g carbohydrates

Starbucks

REPORT CARD

C-

As any caffeine-addicted parent knows, there are few options for kids at a coffee shop. Starbucks is no exception. Whether due to an excess of sugar or a surge of caffeine (or both), nearly every drink here will have your kid treating your furniture like a trampoline. The food isn't any better; most snacks here are based on refined flour and sugar.

SURVIVAL STRATEGY
Get your kid hooked on lightly sweetened Tazo tea and you're golden. If not, skim milk with a shot of chocolate sauce is as safe as it gets.

GREAT GROWN-UP GRUB

Multigrain Bagel

360 calories, 5 g fat (0 g saturated), 420 mg sodium

This is one of the few things on the menu not too sweet for everyday consumption. It's packed with free-radical–fighting sunflower seeds. Couple that with 4 grams of fiber and 13 grams of protein, and your body might actually thank you for for the trip.

Eat This

Grande Tazo® Green Shaken Iced Tea Lemonade

with Mini Black and White Cookies (2)

370 calories
12 g fat (1 g saturated)
55 g sugars

You know a place has food issues when cookies are one of the healthiest items on the menu. While most muffins and cakes weigh in around 400 calories, these cookies have 240 calories and 1 gram of saturated fat.

Green tea is loaded with catechins, powerful antioxidants that have been shown to encourage weight loss and fight cancer. If you're worried about the small amount of caffeine, switch to the Passion Shaken Iced Tea Lemonade, which has many of the same antioxidant benefits.

Other Picks

Grande Chocolate Milk
(nonfat milk with two shots of mocha syrup)

330 calories
3.5 g fat (0.5 g saturated)
54 g sugars

Cinnamon Raisin Bagel

330 calories
0 g fat
13 g sugars

Petite Vanilla Bean Scone

130 calories
5 g fat (3 g saturated)
9 g sugars

1,000 calories
52 g fat
(19 g saturated)
72 g sugars

Not That!

Grande White Hot Chocolate

(whole milk) with No Sugar Added Banana Nut Coffee Cake

Even with no sugar added, this cake still contains 420 calories and 28 grams of fat. Its sweetness comes from 36 grams of sugar alcohols, which, if ingested in excess, can create digestive problems.

Dark chocolate at least has antioxidants, but white chocolate isn't real chocolate at all. It's made from cocoa solids and corn syrup, and its role in this drink is deleterious: Combined with milk and whipped cream, it packs 520 calories and 61 grams of sugar.

Other Passes

570 calories
15 g fat (9 g saturated)
83 g sugars

Grande Strawberries & Crème Frappuccino® Blended Crème

430 calories
18 g fat (2 g saturated)
26 g sugars

Walnut Bran Muffin

480 calories
22 g fat (12 g saturated)
24 g sugars

Blueberry Scone

Genius PARENT TRICK

Don't let the suits at Starbucks headquarters dictate what your kids drink. Instead, help them customize their own beverages using any of the variety of flavored sugar-free syrups. At zero calories a pump, the price is right for a creative low-cal masterpiece.

HIDDEN DANGER

Maple Oat Nut Scone

This little quick bread looks like a harmless snack, but it's actually a miniature nutritional nightmare. It has as much fat and calories as two slices of pepperoni pizza and more sugar than a pack of Reese's Peanut Butter Cups.

490 calories, 21 g fat (8 g saturated), 32 g sugar, 370 mg sodium

Subway

REPORT CARD A-

A menu based on lean protein and vegetables is always going to score well in our book. With more than half a dozen kid-friendly sandwiches under 300 calories, plus a slew of soups and healthy sides to boot, Subway can satisfy even the pickiest eater without breaking the caloric bank. But, despite what Jared may want you to believe, Subway is not nutritionally infallible: Those rosy calorie counts posted on the menu boards include neither cheese nor mayo (add 160 calories per 6-inch sub) and some of the toasted subs, like the Meatball Marinara, contain hefty doses of calories, saturated fat, and sodium.

SURVIVAL STRATEGY
Cornell researchers have discovered a "health halo" at Subway, which refers to the tendency to reward yourself or your kid with chips, cookies, and large soft drinks because the entrée is healthy. Avoid the halo and all will be well.

Eat This

Roast Beef Sub

6" with cheese on a wheat bun

340 calories
9.5 g fat (4.5 g saturated)
930 mg sodium

This sandwich has more of everything: more fiber, more protein, more nutrients from the vegetable toppings, and, being 50 percent larger than the mini subs, a lot more substance.

Other Picks

Oven-Roasted Chicken Breast Sub
6"

310 calories
5 g fat (1.5 g saturated)
830 mg sodium

Steak & Cheese
6"

400 calories
12 g fat (6 g saturated)
1,110 mg sodium

Chili Con Carne

290 calories
8 g fat (3.5 g saturated)
990 mg sodium
12 g fiber

370 calories
22.5 g fat
(7 g saturated)
720 mg sodium

Not That!

Tuna Mini Sub

Approx. 4" with cheese on a white bun

This tuna sub suffers the same fat-tinged, mayo-bound fate of nearly every other tuna sandwich in America.

Other Passes

410 calories
10 g fat (3 g saturated)
1,070 mg sodium

Chicken Breast Wrap

560 calories
24 g fat (11 g saturated)
1,590 mg sodium

Meatball Marinara
6"

200 calories
12 g fat (5 g saturated)
1,180 mg sodium
2 g fiber

Golden Broccoli & Cheese Soup

Genius PARENT TRICK

Use the custom-sub shtick to your advantage. Load your kid up on veggies and you can easily knock out a couple servings for the day. Push for tomatoes, olives, sweet banana peppers, and spinach leaves.

SMART SIDES

Raisins
One little-known benefit of raisins is that they help fight cavities. Raisins contain oleanolic acid, a phytonutrient that kills the cavity-causing bacteria inside the mouth.

SUGAR SPIKES

Sweet Onion Chicken Teriyaki Sandwich (6")

The Impact: 19 g sugars

Do you really want five teaspoons of sugar dumped on your sandwich—especially one that Subway considers a weight-loss option?

T.G.I. Friday's

REPORT CARD **F**

We do applaud Friday's efforts to offer reduced portion sizes for high-calorie bombs, but we don't approve of their reluctance to provide hard data on any of their dishes. Between the array of deep-fried starters and mammoth sandwiches, it's clear they have something to hide.

SURVIVAL STRATEGY
The Lighter Side of Fridays contains five items with approximately "10 grams of fat and 500 calories." It's a sorry attempt at transparency, but until they offer real data, it's the best option.

GUILTY PLEASURES

Zen Chicken Pot Stickers

330 calories, 16 g fat (6 g saturated), 560 mg sodium

Dumplings normally get the pan- or deep-fried treatment, so your gut will relish Friday's less-fattening, fire-grilled version. Plus the veggie stuffing and pico de gallo on top help bring serenity to this tasty Asian treat.

Eat This

Half Rack of Ribs

500 calories
18 g fat
650 mg sodium

One of the few times you'll ever find ribs on the *Eat This* page, partly because much of the rest of the menu is so lackluster. Be extra careful with sides: Forget about the fries and ranch-accompanied salad and carrots and go with the mandarin oranges.

Because T.G.I. Friday's doesn't offer nutritional information to its customers, many of the numbers on this page are estimates drawn from independent research and consultation with nutritionists in order to help you determine what the restaurant is feeding your child.

Other Picks

Dragonfire Chicken
500 calories
10 g fat
825 mg sodium

Kid's Mac & Cheese
240 calories
7 g fat
770 mg sodium

Kid's Sherbet
150 calories
0 g fat
22 g sugars

1,430 calories
82 g fat
1,450 mg sodium

Not That!

Loaded Potato Skins

(½ order)

Even a half order of these kiddie favorites means nearly an entire day's worth of calories for your child.

76

The percentage of 300 chefs recently surveyed who felt that they were serving regular-size portions of steak and pasta. In reality, the average serving was 2 to 4 times bigger than the government-recommended portion size!

UNHAPPY MEALS

Peruvian Herb Roasted Chicken

1,320 calories

In real life, roasted chicken is a reliably nutritious meal for busy parents the world over, but whichever Friday's chef crossed the equator to drag back this monstrous bird should lose his job. The restaurant manages to turn a reliably nutritious meal into the caloric equivalent of six scoops of ice cream.

Other Passes

1,360 calories
78 g fat
1,890 mg sodium

Friday's Chicken Sandwich

600 calories
20 g fat
1,100 mg sodium

Kid's Spaghetti

310 calories
14 g fat
28 g sugars

Kid's Ice Cream

Taco Bell

REPORT CARD
C

Diners live and die by the mix-and-match opportunities Taco Bell presents, where any two items can either be a reasonable 400-calorie meal or a 900-calorie saturated-fat fest.

SURVIVAL STRATEGY
Cut out the big-ticket items like Mexican Pizzas and Nachos and direct your kid's attention to the crunchy tacos, bean burritos, and anything on the Fresco menu.

HIDDEN DANGER
Fiesta Taco Salad

Hearing that your kid actually wants to eat salad might sound exciting at first, but not when that salad packs as much fat as 15 slices of bacon. Here's a no-fail rule to establish in your family: Nothing is to be eaten out of oversize fried tortilla bowls.

840 calories, 45 g fat (11 g saturated, 1.5 g trans), 1,780 mg sodium

Eat This

Fresco Crunchy Beef Tacos
(2)

300 calories
16 g fat
(5 g saturated)
740 mg sodium

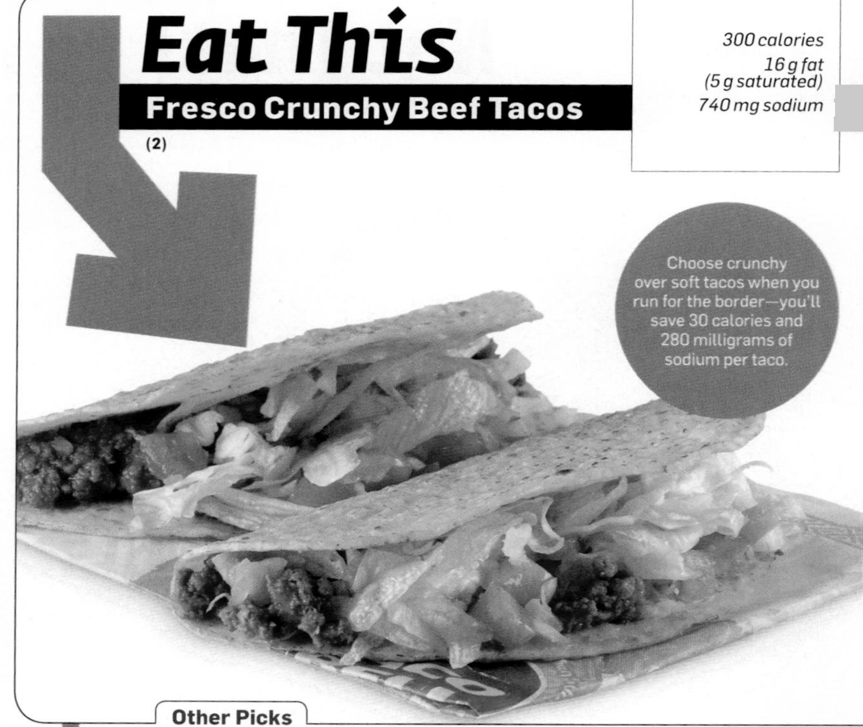

Choose crunchy over soft tacos when you run for the border—you'll save 30 calories and 280 milligrams of sodium per taco.

Other Picks

Steak Gordita
Nacho Cheese

270 calories
12 g fat (2 g saturated, 1 g trans)
680 mg sodium

Chicken Grilled Taquitos

310 calories
11 g fat (4.5 g saturated)
980 mg sodium

Pintos 'n Cheese

160 calories
6 g fat (3 g saturated)
670 mg sodium

540 calories
28 g fat (8 g saturated)
1,640 mg sodium

Not That!

Ranchero Chicken Soft Tacos

(2)

These tacos may seem similar, but with the soft tacos you're getting nearly twice the calories, 75 percent more fat, and more than double the sodium.

Other Passes

340 calories
19 g fat (3.5 g saturated, 2.5 g trans)
670 mg sodium

Steak Chalupa
Nacho Cheese

520 calories
28 g fat (12 g saturated)
1,420 mg sodium

Chicken Quesadilla

290 calories
17 g fat (4 g saturated)
830 mg sodium

Cheesy Fiesta Potatoes

Genius PARENT TRICK

Defang this cheesy, saucy menu by ordering everything Fresco style. This simple, free designation substitutes the cheese and sauce for Fiesta Salsa—a blend of diced tomatoes, onions, and cilantro. Most items outside the Fresco Menu can still be ordered this way.

UNHAPPY MEALS

Grilled Beef Stuft Burrito

680 calories, 30 g fat (10 g saturated, 1 g trans), 2,120 mg sodium

This burrito earns its big figures on sheer size; it's more than twice as big as a chalupa. When it comes to feeding your kids on the fly, remember to stick with the rational rations.

Uno Chicago Grill

REPORT CARD

C-

The fact that Uno invented deep-dish pizza, one of the most fat- and calorie-dense foods on the planet, merits an automatic F, but we'll look past that to the more reasonable flat-bread pizzas and the handful of redeeming entrées, like the Kid's Grilled Chicken and the Kid's Pasta.

SURVIVAL STRATEGY

Do not, under any circumstances, order deep-dish pizza—a single "individual" pizza can house up to 2,300 calories. Instead, split a couple of flatbread pies and large house salads with the family.

SUGAR SPIKES

Uno Deep Dish Sundae (1/2)

The Impact: 68 g sugars

This dessert slaps a load of sugar onto the end of the meal, not to mention 700 calories and 18 grams of saturated fat. If you plan to order indulgences like this, split them with as many people as you can wrangle over to the table.

Eat This

Cheese & Tomato Flatbread Pizza

(1/2) and House Side Salad with fat-free vinaigrette

420 calories
15 g fat (7.5 g saturated)
1,170 mg sodium

The difference between this pizza and the deep-dish cheese pizza is 360 calories per serving. Balance a slice of Uno's admirable thin crust with a side salad; just be sure to avoid the creamy dressings like ranch, blue cheese, and Caesar.

Other Picks

Grilled & Skewered BBQ Shrimp
and brown rice with Craisins® and mango

430 calories
7 g fat (0.5 g saturated)
1,085 mg sodium

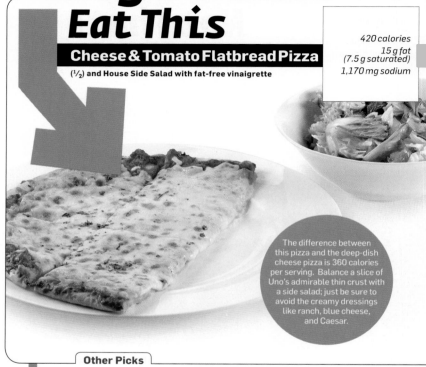

Kid's Grilled Chicken

180 calories
6 g fat (0 g saturated)
840 mg sodium

Kid's Slush

140 calories
0 g fat
32 g sugars

Not That!

Kid's Cheese Pizza

700 calories
26 g fat (12 g saturated)
1,640 mg sodium

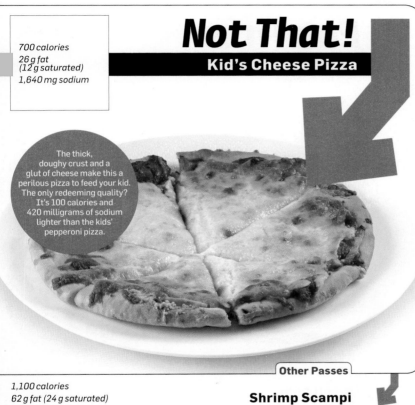

The thick, doughy crust and a glut of cheese make this a perilous pizza to feed your kid. The only redeeming quality? It's 100 calories and 420 milligrams of sodium lighter than the kids' pepperoni pizza.

Other Passes

1,100 calories
62 g fat (24 g saturated)
1,640 mg sodium

Shrimp Scampi

320 calories
20 g fat (4 g saturated)
780 mg sodium

Kid's Chicken Caesar Salad

840 calories
36 g fat (18 g saturated)
98 g sugars

Kid's Sundae

1.8

The number of times around the world Uno Chicago Grill could wrap the pasta it sells each year.

MENU DECODER

PHASE: A mix of partially hydrogenated soybean oil and artificial flavoring that Uno uses to season the Kid's Corn. If they go for the corn, ask for the corn Phase-free.

SMART SIDES

Brown Rice with Craisins® and Mango

170 calories, 5 g fat (0.5 g saturated), 30 g carbohydrates

Whole grains are the foundation of good nutrition, and this brown-rice dish makes whole grains taste delicious. It's sweetened with real fruit, and a splash of olive oil gives it a rich flavor and a healthy dose of omega-3s.

Wendy's

Wendy's official kid's menu may be a tiny concession to the little ones, but it is free of the belly-busters that hamper most menus. Plus, the rest of the menu offers ample options for a growing kid; a cup of chili and a baked potato, chicken salad, even a burger with a cup of mandarin oranges all qualify as nutritionally commendable meals.

SURVIVAL STRATEGY
The Super Value Menu® is full of solid choices, as long as you avoid the 480-calorie add-on of fries and a regular soft drink.

SUGAR SPIKES

Vanilla Frosty™ Float with Coca-Cola®

The Impact:
69 g sugars

This is a cloying combination of two hyper-sweetened drinks, so you can't expect the outcome to be good. Settle for a junior Frosty and cut two-thirds of the sugar. If your kid wants dessert, stick to the classic chocolate Frosty, junior-size, for 160 calories and 21 grams of sugar.

Eat This

Single Burger with Everything

430 calories
20 g fat
7 g saturated)
870 mg sodium

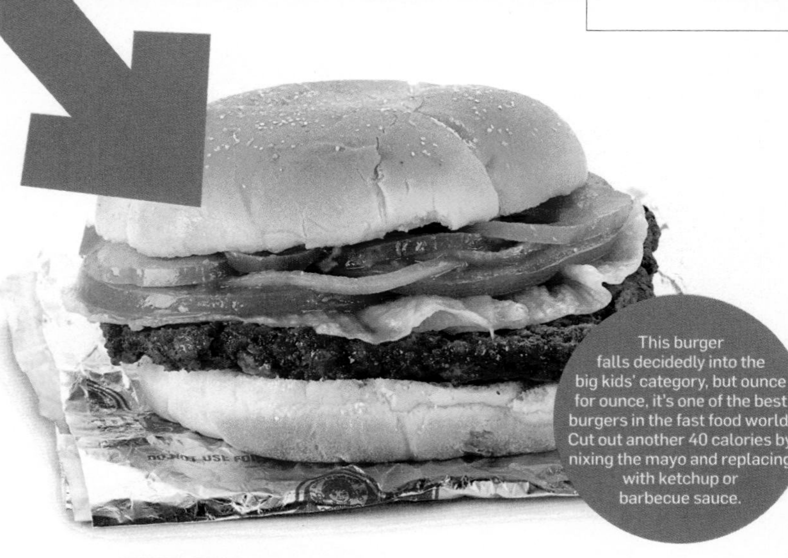

This burger falls decidedly into the big kids' category, but ounce for ounce, it's one of the best burgers in the fast food world. Cut out another 40 calories by nixing the mayo and replacing with ketchup or barbecue sauce.

Other Picks

Small Chili
with a broccoli and cheese baked potato

540 calories
8 g fat (3.5 g saturated)
1,240 mg sodium

Crispy Chicken Sandwich

330 calories
14 g fat (2.5 g saturated)
670 mg sodium

Jr. Cheeseburger

270 calories
11 g fat (5 g saturated)
690 mg sodium

540 calories
25 g fat
(8 g saturated)
1,360 mg sodium

Not That!

Chicken Club Sandwich

Chicken doesn't always trump beef, especially when it's dressed with bacon and cheese. At 320 calories, the Ultimate Chicken Grill sandwich is the best chicken sandwich on the menu.

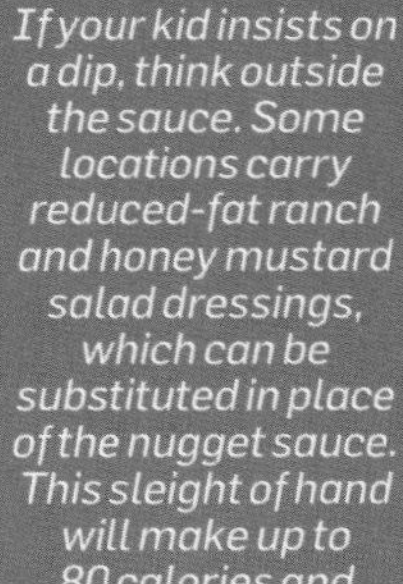

If your kid insists on a dip, think outside the sauce. Some locations carry reduced-fat ranch and honey mustard salad dressings, which can be substituted in place of the nugget sauce. This sleight of hand will make up to 80 calories and 13 grams of fat disappear from your child's meal.

Other Passes

670 calories
39 g fat (16.5 g saturated, 1.5 g trans)
1,530 mg sodium

Southwest Taco Salad
with reduced fat sour cream

360 calories
27 g fat (5 g saturated)
740 mg sodium

Crispy Chicken Nuggets
(5 pieces) with Honey Mustard Nuggets Sauce

320 calories
16 g fat (4.5 g saturated)
860 mg sodium

Homestyle Chicken Go Wrap

SAUCE DECODER
(1 OZ EACH)

- **ZESTY ONION:** 150 calories, 15 g fat (2.5 g saturated)
- **RANCH:** 140 calories, 15 g fat (2.5 g saturated)
- **HONEY MUSTARD:** 90 calories, 6 g fat (1 g saturated)
- **BUFFALO:** 80 calories, 8 g fat (1.5 g saturated)
- **SWEET & SOUR:** 45 calories, 0 g fat
- **BARBECUE:** 40 calories, 0 g fat

MENU DECODER

Your Ticket to Eat Anywhere

Maybe your family doesn't eat out at chain restaurants, or maybe you're fortunate enough to live in a city where your eating options extend beyond the world of Big Macs and Bloomin' Onions. Or maybe you just like to balance your Taco Bell with tuna rolls. Either way, parents need to know exactly what they're getting into when they decide to eat out, whether the restaurant of choice is a mom-and-pop pizza parlor or a neighborhood sushi joint.

We know what you're thinking: There's no way my kid's going to eat at a sushi restaurant. While she might not be ready for the raw sea urchin nigiri or the fugu-tasting menu, there are a surprising number of great options at sushi restaurants, each perfectly suited to a young eater's taste buds. Same goes for Indian, Spanish, Thai, and all of the other great cuisines you tend to ignore when a chicken nugget-craving crew of youngsters is in tow.

These cuisines—increasingly available everywhere from suburban strip malls to the far-flung corners of this country—are built around a variety of vegetables, lean proteins, and antioxidant-packed spices and flavor agents that make them a pleasure to eat and a boon to your kid's overall health.

It would be a shame to miss out on the melting pot of menus this country has to offer. Take a chance from time to time. That way, your kids get to explore and appreciate new foods from an early age, reaping the culinary and nutritional benefits of a well-rounded eater. And you get a break from the stovetop and the drive-thru window. Everybody wins.

In this chapter, we'll show you how to navigate a world of cuisine and become master of your children's nutritional universe.

Learn how to eat well and shed pounds at your favorite neighborhood restaurants with the Ultimate Menu Decoder interactive tool at ***eatthis.com***

5 Ways to Win Over a Picky Eater

Exasperated moms and dads will try anything to win over a finicky eater: begging, bribing, even sneaking new foods into their kids' diets in hopes of a breakthrough at the dinner table. Thwarted and dejected, they form support groups and commiserate over chicken-finger lust and mac-and-cheese mania.

But it doesn't have to be this way. True, kids aren't born with an innate desire to devour lima beans and Dover sole, but parents have tools for teasing out their kids' more sophisticated taste buds. Follow these five simple rules and you'll be well on your way to raising an adventurous eater.

1. **START YOUNG.** Let your child cruise through his early years with nary a vegetable on his fork and you'll have raised a picky eater for life.
2. **HONE THE TASTE BUDS AT HOME.** Kids are more likely to try new foods in a familiar setting. Once they've seen or tasted something mom or dad has cooked for them, they'll be more willing to seek it out on a restaurant menu.
3. **BUILD OFF OF FAMILIAR FOODS.** Barbecued chicken is a staple in most American homes, so use that as a jumping-off point for exploring new cuisines. Indians have tandoori chicken, Thais have chicken satay, and the Japanese have chicken teriyaki—all twists on that comfortable kid-favorite with hints of exotic flavors. By accustoming their taste buds to foreign flavors with familiar vehicles, you'll slowly open up new doors.
4. **PLAY "FIRST BITE, LAST BITE."** In his book *The Parking Lot Rules and 75 Other Ideas for Raising Children*, author Tom Sturges suggests this simple strategy: To get a child to try a new food, promise him he can have the last bite of your dessert if he tries a first bite of a new food. Whether it's poached salmon or simply a strange new fruit, he doesn't need to eat the whole thing, he just needs to try the first bite. Maybe he'll hate it, but who knows? Maybe he'll discover something new, healthy, and delicious!
5. **DON'T INSULT THEIR TASTE BUDS.** It's true, kids have sensitive palates, and it's important to avoid excess spice on your way to introducing them to new flavors. But that doesn't mean food should be boring. A splash of soy sauce, a touch of Tabasco, or a bit of balsamic vinegar could be the difference between outright rejection and love at first bite.

Breakfast Diner

HOME FRIES

The equivalent of starting your day with a big plate of French fries. Stick with the grits, or sub in fresh fruit instead —many diners will do it free of charge.

TOAST

Insist that all toast brought to the table be of the wheat variety. One of the main nutrients you and your kids need for breakfast is belly-filling fiber, and making the simple switch from white to wheat will give you a much-needed 5-gram fiber boost.

FRENCH TOAST, PANCAKES, AND WAFFLES

Each of these three breakfast favorites makes for a less-than-ideal start to your kid's day. That's because all are based on refined flour, and all eventually get covered in sugary syrup. The surge of quick-burning carbohydrates spikes blood sugar and signals the body to start storing fat. And when the blood sugar levels come crashing down, so do your kid's energy levels and attention span.

BACON OR SAUSAGE

This might seem like an insignificant decision, since most people consider both of these breakfast meats to be equally treacherous. The truth is, two sausage links have about 160 calories and 12 grams of fat, whereas two strips of bacon contain 80 calories and 8 grams of fat.

BREAKFAST SPECIALS

Our value-oriented breakfast specials come with your choice coffee or tea and a small juice.

MT. AIRY
TWO EGGS, ANY STYLE, with your choice of breakfast meat, home fries, grits or white cheddar grits. White, wheat or rye toast. 7.95
Add Bagel or English muffin for .... $.50.

WAYNE JUNCTION
CLASSIC EGGS BENEDICT Grilled Canadian bacon served under poached eggs and rich Hollandaise neatly stacked on a toasted English muffin. Comes with your choice of home fries, grits or white cheddar grits. 8.95

WYNDMOOR
THREE THICK-CUT SLICES OF CINNAMON-RAISIN CHALLAH FRENCH TOAST with your choice of breakfast meat. Served dusted with powdered sugar. 7.95

GRAVERS
THREE FLUFFY BUTTERMILK PANCAKES with your choice of breakfast meat 7.45
Add bananas, blueberries or strawberries 1.00

UPSAL
GOLDEN MALTED BELGIAN WAFFLE with your choice of breakfast meat. 7.45
...dd bananas, blueberries or strawberries and whipped cream 1.00

...MARTIN'S
...HONEY-BUCKWHEAT PANCAKES
...ith bananas and served with your choice of breakfast meat. 8.50
...eberries or chocolate chips 1.00

FRENCH TOAST, PANCAKES, WAFFLES

cooked on our griddle and served with butter and syrup.
Top your griddles with bananas, blueberries, chocolate chips or strawberry topping for 1.00

...NCAKES
...STACK (3)
...RT STACK (2)
...TERMILK PANCAKES
...Stack 4.25
...t Stack 3.75
...EY BUCKWHEAT PANCAKES
...Stack 5.50
...t Stack 4.75
...OLE GRAIN PANCAKES
...Stack 5.50
...t Stack 4.75

FRENCH TOAST
TEXAS STYLE FRENCH TOAST
Full Stack 3.50
Short Stack 2........ 2.75

BELGIAN WAFFLE
BELGIAN WAFFLE 3.50

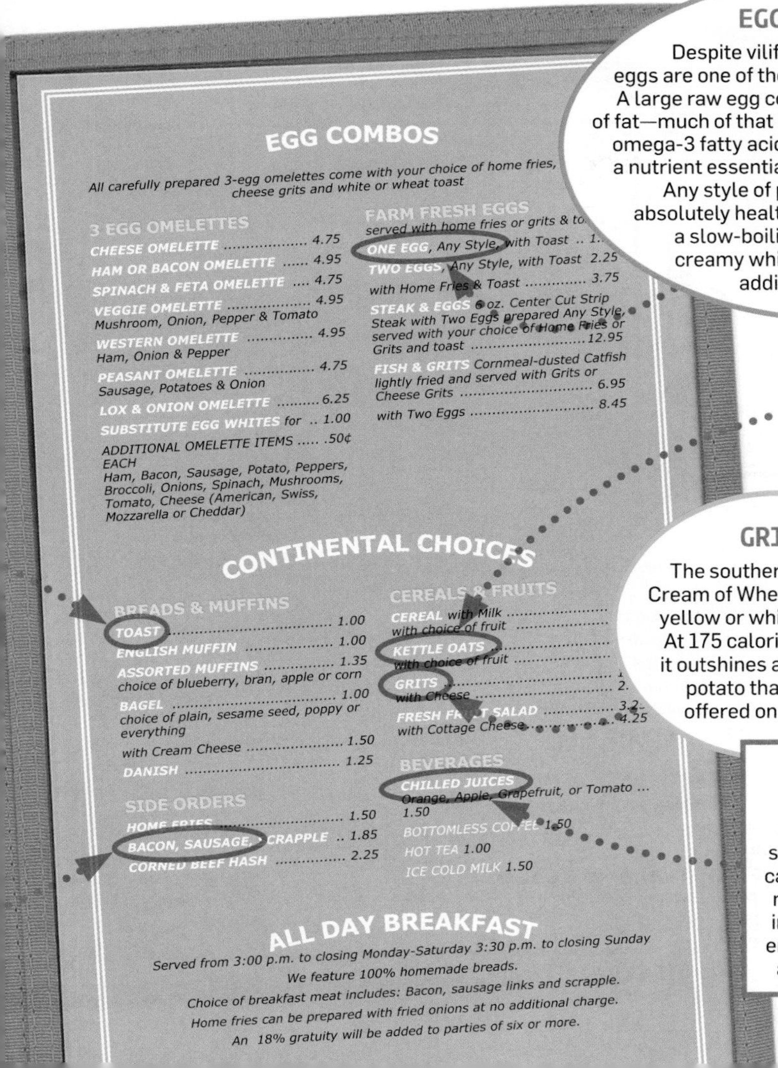

EGG COMBOS

All carefully prepared 3-egg omelettes come with your choice of home fries, cheese grits and white or wheat toast

3 EGG OMELETTES

CHEESE OMELETTE 4.75
HAM OR BACON OMELETTE 4.95
SPINACH & FETA OMELETTE 4.75
VEGGIE OMELETTE 4.95
Mushroom, Onion, Pepper & Tomato
WESTERN OMELETTE 4.95
Ham, Onion & Pepper
PEASANT OMELETTE 4.75
Sausage, Potatoes & Onion
LOX & ONION OMELETTE 6.25
SUBSTITUTE EGG WHITES for .. 1.00
ADDITIONAL OMELETTE ITEMS ..... .50¢ EACH
Ham, Bacon, Sausage, Potato, Peppers, Broccoli, Onions, Spinach, Mushrooms, Tomato, Cheese (American, Swiss, Mozzarella or Cheddar)

FARM FRESH EGGS

served with home fries or grits & to...

ONE EGG, Any Style, with Toast .. 1...
TWO EGGS, Any Style, with Toast 2.25
with Home Fries & Toast 3.75
STEAK & EGGS 6 oz. Center Cut Strip Steak with Two Eggs prepared Any Style, served with your choice of Home Fries or Grits and toast 12.95
FISH & GRITS Cornmeal-dusted Catfish lightly fried and served with Grits or Cheese Grits 6.95
with Two Eggs 8.45

CONTINENTAL CHOICES

BREADS & MUFFINS

TOAST 1.00
ENGLISH MUFFIN 1.00
ASSORTED MUFFINS 1.35
choice of blueberry, bran, apple or corn
BAGEL 1.00
choice of plain, sesame seed, poppy or everything
with Cream Cheese 1.50
DANISH 1.25

SIDE ORDERS

HOME FRIES 1.50
BACON, SAUSAGE, SCRAPPLE .. 1.85
CORNED BEEF HASH 2.25

CEREALS & FRUITS

CEREAL with Milk ....
with choice of fruit ....
KETTLE OATS ....
with choice of fruit ....
GRITS .... 1...
with Cheese .... 2.
FRESH FRUIT SALAD .... 3.2...
with Cottage Cheese 4.25

BEVERAGES

CHILLED JUICES
Orange, Apple, Grapefruit, or Tomato ... 1.50
BOTTOMLESS COFFEE 1.50
HOT TEA 1.00
ICE COLD MILK 1.50

ALL DAY BREAKFAST

Served from 3:00 p.m. to closing Monday-Saturday 3:30 p.m. to closing Sunday
We feature 100% homemade breads.
Choice of breakfast meat includes: Bacon, sausage links and scrapple.
Home fries can be prepared with fried onions at no additional charge.
An 18% gratuity will be added to parties of six or more.

EGGS, ANY STYLE

Despite vilification by the food police, eggs are one of the healthiest foods on the planet. A large raw egg contains 75 calories and 5 grams of fat—much of that healthy, unsaturated fat, including omega-3 fatty acids. Plus, eggs are rich in choline, a nutrient essential to brain and memory function. Any style of preparation will do, but the absolutely healthiest choice here is poaching, a slow-boiling method that produces creamy whites and yolks without the addition of cooking fat.

OATMEAL

The best choice on the menu. Oats are low in fat and sodium and contain plenty of soluble fiber, which helps lower bad cholesterol and regulate blood sugar levels.

GRITS

The southern version of Cream of Wheat®, made with yellow or white cornmeal. At 175 calories for a side, it outshines any breakfast potato that might be offered on the menu.

FRESHLY SQUEEZED OJ

Yes, it might constitute a serving of fruit for your child, but that serving comes with as much as 150 calories and 35 grams of sugar. That much sugar that early in the morning might provide an initial surge of energy but it eventually gives way to a good old-fashioned sugar crash.

Pizzeria

BREADSTICKS

Skip 'em. First of all, you're already eating pizza, so what's the need for another version of oil-soaked bread? On top of that, the tub of garlic sauce the pizza places so thoughtfully provide for dipping is really just a slurry of trans fat–bearing partially hydrogenated oils. That one tub has as many calories as two slices of pizza. Which would you prefer?

MOZZARELLA STICKS

Few things on this planet are worse for you than breaded and fried cheese. They might be a kid favorite, but at 125 calories and a heap of saturated fat per small stick, they are a parent's nightmare. Curb the cheese craving with an 80-calorie string cheese.

CALZONE

These football-size dough pockets hold an ungodly amount of cheese and toppings; even a small hunk of calzone could run up to 500 calories and 25 grams of fat. If it's cheese and sauce you seek, stick to pizza.

KIDS' PIZZA

It's almost always better to give your kids a slice or two from a large pizza than it is to order the kids' pizza. That's because kids' portions are often the same exact serving as a personal pizza that any adult might order on his or her own—and those pack anywhere between 550 and 750 calories.

APPETIZERS & SIDES

Breadsticks *A 12" roll covered with fresh garlic. Served with garlic dipping sauce. 2.99*

French Fries *A large order of our delicious golden fries. 3.29*

Onion Rings *A large order of our golden battered onion rings. 3.99*

Mozzarella Sticks *Six lightly seasoned breaded mozzarella sticks served with marinara sauce. 8.99*

Cheese Fries *A large order of fries, smothered in cheese sauce 3.79*

Buffalo Wings *Tender Chicken wings, golden fried, then tossed in buffalo sauce. Served with blue cheese dressing. (24) 12.49*

OUR SPECIALS

Red or White Pie *Red, Our version of the traditional Neapolitan, cheese pizza. White, A delicious blend of fresh garlic, oregano, Romano, Mozzarella, and our special white herb sauce! 9.59*

Calzone *Traditional style with pepperoni, sausage, meatballs, peppers, onions, fresh garlic, Romano and Mozzarella all wrapped up in our homemade pizza dough! 11.59*

KIDS MENU

Mac 'n' Cheese *Just like Mom makes. 4.99*

Kids Pizza *A 5" thin crust cheese pizza with your choice of dipping sauce. 5.99*

Chicken Fingers *Breaded chicken breast tenderloins, fried to golden brown perfection. Served with your choice of dipping sauce. 4.99 with French Fries 5.99*

Burger and Fries *A quarter-pound meat patty and cheddar cheese served with French Fries 5.99*

TOPPING TOTEM POLE

(nutritional info is for one medium slice)

- **Mushrooms/Onions/Olives/Tomatoes/Peppers:** ~5 cal/0 g fat
- **Ham:** 10 calories, 1 g fat (0 g saturated)
- **Chicken:** 20 calories, 1 g fat (0 g saturated)
- **Ground beef:** 30 calories, 2 g fat (1 g saturated)
- **Extra cheese:** 40 calories, 3 g fat (1.5 g saturated)
- **Sausage:** 50 calories, 3.5 g fat (2 g saturated)
- **Pepperoni:** 50 calories, 4 g fat (2 g saturated)

OUR PIZZA PIES

3 Cheese Pizza *Mozzarella, Romano, and Gruyere with our marinara*

Pizza Marinara *No Cheese, Vegan option! 8.59*

Veggie Lovers Pizza *A mountain of fresh vegetables piled high onto ou*

Meat Lovers Pizza *5 toppings - Bacon, Beef, Ham, Pepperoni, and Sausage*

The Cheese Steak Pizza *with Fresh Grilled Rib Eye Steak, Cheese, Mushrooms & Onions 15.59*

Sicilian Pizza *with tomatoes, onion, sausage, anchovies, parmesan and herbs 15.99*

Hawaiian Style Pizza *A red pie topped with tender diced ham & juicy pineapple chunks 12.99*

Buffalo Chicken *A red pie topped with tender cooked chicken breast, marinated in our own special buffalo sauce. 13.59*

Thick Crust American *A combination of ground beef, Cheddar cheese, tomatoes, onions and peppers with sauce on top 11.59*

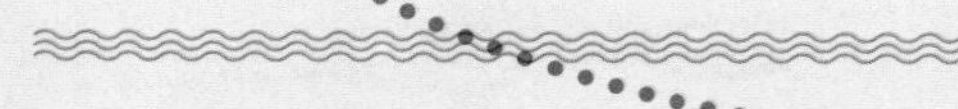

OLD WORLD SALADS

House Salad *Fresh chopped Romaine lettuce, red onions, black olives & tomatoes. with blue cheese, ranch or red wine vinaigrette 5.50*

Caesar Salad *Fresh chopped Romaine lettuce, croutons, black olives, and shredded parmesan cheese with Caesar dressing served on the side 6.50*

Antipasto Salad *Quality Italian meats & cheese over a bed of romaine lettuce topped with olives, onions, roasted peppers, shredded parmesan & red wine vinaigrette 8.50*

Chicken and Veggie Salad *our house salad with broccoli, carrots, celery, cucumbers topped with seasoned, grilled chicken breast. 8.50*

Buffalo Chicken Salad *Breaded chicken tenderloin strips, tossed in buffalo sauce, on top of our house salad. 8.50*

VEGGIE PIZZA

Consider this a vegetable-eaters starter kit, complete with enough cheese and sauce to make those veggies go down easier. Seriously, considering the lack of vegetables in most kids' diets, you need to take advantage of any opportunity to slip in a serving of produce.

SICILIAN PIZZA

Don't be fooled by the authentic-sounding place of origin: This is just a code word for a thick, oily crust with little of the stuff—marinara, vegetables—that your kid actually needs.

THICK CRUST

Not only does the extra dough mean a 75-calorie premium on every slice, it also lends the pizza the structural integrity to withstand a heavier bombardment of toppings. In total, figure double the calories for thick over thin crust.

CHICKEN AND BROCCOLI

Broccoli contains sulforaphane and chicken is packed with selenium. While both have been shown to be potent cancer- and disease-fighters on their own, studies show that eating the two together may multiply their beneficial effects by as much as 13 times.

Family Restaurant

SECRET SAUCE

There's no secret here: Nearly every mysterious sauce across this great land consists of 80 percent mayonnaise and 20 percent ketchup, usually with a smattering of chopped pickles thrown in. Replace it with decidedly less-secretive barbecue sauce and save 100 calories.

FRENCH DIP

We have no idea what makes this sandwich French—it was invented in Los Angeles—but it's a surprisingly safe choice. Roast beef is nearly every bit as lean as roast turkey, and the beef stock dipping sauce only adds about 25 calories to the total.

CHICKEN SANDWICH

Not always as safe as it seems. An array of variables can make this either the healthiest choice on the menu or one of the most deceptively bad. Here's the quick checklist: Is it fried? Is there mayo or ranch? Does it come with cheese? Answer yes to more than one of these questions, and your kid may as well eat a cheeseburger.

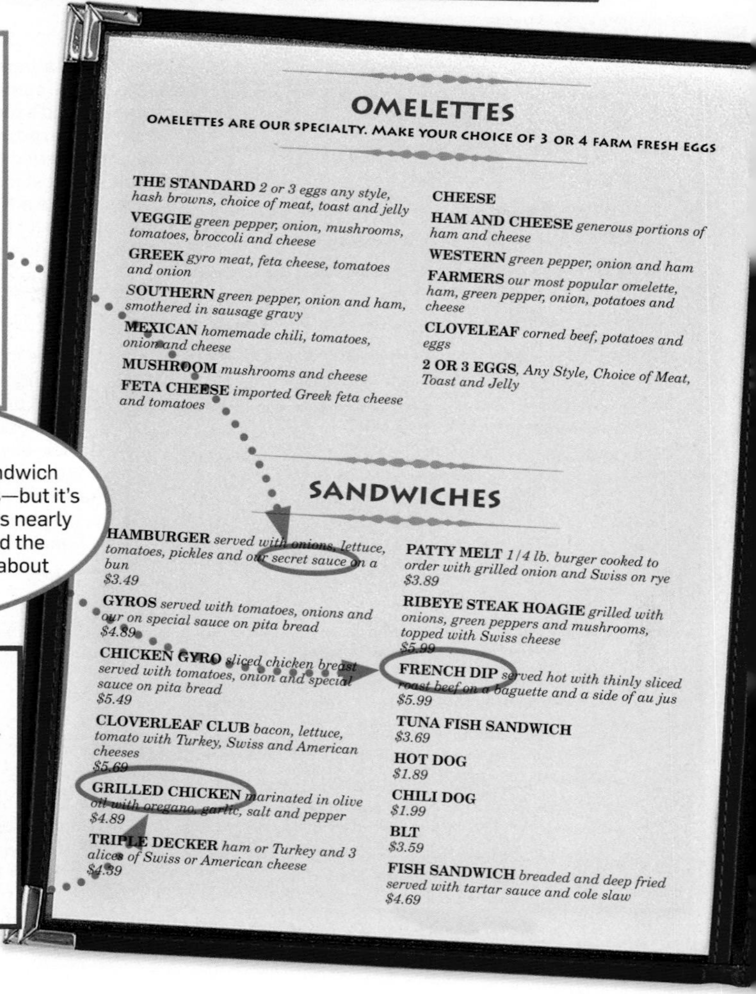

OMELETTES

OMELETTES ARE OUR SPECIALTY. MAKE YOUR CHOICE OF 3 OR 4 FARM FRESH EGGS

THE STANDARD *2 or 3 eggs any style, hash browns, choice of meat, toast and jelly*

VEGGIE *green pepper, onion, mushrooms, tomatoes, broccoli and cheese*

GREEK *gyro meat, feta cheese, tomatoes and onion*

SOUTHERN *green pepper, onion and ham, smothered in sausage gravy*

MEXICAN *homemade chili, tomatoes, onion and cheese*

MUSHROOM *mushrooms and cheese*

FETA CHEESE *imported Greek feta cheese and tomatoes*

CHEESE

HAM AND CHEESE *generous portions of ham and cheese*

WESTERN *green pepper, onion and ham*

FARMERS *our most popular omelette, ham, green pepper, onion, potatoes and cheese*

CLOVELEAF *corned beef, potatoes and eggs*

2 OR 3 EGGS, *Any Style, Choice of Meat, Toast and Jelly*

SANDWICHES

HAMBURGER *served with onions, lettuce, tomatoes, pickles and our secret sauce on a bun*
$3.49

GYROS *served with tomatoes, onions and our on special sauce on pita bread*
$4.89

CHICKEN GYRO *sliced chicken breast served with tomatoes, onion and special sauce on pita bread*
$5.49

CLOVERLEAF CLUB *bacon, lettuce, tomato with Turkey, Swiss and American cheeses*
$5.69

GRILLED CHICKEN *marinated in olive oil with oregano, garlic, salt and pepper*
$4.89

TRIPLE DECKER *ham or Turkey and 3 alices of Swiss or American cheese*
$4.39

PATTY MELT *1/4 lb. burger cooked to order with grilled onion and Swiss on rye*
$3.89

RIBEYE STEAK HOAGIE *grilled with onions, green peppers and mushrooms, topped with Swiss cheese*
$5.99

FRENCH DIP *served hot with thinly sliced roast beef on a baguette and a side of au jus*
$5.99

TUNA FISH SANDWICH
$3.69

HOT DOG
$1.89

CHILI DOG
$1.99

BLT
$3.59

FISH SANDWICH *breaded and deep fried served with tartar sauce and cole slaw*
$4.69

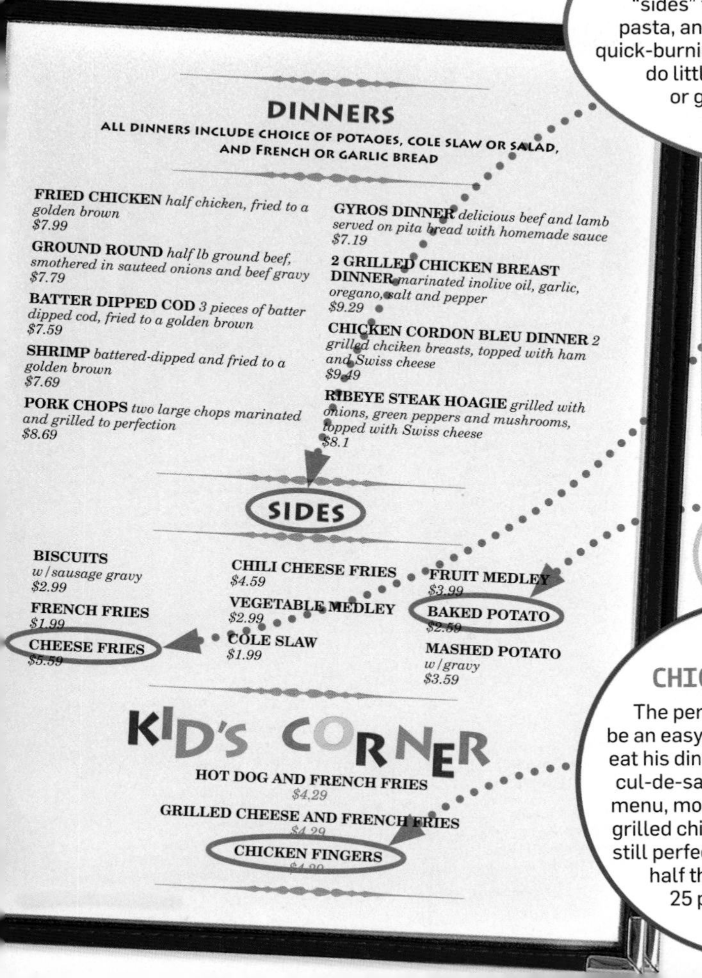

DINNERS

ALL DINNERS INCLUDE CHOICE OF POTAOES, COLE SLAW OR SALAD, AND FRENCH OR GARLIC BREAD

FRIED CHICKEN *half chicken, fried to a golden brown*
$7.99

GROUND ROUND *half lb ground beef, smothered in sauteed onions and beef gravy*
$7.79

BATTER DIPPED COD *3 pieces of batter dipped cod, fried to a golden brown*
$7.59

SHRIMP *battered-dipped and fried to a golden brown*
$7.69

PORK CHOPS *two large chops marinated and grilled to perfection*
$8.69

GYROS DINNER *delicious beef and lamb served on pita bread with homemade sauce*
$7.19

2 GRILLED CHICKEN BREAST DINNER *marinated inolive oil, garlic, oregano, salt and pepper*
$9.29

CHICKEN CORDON BLEU DINNER *2 grilled chciken breasts, topped with ham and Swiss cheese*
$9.49

RIBEYE STEAK HOAGIE *grilled with onions, green peppers and mushrooms, topped with Swiss cheese*
$8.1

SIDES

BISCUITS
w/sausage gravy
$2.99

FRENCH FRIES
$1.99

CHEESE FRIES
$5.59

CHILI CHEESE FRIES
$4.59

VEGETABLE MEDLEY
$2.99

COLE SLAW
$1.99

FRUIT MEDLEY
$3.99

BAKED POTATO
$2.59

MASHED POTATO
w/gravy
$3.59

KID'S CORNER

HOT DOG AND FRENCH FRIES
$4.29

GRILLED CHEESE AND FRENCH FRIES
$4.29

CHICKEN FINGERS
$4.29

SIDES

When it comes to eating at American-style family restaurants, nutritional battles are won and lost on the "sides" front. As a rule, starches—including rice, pasta, and potato dishes—are losers, packed full of quick-burning carbohydrates that spike blood sugar and do little to fill your kids up. Steamed, roasted, or grilled vegetables; fresh fruit; or even applesauce are the winners in the bunch.

CHEESE FRIES

Pretty much the worst thing anyone—kid or parent—can put in his or her body. A single appetizer-size order with a side of ranch is the caloric equivalent of 14 Taco Bell® beef tacos. Even if you split an order among four people, you're still looking at nearly 700 calories and 40 grams of fat per serving.

BAKED POTATO

Loaded baked potatoes are too caloric to be considered a healthy side, but a jacket stuffed with steamed broccoli and a bit of melted cheese makes a filling, nutritious, 400-calorie meal for a kid.

CHICKEN FINGERS

The perennial favorite might be an easy way to get your child to eat his dinner, but it's a nutritional cul-de-sac. Even if it's not on the menu, most kitchens will cook up grilled chicken fingers, which are still perfect for dunking but carry half the calories and only 25 percent of the fat.

Chinese Takeout

DUMPLINGS

Filled with vegetables, chicken, pork, or some combination thereof, these make a much more suitable start to a meal than the old standby, the egg roll. Just be sure to ask for your dumplings steamed; otherwise they'll come fried in an inch of oil.

SESAME/ORANGE/GENERAL TSO'S

These three popular dishes have a few unfortunate traits in common: They're all fried; they're all covered in a viscous, sugar-spiked sauce; and they're all incredibly appealing to kids. Oh, and at around 1,300 calories and 70 grams of fat per order, they're part of an unholy trinity comprising the worst of the Chinese takeout menu.

KUNG PAO CHICKEN

One of the better options on the menu. Yes, there is still the issue of excessive oil (anything that goes into the wok will have this problem), but its grip on this dish is nowhere near as pronounced as in most others, and it's offset by a slew of vegetables—onions, zucchini, and peppers. If your child is sensitive to spice, ask them to go easy on the dried chiles.

FORTUNE COOKIES

They're not technically Chinese (they were invented in San Francisco), but at a mere 30 calories a serving, they make an authentically safe ending to a meal.

Noodle Corner

HOURS OF OPERATION
11:00AM-12:00 MIDNIGHT
FREE OUTGOING DELIVERY

TEL 245-5896

APPETIZERS

A1. PuPu Plat ter (for 2) $7.25
Egg Rolls, Chicken Fingers, Spareribs, Teriyaki Beef, Chicken Wings, Crab Rangoon
A10. Chicken Fingers $7.25
A2. Mini Pu Pu Platter $9.95
Teriyaki Beef (2), Boneless Spare Ribs, Chicken Wings (2), Crab Rangoon (2), Chicken Teriyaki (2)
A11. Dumplings (Pork or Vegetable) (6) $3.95
A3. Beef Teriyaki (6) $7.55
A12. Crab Rangoon (6) $4.25
A4. Egg Roll (2) $3.75
A13. Dim Sim Siu Mi (6) $4.75
A5. Shanghai Spring Rolls (2) $3.95
A14. Chicken Teriyaki $7.55
A15. Vegetable Egg Rolls(2) $3.95
A7. Chicken Wings (7) $5.95
A8. Fried Shrimps (6) $7.55
A17. Scallion Pancake $7.55
A9. Spareribs $3.95
A18. Boneless Spareribs $7.25

SOUP

n Soup $2.05
d Sour Soup $2.05
rop Soup $1.65
se Vegetable Soup $2.05
use Special Soup $7.55

BEEF

B1. Beef with Green Peppers $9.55
B10. Beef with Mushrooms $10.25
Beef with Broccoli $9.55
Beef in Szechuan Sauce $9.55
Beef with Pea Pods $9.55
Spicy Beef with Peanuts and Peppers $9.55
Crispy Beef with Pea Pods $9.55
Spicy Shredded Beef in Garlic Sauce $9.55
B5. Beef with Pea Pods and Bamboo Shoots $10.25
B14.* Hunan Spiced Beef $9.55
B6. Mongolian Barbecued Beef $10.25
B15.* Beef with Black Bean Sauce $9.55
B7. Beef with Scallions $9.55
B16.* Orange Flavored Beef $10.55
B8. Beef with Chinese Vegetables $9.55
B17.* House Special Lamb $11.95
B9. Sesame Beef $10.95

PORK

P1. Pork with Pea Pods $8.95
P5.* Spicy Double Cooked Pork $8.95
P2. Pork with Broccoli $8.95
P6.* Spicy Shredded Pork in Garlic Sauce $8.95
P3. Pork with Scallions $8.95
P7.* Hunan Pork $8.95
P4. Three Delights with Pork, Shrimp, or Chicken $9.55

POULTRY

C1. Chicken with Cashews $9.05
C12.* Kung Pao Chicken $9.05
C2. Chicken with Pea Pods $9.05
C13.* Tender Chicken w/Black Bean Sauce $9.05
C3. Moo Goo Gai Pan $9.05
C14.* Orange Flavor Chicken $9.75
C4. Eight Treasure Chicken $9.05
C15.* Curried Chicken $9.05
C5. Chicken with Broccoli $9.05
C16.* Jordan Chicken (General Gau's Chicken) $9.75
C17.* Chef's Chicken Delight with Spicy Sesame $9.95
C6. Chicken with Pineapple $9.05
C18.* Sesame Crispy Chicken $9.95
C7.* Spicy Szechuan Chicken with Peanuts $9.05
C19.* Fresh String Beans with Chicken and Beef $9.05

"LIGHT ON THE SAUCE"

You won't see this phrase anywhere on the menu, but it's one you should rely on when ordering Chinese food. Real Chinese food comes lightly sauced, not drowning in a gloppy tide of sugary goo. Employ this phrase for a touch of authenticity and a savings of hundreds of calories for your family.

LUNCHEON SPECIALS

Served daily 11:30 a.m. to 2:30 p.m. (except Sunday & Holidays). Served with choice of Pork Fried Rice or S choice of Hot and Sour Soup, Egg Drop Soup or Wonton Soup. (Soup not included with Take-Out c

1. Chicken Wings (3), Egg Roll $5.25
12.* Spicy Chicken with Peanuts, Spareribs $6.55
2. Teriyaki Beef (2), Chicken Wings (2), Egg Roll .. $5.95
13. Eight Treasure Chicken, Teriyaki Beef $6.75
3. Boneless Spareribs (4), Egg Roll $5.95
14. Chicken with Pea Pods, Chicken Fingers (3) ... $6.25
4. Teriyaki Beef (2), Spareribs (2), Shrimp (2) $6.95
15.* General Tso's Chicken, Egg Roll $7.25
5. Chicken Fingers (4), Chicken Wings (2) $5.55
16. Combo Lo Mein, Boneless Spareribs $5.75
6. Sweet and Sour Pork, Egg Roll $5.25
17.* Shrimp with Garlic Sauce, Egg Roll $7.25
7. Sweet and Sour Chicken, Egg Roll $5.25
18. Shrimp with Lobster Sauce, Egg Roll $7.25
8. Beef with Green Pepper, Egg Roll $6.25
19.* Szechuan String Beans, Egg Roll .... $5.
9. Beef with Broccoli ....
20. Vegetarian's Delight, Egg Roll ....
10.* Spicy Double Cooked Pork, Egg Roll ....
21.* Meatless Chow Mein, Egg Roll .... (Or choice of Chicken, Shrimp, Beef or Pork Ch Mein) .... $4.
11. Pork with Broccoli, Egg Roll $5.75
22.* Shredded Beef Szechuan Style (Or choice of Chicken, Shrimp, or Pork ....

BEEF AND BROCCOLI

Not the healthy dish it pretends to be. That's because the thick brown sauce brings a dangerous amount of saturated fat and sodium to the plate.

WEIGHT WATCHERS

All Weight-Watchers' orders are steamed. There is no seasoning or corn starch used in cooking.

W1. Mixed Vegetables $5.95
W2. Mixed Vegetables (Choice of Pork, Chicken, Beef or Shrimp) $8.95
W3. Broccoli or Snow Pea Pods or Asparagus $5.95

SWEET SOU

SW1. Sweet and Sour Pork ......
SW3. Sweet and Sour Shrimp ......
SW2. Sweet and Sour Chicken ......
SW4. Sweet and Sour Combo ......

STEAMED MIXED VEGETABLES

Expect broccoli, carrots, and snow peas, a potent mix of nutrient-dense vegetables. Make a simple rule in your house: Every time you eat Chinese, everyone (including you) must eat at least one portion of this healthy side.

MOO-SHI

Moo-Shi is a very popular mandarin dish which contains mushrooms, cabbage, fungus, dried lily flower, eggs and meat served with 6 pancakes and Hoi Sin sauce

MI. Moo-Shi (Chicken, Beef, Pork, Shrimp, or Vegetables) $7.95
M2. Moo-Shi Peking Style (Spicy) $8.05

NOODLES

L1. Lo Mein (Choice of Pork, Chicken, B Shrimp) ....
L2. Combo Lo Mein ....
L4. Shanghai Noodles ....
L6. Shanghai Noodles (Meatless) ....
L7. Cold Noodles in Sesame Sauce ....

VEGETABLES

V1. Vegetarian's Delight $6.55
V5. Stir Fried Pea Pods $6.55
V6.* Spicy Eggplant in Garlic Sauce $6.25
V3. Snow Pea Pods with Water Chestnuts .. $6.55
V7.* Spicy Broccoli $6.25
V4. Brocoli in Oyster Sauce $6.55
V8.* String Beans, Szechuan Style (Meatless) $6.25

RICE

R1. Steamed Rice ....
R2. Fried Rice (Choice of Pork, Chicken, B $5.95
R3. Combo Fried Rice ....
R6. Brown Rice ....

RICE

The most seemingly innocent part of the meal is actually one of the most problematic. A single scoop could add 300 calories to a meal, and all of those calories come from fast-burning carbohydrates. If you can't imagine a Chinese meal without rice, try a small scoop of brown rice, which at least brings some fiber to the table.

Genius PARENT TRICK

Make your kids use chopsticks. It takes 20 minutes for our stomachs to convey to our brains that we're full, so working a bit for their food (while refining fine motor skills) is a good way to prevent the overeating.

Italian

BRUSCHETTA

Loaded with chopped tomatoes, garlic, and fresh basil, these crunchy hunks of grilled bread are the Italian take on chips and salsa. At less than 200 calories a serving, it's a solid starter for the table. Sell it to your kid by calling it "fresh tomato pizza."

PASTA E FAGIOLI

Soup is always a good idea (assuming we're not talking about chowder or a soup with cheese in the title) because it provides low-calorie padding for the belly before the unhealthier entrées arrive. This particular soup, found throughout Italy and rich with tomatoes, pasta, and fiber-packed beans, is like a high-octane, more-satisfying version of SpaghettiOs®.

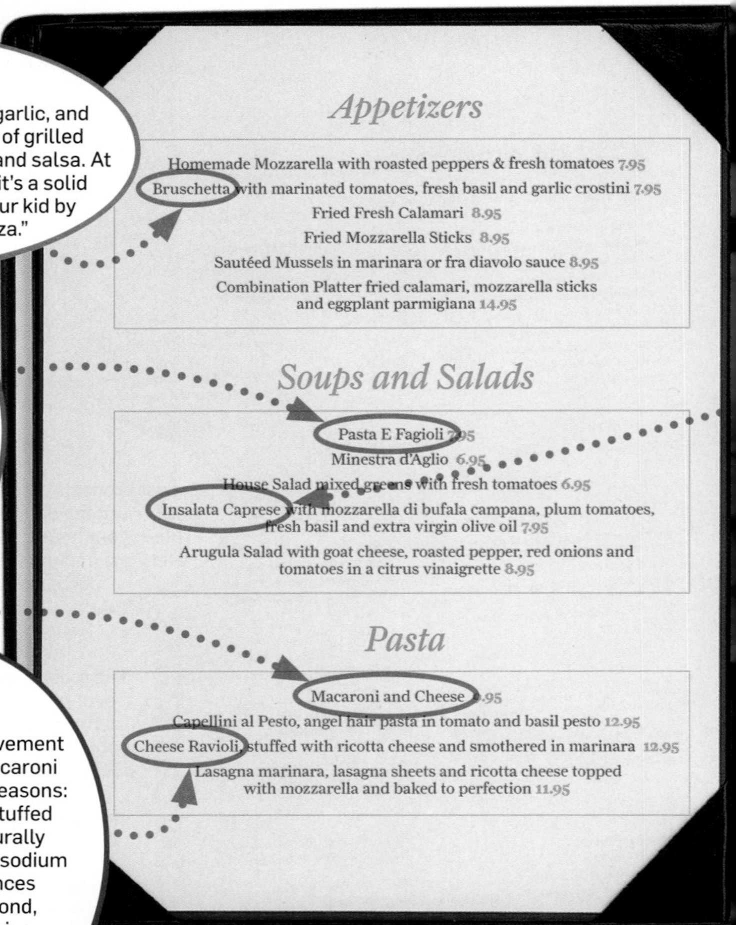

MACARONI AND CHEESE

There is absolutely nothing Italian about macaroni and cheese. So for the sake of authenticity—and your kid's waistline—institute a "No-Mac" policy at Italian restaurants.

CHEESE RAVIOLI

A substantial improvement over the normal macaroni and cheese for two reasons: First, the pasta is stuffed with ricotta, a naturally low-calorie and low-sodium cheese that trounces Cheddar, and second, it's sauced with marinara, the nutritional standard-bearer of the Italian menu.

Appetizers
Homemade Mozzarella with roasted peppers & fresh tomatoes 7.95
Bruschetta with marinated tomatoes, fresh basil and garlic crostini 7.95
Fried Fresh Calamari 8.95
Fried Mozzarella Sticks 8.95
Sautéed Mussels in marinara or fra diavolo sauce 8.95
Combination Platter fried calamari, mozzarella sticks and eggplant parmigiana 14.95
Soups and Salads
Pasta E Fagioli 7.95
Minestra d'Aglio 6.95
House Salad mixed greens with fresh tomatoes 6.95
Insalata Caprese with mozzarella di bufala campana, plum tomatoes, fresh basil and extra virgin olive oil 7.95
Arugula Salad with goat cheese, roasted pepper, red onions and tomatoes in a citrus vinaigrette 8.95
Pasta
Macaroni and Cheese 9.95
Capellini al Pesto, angel hair pasta in tomato and basil pesto 12.95
Cheese Ravioli, stuffed with ricotta cheese and smothered in marinara 12.95
Lasagna marinara, lasagna sheets and ricotta cheese topped with mozzarella and baked to perfection 11.95

Meat

Bistecca Fiorentina 24.95
Homemade Sausage with Sweet Peppers 16.95
Neapolitan Beef Ragu 14.95
Neapolitan Meatballs 15.95
Pork Chops 19.95

Seafood

Shrimp & Scallops in fra diavolo or marinara sauce 19.95
Grilled Prawns in Lemon 19.95
Baked Branzino 23.95
Tuna and Ricotta Fritters 17.95
Grilled Lobsters 25.95

Chicken

Grilled Double Breast Of Chicken with fresh rosemary and herbs over arugula 11.95
Pizzaiola sautéed in marinara with mushrooms and peppers 13.95
Chicken Marsala sautéed in marsala wine with shallots and mushrooms 13.95
Chicken Balsamic sautéed with onions, mushrooms and fresh tomatoes in a sweet balsamic sauce 1
Chicken Francaise lightly dipped in egg and delic sautéed in a butter lemon sauce 13.95

Dolce

Gelato in various flavors 4.95
Panna Cotta topped with wild berries 5.95
Cannoli topped with Nutella 4.95
Tiramisu delicately layered with a hint of coffee

INSALATA CAPRESE

The fresh mozzarella cheese used in this tricolored salad is naturally low in fat and sodium, and the tomatoes and basil add a nice antioxidant hit. This beats out Caesar salad any day of the week.

PIZZAIOLA

It's like chicken Parmesan, minus all the excess calories. This preparation combines a grilled or sautéed meat—usually chicken or veal—with a marinara sauce spiked with peppers and mushrooms. Not only does the pizzaiola treatment save Parm-devotees a few hundred calories, but it also packs a few servings of vegetables into a single dish.

GELATO

Unlike most American ice creams, which are made with heavy cream, gelato is made with milk, making a scoop a relatively low-impact indulgence.

TIRAMISU

Delicious, yes, but this ubiquitous Italian dessert is made from ladyfingers, egg yolks, mascarpone cheese, and chocolate, a dubious combination that leaves even a tiny slice with 450 calories and 25 grams of fat.

SAUCE DECODER

LISTED FROM BEST TO ABSOLUTE WORST:

Marinara
This is virtually fat-free, plus it delivers at least one serving of fruit in the form of antioxidant-packed tomatoes.

Pesto
It's high in fat, but most of that is healthy monounsaturated fat from olive oil. Plus basil and garlic both contain strong cancer-fighting compounds.

Butter and Parmesan
The food of choice for half of this country's young eaters, this simple combination might seem fairly innocent. The problem is, it offers no viable nutrition for your kids—just fat from the sauce and quick-burning carbs from the pasta.

Alfredo
The same as Butter and Parmesan (above), only with the addition of heavy cream. Avoid at all costs.

Sushi

MISO SOUP

Every bit as comforting and approachable as a bowl of chicken noodle soup, but with just 80 calories a bowl. So rich and familiar is the taste of a good miso soup that the kids won't even notice that those little green strands floating about in the clouded broth are seaweed!

YAKITORI

Skewers of lean meat, usually chicken, grilled over an open flame. Lightly sauced, low in calories, and high in quality protein, these are perfectly tailored for the little ones. Plus, what kid can resist food on a stick?

TERIYAKI

This reduction of soy, sweet wine, and sugar comes painted on a variety of meats and vegetables at Japanese restaurants. The sweet-salty sauce makes nearly anything it touches palatable, so why not encourage your kids to try it on salmon? The monster dose of omega-3s is critical for brain development as well as a dozen other bodily functions.

TEMPURA

Japanese chefs use a lighter batter than that reserved for more familiar fried foods, making the shrimp, asparagus, carrots, and other foods they coat and fry less-oil soaked than the onion rings and fried mozzarella sticks most kids crave. Even so, it's still food cooked in boiling fat, so split an order for the whole table.

KRAB

Krab with a K (also called "crab sticks" on menus) refers to imitation crab made from surimi, finely chopped white fish—usually hake or pollock—pressed into logs that resemble crab legs. While it is highly processed, it still contains many of the same health benefits as fish, but without any of the fishy smell or taste that scare most kids away.

appetizers

Miso Soup

House Salad

Roll Appetizer (3pcs California roll, 3pcs crab salad roll, 3pcs takka maki, 3pcs negi hamachi)

Sashimi Appetizer Combo (tuna, white fish & octopus)

Sushi Appetizer Combo (nigiri: tuna, white fish, shrimp, crabstick & 2 pcs tekka maki)

Yakitori (choice of chicken, or roasted with special sauce)

teriyaki

Chicken Teriyaki

Steak Teriyaki

Pork Teriyaki

Salmon Teriyaki

Tofu Teriyaki

Shrimp Teriyaki

Scallop Teriyaki

Tuna Teriyaki

tempura

Vegetable
15 pieces vegetable

Chicken
7 pieces chicken & vegetable

Shrimp
7 pieces shrimp & vegetable

Salmon
7 pieces salmon & vegetable

Tempura Combo
3 pieces shrimp, 3 pieces salmon, 3 pieces chicken & vegetable

nigiri-sushi

One serving consists of two pieces

Alaska King Crab
Amaebi (sweet shrimp)
Blue Fin Tuna
Ebi (boiled shrimp)
Escolar (seared fatty white tuna)
Hamachi (yellowtail)
Hirame (fluke)
Hotategai (scallop)
Ika (squid)
Ikura (salmon roe)
Kanikama (crab stick)

Kanpachi (wild yellowtail)
Saba (spanish mackeral)
Shake (fresh salmon)
Shake (smoked salmon)
Spicy Tuna (original or jalapeno)
Suzuki (bass)
Tai (red snapper)
Tako (boiled octopus)
Tobiko (flying fish roe)
Unagi (fresh water eel)
Uni (sea urchin)

sushi combinations

Served with Miso Soup & Salad

Matsu Sushi Dinner
California roll, spicy tekka maki, 5pcs nigiri sushi consisting of: tuna, shrimp, white fish, tamago and smoked salmon

Traditional Sushi & Sashimi Dinner Traditional Sushi Dinner plus sashimi appetizer

Traditional Sushi Dinner
Nigiri sushi consisting of: tuna, white fish, mackerel, smoked salmon, yellowtail, shrimp, octopus, crab stick, tamago, crab roe & tekka maki

specialty rolls

Black & White (white fish tempura, scallions, black sesame seeds)

Tuna Cubed (blue fin tuna and escolar topped with fatty tuna & wasabi tobiko)

Grand Canyon (unagi, avocado & cucumber topped with broiled escolar, masago & silver sauce)

Green Dragon (Alaska king crab, unagi topped with avocado and tempura crunch)

Hawaiian (spicy salmon, tempura crunch & cucumber topped with avocado & tuna)

Jumbo (crab stick, cucumber, hamachi, unagi & masago)

Fire Island (California roll topped with spicy tuna, scallions and tempura crunch)

Fuji Volcano (shrimp tempura and avocado topped with unagi & spicy masago sauce)

Matsu (unagi, avocado, crabstick, tamago & masago)

maki sushi

One serving consists of 6 pieces unless noted

Alaska Roll (smoked salmon, cream cheese & masago)
California Roll (crab stick & cucumber)
Futomaki 4 pcs (crab stick, shrimp, tamago, pickle & cucumber)
Gobo Maki (pickled burdock)
Ikura Maki (salmon roe)
Kappa Maki
Mexican Roll (boiled shrimp & avocado)
Negi Hamachi Maki (yellowtail & scallions)
Natto Maki (fermented soybeans)
Philadelphia Roll (smoked salmon, cream cheese & masago)
Shrimp Tempura Maki 4 pcs (shrimp tempura, cucumber & crab roe)
Spicy Tekka Maki (spicy tuna original or jalapeno)
Spider Maki 4 pcs (soft shell crab roll & masago)
Unagi Maki (fresh water eel)

SOY SAUCE

While Japanese meals are lean, low-fat, high-protein affairs, one real danger comes from excessive sodium intake. A single tablespoon of soy sauce has over 1,000 milligrams of sodium—half the recommended maximum for a day. Luckily, most sushi places now offer the low-sodium variety, which cuts the sky-high count in half.

TUNA ROLL

Consumption of tuna sushi has recently been linked to high levels of mercury intake, which can negatively affect language, visual-spatial skills, and brain development in young kids. Children under the age of 6 and pregnant women are the most susceptible to mercury's ill effects, so limit your kid to one or two pieces of tuna-based sushi per visit, or just cut it out entirely.

CALIFORNIA ROLL

A mix of sweet (crab), creamy (avocado), and crunchy (cucumber), this popular Americanized roll is the perfect fit for a kid's tastes. Plus, at 300 calories for eight vegetable-stuffed pieces, this might be one of the healthiest kids' meals in America. No, the crab is not likely to be real, but for a kid, that might be a good thing.

PHILADELPHIA ROLL

It's not the healthiest item on the menu, but it's a great beginner roll for kids. The salmon is smoked, so that solves the raw issue most kids might have, plus the avocado and cream cheese give it a nice richness. At 350 calories for 8 pieces, it makes a perfect meal.

Indian

APPETIZERS

If there's one area where normally healthy Indian cuisine hits a nutritional pothole, it's with the starting dishes. From potato-stuffed samosas to the crispy fritters called *pakora*, a vast majority of the appetizers make a pit stop in boiling oil on the way to your plate. That means that they also pick up an unnecessary dose of calories and saturated fat in transit.

NAAN AND ROTI

Both are hot flatbreads baked up soft and pillowy in the tandoori oven, and both are absolutely addictive. Stick to a single basket, but make it roti instead of naan—roti is made with whole-wheat flour, giving it an extra dose of fiber.

VINDALOO

Proceed with caution: Many versions of this fragrant chicken stew come with a serious dose of dried chiles, and the heat may be overwhelming to a sensitive palate.

CURRY

Many kids are turned off by the pervasive smell, but Indian curry contains turmeric, a miracle spice known to fight cancer and cardiovascular disease, slow mental decline, and boost insulin resistance. If they won't do curry, Indian yellow rice and tandoori chicken also contain turmeric.

APPETIZERS

VEGETABLE SAMOSA *Two crisp turnovers, stuffed with spiced potatoes, peas, and herbs. $2.50*

VEGETABLE PAKORA *Assorted vegetable fritters gently seasoned and deep fried. $2.50*

CHICKEN PAKORA *Chicken fritters. $3.25*

SHRIMP PAKORA *Shrimp dipped in spiced batter, deep fried. $5.95*

HOUSE SPECIAL PLATTER *A fine presentation of our choice appetizers, recommended for two. $6.95*

VEGETARIAN PLATTER *Assorted vegetable appetizers, recommended for two. $5.95*

PANEER PAKORA *Pieces of homemade cheese, dipped in chickpea flour and fried.$3.25*

SOUPS AND SALADS

VEGETABLE SOUP *Soup made from fresh vegetable, lentils, spices and delicate herbs. $2.50*

MULLIGATAWNY SOUP *A traditional chicken soup with lentils and spices. $2.50*

RAITA *Homemade whipped yoghurt with cucumbers, potatoes and fresh mint. $2.50*

GREEN SALAD *Lettuce, tomatoes, green peppers, and onions. $2.50*

BREADS

NAAN *Leavened bread, soft and fluffy. $2.25*

ROTI *Whole wheat bread $1.50*

ALOO PARATHA *Whole wheat bread, stuffed with potatoes $2.50*

PANEER KULCHA *Naan stuffed with homemade cheese, spices, and herbs $2.50*

RICE SPECIALTIES

CHICKEN BIRYANI *Classic mulgai dish of curried rice with chicken, dried fruits and nuts $9.95*

LAMB BIRYANI *Curried rice with lamb, dried fruits and nuts $10.95*

HOUSE SPECIAL BIRYANI *Our special biryani cooked with chicken, lamb, shrimp, vegetables, dried fruits and nuts $13.95*

PEAS PULLAO *Rice cooked with peas, raisins and nuts $3.95*

OUR CHEF RECOMMENDS

SEAFOOD FANTASY *Start with tandoori fish and tandoori shrimp, followed by your choice of shrimp masala or shrimp cury, dal, naan, pullao and green salad. $19.95*

THALI HOUSE VEGETARIAN *A traditional Indian meal served on a silver platter with dal, chana masala, mattar paneer, rice, poori or roti, raita and gulab jamun. $12.95*

VEGETABLE SEEKHAM *Fresh carrots, cauliflower, green peas, homemade cheese, pineapple chunks cooked with spices, sauce and nuts. $9.95*

LAMB DANSHIK *Tender lamb and chick peas lentils cooked with pineapple and herbs. $11.95*

LAMB KASHMIRI *Lamb cooked in an onion, ginger, garlic and peach sauce. $11.95*

CHICKEN LA-JAWAB *Tender boneless chicken pieces and apple chunks cooked in ginger, garlic sauce and nuts. $11.95*

CHICKEN

CHICKEN MAKHANI *The legendary tandoori chicken, cooked in tomato and garlic sauce $10.95*

CHICKEN VINDALOO *Boneless chicken and potatoes in a highly spiced sauce $9.95*

CHICKEN SHAHI KORMA *Tender chicken cooked in a rich sauce with nuts and cream $9.95*

CHICKEN SAAGWALA *Boneless chicken cooked with creamed spinach $9.95*

CHICKEN TIKKA MUGLAI *Tandoori chicken and mushrooms cooked in tomato and garlic $10.95*

CHICKEN TIKKA BHUNA *Chicken tikka cooked dry with onions, tomato and bell peppers $9.95*

CHICKEN TIKKA MASALA *Tandoori roasted chicken tikka, in a tomato and butter sauce $10.95*

CHICKEN CURRY *The original cooked in onions, garlic, ginger, yoghurt, and spices $9.95*

CHICKEN JALFEREZI *Tender, boneless chicken cooke with onions,tomato and bell peppers $9.95*

CHICKEN DILRUBA *Chicken cooked with mushrooms $9.95*

CHICKEN ASPARAGUS *Chicken cooked with aspara gus and fresh spices sauce $10.95*

CHICKEN ACHAR *Chicken cooked in tomato, onior gravy with pickled spices $9.95*

CHICKEN CHILLY *Tendar boneless chicken pieces, onions, tomatoes, bell peppers cooked in swee and sour sauce, mint flavored $10.95*

MENU DECODER

LAMB

LAMB SHAHI KORMA *Tender lamb, in a rich sauce with nuts and cream $10.95*

LAMB SAAGWALA *Chunks of lamb in creamed spinach $10.95*

LAMB BHUNA *Pan-broiled lamb, cooked in specially prepared herbs and spices with a touch of ginger and garlic $10.95*

LAMB VINDALOO *Lamb and potatoes cooked in a sharply spiced tangy sauce $10.95*

KEMMA MATTAR *Ground lamb cooked with peas and herbs $10.95*

BOTI KABAB MASALA *Tandoor broiled lamb sauteed in our special exquisite curry to gastronomic satisfaction $11.95*

LAMB ACHAR *Tender lamb cooked in tomato, onion, gravy with pickled spices $10.95*

LAMB ASPARAGUS *Lamb and asparagus cooked in a special ginger, garlic and onion sauce $11.95*

VEGETABLE

NAVRATAN CURRY *Nine assorted garden fresh vegetables sauteed in a traditional onion and tomato sauce $8.95*

DAL MAKHANI *Black lentils and beans, cooked in onions, with tomatoes and cream $8.95*

SAAG PANEER *Chunks of homemade cheese in creamed spinach and fresh spices $8.95*

ALOO SAAG *Spinach and potatoes with fresh spices $8.95*

ALOO GOBHI MASALA *Fresh cauliflower and potatoes, cooked dry in onions, tomatoes and herbs $8.95*

MATTAR PANEER *Fresh homemade cheese, cooked with tender garden peas and fresh spices $8.95*

ALOO MATTAR *Garden fresh green peas and potatoes with fresh spices $8.95*

MATTAR MUSHROOMS *Garden fresh peas and mushroms cooked with garlic, ginger, and onions $8.95*

BAIGAN BHARTHA *Roasted eggplant sauteed in onion, tomatoes and green peas $8.95*

MALAI KOFTA KASHMIRI *Garden fresh vegetables and homemade cheeseballs cooked in a rich sauce with nuts and cream $9.95*

CHANNA MASALA PUNJABI *A North Indian specialty, subtly flavored chick peas, tempered with ginger $8.95*

KADI PAKORA SINDHI *Dumpling of mixed vegetables, cooked in chick peas flour, yoghurt and mustard sauce $8.95*

PANEER SHAHI KORMA *Tender chunks of homemade cheese, cooked with nuts and a touch of cream in fresh herbs and spices $9.95*

PANEER MASALA *Tender chunks of homemade cheese, cooked with tomato and butter $9.95*

PANEER ACHAR *Homemade cheese cooked in tomato onion gravy with pickled spices $9.95*

PANEER CHILLY *Homemade cheese, onions, tomatoes, bell peppers cooked in sweet and sour sauce, mint flavored $9.95*

TANDOORI

TANDOORI CHICKEN *Chicken marinated in yoghurt and freshly ground spices, then broiled in the tandoor (half) $9.95*

TANDOORI FISH *Swordfish marinated in an exotic recipe of exciting spices and herbs, broiled on charcoal $13.95*

TANDOORI SHRIMP *Jumbo shrimp seasoned with spices and herbs, baked in the tandoor $14.95*

CHICKEN TIKKA *Boneless, tender chicken, gently broiled $9.95*

RESHMI KABAB *Mild, tender, pieces of chicken breast, marinated in a very mild sauce, barbecued on a skewer in the tandoor $10.95*

BOTI KABAB *Juicy cubes from leg of lamb, broiled to perfection in the tandoor $10.95*

SEEK KABAB *Finger rolls of ground lamb, spiced with fresh ginger $10.95*

DRINK SPECIALTIES

LASSI SWEET *$2.25*

MANGO LASSI *$2.75*

MANGO JUICE *$2.00*

STRAWBERRY LASSI *seasonal $2.75*

SODAS *$1.25*

KESAR PISTA SHAKE *seasonal $2.75*

ACCOMPANIMENTS

MANGO CHUTNEY *spicy, sweet & sour relish 4.00*

PICKLES *mango, lemon, chili 3.00*

PAPADUM *thin bean wafers 3.00*

RAITA *tomato and cucumber in a yogurt sauce 3.00*

TANDOORI

The perfect place to find approachable food for a youngster. Tandoori dishes have been roasted at high heat in a tandoor —a scorching clay oven. Chicken is the obvious choice for this healthy treatment, but shrimp and fish make for an even healthier dinner.

DAL

Lentils stewed with a variety of flavorful Indian spices. Packed full of fiber, protein, and antioxidants, you'd be hard-pressed to find a better dish to feed your family in the restaurant world.

CHICKEN TIKKA

Lean chicken marinated in yogurt and spices, then roasted tandoori-style. Not only is this the most kid-friendly dish on the menu, it's also one of the healthiest. A single serving weighs in at a svelte 250 calories.

LASSI

Blended fruit drinks made with yogurt, milk, and just a touch of sugar. The most popular is blended with mango and makes for a great low-calorie dessert that kids will beg for once they get a taste. Go ahead, let 'em have one.

CONDIMENTS

While sauces and condiments can be the most destructive parts of American-style meals, the table sauces that come with Indian food are one of the healthiest parts of the meal. Both raita, a cool yogurt and cucumber sauce, and chutney, a salsa-like condiment made with mango or fresh mint, are perfectly suited for a kid's appetite and should be used with reckless abandon.

Deli

OIL AND VINEGAR

Seems like a harmless splash to lubricate the sandwich and make it all go down easier, right? Not exactly. The vinegar is harmless, but the oil used in most sub shops is of the low-grade soy variety, carrying a 100-calorie penalty for every few inches of sandwich.

BLT

Probably not as bad as you think. With four strips of bacon and a light coating of mayo, this sandwich still manages to hover right around the 400-calorie mark.

WRAP

Beware the healthy foods that aren't! The tortilla this comes wrapped in packs up to 300 calories on its own and provides ample surface area for a surplus of cheese and dressing. All told, the average chicken wrap weighs in at 600 calories—about 50 percent more than the average grilled chicken sandwich.

ITALIAN HERO

This popular combo order combines a mountain of the fattiest, saltiest meats around: pepperoni, salami, capicolla. Add to that Italian dressing and sodium-laden provolone cheese, and even a small sandwich will top 600 calories and approach 2,000 milligrams of sodium.

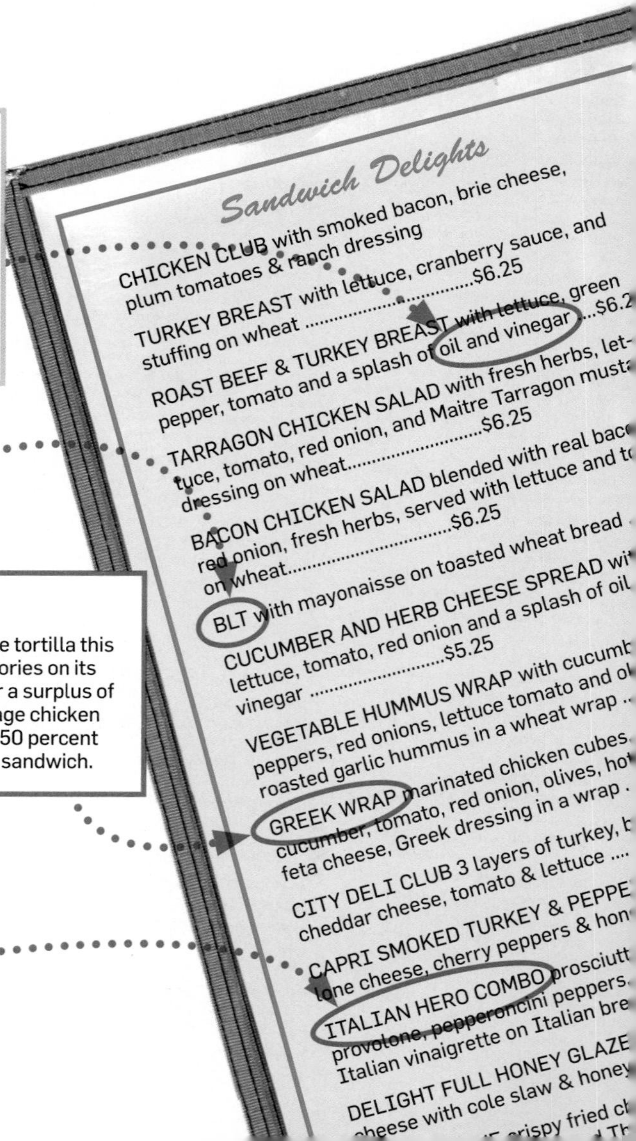

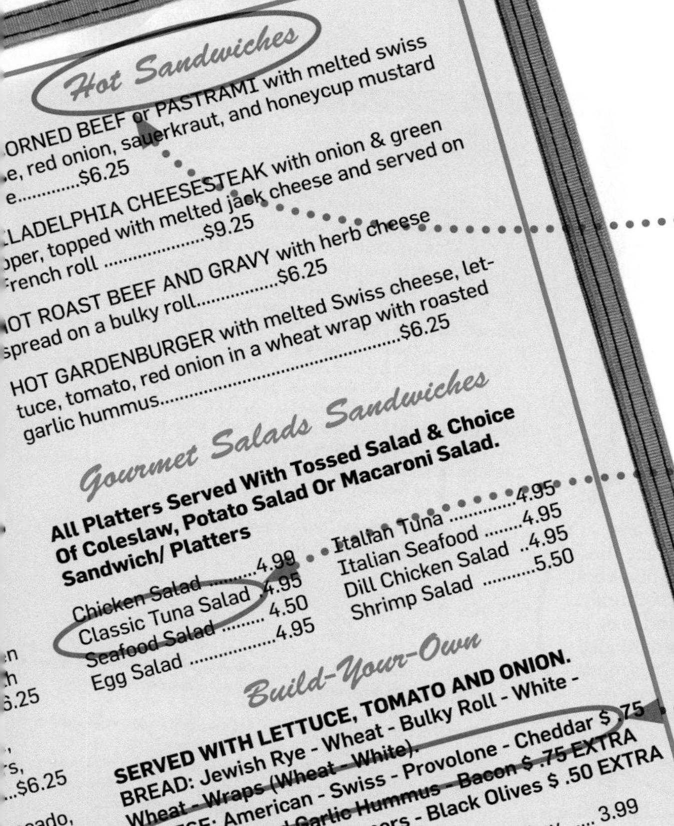

Hot Sandwiches
ORNED BEEF or PASTRAMI with melted swiss
e, red onion, sauerkraut, and honeycup mustard
e..............$6.25
LADELPHIA CHEESESTEAK with onion & green
pper, topped with melted jack cheese and served on
French roll $9.25
HOT ROAST BEEF AND GRAVY with herb cheese
spread on a bulky roll.................$6.25
HOT GARDENBURGER with melted Swiss cheese, let-
tuce, tomato, red onion in a wheat wrap with roasted
garlic hummus.......................................$6.25
Gourmet Salads Sandwiches
All Platters Served With Tossed Salad & Choice
Of Coleslaw, Potato Salad Or Macaroni Salad.
Sandwich/ Platters
Chicken Salad 4.99
Classic Tuna Salad 4.95
Seafood Salad 4.50
Egg Salad 4.95
Italian Tuna 4.95
Italian Seafood 4.95
Dill Chicken Salad ..4.95
Shrimp Salad 5.50
Build-Your-Own
SERVED WITH LETTUCE, TOMATO AND ONION.
BREAD: Jewish Rye - Wheat - Bulky Roll - White -
Wheat - Wraps (Wheat - White).
CHEESE: American - Swiss - Provolone - Cheddar $ .75
EXTRA: Roasted Garlic Hummus - Bacon $ .75 EXTRA
Cucumbers - Green Peppers - Black Olives $ .50 EXTRA
Boiled Ham 3.99
Turkey Breast 3.99
Roast Beef 4.50
Pastrami 3.99
Corned Beef 3.99
Genoa Salami 3.99
Hard Salami 3.99
Smoked Turkey 3.99
Virginia Ham 3.99
Cappicola Ham 3.99
Prosciutto 3.50
Liverwurst
Bologna
Spiced Ham
Black Forest Ham

HOT SANDWICHES

Stay away! Calories at delis rise in direct proportion to the temperature of the sandwich being made. Among the worst offenders in the hot sandwich department: hot pastrami and Swiss, meatball, sausage and peppers, and, of course, the disastrous cheesesteak.

TUNA SALAD

Tuna and salad may each be perfectly healthy on their own, but when smashed together they become one of the most consistently bad orders in a sandwich shop. "Salad" in this case is a euphemism for a bucket of mayo, making a small scoop of this menu item three times as caloric as a serving of turkey or ham.

CHEESE

Choose Swiss and mozzarella over Cheddar and provolone. Not only are they lower in fat and calories, but Swiss in particular has only a fraction of the sodium.

YOUR CHOICE OF HAM, TURKEY, OR ROAST BEEF

Surprisingly, there is only a marginal caloric and fat discrepancy among these three ubiquitous cuts. All contribute about 100 calories and 8 grams of fat to a small sandwich. One warning: Watch out for smoked ham and turkey, which tend to have precariously high sodium levels.

Mexican

CHIPS AND SALSA

Salsa is the world's greatest condiment, with only 15 calories and 0 grams of fat in a generous scoop, plus a ton of lycopene from the tomatoes. Problem is, a basket of chips will cost you at least 600 calories, and when they're complimentary, those calories can pile up quickly. Limit the family to one basket and save any leftover salsa to lavish generously on your entrées.

TORTILLAS

No, not all tortillas are created equally. In fact, the wrong tortilla can be your worst enemy at a Mexican restaurant, packing up to 400 calories on its own. To dampen the damage, have all tacos and fajitas made with corn tortillas; they're lower in calories and higher in fiber than standard flour tortillas.

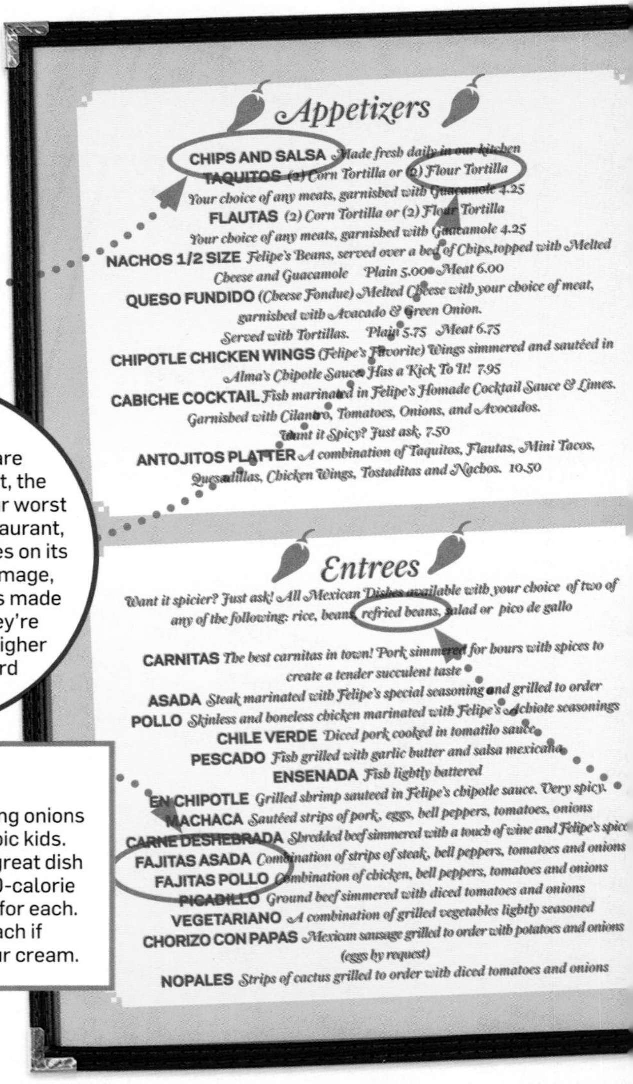

FAJITAS

The sizzling skillet has a magical way of making onions and peppers more appealing to veggie-phobic kids. Because the serving size is so massive, it's a great dish to split between two kids, which cuts the 900-calorie entrée into a reasonable 450-calorie portion for each. You can knock off another 150 calories each if you ask the server to hold the cheese and sour cream.

Appetizers

CHIPS AND SALSA *Made fresh daily in our kitchen*
TAQUITOS *(2) Corn Tortilla or (2) Flour Tortilla*
Your choice of any meats, garnished with Guacamole 4.25
FLAUTAS *(2) Corn Tortilla or (2) Flour Tortilla*
Your choice of any meats, garnished with Guacamole 4.25
NACHOS 1/2 SIZE *Felipe's Beans, served over a bed of Chips, topped with Melted Cheese and Guacamole Plain 5.00 Meat 6.00*
QUESO FUNDIDO *(Cheese Fondue) Melted Cheese with your choice of meat, garnished with Avacado & Green Onion. Served with Tortillas. Plain 5.75 Meat 6.75*
CHIPOTLE CHICKEN WINGS *(Felipe's Favorite) Wings simmered and sautéed in Alma's Chipotle Sauce Has a Kick To It! 7.95*
CABICHE COCKTAIL *Fish marinated in Felipe's Homade Cocktail Sauce & Limes. Garnished with Cilantro, Tomatoes, Onions, and Avocados. Want it Spicy? Just ask. 7.50*
ANTOJITOS PLATTER *A combination of Taquitos, Flautas, Mini Tacos, Quesadillas, Chicken Wings, Tostaditas and Nachos. 10.50*

Entrees

Want it spicier? Just ask! All Mexican Dishes available with your choice of two of any of the following: rice, beans, refried beans, salad or pico de gallo

CARNITAS *The best carnitas in town! Pork simmered for hours with spices to create a tender succulent taste*
ASADA *Steak marinated with Felipe's special seasoning and grilled to order*
POLLO *Skinless and boneless chicken marinated with Felipe's Achiote seasonings*
CHILE VERDE *Diced pork cooked in tomatilo sauce*
PESCADO *Fish grilled with garlic butter and salsa mexicana*
ENSENADA *Fish lightly battered*
EN CHIPOTLE *Grilled shrimp sauteed in Felipe's chipotle sauce. Very spicy.*
MACHACA *Sautéed strips of pork, eggs, bell peppers, tomatoes, onions*
CARNE DESHEBRADA *Shredded beef simmered with a touch of wine and Felipe's spice*
FAJITAS ASADA *Combination of strips of steak, bell peppers, tomatoes and onions*
FAJITAS POLLO *Combination of chicken, bell peppers, tomatoes and onions*
PICADILLO *Ground beef simmered with diced tomatoes and onions*
VEGETARIANO *A combination of grilled vegetables lightly seasoned*
CHORIZO CON PAPAS *Mexican sausage grilled to order with potatoes and onions (eggs by request)*
NOPALES *Strips of cactus grilled to order with diced tomatoes and onions*

TACOS
All tacos are served on a soft flour tortilla with cheese and lettuce. Hard shell or corn tortilla by request.

Taco filled with...
- *Asada, Fajitas Asada 3.50*
- *Carne Desbebrada, Carne Desbebrada, Carnitas, Pollo, Picadillo, Fajitas Pollo, Chorizo con Papas, Nopales, Machacha, Chile Verde 3.25*
- *Ensenada or Pescado 3.50*

TACO SALAD
Lettuce, rice, beans, jack and cheddar cheese, fresh salsa, guacamole, sour cream served with or without crisp shell

BURRITOS
A meal in itself that starts with a large flour tortilla and your choice of any meat, then we add rice, beans and cheese all wrapped inside. Frijoles de la olla by request.

Burrito filled with...
- *Fajitas Asada, Chile Relleno 8.00*
- *Carne Desbebrada, Carnitas, Pollo, Picadillo, Fajitas Pollo, Vegetariano, Chorizo con Papas,*
- *Nopales, Machaca, Chile Verde 7.25*
- *Ensenada or Pescado 8.50*

TOSTADAS
A crisp corn tortilla spread with beans, your choice of entree, topped with fresh lettuce, guacamole and cheese.

Tostadas with...
- *Asada, Fajitas Asada 8.00*
- *Carne Desbebrada, Carnitas, Pollo, Picadillo,*
- *Fajitas Pollo, Vegetariano 7.25*

NACHOS
First we start with a good portion of fresh chips, add beans, your favorite meat and cover it with melted cheese and garnished with guacamole.

Nachos with...
- *Asada, Fajitas Asada 8.50*
- *Carne Desbebrada, Carnitas, Pollo, Picadillo 7.50*

QUESADILLAS
Your choice of meat and melted cheese in between two flour tortillas, garnished with guacamole.

Quesadillas with...
- *Asada 8.00*
- *Carne Desbebrada, Carnitas, Pollo, Picadillo 7.45*

ENCHILADAS
A soft corn tortilla, stuffed with cheese or meat, and smothered with enchilada sauce or tomatillo sauce then topped with melted cheese and lettuce.

Enchiladas with...
- *Carne Desbebrada, Carnitas, Pollo 4.25*
- *Cheese 4.25*

EMPANADAS
Corn pastry filled with cheese and your choice of meat and vegetable.

Empanadas with...
- *Carne Desbebrada, Carnitas, Pollo 4.25*
- *Cheese 4.25*

CHILE RELLENO
A Chile Poblano stuffed with cheese and topped with special sauce.

QUESADILLAS

Mexico's thin, crispy answer to that American kid favorite, grilled cheese, has nothing even closely resembling nutrition to offer your loved ones. Whereas a homemade quesadilla might contain $^1/_2$ cup of shredded cheese on a small tortilla, the restaurant equivalent is a hubcap-size wrap housing up to 2 cups of Cheddar and Jack cheeses. The damage? 700 calories and 40 grams of fat.

GUACAMOLE

Yes, avocados are loaded with heart-healthy fats, but they're also stuffed full of belly-expanding calories, making a small bowl of guacamole a 400-calorie proposition. Go ahead and order the guac—just make sure it's shared with the rest of the table, okay?

EMPANADAS

This South American staple has migrated onto many a Mexican menu in this country. Which is rather unfortunate, considering that it's a fried meat-and-cheese filled pastry. Ouch.

REFRIED BEANS

Don't be scared by the name: While this popular Mexican staple carries a bit of fat with each serving, refried beans also come with a big dose of protein, fiber, and antioxidants. (Yes, refried beans pack quite an antioxidant punch.) All of these factors make the beans considerably better for you than the rice they're served with.

Seafood

SHRIMP COCKTAIL

There are few better ways to start any meal in the restaurant world. Shrimp are virtually fat-free and are loaded with protein, which is a vital component of satiety. Studies show that starting a meal with lean protein makes you less likely to overeat come entrée and dessert time.

CLAM CHOWDER

The cream-based New England variety might be the better-known chowder, but nutritionally, it can't hold a candle to tomato-based Manhattan-style chowder.

CRAB LEGS

Young boys might be tempted to try to scare their sisters with these giant claws, but trapped inside is a sweet, nonfishy, lean meat that is pitch-perfect for a young eater's taste buds.

MELTED BUTTER

It might look like a small ramekin, but those 2 tablespoons of melted butter contain over 200 calories and a full day's worth of saturated fat, all but erasing any benefits your family is getting from eating seafood.

GREAT STARTERS
OYSTERS ON THE HALF SHELL Six market oysters served with a shallot and vinegar mignonette or cocktail sauce $7.99
SHRIMP COCKTAIL 8 of our butterfly shrimp served with our homemade cocktail sauce $5.99
MOZZARELLA STICKS Mozzarella cheese lightly breaded and golded fried. Served with marinara $5.99
SAUTEED MUSHROOMS Broiled in lemon, white wine and butter $5.99
CIAPPINO Variety of fresh seafood in a rich spicy tomato broth $5.99
APPETIZER SAMPLER A sharable platter of Harbor House favorites. Shrimp cocktail, sautéed mushrooms and popcorn shrimp $7.99
BROCCOLI BITES Tender broccoli and creamy American cheese double dipped in a light batter and fried $5.99
SOUP
New England clam chowder Cup $2.99 Bowl $3.99
Seafood gumbo Cup $2.99 Bowl $3.99
SEAFOOD BUFFET
Features snow crab legs, steamed shrimp, steamed mussels, steamed clams, crawfish, fresh fish, hot and cold pasta dishes, seafood gumbo, fresh fruit, salad bar, and much more $24.99
SPECIALTY DISHES
The following served with one trip salad bar and choice of baked potato or fries. Add 50 for sweet potato.
9 oz. USDA choice ribeye grilled on open flame and one whole steamed lobster served with lemon and melted butter $MP
RIBEYE STEAK Top quality black angus ribeye steak grilled on open flame to your specifications $21.99
LOBSTER THERMIDOR Baked in a rich cream sauce with a touch of Sherry $27.95

OVEN BROILED SEAFOOD

BROILED FISH Choose from Alaskan whitefish, Flounder or Catfish. Seasoned and grilled over an open flame. Served over rice pilaf **$10.99**

SWORDFISH a thick steak covered in herb butter and broiled. Served over rice pilaf **$12.99**

BROILED ATLANTIC SALMON An 8 oz. portion of delicious pink salmon broiled in our special seasonings. Served over rice pilaf **$10.99**

BUTTERFLY SHRIMP 12 pieces of shrimp basted in our unique mixture of seasonings, then broiled. Served over rice pilaf **$1**

SCALLOPS Fresh sea scallops perfectly seasoned and broile Served over rice pilaf **$15.99**

BLACKENED AHI TUNA with ginger-citrus sticky rice, sesame sugar snaps and wasabi **$22.99**

STUFFED LOBSTER Whole lobster oven broiled and stuffed with crab mea dressing **$36.95**

FRIED PLATTERS

Served with slaw, hushpuppies and tartar sauce.

Popcorn Shrimp 7.99
Fish & Popcorn Shrimp 10.49
Clam Strips 7.99
Sea Scallops 13.99
Oysters 13.99
Butterfly Shrimp 12.99
Fish & Chips 7.99
Skinless, Boneless Flounder 7.99
Farm Raised Catfish Filets 7.99

CATFISH

A great introductory fish for finicky eaters who refuse to try anything but fried shrimp at seafood restaurants. The flaky white flesh is relatively low in fat, which means that it's low in the fishy flavor that repels many a young diner.

BROILED SALMON

When it comes to fish, conventional nutritional wisdom is turned on its head: The fattier the fish, the better. That's because most of the fat is of the omega-3 variety, the kind proven to aid in the fight against everything from diabetes to asthma. Fatty salmon leads the way in omega-3s.

BLACKENED

The best flavor masker in the kitchen, this combination of dried spices such as paprika, onion powder, and cayenne can make a mild white fish like snapper, tilapia, or catfish taste like something close to chicken. Bonus: The spices in the blackening blend are calorie-free and loaded with antioxidants.

POPCORN SHRIMP

It's too bad that 75 percent of kids eating at seafood spots opt for these crunchy morsels. Even though they're tiny, they still weigh in at a hefty 500 calories.

FISH AND CHIPS

The biggest calorie bomb on the menu by an unhealthy measure. Add tartar sauce to the mix and you're looking at three-quarters of an 8-year-old's calorie allotment for the day. Yikes.

BBQ

PORK CHOP

In the world of barbecued meats, this is a relatively lean choice. At about 300 calories for a 4-ounce chop, this weighs in considerably lighter than the fat-speckled ribs and brisket.

SMOKED CHICKEN

Even with the skin on and slathered in barbecue sauce, this takes the prize for best entrée on the menu. Either white or dark meat will do, though the breast will save your kid about 75 calories over the leg.

SWEET TEA

The drink of choice at most 'cue shacks across the South, but would you put 9 spoonfuls of sugar in your cup of tea if you were making it at home? Well, then you shouldn't let your kids order it here, because ounce for ounce, true sweet tea has nearly as much sugar as a Mountain Dew®.

OUR MEATS

NORTH CAROLINA PULLED PORK	6.29
KANSAS CITY BURNT ENDS	6.29
TEXAS SLICED BEEF BRISKET	6.29
BARBECUED PORK CHOP	6.29
RED HOT SMOKED SAUSAGE	6.29
MEMPHIS DRY-RUBBED BARBECUED RIBS	
Lone Bone (one rib)	2.75
Rib Sandwich (2 ribs)	6.29
1/3 Slab (3-4 ribs)	11.95
1/2 Slab (5-6 ribs)	13.95
Full Slab (12 Ribs)	21.95
SMOKED CHICKEN	
1/4 Chicken	5.95
1/2 Chicken	9.95
Whole Chicken	16.95

BARBECUED BURRITO 5.29

arge flour tortilla stuffed with rice & ...s, cheese, cabbage, salsa, sour ...nd cilantro

...d pork, chicken, or burnt ends 6.29

OUR MEALS

OUR $60 VALUE

- (1) Slab of Ribs
- (1) Pint of Pulled Pork, Burnt Ends, Beef Brisket, Pulled Chicken, or Hot Sausage
- (1) Barbecued or Jamaican Jerk Half Chicken
- (1) Pint each, Baked Beans & Cole Slaw
- (4) Biscuits
- (2) Quarts of Lemonade or Iced Sweet Tea
- Half-pints of BBQ sauces

OUR $97 VALUE

- (2) Slabs of Ribs
- (2) Pints of Pulled Pork, Burnt Ends, Beef Brisket, Pulled Chicken, or Hot Sausage
- (2) Barbecued or Jamaican Jerk Half Chickens
- (1) Quart each, Baked Beans, Collard Greens, Black-eyed Corn & Cole Slaw
- (6) Biscuits
- (2) Quarts of Lemonade or Iced Sweet Tea
- Half-pints of BBQ sauces

See our **BAR MENU** for specialty drinks and beers on tap. Also serving homeade Lemonade and Iced Sweet Tea.

OUR OTHERS

BIG GREEN SALAD WITH CORNBREAD 4.75
Choice of or Italian
With pulled chicken or spicy chicken salad 6.29

HOT OPEN-FACED BRISKET SANDWICH 8.95
With mashed potatoes, pan gravy, collard greens and cornbread

FRIED CATFISH 10.75
Cornmeal crusted and served with cole slaw, hush puppies and mash potatoes

BLACKENED CATFISH 10.75
Grilled in spices and served with cole slaw, mash potatoes and black-eyed corn

PEEL 'N' EAT SHRIMP 12.95

POTLIKKER WITH BISCUITS 1.95
Ask and we'll tell ya

OUR SWEETS

PIE 2.95

KEY LIME PIE 2.95

FRUIT COBBLER WITH WHIPPED CREAM 2.95

DREAM BAR 1.95

OUR SIDES

BAKED BEANS 1.95 cup / 3.95 pint / 6.95 quart

HUSH PUPPIES $.95 / 1.9 / 3.95

BLACK-EYED CORN 3.9 / 6.95 q

HOMEMADE PICKLES 1.95 half pint

PAN GRAVY 3

COLE SLAW 3 / 6.9

BISCUITS $.

GREEN BEANS 3 / 6.9

MASH POTATOES 3 / 6.9

COLLARD GREENS 3.95 pint / 6.95 quart

RICE & BEANS 1.95 cup / 3.95 pint / 6.95 quart

ALL PLATTERS
served with choice of two sides, hush puppies and a biscuit.

HUSH PUPPIES

Fried balls of cornbread, often dipped by eager Southerners into tubs of whipped butter. If your kid gets one taste of these little weapons of mass destruction, a dangerous addiction will be born.

PEEL 'N' EAT SHRIMP

A superfood for growing boys and girls. Shrimp are high in vitamin B_{12} and vitamin D, which work together to help build strong, dense bones. And this low-calorie, protein-rich finger food is just messy enough to make it fun to eat.

BISCUITS

Though most restaurants have found a way to swap out the partially hydrogenated frying oils that used to saturate French fries and chicken nuggets in trans fats, no one seems to know how to make a trans fat–free biscuit. Restaurants rely on lard and semisolid fats to make biscuits flaky, and until a suitable replacement is made available, biscuits—with up to three times the amount of trans fats one should consume in a day—should be avoided at all costs.

COLLARD GREENS

The best side on this menu, and any menu, for that matter. Even if they're stewed with a ham hock, these bitter greens have an obscenely high level of vitamins A, C, and K, plus a punch of phytochemicals.

Thai

SPRING ROLLS

A healthy dose of carrots, cucumbers, and fresh herbs await inside, but Thai rolls come in two seasons: spring rolls, which are deep fried, and summer rolls, which are not. Now choose accordingly.

GREEN PAPAYA SALAD

It might sound strange to your kid, but the mix of shredded fruit, tomatoes, lime juice, peanuts, and a touch of palm sugar make for a perfectly refreshing and healthy starter. No offense, Mom, but it's 10 times more exciting than the iceberg salad you serve at home.

CHICKEN SATAY

This classic Thai street food combines two kid-favorite—chicken and peanuts—on a stick. Considering that an entrée portion contains less than 300 calories, mostly from lean protein, there's nothing not to love about satay.

TOFU

It might have the reputation as a low-calorie source of protein, but the soybean slab also serves as an edible sponge, so any treatment that involves oil—especially deep frying—will carry with it a few hundred calories of extra baggage.

APPETIZERS

SPRING ROLLS Vegetables $5.95

VIETNAMESE SUMMER ROLLS Shrimp or tofu $6.95

FRIED WONTON Chicken $6.95

STEAMED DUMPLING Chicken or vegetables $5.95

FRIED TOFU
Deep-Fried Fresh Tofu. Served with sweet sauce topped with crushed peanuts $4.50

PEAK GAI YANG
Special Thai B.B.Q. Wings marinated with Thai sauce $5.95

CHICKEN SATAY
Skewered chicken breast with peanut sauce dressing $7.95

PLA MUOK TOD
Deep fried squid served with sweet Chili sauce $6.95

MEE GROB
The most famous Thai crispy noodle with tomato-Tamarind sauce, tofu, bean sprouts $4.50

KA-NA-NAM-MAN-HOI
Steamed broccoli with oyster sauce, sesame oil and fried onion $4.50

SALADS

CUCUMBER SALAD
With sweet and sour sauce $4.00

THAI SALAD
Green salad, bean curd, cucumber, carrot with peanut sauce dressing $4.50

THAI CHICKEN SALAD
With chicken breast and peanut sauce dressing $8.95

TOFU SALAD
Steamed tofu tossed with spicy lime dressing $8.95

GREEN PAPAYA SALAD
Lime juice, string beans, tomato, crushed peanuts $4.50

YUM WOON SEN
Glass noodle with chicken tossed with spicy lime dressing $8.95

YUM YAI
Boiled chicken, egg, and shrimp over a bed of lettuce topped wit fresh peanuts and sweet & sour sauce $9.95

SPICY BBQ BEEF SALAD
Tossed with spicy lime dressing $9.95

VEGETABLES & TOFU

SAUTEED SPINACH $10.95

SZECHWAN STRING BEANS $10.95

GARLIC EGGPLANT $10.95

ORANGE TOFU .$10.95

SPECIALTIES

THAI BBQ CHICKEN .$10.95

BBQ PORK RIBS. $10.95

ORANGE CHICKEN $11.95

TERIYAKI CHICKEN $10.95

HONEY DUCK
Topped with house honey and hoisin sauce $12.95

GARLIC SCALLOPS $12.95

FISH WITH BLACK BEAN SAUCE $12.95

THAI CHILLI FISH
Lightly fried and topped with thai chilli sauce... $12.95

PLA LARD PRIK
Crispy snapper with chili, garlic and tamarind $12.95

NOODLE

PAD THAI
Stir-fried Thai noodles with shrimp, chicken, or vegetable, crushed peanuts, beansprouts & scallions. $7.95

PAD SEE YU
A traditional Thai broad noodles stir fried with broccoli, egg sweet soy sauce. (chicken or beef) $7.95

LAD NARD
Stir- fried broad noodles sweet soy sauce topped with gravy bean oyster and broccoli, carrot. (chicken or beef) $7.95

MEE GROB LAD NARD
Crispy egg noodles topped with brown gravy sauce, mushrooms, vegetables and chicken $7.95

BA MEE
Egg noodle topped with ground chicken, lime juice, ground peanut, and bean sprouts $7.95

PAD WOON SEN
Stir-fried glass noodle with shrimp, mushroom, egg, onion, tomato & cabbage in soy bean sauce $7.95

RICE

THAI FRIED RICE
With onion, carrot, pineapple, choice of chicken or beef $7.95

SPICY BASIL FRIED RICE
With chili, onion, and fresh basil. (chicken or beef) $7.95

VEGETABLES FRIED RICE $7.95

MANGO STICKY RICE $2 .50

RICE $1.00

PAD THAI

The perfect dish for all the spaghetti-loving boys and girls out there. Glass noodles are tossed with eggs, peanuts, cilantro, fresh lime juice—and often chicken, shrimp, or tofu. A kid-size portion has 450 calories, with only a small amount of (healthy) fat from the peanuts.

CRISPY NOODLES

There's only one way for noodles to end up crispy: a sizzling bath in hot oil. Expect dishes containing them to outpace stir-fried noodle dishes by 200 calories and 10 grams of fat.

THAI FRIED RICE

The only thing that keeps this rice from sticking to the giant woks chefs fry it in is a small pond of oil, most of which ends up in the dish.

MANGO STICKY RICE

Don't be fooled by the fruit: This dessert is a carb catastrophe. Go for the mango sorbet, instead.

4

AT THE SUPERMARKET

Win the Supermarket Sweepstakes

It is a place as colorful as a park in July, as full of wonder as a Disneyland vacation—and as dangerous to our children's health as a minefield with a play set in the middle of it. I'm talking, of course, about the American supermarket, that dazzling monstrosity of concrete and cinder block where food marketers compete for our attention—and the attention of our children.

Supermarkets are intricately constructed to extract the maximum amount of money from your pocket while loading as many cheap calories into your cart as possible. Next time you're in the market, take a look—literally—at what's on offer, specifically about 5 feet off the ground, where your eyes fall. You'll see lots of appealing, unhealthy, and often high-priced foods placed there, while the more healthful stuff is a little higher—you just have to search a bit for it.

Indeed, searching the shelves in a state of confusion is a common experience. Have you ever gone into the market for what you thought was a quick stop and found yourself still trapped in the aisles 45 minutes later, frantically searching for that one last item—and maybe thinking that memory loss has set in early? In fact, it's not you, it's your supermarket—many grocery store chains intentionally switch around the placement of their products from time to time to cause shoppers confusion, because more time spent in the market means, in most cases, more money spent. Often, they'll try to get you to try a new, more-expensive brand of, say, jam, by putting it in the exact place where their best-selling brand usually rests. And there you are, scratching your head, as though it's your fault. (Hey, it happens to me, too!)

If you really want a lesson in food marketing, go to the cereal aisle. Where are the cereals targeted to you? Right at eye level. Where are the cereals with the dancing leprechauns, chocolaty vampires, and cuddly honey bears? At about hip level, right where kids can spot them. Oh, and here's the rub: Where's the candy? In most markets, the candy aisle is directly across from the cereal aisle—because all parents with kids need cereal, and all kids love candy, and . . .

You get the gist. Now, where can you find the milk, the eggs, the butter—the stuff every shopper needs? Invariably, they're all the way at the back of the store, so even a quick pop-in to get one of these staples with the kids in tow means that they'll be exposed to as many swaggering pirates, smiling clowns, and cereal-chowing sports heroes as possible.

Instead of falling victim to modern marketing, use these tricks to protect your children—and your paycheck.

STICK TO THE EDGE. Think of the grocery store as a battleground, and the edges of the store—where the produce, dairy, and meat are sold—as your green zone. Keep your kids there, and make only strategic, solo incursions into the middle aisles to snag beans and whole-grain cereals—lest your little ones be abducted by cartoon pitchmen hawking sugar.

CHOOSE REAL FRUIT. Believe it or not, 51 percent of children's food products have pictures of fruit on the package, but no actual fruit inside. Even fruit juices can be deceiving—most are just flavored sugar water. So stick to the fresh stuff. You can get all the vitamin C you need in one day from just one orange—with only half the calories of a glass of OJ.

KNOW YOUR GRAINS. If the label says, "Made with whole grain," that doesn't mean it's healthy—just pick up a box of Franken Berry and you'll see what we mean. A product only needs to be made of 51 percent whole grain ingredients in order to carry this label. To make sure, check that the word "whole" is next to every flour listed in the ingredients.

DON'T GO AU NATURAL. The phrase *all natural* has no specific FDA definition, and there is no legislation or standards for it. Just about anything can be called "all natural."

BANISH TECHNOSUGAR. Sugar shows up in so many products, and under so many different names, that you may not even know that it's there. Look for these aliases: maltose, sorghum, sorbitol, dextrose, lactose, fructose, high-fructose corn syrup (HFCS), and glucose. And then there are the healthy-sounding versions: molasses, brown rice sugar, fruit juice, turbinado, barley malt, honey, and organic cane juice. All sugars spike insulin levels and affect the body in the same way. A good rule of thumb is to skip any product that lists sugar as one of its first four ingredients.

SKIP THE COCKTAILS. Stay away from beverages containing the words "drink," "cocktail," "punch," "beverage," or "-ade." Unless something is called "100 percent fruit juice," it's not. Even 100 percent fruit juices provide minimal nutritional value and contain as many or more calories as soft drinks. That being said, fruit juice can be a healthier alternative to soda. Mix 100 percent fruit juices with seltzer water to make a fruit spritzer, which is carbonated like soda, but has fewer calories.

KICK THE RABBIT. A cartoon character pitching food is always a bad sign. Case in point: Trix yogurt, which touts itself as "the most fun and colorful yogurt" (this is the yogurt of choice in some elementary school cafeterias). For the best nutritional value, opt for unsweetened yogurt and add your own fruit.

DON'T BE FRESH. The idea of "fresh" fruits and vegetables is great, but unless you're buying strawberries in June or tomatoes in August, that produce was probably picked unripe, trucked thousands of miles, and set to ripen under the loving, all-natural fluorescent lighting of your supermarket chain. Frozen produce, on the other hand, is usually allowed to ripen on the vine and is then frozen immediately, so it often contains more nutrients—and flavor. If you want fresh, only buy it if you're going to eat it within 3 or 4 days.

TRICK THEM WITH FRUIT. Canned pineapple, mandarin oranges, and peaches are a genius way of satisfying a kid's sweet tooth without giving them actual sweets. Just avoid the ones packed in sweetened syrup.

LEAN ON BEANS. Think of beans—which are packed with protein, fiber, and nutrients—as miniature weight-loss pills. Buy them in cans and add them to pastas, soups, salad, dips, and burritos—wherever you can disguise them.

ADD RAISINS. Raisins are packed with vitamins and minerals, but most commercial cereals coat their raisins with sugar. Be smart—buy straight-up bran and add your own, far healthier, raisins.

DON'T GET BITTEN. Frostbite sets in after 3 to 4 months in the freezer. Don't buy big economy bags of foodstuffs and think you'll save money by storing them; you'll just wind up throwing a lot out.

SNACK BEFORE SHOPPING. One of the sneakiest supermarket tricks isn't played on your eyes or your ears, it's played on your nose. Even supermarkets that don't bake bread on premises—and most don't—seem to smell like a bakery because they often pull baked goods from the freezer and nuke them to create a "lovin'-from-the-oven" scent. Whole Foods Markets are geniuses at the "scents-make-sense" game: Note the chocolate-making stations and the chicken rotisseries at the fronts of the stores. To keep your nose from triggering your salivary glands—which are, by the way, directly tied to your wallet—make sure you and your kids are fed before you shop. (Sugar-free gum or other smart ways to keep their mouths working can also cut down on the "screaming-bloody-murder-until-you-buy-me-that" tantrums.)

HOW TO USE THIS SECTION

As any parent knows, kids have very specific tastes, which is why this section focuses on comparisons between similar foods (peanut butter cookies vs. peanut butter cookies; apple juice vs. apple juice)—so that you can find the healthiest versions of all of the foods they love most. The boxes are color-coded to help you find the relevant comparisons. Happy shopping!

Check out even more great grocery store pics, along with the 125 best foods for you and your family, at ***eatthis.com***

What You Can Learn from Labels

Nutrition Facts

Serving Size 1 Cup (32g/1.1 oz.)
Servings Per Container About 10

Amount Per Serving	Cereal	Cereal with ½ Cup Vitamins A&D Fat Free Milk
Calories	120	160
Calories from Fat	10	10
	% Daily Value**	
Total Fat 1g*	2%	2%
Saturated Fat 0.5g	3%	3%
Trans Fat 0g		
Cholesterol 0mg	0%	0%
Sodium 150mg	6%	9%
Potassium 35mg	1%	7%
Total Carbohydrate 28g	9%	11%
Dietary Fiber 1g	4%	4%
Sugars 15g		
Other Carbohydrate 12g		
Protein 1g		
Vitamin A	10%	15%
Vitamin C	25%	25%
Calcium	0%	15%
Iron	25%	25%
Vitamin D	10%	25%
Thiamin	25%	30%
Riboflavin	25%	35%
Niacin	25%	25%
Vitamin B_6	25%	25%
Folic Acid	25%	25%
Vitamin B_{12}	25%	35%
Phosphorus	2%	15%
Zinc	10%	15%

* Amount in cereal. One half cup of fat free milk contributes an additional 40 calories, 65mg sodium, 6g total carbohydrates (6g sugars), and 4g protein.

** Percent Daily Values are based on a 2,000 calorie diet. Your daily values may be higher or lower depending on your calorie needs:

	Calories	2,000	2,500
Total Fat	Less than	65g	80g
Saturated Fat	Less than	20g	25g
Cholesterol	Less than	300mg	300mg
Sodium	Less than	2,400mg	2,400mg
Potassium		3,500mg	3,500mg
Total Carbohydrate		300g	375g
Dietary Fiber		25g	30g

Calories per gram: Fat 9 • Carbohydrate 4 • Protein 4

INGREDIENTS: SUGAR; CORN FLOUR; WHEAT FLOUR; OAT FLOUR; PARTIALLY HYDROGENATED VEGETABLE OIL (ONE OR MORE OF: COCONUT, COTTONSEED, AND SOYBEAN); SALT; SODIUM ASCORBATE AND ASCORBIC ACID (VITAMIN C); NIACINAMIDE; REDUCED IRON; NATURAL ORANGE, LEMON, CHERRY, RASPBERRY, BLUEBERRY, LIME, AND OTHER NATURAL FLAVORS; RED #40; BLUE #2; ZINC OXIDE; YELLOW #6; TURMERIC COLOR; PYRIDOXINE HYDROCHLORIDE (VITAMIN B_6); BLUE #1; RIBOFLAVIN (VITAMIN B_2); THIAMIN HYDROCHLORIDE (VITAMIN B_1); ANNATTO COLOR; VITAMIN A PALMITATE; BHT

The Food and Drug Administration requires all manufacturers to provide accurate and comprehensive information on ingredients and nutritional content on the back labels of packaged products. But all those random numbers and eight-syllable words can be daunting even for nutritionists, so to make matters easy on you, we've concocted a super simple four-step plan for choosing the healthiest product in every supermarket category. Start with number 1 and start eliminating products.

1 CALORIES After all, they're the largest contributor to obesity and the cluster of serious maladies—diabetes, heart disease—that come with it. If two similar products have servings within 25 calories of each other, move on to 2.

2 UNHEALTHY FATS If it contains trans fat (look for partially hydrogenated oils), or if "interesterified" oils or "stearate-rich" appear in the ingredients, find another product. Safe? Move on to 3.

3 SUGARS Always choose the food with the least amount. If sugars are within 3 grams, go on to 4.

4 FIBER The more, the better. Still a close call? Check out the tiebreaker.

THE TIEBREAKER NUMBER OF INGREDIENTS The product that has the least wins.

Food manufacturers will put anything on their packages in hopes of persuading a busy mom to fill up her cart with their goods—no matter how dubious they might be. Unfortunately, the FDA does little to regulate the vagaries that clutter the fronts of cookie boxes and juice containers. As a result, most of these health claims have, at best, a tenuous relationship with the truth.

We've picked out four products with glitzy front labels that tell one tale and back labels that tell quite another. There are hundreds of other products cluttering the aisles guilty of the same offense, so spot the tricks on these labels and use your BS detector on everything else in the supermarket.

Lunchables

Be skeptical of packages adorned with cartoon characters, Hollywood heroes, or promises of toys inside. Studies show that products marketed directly to children are often poorer in terms of nutrition than regular packaged goods.

This isn't "sensible"—it's a science project gone awry. The ingredient list takes the better part of an afternoon to read through and requires a chemistry book even to begin to understand. All told, there are no fewer than 70 ingredients on the list, from the undesirable (partially hydrogenated soybean oil, high-fructose corn syrup, sodium nitrite) to the unpronounceable (acesulfame potassium, sodium stearoyl lactylate).

According to Kraft, "The Sensible Solution green flag on package labels is an easy way to identify better-for-you choices from among many food and beverage products. Sensible Solution criteria require that ALL qualifying products contain limited amounts of calories, fat (including saturated and trans fat), sodium, and sugar." A panel of Kraft nutritionists use US Dietary Guidelines in determining which of their products are worthy of recognition. Despite the seemingly strict standards this green flag is meant to represent, the Maxed Out Deep Dish pizza contains 510 calories and 36 g sugars.

INGREDIENTS: WATER - NATURAL SPRING WATER. **PIZZA CRUST** - ENRICHED WHEAT FLOUR (WHEAT FLOUR, NIACIN, REDUCED IRON, THIAMIN MONONITRATE [VITAMIN B1], RIBOFLAVIN [VITAMIN B2], FOLIC ACID), WATER, YEAST, HIGH FRUCTOSE CORN SYRUP, SOYBEAN OIL, CONTAINS LESS THAN 2% OF WHEY (FROM MILK), SALT, POTASSIUM CHLORIDE, SODIUM STEAROYL LACTYLATE, RICE BRAN EXTRACT, MONO- AND DIGLYCERIDES, CALCIUM PROPIONATE (PRESERVATIVE), DRIED GARLIC, ALPHA CELLULOSE, PECTIN, CELLULOSE GUM, NATURAL AND ARTIFICIAL FLAVOR, ENZYMES, L-CYSTEINE. **CONTAINS: WHEAT, MILK. PIZZA SAUCE** - WATER, TOMATO PASTE, HIGH FRUCTOSE CORN SYRUP, MODIFIED FOOD STARCH, CONTAINS LESS THAN 2% OF SALT, SPICE, ONION POWDER, CITRIC ACID, XANTHAN GUM, POTASSIUM SORBATE (PRESERVATIVE), NATURAL FLAVOR, SOY LECITHIN. **CONTAINS: SOY. 2% MILK NATURAL REDUCED FAT MOZZARELLA CHEESE** - REDUCED FAT MOZZARELLA CHEESE (PASTEURIZED PART-SKIM MILK, CHEESE CULTURE, SALT, ENZYMES, VITAMIN A PALMITATE), CELLULOSE POWDER ADDED TO PREVENT CAKING, NATAMYCIN (A NATURAL MOLD INHIBITOR). **CONTAINS: MILK. ARTIFICIALLY FLAVORED CANDY** - SUGAR, CORN SYRUP, MALTODEXTRIN, DEXTROSE, MODIFIED FOOD STARCH (CORN), PARTIALLY HYDROGENATED SOYBEAN OIL, CITRIC ACID, WATER, ARTIFICIAL FLAVOR, RED 40. **MANUFACTURED IN A FACILITY THAT PROCESSES WHEAT FLOUR. CONTAINS: WHEAT. PEPPERONI FLAVORED SAUSAGE** - PORK, WATER, PEPPERONI (PORK, SALT, SPICES, DEXTROSE, GARLIC POWDER, LACTIC ACID STARTER CULTURE, SODIUM NITRITE), CONTAINS LESS THAN 2% OF SALT, DEXTROSE, POTASSIUM CHLORIDE, FLAVOR, MALTODEXTRIN, LACTIC ACID STARTER CULTURE, EXTRACTIVES OF PAPRIKA, SODIUM ASCORBATE, SODIUM NITRITE. **TROPICAL PUNCH ARTIFICIAL FLAVOR SOFT DRINK MIX** - SUGAR, FRUCTOSE, CITRIC ACID (PROVIDES TARTNESS), CONTAINS LESS THAN 2% OF NATURAL AND ARTIFICIAL FLAVOR, ASCORBIC ACID (VITAMIN C), VITAMIN E ACETATE, CALCIUM PHOSPHATE (PREVENTS CAKING), ACESULFAME POTASSIUM AND SUCRALOSE (SWEETENERS), ARTIFICIAL COLOR, RED 40, BLUE 1, BHA (PRESERVES FRESHNESS). **CHEESY FLAVORED SEASONING - ARTIFICIALLY FLAVORED** - MALTODEXTRIN, NATURAL BUTTER FLAVOR (AUTOLYZED YEAST EXTRACT, NATURAL FLAVOR [CONTAINS MILK], TAPIOCA MALTODEXTRIN, MALTODEXTRIN, CULTURED WHEY, CALCIUM PHOSPHATE, SILICON DIOXIDE, WHEAT BRAN, SALT, WHEAT, MOLASSES, NATURAL FLAVOR [MALTODEXTRIN, MEDIUM CHAIN TRIGLYCERIDES, MODIFIED FOOD STARCH, NATURAL FLAVOR], CALCIUM PHOSPHATE, TRIETHYL CITRATE), NATURAL FLAVOR (PARTIALLY HYDROGENATED SOYBEAN OIL, NATURAL FLAVOR), SILICON DIOXIDE AS AN ANTICAKING AGENT, ALUMINUM OXIDE, YELLOW 6 LAKE, YELLOW 5. **CONTAINS: MILK, WHEAT.**

DISTRIBUTED BY KRAFT FOODS GLOBAL, INC. NORTHFIELD, IL [illegible] USA

Smart Start Cereal

The front of the cereal box is dominated by a slew of vague terms that hit on current "healthy" buzz words in the packaged food industry, but ultimately deliver scarcely little substance.

"Strong Heart": With no formal definition from the FDA, it's difficult to discern what it actually refers to. Perhaps the 5 grams of fiber, which *have* been shown to help stabilize cholesterol levels? Or maybe the 38 items that clutter the ingredients list, which include a barrage of preservatives, synthetic sweeteners, and artificial flavorings?

"Antioxidants": Most cereals can make the same claim, since most are fortified with a near-standard mix of minerals and antioxidant-carrying vitamins like A, C, and E.

"Smart Start": The most misleading term of them all. A real smart start would mean a cereal high in fiber, low in sugar, and with a relatively short ingredient list. Unfortunately, this cereal only meets one of the criteria.

Kellogg's

SMART START

STRONG HEART

Whole-Grain Oats, Antioxidants, & Low Sodium

NEW LOOK!

Maple Brown Sugar

Lightly sweetened, maple & brown sugar, toasted flakes with whole-grain oats and crunchy oat clusters

NET WT. 15.2 OZ. (431g)

This cereal is anything but "lightly sweetened." In fact, each flake is battered with a barrage of sweeteners, including sugar, molasses, honey, corn syrup, and high-fructose corn syrup.

All told, there are eight references to sweeteners in the ingredients list, more than any other cereal we've found in the supermarket aisles.

The resulting 17 grams of sugar make Smart Start one of the sweetest cereals on the market—just 3 grams of sugar shy of a Haagen Dazs Vanilla and Almond Ice Cream bar.

Among the many sweetened kids' cereals with less sugar per serving than Smart Start: Lucky Charms, Frosted Flakes, Trix, Froot Loops, Cocoa Pebbles.

SMART START®

Maple Brown Sugar

Nutrition Facts

Serving Size 1¼ Cups (60g/2.1 oz.)

Servings Per Container About 7

Amount Per Serving	Cereal	Cereal with ½ Cup Vitamins A&D Fat Free Milk
Calories	220	260
Calories from Fat	20	20
	% Daily Value**	
Total Fat 2.5g*	4%	4%
Saturated Fat 0.5g	3%	3%
Trans Fat 0g		
Cholesterol 0mg	0%	0%
Sodium 140mg	6%	8%
Potassium 380mg	11%	17%
Total Carbohydrate 47g	16%	18%
Dietary Fiber 5g	19%	19%
Soluble Fiber 2g		
Insoluble Fiber 3g		
Sugars 17g		
Other Carbohydrate 25g		
Protein 6g		
Vitamin A (10% as beta carotene)	25%	30%
Vitamin C	25%	25%
Calcium	2%	15%
Iron	25%	25%
Vitamin D	10%	25%
Vitamin E	100%	100%
Thiamin	25%	30%
Riboflavin	25%	35%
Niacin	25%	25%
Vitamin B_6	25%	25%
Folic Acid	25%	25%
Vitamin B_{12}	25%	35%
Pantothenate	25%	30%
Phosphorus	25%	35%
Magnesium	20%	20%
Zinc	25%	25%

* Amount in cereal. One half cup of fat free milk contributes an additional 40 calories, 65mg sodium, 6g total carbohydrates (6g sugars), and 4g protein.

** Percent Daily Values are based on a 2,000 calorie diet. Your daily values may be higher or lower depending on your calorie needs:

	Calories	2,000	2,500
Total Fat	Less than	65g	80g
Sat. Fat	Less than	20g	25g
Cholesterol	Less than	300mg	300mg
Sodium	Less than	2,400mg	2,400mg
Potassium		3,500mg	3,500mg
Total Carbohydrate		300g	375g
Dietary Fiber		25g	30g

Calories per gram: Fat 9 • Carbohydrate 4 • Protein 4

INGREDIENTS: OAT BLEND (WHOLE OATS, OAT BRAN), RICE, SUGAR, MAPLE AND BROWN SUGAR FLAVORED OAT CLUSTERS (SUGAR, TOASTED OATS [ROLLED WHOLE OATS, SUGAR, CANOLA OIL WITH TBHQ AND CITRIC ACID TO PRESERVE FRESHNESS, MOLASSES, HONEY, BHT FOR FRESHNESS, SOY LECITHIN], WHEAT FLAKES, CRISP RICE [RICE, SUGAR, MALT, SALT], CORN SYRUP, POLYDEXTROSE, HONEY, NATURAL AND ARTIFICIAL FLAVORS, CINNAMON, BHT FOR FRESHNESS, ARTIFICIAL VANILLA FLAVOR), HIGH FRUCTOSE CORN SYRUP, MALT FLAVORING, POTASSIUM CHLORIDE, SALT, NATURAL AND ARTIFICIAL FLAVOR, VITAMIN A PALMITATE, BAKING SODA, ASCORBIC ACID (VITAMIN C), NIACINAMIDE, ZINC OXIDE, CALCIUM PANTOTHENATE, REDUCED IRON, VITAMIN D, ALPHA TOCOPHEROL ACETATE (VITAMIN E), BHT (PRESERVATIVE), PYRIDOXINE HYDROCHLORIDE (VITAMIN B_6), RIBOFLAVIN (VITAMIN B_2), THIAMIN HYDROCHLORIDE (VITAMIN B_1), BETA CAROTENE (A SOURCE OF VITAMIN A), FOLIC ACID, VITAMIN B_{12}.

CONTAINS WHEAT AND SOY INGREDIENTS.

Exchange: 3 Carbohydrates

The dietary exchanges are based on the *Exchange Lists for Meal Planning*, ©2003 by The American Diabetes Association, Inc. and The American Dietetic Association.

Distributed by Kellogg Sales Co. Battle Creek, MI 49016 USA ®, TM, © 2007 Kellogg NA Co.

†® American Heart Association

Visit **Kelloggs.com** for information on promotions, recipes, products, and FAQs.
To check your offer order status go to **Kelloggs.com/orders**
Phone us at 1-800-962-1413
Write to P.O. Box CAMB, Battle Creek, MI 49016-1986
Provide production code on package.

Whole grain, yes, but wholesome? Hardly. These oats are covered in an unsavory mix of "sugar, canola oil with TBHQ and citric acid to preserve freshness, molasses, honey, BHT for freshness, soy lecithin." Try to avoid ingredients with their own acronyms.

The FDA defines "low sodium" as anything under 140 milligrams, which is exactly what this cereal has. Most cereals can claim the same, though, since it's a sugar- (not salt-) driven product.

Pop-Tarts

Yes, thankfully, there are actual strawberries in strawberry Pop Tarts. Problem is, it's the ninth ingredient in the list, six slots below high-fructose corn syrup.

The vitamin list? 10 percent of vitamin A, iron, niacin, thiamin, B_6, riboflavin, and folic acid. In accordance with USDA regulations, in order for a food product to claim that it is a "good source" of something, it must contain at least 10 percent of the recommended daily intake. The problem is that this system fails to consider the other junk that comes along with it, things like saturated fat and sugar. So Pop-Tarts can call itself a good source of vitamins, and if your child eats 10 of these toaster pastries, she will have earned her daily intake of seven vitamins plus well over 2,000 calories. Sort of makes you wonder what a bad source of vitamins would be. So a 900-calorie pizza with 10 percent of the recommended daily intake of vitamin A can stamp "Good source of vitamin A!" on its box.

Unfortunately, two of the lowest numbers on the box also happen to be the most important, especially for something you might consider feeding to your kids for breakfast.

It's important to start the day with a bit of protein, as protein wakes up our metabolism and gets us burning calories early in the day.

Fiber is important because it helps control blood sugar levels, which makes it a potent defense mechanism against type 2 diabetes, a rising epidemic with kids in this country. And by slowing the rate at which food leaves the stomach, fiber is also a vital component of satiety, which means your child won't run out of fuel midmorning.

Nutrition Facts
Serving Size 1 Pastry (52g)
Servings Per Container 8
Amount Per Serving
Calories 210 Calories from Fat 50
% Daily Value*
Total Fat 6g 9%
Saturated Fat 2g 10%
Trans Fat 0g
Cholesterol 0mg 0%
Sodium 180mg 8%
Total Carbohydrate 37g 12%
Dietary Fiber less than 1g 3%
Sugars 16g
Protein 2g
Vitamin A 10% • Vitamin C 0% • Calcium 0%
Iron 10% • Thiamin 10% • Riboflavin 10%
Niacin 10% • Vitamin B6 10% • Folic Acid 10%
* Percent Daily Values are based on a 2,000 calorie diet. Your daily values may be higher or lower depending on your calorie needs:
Calories 2,000 2,500
Total Fat Less than 65g 80g
Sat. Fat Less than 20g 25g
Cholesterol Less than 300mg 300mg
Sodium Less than 2,400mg 2,400mg
Total Carbohydrate 300g 375g
Dietary Fiber 25g 30g
Calories per gram: Fat 9 • Carbohydrate 4 • Protein 4
INGREDIENTS: ENRICHED FLOUR (WHEAT FLOUR, NIACINAMIDE, REDUCED IRON, THIAMIN MONONITRATE [VITAMIN B1], RIBOFLAVIN [VITAMIN B2], FOLIC ACID), CORN SYRUP, HIGH FRUCTOSE CORN SYRUP, DEXTROSE, VEGETABLE OIL (SOYBEAN, COTTONSEED AND HYDROGENATED COTTONSEED OIL† WITH TBHQ AND CITRIC ACID FOR FRESHNESS), CRACKER MEAL. CONTAINS TWO PERCENT OR LESS OF WHEAT STARCH, SALT, DRIED STRAWBERRIES, DRIED APPLES, DRIED PEARS, LEAVENING (BAKING SODA, SODIUM ACID PYROPHOSPHATE, MONOCALCIUM PHOSPHATE), CITRIC ACID, MODIFIED WHEAT STARCH, CORNSTARCH, CARAMEL COLOR, XANTHAN GUM, SOY LECITHIN, NIACINAMIDE, REDUCED IRON, RED #40, YELLOW #6, VITAMIN A PALMITATE, PYRIDOXINE HYDROCHLORIDE (VITAMIN B6), RIBOFLAVIN (VITAMIN B2), THIAMIN HYDROCHLORIDE (VITAMIN B1), FOLIC ACID.
†LESS THAN 0.5g TRANS FAT PER SERVING.
CONTAINS WHEAT AND SOY INGREDIENTS.
Distributed by Kellogg Sales Co., Battle Creek, MI 49016 USA
®, TM, © 2006 Kellogg NA Co.
Have you tried these flavors frozen?
Chocolate Chip Cookie Dough
Strawberry Milkshake
Chocolate Fudge
Cookies & Creme
Chocolate Chip
Mint Chocolate Chip
Hot Fudge Sundae
Which flavor will you try next?

Dole Mandarins in Orange Gel

Chefs may know a thing or two about taste, but judging by the calorie bombs served up in most restaurants across the country, most care little of nutrition. They say so themselves on their Web site: "To receive a ChefsBest Certified Award, a product must meet the high quality standards set by the ChefsBest judges. Because of widely differing opinions, ChefsBest does not make a judgment on a product's stated nutritional or performance claims."

Unfortunately, "all natural" means very little when placed on a package, since the FDA doesn't have a definition for this claim. Although the fruit itself is real, it's gelled into a decidedly unnatural blend of additives and preservatives.

The ingredients include: sugar, natural and artificial flavors, sodium citrate, locust bean gum, malic acid, fumaric acid, potassium citrate, and FD&C yellow #6—a far cry from natural ingredients.

Dole puts this claim on a lot of their fruit cups, including those packaged with sugary syrup.

A medium mandarin, one of the naturally sweetest fruits on earth, contains 9 grams of sugar, so the remaining 13 grams are added sugars found in the gel.

That same medium tangerine has 47 calories and 2 grams of fiber, which means that with Dole's clever concoction here your kid gets twice the calories and half the fiber of the real thing.

Alternative Sweeteners

While there is a robust debate among scientists about the potential dangers of alternative sweeteners, research is still too new to make any final judgments. With little evidence to support cancer-causing claims made by those who oppose aspartame and its ilk, and a supermarket's worth of research clearly documenting the ill effects of sugar, we see no clear reason to cut out artificial sweeteners entirely, if it means decreasing sugar in your kid's diet. That being said, not all alternative sweeteners are created equal, and it's best to avoid excessively sweetened foods, artificial or not. When possible, shoot for natural ingredients and a short ingredients list.

ASPARTAME

What Is It? A low-calorie artificial sweetener made by joining two amino acids with an alcohol

How Sweet Is It? 180 times sweeter than sugar

Potential Dangers: Some researchers claim to have linked aspartame to brain tumors and lymphoma, but the FDA insists that the sweetener is safe for humans. A list of complaints submitted to the Department of Health and Human Services includes headaches, dizziness, diarrhea, memory loss, and mood changes. The Center for Science in the Public Interest states that children should avoid drinks sweetened with aspartame.

Found in: NutraSweet, Equal, Diet Coke, Sugar Free Popsicle

Limit

ACESULFAME POTASSIUM

What Is It? A zero-calorie sweetener that often appears with sucralose or aspartame to create a flavor closer to sugar

How Sweet Is It? 200 times sweeter than sugar

Potential Dangers: In 2003, the FDA approved acesulfame-K for everything besides meat and poultry. Although the FDA does not recognize the sweetener as a carcinogen, some experts disagree. They point to flawed tests as the basis for the FDA's acceptance of the additive. Large doses have been shown to cause problems in the thyroid glands of rats, rabbits, and dogs.

Found in: PowerAde Zero, Coke Zero, Breyers No Sugar Added Vanilla Ice Cream

Limit

SUCRALOSE

What Is It? A zero-calorie sugar derivative made by joining chlorine particles to sugar molecules

How Sweet Is It? 600 times sweeter than sugar

Potential Dangers: After reviewing more than 110 animal and human studies, the FDA decided in 1999 to approve sucralose for use in all foods. Sucralose opponents argue that the amount of human research is inadequate, but even groups like the Center for Science in the Public Interest have deemed it safe.

Found in: Splenda, Minute Maid Fruit Falls, Dannon Light & Fit

Safe

SUGAR ALCOHOLS

What Is It? A group of alcohols such as lactilol, sorbitol, and mannitol that provide roughly 25 percent fewer calories than sugar

How Sweet Is It? They vary from one alcohol to another, but generally they're slightly less sweet than sugar.

Potential Dangers: Sugar alcohols are applauded for not causing tooth decay and providing a smaller impact on blood sugar. Because they are not well digested, however, sugar alcohols may cause intestinal discomfort, gas, and diarrhea. Some people also report carb cravings after ingesting too much of these sweeteners.

Found in: Smuckers Sugar Free Breakfast Syrup, Wrigley's Gum, Jell-O Sugar Free cups

Limit

SACCHARIN

What Is It? A chemically complex zero-calorie sweetener

How Sweet Is It? 300 times sweeter than sugar

Potential Dangers: Between 1977 and 2000, the FDA mandated that saccharin-containing products carry a label warning consumers about the risk of cancer, due largely to the development of bladder tumors in saccharin-consuming rats. Saccharin still isn't in the clear. One recent study funded by Purdue and the National Institute of Health showed that rats with a saccharin-rich diet gained more weight than those with high-sugar diets.

Found in: Sweet'N Low

Avoid

Cereal

Eat This

Kashi® 7 Whole Grain Honey Puffs
(1 c)
120 calories
1 g fat (0 g saturated)
6 g sugars
2 g fiber

This cereal packs 22 grams of whole grains per serving.

Dora the Explorer™ Cereal (¾ c/27 g)
100 calories
1.5 g fat
(0 g saturated)
6 g sugars
3 g fiber
Dora provides kids with a healthy mix of iron and B vitamins.

MultiGrain Cheerios®
(1 c/29 g)
110 calories
1 g fat
(0 g saturated)
6 g sugars
3 g fiber
Of all the Cheerios-branded cereals, this one is second only to the original Cheerios.

Berry Burst Cheerios®
(¾ c/27 g)
100 calories
1 g fat
(0 g saturated)
8 g sugars
2 g fiber
The "burst" comes in the form of real freeze-dried strawberries, raspberries, and blueberries.

Kix® (1¼ c/30 g)
110 calories
1 g fat
(0 g saturated)
3 g sugars
3 g fiber
This low-cal cereal contains nearly half of your child's recommended daily intake of folic acid and iron.

Cinnabon™ Cinnamon Crunch (1 c/40 g)
150 calories
1.5 g fat
(0 g saturated)
10 g sugars
3 g fiber
Much of the sugar comes from concentrated fruit juice and honey.

All-Bran® Yogurt Bites
(1¼ c/56 g)
190 calories
3 g fat
(1.5 g saturated)
7 g sugars
10 g fiber
A single bowl has almost one-third of a child's daily fiber.

Kashi® Mighty Bites™ (1 c/33 g)
120 calories
1.5 g fat
(0 g saturated)
5 g sugars
3 g fiber
Kashi's cereals have a mix of healthy grains; this one contains 25% of the day's calcium and half of the day's iron.

Cascadian Farm® Clifford™ Crunch (1 c/30 g)
100 calories
1 g fat
(0 g saturated)
6 g sugars
5 g fiber
Whole grain oat and barley flours give this cereal a healthy boost of fiber.

Not That!

Cap'n Crunch®
(3/4 c/27 g)
110 calories
1.5 g fat
(1 g saturated)
12 g sugars
1 g fiber
Yellow 5, used to color Cap'n Crunch, has been linked to hyperactivity and attention-deficit disorder.

Apple Cinnamon Cheerios®
(3/4 c/30 g)
120 calories
1.5 g fat
(0 g saturated)
12 g sugars
1 g fiber
Grains are only good when they're not covered in sugar.

Honey Smacks®
(3/4 c/27 g)
100 calories
0.5 g fat (0 g saturated)
15 g sugars
1 g fiber

Calorie for calorie, this is the sweetest cereal in the supermarket.

Fruity Pebbles®
(3/4 c/30 g)
110 calories
1 g fat
(1 g saturated)
11 g sugars
3 g fiber

Corn Pops®
(1 c/31 g)
120 calories
0 g fat
14 g sugars
< 1 g fiber
The basic formula for this cereal is milled corn soaked in sugar and corn syrup.

Nature's Path EnviroKidz™ Organic Gorilla Munch® (3/4 c/30 g)
120 calories
0 g fat
(0 g saturated)
8 g sugars
2 g fiber
The ratio of sugar to nutrients is concerningly high.

Golden Grahams®
(3/4 c/31 g)
120 calories
1 g fat
(0 g saturated)
15 g sugars
1 g fiber
We're glad General Mills is commited to whole grains, but we can't get past all that sugar.

Yogurt Burst® Cheerios®
(3/4 c/30 g)
120 calories
1.5 g fat
(0.5 g saturated)
9 g sugars
2 g fiber
It looks innocent, but almost one-third of this cereal's calories come from sugars.

French Toast Crunch®
(1 c/41 g)
173 calories
4 g fat
(0 g saturated)
15 g sugars
1 g fiber

Cereal

Eat This

Frosted Mini-Wheats® Bite Size (12 biscuits/30 g)

100 calories
0.5 g fat (0 g saturated)
6 g sugars
4 g fiber

Not only does it have 3 grams of protein, but it also has 45 percent of your child's daily iron and a whole host of B vitamins.

Kashi® GOLEAN® (1 c)

140 calories
1 g fat
(0 g saturated)
6 g sugars
10 g fiber

One of our favorite cereals, with enough sweetness for a kid to enjoy, plus major fiber to boot.

All-Bran® Complete® Wheat Flakes (1 c)

120 calories
1 g fat
(0 g saturated)
7 g sugars
7 g fiber

The same fiber hit for a fraction of the calories.

Quaker® Oatmeal Squares Brown Sugar (1 c/56 g)

210 calories
2.5 g fat
(0.5 g saturated)
10 g sugars
5 g fiber

All of the fiber of granola, without the sugar surge.

Grape-Nuts® Flakes (¾ c/29 g)

110 calories
1 g fat
(0 g saturated)
4 g sugars
3 g fiber

A hint of sweetness, plus enough fiber to keep their bellies full until lunch.

Full Circle® Raisin Bran (1 c)

190 calories
1 g fat
(0 g saturated)
13 g sugars
6 g fiber

Instead of being battered in sugar, Full Circle's raisins are coated in cane juice.

Cheerios
Toasted Whole Grain Oat Cereal
Whole Grain Guaranteed
OATS
TO HELP NATURALLY LOWER CHOLESTEROL

Cheerios® (1 c)

100 calories
2 g fat
(0 g saturated)
1 g sugars
3 g fiber

Classic for a reason: It's low-sugar, low-cal, and even contains a decent dose of fiber. It's screaming out for sliced banana.

Not That!

Quaker® Natural Granola Oats, Honey & Raisins
(½ c/51 g)
420 calories
6 g fat
(3.5 g saturated)
15 g sugars
3 g fiber

Frosted Flakes®
(¾ c/30 g)
110 calories
0 g fat
11 g sugars
1 g fiber

Where the Mini-Wheats use whole grain wheat, the Frosted Flakes use milled corn, a cheap and nutritionally empty filler food.

Smart Start® Original Antioxidants
(1 c)
190 calories
0.5 g fat
(0 g saturated)
14 g sugars
3 g fiber

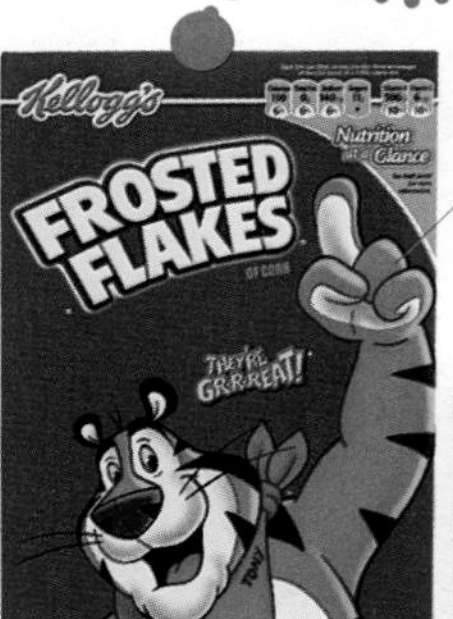

Raisin Nut Bran
(¾ c/49 g)
180 calories
3 g fat
(0.5 g saturated)
14 g sugars
5 g fiber

Sugar comes before raisins on the list of ingredients.

Kashi® GOLEAN® Crunch!® Honey Almond Flax
(1 c/53 g)
200 calories
4.5 g fat
(0 g saturated)
12 g sugars
8 g fiber

Sugar and calories cancel out the fiber.

Rice Krispies®
(1¼ c/33 g)
120 calories
0 g fat
3 g sugars
0 g fiber

You can't afford to feed your kid a cereal with zero fiber.

Wheat Chex®
(¾ c/47 g)
160 calories
1 g fat
(0 g saturated)
5 g sugars
5 g fiber

Hot Cereals

Eat This

Quaker® Instant Oatmeal Lower Sugar Maple and Brown Sugar (1 packet)
120 calories
2 g fat (0 g saturated)
4 g sugars 3 g fiber

Because it has oatmeal's usual high protein and fiber content, Quaker's Lower Sugar line is a perfect compromise for kids who can't forgo the sweet and flavored varieties.

Kashi® GOLEAN™ Creamy Truly Vanilla™ Instant Hot Cereal (1 packet)
150 calories
2 g fat
(0 g saturated)
6 g sugars
7 g fiber

Hodgson Mill® Oat Bran Hot Cereal (¼ c dry)
120 calories
3 g fat
(1 g saturated)
0 g sugars
6 g fiber

Trading this for Malt-O-Meal for one week will add 35 grams of fiber to your child's diet.

Old Fashioned Quaker® Oats (½ c dry)
150 calories
3 g fat
(0.5 g saturated)
1 g sugars
4 g fiber

You can spare the 5 minutes it takes to cook Old Fashioned Oats—your kid's worth it.

McCann's® Quick & Easy Steel-Cut Irish Oatmeal (¼ c dry)
150 calories
2 g fat
(0 g saturated)
0 g sugars
4 g fiber

Steel-cut oats have a rich texture.

Hodgson Mill® Bulgur Wheat with Soy Hot Cereal (¼ c dry)
115 calories
1 g fat
(0 g saturated)
0 g sugars
3 g fiber

Bulgur wheat has a gentle effect on blood sugar.

Quaker® Instant Oatmeal Weight Control Cinnamon (1 packet)
160 calories
3 g fat
(0.5 g saturated)
1 g sugars
6 g fiber

Not That!

Quaker® Organic Instant Maple Brown Sugar
(1 packet)
150 calories
2 g fat (0 g saturated)
12 g sugars 3 g fiber

Forgo the heavily sweetened flavored varieties; the high sugar intake cancels out any benefit your kid might get from the fiber.

Quaker® Instant Oatmeal Cinnamon & Spice (1 packet)
170 calories
2 g fat
(0.5 g saturated)
15 g sugars
3 g fiber

Nature's Path® Organic Instant Original Hot Oatmeal
(1 packet)
190 calories
4 g fat
(0 g saturated)
0 g sugars
4 g fiber

Quaker® Oatmeal Crunch Maple & Brown Sugar (1 packet)
190 calories
2.5 g fat
(0.5 g saturated)
14 g sugars
3 g fiber

Cream of Wheat Original Flavor
(3 Tbsp dry)
120 calories
0 g fat
0 g sugars
1 g fiber
Oatmeal prevails in the battle of the classic hot cereals, packing more than double the fiber.

Malt-O-Meal® Original Hot Wheat Cereal
(3 Tbsp dry)
130 calories
0.5 g fat
(0 g saturated)
0 g sugars
1 g fiber
No real nutrition makes Malt-O-Meal a breakfast worth passing on.

Quaker® Simple Harvest™ Apples with Cinnamon
(1 packet)
150 calories
1.5 g fat
(0 g saturated)
12 g sugars
4 g fiber

Granola and Breakfast

Eat This

Quaker® Chewy® Peanut Butter Chocolate Chip Bar with 25% Less Sugar (1 bar)

100 calories
3 g fat
(1 g saturated)
5 g sugars
3 g fiber

Clif® Kid™ Organic Chocolate Brownie ZBar (1 bar)

120 calories
3 g fat
(1 g saturated)
12 g sugars
3 g fiber

More of all the things that matter most.

All-Bran® Apple Cinnamon Streusel Fiber Bar (1 bar)

130 calories
2.5 g fat
(1 g saturated)
10 g sugars
10 g fiber

One-third of a 10-year-old's fiber RDA.

Rice Krispies Treats® (1 treat)

90 calories
2.5 g fat (1 g saturated)
7 g sugars

Nutri-Grain® Cranberry, Raisin, and Peanut Fruit & Nut Bars (1 bar)

120 calories
3.5 g fat
(1 g saturated)
11 g sugars
3 g fiber

If you need to reward a well-behaved kid, use a Rice Krispies Treat. It's the least dangerous of the sugary-snack bars.

All-Bran® Strawberry Drizzle Fiber Bar (1 bar)

120 calories
2.5 g fat
(1 g saturated)
9 g sugars
10 g fiber

Twice the protein and 10 times the fiber.

Quaker® Oats, Nuts & Honey Sweet & Salty Crunch (2 bars)

150 calories
6 g fat
(1 saturated)
8 g sugars
2 g fiber

Why not save 30 calories per serving?

Quaker® Chewy® 90 Calorie Peanut Butter Granola Bar (1 bar)

90 calories
2 g fat
(0 g saturated)
7 g sugars
1 g fiber

Light on the fiber, but also light on sugar.

Quaker® Simple Harvest™ Cinnamon Brown Sugar Bar (1 bar)

140 calories
3 g fat
(0 g saturated)
10 g sugars
2 g fiber

Kashi® GOLEAN® Crunchy! Chocolate Almond Protein & Fiber Bar (1 bar)

170 calories
5 g fat
(2.5 g saturated)
13 g sugars
5 g fiber

Bars Not That!

Cascadian Farm® Organic Vanilla Chip Chewy Granola Bars
(1 bar)
140 calories
3 g fat (2 g saturated)
13 g sugars

Kudos® Peanut Butter Whole Grain Bars
(1 bar)
130 calories
6 g fat
(3 g saturated)
12 g sugars
1 g fiber
This bar would be more at home in the candy aisle.

Nature Valley® Chewy Trail Mix Bars
(all flavors) (1 bar)
140 calories
4 g fat
(0.5 g saturated)
13 g sugars
1 g fiber

Crunchy Nut® Peanut Butter Sweet & Salty Granola Bars
(1 bar)
150 calories
8 g fat
(3 g saturated)
10 g sugars
2 g fiber

Quaker® Brown Sugar Cinnamon Oatmeal to Go
(1 bar)
220 calories
4 g fat
(1 g saturated)
19 g sugars
5 g fiber

Kashi® GOLEAN® Chewy Cookies 'N Cream Protein & Fiber Bar
(1 bar)
290 calories
6 g fat
(4 g saturated)
35 g sugars
6 g fiber

Cinnamon Toast Crunch® Milk 'n Cereal Bars (1 bar)
180 calories
4 g fat
(2 g saturated)
15 g sugars
1 g fiber
75% of the sugar and less fiber than its parent cereal.

Health Valley® Peanut Crunch Chewy Granola Bars
(1 bar)
110 calories
2.5 g fat
(1 g saturated)
10 g sugars
<1 g fiber
40% of its calories are from sugar.

Nature Valley® Oats 'N Honey Granola Bars
(2 bars)
180 calories
6 g fat
(0.5 g saturated)
11 g sugars
2 g fiber

Nutri-Grain® Strawberry Cereal Bars
(1 bar)
140 calories
3 g fat
(0.5 saturated)
13 g sugars
<1 g fiber
Loaded with high-fructose corn syrup.

Just because it's organic doesn't mean it's good for you. This one has a load of sugar and very little protein or fiber.

Yogurt

Eat This

Oikos™ Greek Vanilla (5.3 oz)
110 calories
0 g fat
11 g sugars

Dannon® All Natural Strawberry (4 oz)
110 calories
1 g fat
(0.5 g saturated)
19 g sugars
Dannon's All-Natural line is made with real fruit and no chemicals.

Greek-style yogurt involves straining the whey (the liquid part) from the yogurt, leaving a creamier cup with nearly twice the protein of regular American yogurt.

Stonyfield Farm® Organic YoBaby® Simply Plain (1 c/4 oz)
90 calories
4.5 g fat
(1 g saturated)
6 g sugars

Yoplait® Kids™ Strawberry Banana Yogurt Drink (3.2 oz)
70 calories
1.5 g fat
(1 g saturated)
10 g sugars
Unlike most children's squeezable and drinkable yogurts, this one's made with real fruit puree.

Breyers™ YoCrunch® Light Strawberry (6 oz)
120 calories
1 g fat
(0 g saturated)
11 g sugars
Take advantage of the creamy-crunchy blend to turn this yogurt-granola combo into a super healthy dessert.

Brown Cow Low Fat Maple (6 oz)
130 calories
2.5 g fat
(1.5 g saturated)
20 g sugars
This one contains almost one-quarter of your child's recommended daily calcium.

Not That!

Stonyfield Farm® All Natural O'Soy® Strawberry (6 oz)

170 calories
2.5 g fat
(0 g saturated)
27 g sugars

Some of the "healthier" brands tend to overdo it with the cane sugar.

Horizon® Organic Fat-Free Vanilla (6 oz)

80 calories
0 g fat
24 g sugars

Stonyfield Farm® Organic Lowfat Caramel (6 oz)

180 calories
1.5 g fat
(1 g saturated)
35 g sugars

This cup of yogurt has 15 grams more sugar than a ½-cup serving of Stonyfield's After Dark Chocolate Ice Cream.

Dannon® la Crème® Raspberry (4 oz)

140 calories
5 g fat
(3 g saturated)
18 g sugars

If you want a creamy yogurt that tastes like dessert, try the Greek-style cups from Oikos.

Danimals® Drinkables Swingin' Strawberry-Banana™ (6 oz)

180 calories
3 g fat
(2 g saturated)
30 g sugars

Stonyfield Farm® Organic YoBaby® Peach (4 oz)

110 calories
4 g fat
(1 g saturated)
13 g sugars

This cup contains more than 3 grams of sugar per ounce of yogurt.

Who cares if the yogurt is organic if it still contains more sugar than a Häagen-Dazs ice cream bar?

Breakfast Breads and

Eat Thi[illegible]

Sara Lee® Blueberry Crumble Bakery Bread (2 slices)

180 calories
2.5 g fat (1 g saturated)
10 g sugars
4 g fiber

Still a sweet breakfast, but with 5 grams of protein and 4 grams of fiber.

Pepperidge Farm® Brown Sugar Cinnamon Mini Bagels (2 bagels)

240 calories
1 g fat
(0 g saturated)
12 g sugars
4 g fiber

Four times the fiber and protein and no saturated fat.

Sunbelt® Fruit & Grain Strawberry Cereal Bars (1 bar)

140 calories
3 g fat
(1 g saturated)
17 g sugars
1 g fiber

Plenty of sweetness in this bar, but unlike Pop-Tarts, it contains real fruit and no high-fructose corn syrup or hydrogenated oils.

Pillsbury® Reduced Fat Cinnamon Rolls with Icing (1 roll)

140 calories
2.5 g fat
(1 g saturated)
10 g sugars
< 1 g fiber

The lesser of the many evils in the world of cinnamon rolls. Eat in moderation—there are partially hydrogenated oils hidden in this bread.

Thomas'® Hearty Grains 100% Whole Wheat English Muffins (1 muffin)

130 calories
1 g fat
(0 g saturated)
2 g sugars
3 g fiber

English muffins contain half the calories that a bagel does.

Pepperidge Farm® 100% Whole Wheat Bagels (1 bagel)

250 calories
1.5 g fat
(0 g saturated)
9 g sugars
6 g fiber

Get more protein and twice the fiber of plain bagels with the whole wheat option.

Pastries

Not That!

Pepperidge Farm® Plain Bagels (1 bagel)

260 calories
1 g fat
(0 g saturated)
10 g sugars
3 g fiber

The refined flour found in white breads can cause blood sugar to soar. Studies found that the resulting metabolic changes from these foods caused obese boys to overeat.

Hostess® Blueberry Mini Muffins (1 pouch)

270 calories
15 g fat (2.5 g saturated)
19 g sugars
< 1 g fiber

Remember this: Blueberries are good for you. Blueberry muffins are not.

Hostess® Donettes® Frosted Mini Donuts (4 donuts)

240 calories
14 g fat (10 g saturated)
16 g sugars
<1 g fiber

There's nothing mini about the effects of frosted donuts. The main ingredient is sugar, and with zero fiber, your child will be hungry before first bell.

Thomas'® Cinnamon Raisin English Muffin (1 muffin)

140 calories
1 g fat
(0 g saturated)
9 g sugars
2 g fiber

Pillsbury® Flaky Cinnamon Twists with Glaze (2 twists)

180 calories
9 g fat (2.5 g saturated, 2.5 g trans)
10 g sugars
0 g fiber

If you're going to go through the effort of cooking, why waste the effort on something nutritionally empty?

Pop-Tarts® Low Fat Frosted Strawberry (1 pastry)

190 calories
3 g fat
(1 g saturated)
20 g sugars
< 1 g fiber

Low fat or not, this gooey tart packs unhealthy doses of high-fructose corn syrup.

Breakfast Condiments

Eat This

Smucker's® Sugar Free Breakfast Syrup
(¼ c)
25 calories
0 g fat
0 g sugars

Kraft® Philadelphia® Whipped Cream Cheese (2 Tbsp)
60 calories
6 g fat
(3.5 g saturated)
Easier to spread and less caloric. What more could you want?

Shedd's Spread Country Crock® Omega Plus (1 Tbsp)
50 calories
5 g fat
(1 g saturated)
Contains 310 milligrams of omega-3 fats.

Smucker's® Simply Fruit® Blueberry Spreadable Fruit (2 Tbsp)
80 calories
0 g fat
16 g sugars
Perfect as a syrup substitute. Most of the sugars here come from real fruit.

Kraft® Philadelphia® Strawberry Cream Cheese (2 Tbsp)
90 calories
8 g fat
(4.5 g saturated)
4 g sugars
Flavored with real strawberry.

Peanut Butter & Co® Dark Chocolate Dreams® (2 Tbsp)
170 calories
13 g fat
(2.5 g saturated)
7 g sugars

Land O Lakes® Unsalted Whipped Butter (1 Tbsp)
50 calories
6 g fat
(3.5 g saturated)
Whipping air into the butter decreases the caloric density—plus it makes for easier spreading.

Not That!

Lite syrups are essentially just watered-down versions of regular syrups.

Mrs. Butterworth's® Lite Syrup
(¼ c)
100 calories
0 g fat
24 g sugars

Land O'Lakes® Stick Margarine (1 Tbsp)
100 calories
11 g fat
(2 g saturated, 2.5 g trans)
Stick margarine trades saturated fat for more-dangerous trans fats.

Nutella® (2 Tbsp)
200 calories
11 g fat
(2 g saturated)
20 g sugars
This chocolate-hazelnut spread may be a favorite in Europe, but it has no place on the breakfast table.

Horizon® Organic Cream Cheese (2 Tbsp)
110 calories
10 g fat
(6 g saturated)
0 g sugars

Smucker's® Blueberry Syrup (2 Tbsp)
200 calories
0 g fat
44 g sugars
Although it does have a small amount of blueberry puree, this syrup is still mostly corn syrup and high-fructose corn syrup.

Land O Lakes® Light Butter (1 Tbsp)
50 calories
6 g fat
(3.5 g saturated)
Not a bad choice, as far as butters go, but swap with the Crock and you'll trade saturated fat for healthy omega-3s.

Kraft® Philadelphia® Regular Cream Cheese (2 Tbsp)
90 calories
9 g fat
(5 g saturated)

Peanut Butter and Jell

Eat This

Smucker's® Simply Fruit® Seedless Black Raspberry Spreadable Fruit (1 Tbsp)

40 calories
0 g fat
8 g sugars

This is a great alternative to ultrasweet grape jelly.

Smucker's® Reduced Sugar Strawberry Fruit Spread (1 Tbsp)

20 calories
0 g fat
5 g sugars

Make the switch to reduced sugar twice a week and you'll save your kid 4 cups of added sugar by the end of the year.

Kettle™ Creamy Almond Butter (1 oz)

184 calories
16 g fat
(2 g saturated)

The same smooth sweetness of peanut butter, almonds have more heart-healthy fats and antioxidants than peanuts.

Skippy® Natural Creamy Peanut Butter (2 Tbsp)

180 calories
16 g fat
(3.5 g saturated)

Unlike most peanut butters, Skippy Natural doesn't contain hydrogenated oils.

Musselman's® Apple Butter (3 Tbsp)

90 calories
0 g fat
18 g sugars

No actual butter in this one, just apples cooked down long and slow until the fruit has a creamy consistency. Make this your kid's favorite condiment.

MaraNatha® Crunchy & Roasted Peanut Butter (2 Tbsp)

190 calories
16 g fat
(2 g saturated)

Just dry roasted peanuts and sea salt.

Not That!

It might be organic, but the first ingredient is still sugar.

Smucker's® Organic Concord Grape Jelly (1 Tbsp)

50 calories
0 g fat
12 g sugars

Simply Jif® Creamy Peanut Butter (2 Tbsp)

190 calories
16 g fat
(3 g saturated)

Contains fully hydrogenated vegetable oils.

Smucker's® Goober Grape® Peanut Butter and Grape Jelly Stripes (3 Tbsp)

240 calories
13 g fat
(2.5 g saturated)
21 g sugars

The Goober must be the mass of sugar holding this sludge together.

Peter Pan® Creamy Peanut Butter (2 Tbsp)

190 calories
17 g fat
(3.5 g saturated)

SunGold® Natural SunButter® (2 Tbsp)

200 calories
16 g fat
(2 g saturated)

This is a good alternative for kids with peanut allergies, but otherwise too high in calories for regular consumption.

Welch's® Squeezable Strawberry Spread (1 Tbsp)

50 calories
0 g fat
13 g sugars

Granted some of it is natural, but two tablespoons of this spread has nearly as much sugar as a Snickers bar.

Breads

Eat This

This is the best tortilla at your supermarket. It's a fiber-and-protein-rich rarity among wraps, and it contains only polyunsaturated and monounsaturated fats—both of which are good for you and your child.

La Tortilla Factory® Whole Wheat Low Carb/ Low Fat Tortilla (1 tortilla)
50 calories
2 g fat (0 g saturated)
8 g fiber

Sara Lee® Heart Healthy Wheat Hot Dog Buns (1 bun)
110 calories
1 g fat
(0 g saturated)
2 g fiber
This small swap will still add a couple grams of fiber to your dog.

Alexia® Whole Grain Rolls (bagged, frozen) (1 roll)
90 calories
1 g fat
(0 g saturated)
3 g fiber
Frozen or not, this is as good as it gets for a dinner roll.

Wonder® Whole Grain White Bread (2 slices)
130 calories
2 g fat
(0.5 g saturated)
4 g fiber
If you must eat white bread, look for a white-wheat hybrid with at least 4 grams of fiber.

Toufayan® Low Carb Pita (1 pita)
130 calories
2.5 g fat
(0 g saturated)
9 g fiber
Contains no sugar and an amazing 11 grams of protein.

Boboli® Thin Crust (1 crust/12")
850 calories
17.5 g fat
(7.5 g saturated)
5 g fiber
Or try the new whole wheat thin crust, which has an impressive 25 grams of fiber per crust.

Pepperidge Farm® 100% Whole Wheat Buns (1 bun)
120 calories
2 g fat
(0 g saturated)
2 g fiber
The term "wheat" can be misleading. Make sure the label says "100% whole wheat."

Not That!

Mission® Garden Spinach Herb Wrap
(1 tortilla)
210 calories
5 g fat (1.5 g saturated)
2 g fiber

The "spinach" in this garden-herb wrap is actually spinach powder, which does not count as a serving of vegetables.

Pepperidge Farm® Farmhouse Sandwhich Rolls Country Wheat (1 roll)
220 calories
4.5 g fat
(1 g saturated)
1 g fiber

Boboli® Original Crust (1 crust/12")
1,120 calories
20 g fat
(8 g saturated)
8 g fiber
Tack on 192 grams of carbs and more than 2,000 milligrams of sodium—and that's before toppings!

Toufayan® Wheat Flat Bread (1 piece)
260 calories
9 g fat
(1.5 g saturated)
3 g fiber
Just because it's thin doesn't mean it's light.

Wonder® Classic (2 slices)
120 calories
1 g fat
(0 g saturated)
0 g fiber
Run-of-the-mill white breads have little to offer in the way of nutrition.

King's Hawaiian® 100% Whole Wheat Rolls (1 roll)
100 calories
3 g fat
(1 g saturated)
2 g fiber
Whole wheat, sure, but loaded with sugar and margarine.

Sara Lee® Whole Grain White Hot Dog Buns (1 bun)
120 calories
1.5 g fat
(0 g saturated)
1 g fiber

Cheeses

Eat This

Kraft® Polly-O® Twists
(1 twist)
60 calories
4 g fat
(2.5 g saturated)
140 mg sodium

A fun "twist" on the classic string cheese, these low-calorie snacks provide 15 percent of your child's recommended daily calcium.

Kraft® 2% American Singles
(1 slice/21 g)
45 calories
2.5 g fat (1.5 g saturated)
260 mg sodium

Each slice contains 10 percent of your daily vitamin D and a full quarter of your daily calcium.

Kraft® Natural Low-Moisture Part-Skim Mozzarella Shreds (¼ c)
80 calories
5 g fat
(3.5 g saturated)
220 mg sodium

Mozzarella beats cheddar every time.

Treasure Cave® Traditional Crumbled Feta Cheese (¼ c)
80 calories
6 g fat
(4 g saturated)
320 mg sodium

Adds a nice hit of protein and calcium to a salad.

The Laughing Cow® Original Creamy Swiss Wedges
(1 wedge/21 g)
50 calories
4 g fat
(2.5 g saturated)
250 mg sodium

Pair with whole grain crackers for a tasty after-school snack.

Breakstone's® 2% Milkfat Cottage Cheese (½ c)
90 calories
2.5 g fat
(1.5 g saturated)
400 mg sodium

Almost pure protein. Add a drizzle of honey or a handful of blueberries and let your kids dig in.

Sargento® Reduced Fat 4 Cheese Mexican (¼ c)
80 calories
6 g fat
(3 g saturated)
200 mg sodium

Melt a serving inside a whole-grain tortilla and you've got one-quarter of the day's calcium.

Not That!

Kraft® Deli Deluxe Sharp Cheddar (2 slices/19 g)
110 calories
8 g fat (5 g saturated)
150 mg sodium

Kraft® Snackables® Cubes Natural Cheddar & Monterey Jack Cheeses (5 pieces)
72 calories
7 g fat
(4.5 g saturated)
132 mg sodium

Why triple your kid's fat intake when a perfectly fine substitute is readily available?

Kraft® Natural Shredded Sharp Cheddar (¼ c)
110 calories
9 g fat
(6 g saturated)
180 mg sodium

Horizon® Organic Cottage Cheese (½ c)
120 calories
5 g fat
(3 g saturated)
390 mg sodium

WisPride® Sharp Cheddar (2 Tbsp/28 g)
90 calories
7 g fat
(3.5 g saturated)
170 mg sodium
There's nothing sharp about a cheese that's made with xantham gum.

DiGiorno® Shredded Romano Cheese (¼ c)
110 calories
8 g fat
(5 g saturated)
430 mg sodium
The long aging process concentrates the fat and sodium levels in this cheese.

Kraft® Finely Shredded Mild Cheddar (¼ c)
110 calories
9 g fat
(6 g saturated)
180 mg sodium

Deli Meats

Eat This

Applegate Farms® Organic Uncured Turkey Hot Dogs
(1 dog)
80 calories
6 g fat (2 g saturated)
350 mg sodium

You'd be hard pressed to find a better hot dog anywhere.

Oscar Mayer® Deli Fresh Honey Shaved Ham
(6 slices/51 g)
50 calories
1 g fat
(0 g saturated)
650 mg sodium

Sara Lee® Fresh Ideas Oven Roasted Chicken Breast
(6 slices/86 g)
68 calories
1 g fat
(0 g saturated)
645 mg sodium

Hillshire Farm® Deli Select® UltraThin™ Roast Beef
(2 oz)
60 calories
3 g fat
(1 g saturated)
450 mg sodium

Hormel® Natural Choice® 100% Natural Smoked Deli Turkey
(3 slices/56 g)
50 calories
1 g fat
(0 g saturated)
450 mg sodium
No added nitrates.

Hormel® Natural Choice® Canadian Style Bacon
(2 slices/56 g)
70 calories
2 g fat
(1 g saturated)
680 mg sodium

StarKist® Chunk Light Tuna in Water
(2 oz)
60 calories
0.5 g fat
(0 g saturated)
250 mg sodium
The water-packed tuna contains a fraction of the fat and calories.

Oscar Mayer® 98% Fat Free Bologna
(1 slice/28g)
25 calories
0.5 g fat
(0 g saturated)
240 mg sodium

Oscar Mayer® America's Favorite Bacon
(2 slices)
70 calories
6 g fat
(2 g saturated)
290 mg sodium
Whether in a BLT, or as a breakfast side, two slices of bacon is a relatively low-impact indulgence.

Not That!

Oscar Mayer® Deli Fresh® Grilled Chicken Breast Strips
(9 slices/84 g)
110 calories
1.5 g fat
(1 g saturated)
690 mg sodium

Budding® Baked Honey Ham Deli Cuts
(2 oz/57 g)
80 calories
2.5 g fat
(1 g saturated)
650 mg sodium

Oscar Mayer Louis Rich 1/3 Less Fat Turkey Franks
(1 dog)
100 calories
8 g fat
(2.5 g saturated)
510 mg sodium

Oscar Mayer® Turkey Bacon
(2 slices)
70 calories
6 g fat
(2 g saturated)
360 mg sodium
And here you were, thinking that you were doing yourself and your family a favor by using turkey bacon.

Oscar Mayer® Turkey Bologna
(1 slice/28 g)
50 calories
4 g fat
(1 g saturated)
270 mg sodium

StarKist® Chunk Light Tuna in Vegetable Oil
(2 oz)
90 calories
4.5 g fat
(1 g saturated)
170 mg sodium
Tuna is a great source of protein; vegetable oil is not.

Hormel® Turkey Pepperoni
(22 slices/39 g)
90 calories
5 g fat
(2 g saturated)
830 mg sodium

Butterball® Honey Roasted Turkey Breast
(7 slices/56 g)
70 calories
1 g fat
(0.5 g saturated)
550 mg sodium

Hillshire Farm® Deli Select® Ultra Thin Hard Salami
(5 slices/28 g)
110 calories
10 g fat
(4 g saturated)
500 mg sodium
This "thin" salami packs 125 milligrams of sodium per slice.

Trail Mix, Dried Fruit,

Eat This

Sun-Maid® Mixed Fruit
(¼ c/40 g)
100 calories
0 g fat
17 g sugars

Look for a brand with the fewest possible preservatives. And added sugars are absolutely unnecessary, since fruit has enough natural sweetness to satisfy a sweet tooth.

Sunsweet® Pitted Prunes
(5 prunes/40 g)
100 calories
0 g fat
12 g sugars
3 g fiber

Per gram, prunes provide fewer calories, more fiber, and less sugar than raisins.

DAVID® Roasted & Salted Pumpkin Seeds
(¼ c/30 g)
160 calories
12 g fat
(2.5 g saturated)
0 g sugars
940 mg sodium

Jacked full of manganese, magnesium, and iron

Planters® Mixed Nuts and Raisins Trail Mix (1 oz)
150 calories
11 g fat
(1.5 g saturated)
6 g sugars

Ocean Spray® Craisins Orange Flavor
(¼ c/30 g)
98 calories
0 g fat
20 g sugars

When it comes to antioxidants, few fruits can match the concentration found in cranberries.

Emerald® Mixed Nuts (1 oz)
170 calories
16 g fat
(2.5 g saturated)
1 g sugarsa

Peanut-free, so your child gets more cashews, almonds, and walnuts, which have higher levels of healthy fats and antioxidants.

and Mixed Nuts Not That!

Welch's® Mixed Fruit (¾ c/40 g)
130 calories
0 g fat
21 g sugars

As if dried fruit weren't sweet enough already, Welch's adds extra sugar to the mix.

Planters® Mixed Nuts (1 oz)
170 calories
15 g fat (
2 g saturated)
1 g sugars

This mix lists peanuts as the main nut. Technically peanuts are legumes and are lower in healthy fats and antioxidants than more legitimate nuts.

Sun-Maid® Vanilla Yogurt Cranberries (¼ c/30 g)
120 calories
3.5 g fat
(3 g saturated)
20 g sugars

This is really more candy than fruit.

Planters® Nut & Chocolate Trail Mix (1 oz)
160 calories
10 g fat
(2.5 g saturated)
13 g sugars

The sugar doubles when chocolate pieces sneak into the mix.

Frito Lay® Sunflower Seeds (3 Tbsp hulled seeds/28 g)
200 calories
16 g fat
(2 g saturated)
150 mg sodium

Add in the shells and the sodium jumps to 1,230 milligrams.

Sun-Maid® Raisins (¼ c/40 g)
130 calories
0 g fat
29 g sugars
2 g fiber

Crackers

Eat This

With 3 grams of fiber and no added sugars, this is the best cracker for cheese, peanut butter, or just straight snacking.

Nabisco® Triscuit®
(6 crackers/29 g)
120 calories
4.5 g fat (1 g saturated)
180 mg sodium

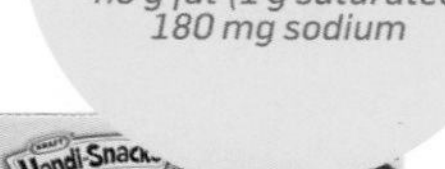

Kashi® TLC™ Fire Roasted Vegetable
(15 crackers/30 g)
130 calories
3.5 g fat
(0 g saturated)
210 mg sodium
Made with Kashi's signature 7 whole grains and real bell peppers, onions, and carrots.

Keebler® Club® Original Cracker
(4 crackers)
70 calories
3 g fat
(0.5 g saturated)
140 mg sodium

Nabisco® Premium® Toasted Onion Saltine Crackers
(10 crackers/30 g)
120 calories
3 g fat
(0 g saturated)
360 mg sodium

Nabisco® Triscuit® Roasted Garlic
(6 crackers/28 g)
120 calories
4.5 g fat
(0.5 g saturated)
140 mg sodium
This tasty twist on original Triscuits boasts 3 grams of fiber per serving.

Kraft® Handi-Snacks® Mister Salty® Pretzels 'n Cheez
(1 packet)
90 calories
3.5 g fat
(1 g saturated)
380 mg sodium
Pretzels make for safer dipping than breadsticks.

Kellogg's® All-Bran™ Garlic Herb Crackers
(18 crackers/30 g)
120 calories
6 g fat
(1 g saturated)
330 mg sodium

Not That!

Nabisco® Wheat Thins®
(16 crackers/31 g)
140 calories
6 g fat (1 g saturated)
260 mg sodium

The ingredients list is 3 inches long and includes such unlikely cracker suspects as malt syrup and HFCS.

Keebler® Town House® Wheat
(10 crackers/32 g)
160 calories
8 g fat
(2 g saturated)
280 mg sodium
These wheat crackers have more partially hydrogenated oil than they do actual whole grain wheat.

Austin® Wheat Crackers with Cheddar Cheese (1 packet)
200 calories
10 g fat
(2 g saturated,
4 g trans)
370 mg sodium
Beware: more than a half-gram of trans fat per cracker!

Keebler® Wheatables®
(17 crackers/30 g)
140 calories
6 g fat
(1.5 g saturated)
340 mg sodium
These offer only 1 gram of fiber.

Nabisco® Chicken in a Biskit®
(12 crackers/31 g)
160 calories
8 g fat
(1.5 g saturated)
300 mg sodium
The liberal use of soybean and palm oils loads each of these crackers with nearly 1 gram of fat.

Keebler® Club® Reduced Fat Crackers
(5 crackers)
70 calories
2 g fat
(0 g saturated)
180 mg sodium
In exchange for one less gram of fat you get more sodium and double the sugar. Keep it original.

Nabisco® Vegetable Thins®
(21 crackers/30 g)
150 calories
7 g fat
(2 g saturated)
320 mg sodium
Thin in name only, these pack partially hydrogenated oils and high-fructose corn syrup.

Crunchy Snacks

Eat This

Pepperidge Farm® Cheddar Goldfish
(55 pieces/ 30 g)
140 calories
5 g fat
(1 g saturated)
250 mg sodium

Nabisco® Garden Harvest® Toasted Chips Apple Cinnamon
(16 chips/1 oz)
120 calories
3 g fat
(0 g saturated)
Half a serving of fruit in each bag.

Doritos® Spicy Nacho
(12 chips/1 oz)
140 calories
7 g fat (1 g saturated)
210 mg sodium

Not the quintessential healthful food option, but the lesser of two spicy evils in the full-flavor chip category.

Baked! Lay's® Original
(15 crisps/1 oz)
120 calories
2 g fat
(0 g saturated)
180 mg sodium
If you're going to have chips in your pantry, this is a good one to stock.

Smart Balance® Light Butter Microwave Popcorn
(4 c popped)
120 calories
4.5 g fat
(1.5 g saturated)
290 mg sodium

Garden of Eatin'® Nacho Cheese
(9 chips/1 oz)
140 calories
6 g fat
(0.5 g saturated)
140 mg sodium

Ritz® Snack Mix 100 Calorie Packs® (1 packet)
100 calories
3 g fat
(0.5 g saturated)
210 mg sodium
When it comes to self-contained snacks, you'd be hard-pressed to find a better one.

Baked! Lays® Barbecue Flavored
(14 chips/1 oz)
120 calories
3 g fat
(0.5 g saturated)
210 mg sodium

New York Style® Whole Wheat Pita Chips
(7 chips/1 oz)
110 calories
3.5 g fat
(1.5 g saturated)
350 mg sodium

Not That!

Pringles® Extreme® Blazin' Buffalo Wing
(15 chips/1 oz)
150 calories
10 g fat (3 g saturated)
280 mg sodium

Seneca® Crispy Apple Chips
(12 chips/1 oz)
140 calories
7 g fat
(1 g saturated)

Nabisco® Cheez-It®
(27 crackers/30 g)
160 calories
8 g fat
(2 g saturated)
250 mg sodium

Stacy's® Simply Naked Pita Chips
(14 chips/1 oz)
130 calories
5 g fat
(0.5 g saturated)
270 mg sodium

Kettle™ Krinkle Cut™ Classic Barbeque
(1 oz)
150 calories
9 g fat
(1 g saturated)
170 mg sodium
Natural it may be, but light it is not.

Keebler® Toast & Peanut Butter Sandwich Crackers
(1 packet)
200 calories
10 g fat
(1.5 g saturated)
410 mg sodium

Tostitos® Multigrain
(8 chips/1 oz)
150 calories
8 g fat
(1 g saturated)
135 mg sodium
Opt for a thinner tortilla chip. It provides just as many salsa-dunks for a fraction of the calories.

Pop Secret® Homestyle Premium Popcorn
(4 c popped)
180 calories
11 g fat
(1.5 g saturated, 5 g trans)
410 mg sodium
The real secret is the amount of trans fat.

SunChips® Original
(16 chips/1 oz)
140 calories
6 g fat
(1 g saturated)
120 mg sodium
For all the good press they get, SunChips are only marginally better for you than real potato chips.

Dips

Eat This

Mission® Cheddar Cheese Dip
(2 Tbsp)
45 calories
3 g fat (0.5 g saturated)
280 mg sodium

Drew's® All Natural Salsa
(2 Tbsp)
10 calories
0 g fat
100 mg sodium

There's no beating a pure, tomato-based salsa. Beyond being a low-calorie condiment, salsa also packs plenty of disease-fighting antioxidants.

Wholly Guacamole™
(2 Tbsp)
50 calories
4 g fat
(0.5 g saturated)
75 mg sodium

It might be a few more calories, but they come from real heart-healthy avocados—not oil and thickening agents.

Annie's Naturals® Organic Buttermilk Dressing
(2 Tbsp)
60 calories
6 g fat
(1 g saturated)
230 mg sodium

The exact flavors of the beloved ranch, with half the calories.

Fritos® Bean Dip Original Flavor
(2 Tbsp)
35 calories
1 g fat
(0 g saturated)
190 mg sodium

Pinto beans, like the ones used in this dip, are an excellent source of fiber.

Wild Garden® Roasted Garlic Hummus Dip
(2 Tbsp)
35 g calories
2 g fat
(0 g saturated)
70 mg sodium

Set up a plate of baby carrots, Triscuits, and hummus for a perfect after-school snack.

Not That!

Ruffles® Rich and Creamy Sour Cream & Chive (2 Tbsp)

60 calories
5 g fat
(0.5 g saturated)
240 mg sodium

Pace® Mexican Four Cheese Salsa (2 Tbsp)

90 calories
7 g fat (1.5 g saturated)
430 mg sodium

Taco Bell® Medium Salsa con Queso (2 Tbsp)

25 calories
2 g fat
(0 g saturated)
220 mg sodium

The first two ingredients are water and soybean oil.

Fritos® Mild Cheddar Dip (2 Tbsp)

50 calories
3.5 g fat
(5g saturated)
330 mg sodium

This dip is easy to confuse with a bean dip, but its base is really milk, and it contains partially hydrogenated oils.

Newman's Own® Ranch Dressing (2 Tbsp)

140 calories
16 g fat
(2.5 g saturated)
310 mg sodium

What with the way kids are dipping these days, a bottle of this stuff in the fridge could be a major health hazard.

Mission® Guacamole Dip (2 Tbsp)

40 calories
3 g fat
(0 g saturated)
150 mg sodium

The first three ingredients are water, canola oil, and food starch. The only mention of avocado is the "avocado powder."

Cookies

Eat This

Newman's Own® Newman-O's® Chocolate Crème Filled Chocolate Cookies
(2 cookies/28 g)
130 calories
4.5 g fat (1.5 g saturated)
10 g sugars

Unlike most cookies on the shelves, you'll actually recognize most of the ingredients in these.

Nabisco® Snack Well's® Creme Sandwich Cookies
(2 cookies/25 g)
110 calories
3 g fat (1 g saturated)
9 g sugars

Keebler® Low Fat Cinnamon Grahams
(1 sheet/28 g)
110 calories
1.5 g fat
(0 g saturated)
9 g sugars

As a rule, graham crackers crush cookies in the calorie and fat department. Up the satiety quotient by spreading the grahams with peanut butter.

Nestlé® Toll House® Chocolate Chip Cookie Dough (1 large cookie)
120 calories
6 g fat
(3 g saturated)
10 g sugars

Nearly identical as the Pillsbury version, but for one big difference: no trans fat.

Nabisco® Ginger Snaps®
(4 cookies/28 g)
120 calories
2.5 g fat
(0.5 g saturated)
11 g sugars

As far as classes of cookies go, ginger snaps are about as safe as it gets.

Not That!

They may look like friendly elves, but Keebler cookies are consistently some of the most caloric in the supermarket.

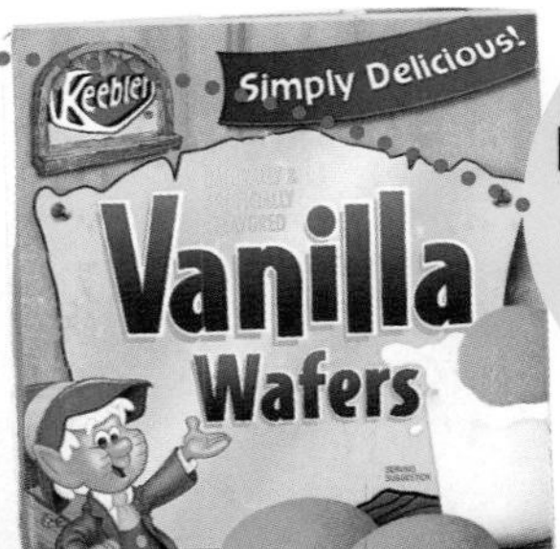

Keebler® E.L. Fudge® Original
(2 cookies/36 g)
180 calories
7 g fat (3 g saturated)
12 g sugars

Keebler® Sandies® Simply Shortbread
(2 cookies/31 g)
170 calories
9 g fat (4 g saturated)
7 g sugars

We applaud Keebler for cutting back on the trans fats, but these cookies still contain partially hydrogenated oils—and 2 grams of saturated fat apiece.

Pillsbury® Ready to Bake Chocolate Chip Cookie Dough
(1 large cookie)
120 calories
6 g fat (2 g saturated, 2 g trans)
10 g sugars

The trans fat comes from the partially hydrogenated soybean and cottonseed oils in the recipe.

Keebler® Vanilla Wafers
(8 cookies/30 g)
140 calories
6 g fat
(2 g saturated)
9 g sugars

Keebler® Vienna Fingers
(2 cookies/31 g)
150 calories
6 g fat (2 g saturated)
10 g sugars

Pudding

Eat This

Kraft® Handi-Snacks® Sugar Free Vanilla Pudding (1 c)

45 calories
1 g fat (.5 g saturated)
0 g sugars

You only gain 1 gram of fat and save 35 calories and 14 grams of sugar!

Jell-O® Fruit Passions® Pineapple in Tropical Fusion Gelatin (1 c)

35 calories
0 g fat
6 g sugars

Might as well use the Jell-O snack as an opportunity to slip in a serving of good fruit.

Jell-O® Cook & Serve Custard (¼ package)

80 calories
0 g fat
17 g sugars

Try instant custard over pudding. There's no point in eating saturated fat when what you're really craving is sugar.

Jell-O® Sugar Free/Fat Free Cook & Serve Chocolate Pudding (¼ package)

30 calories
0 g fat
0 g sugars

Jell-O® Sugar Free Cinnamon Rice Pudding (1 c)

70 calories
2 g fat
(1.5 g saturated)
0 g sugars

Jell-O® Sugar Free Dulce De Leche Pudding (1 c)

60 calories
1 g fat
(1 g saturated)
0 g sugars

Not That!

Food manufacturers love to remove fat only to replace it with a ton of sugar.

Snack Pack® Fat Free Tapioca Pudding
(1 c)
80 calories
0 g fat
14 g sugars

Kraft® Handi-Snacks® Baskin Robbins Chocolate Vanilla Sundae
(1 c)
100 calories
1 g fat
(1 g saturated)
16 g sugars

Kozy Shack® No Sugar Added Rice Pudding
(1 c)
90 calories
3 g fat
(2 g saturated)
4 g sugars

Jell-O® Instant Chocolate Pudding (1 c)
100 calories
0 g fat
19 g sugars
The first two ingredients are sugar and starch.

Jell-O® Instant Coconut Cream Pudding & Pie Filling (1/4 package)
100 calories
2.5 g fat
(2.5 g saturated)
16 g sugars
Don't let the "Calci-YUM!" declaration on the front of the box fool you; there's no calcium inside.

Jell-O® Gelatin Snacks Strawberry/Orange
(1 c)
70 calories
0 g fat
17 g sugars

Juice

Eat This

Ocean Spray® Cranergy™ Cranberry Lift (12 oz)

50 calories
12 g sugars

This alternative to straight cranberry juice has an energizing mix of B vitamins and green tea extracts.

Pom® Pomegranate Lychee Green Tea (8 oz)

70 calories
16 g sugars

Part green tea and part pomegranate juice, this packs a walloping dose of antioxidants for the little ones.

Santa Cruz® Raspberry Lemonade (8 oz)

100 calories
22 g sugars

V8 V-Fusion® Pomegranate Blueberry 100% Juice (8 oz)

100 calories
0 g fat
23 g sugars

One serving of fruit *and* a serving of vegetables in every 8-ounce glass.

Mott's for Tots® Apple Juice (1 box/6.8 oz)

50 calories
13 g sugars

This is 100 percent apple juice diluted with purified water. The kids get the sweetness and the nutrition, but avoid the deluge of sugar.

V8 V-Fusion® Strawberry Banana Light (8 oz)

50 calories
0 g fat
10 g sugars

The Fusion line masks V8's vegetable blend with the sweetness of real fruit juice.

Simply Orange® Juice Company's Simply Grapefruit™ (8 oz)

90 calories
18 g sugars

This juice is entirely unadulterated.

Minute Maid® Kids+® 100% Orange Juice (1 box, 6.8 oz)

100 calories
20 g sugars

This orange juice is a step above most because it's fortified with a slew of good vitamins.

Welch's® Light Berry (8 oz)

70 calories
16 g sugars

Drink this and you'll lose nearly half the sugars without sacrificing the tasty and healthful allure of blueberries, blackberries, and raspberries.

Not That!

Minute Maid® Lemonade
(8 oz)
110 calories
29 g sugars

Minute Maid® Enhanced Pomegranate Lemonade
(8 oz)
110 calories
30 g sugars
The first two ingredients are water and high-fructose corn syrup.

Ocean Spray® Cranberry with Calcium
(8 oz)
150 calories
37 g sugars
This juice contains only 27 percent cranberry juice. The rest of the calories come from added sugars.

Lemonade is generally 10 percent lemon juice and 90 percent sugar water and provides little nutritional benefit to your kids.

Juicy Juice® 100% Juice Fruit Punch
(8 oz)
120 calories
26 g sugars
This diluted mix still holds 26 grams of sugar—equal to two servings of Edy's® Loaded Chocolate Peanut Butter Cup ice cream.

Welch's® Orange Pineapple Apple (8 oz)
140 calories
34 g sugars
One of the most sugar-laden "juices" in the supermarket.

Ocean Spray® Ruby Red Grapefruit 100% Juice
(8 oz)
130 calories
29 g sugars
The grapefruit juice is diluted with cheap, high-sugar fillers such as grape and apple juices.

Dole® Orange Strawberry Banana Juice
(8 oz)
120 calories
0 g fat
24 g sugars

Minute Maid® Apple Juice
(1 bottle/10 oz)
140 calories
32 g sugars
There's a simple reason why kids love apple juice so much: it's sweeter than most soft drinks. This bottle is no exception.

Nestlé® Juicy Juice® Berry All-Natural 100% Juice
(8 oz)
120 calories
0 g fat
27 g sugars

Children's Drinks

Eat This

Gatorade® G2®
(8 oz)
25 calories
7 g sugars
Gatorade's new light sports beverage provides all the electrolytes active kids will need without all the sugar or calories. Perfect for game day.

Minute Maid's line of water-based beverages for kids provides the hit of sweetness they crave, but without the heavy caloric cost. Plus each pouch packs a day's worth of vitamin C.

Minute Maid® Fruit Falls™ Tropical Water Beverage
(1 pouch)
5 calories
< 1 g sugars

Nestlé® Nesquik® Chocolate No Sugar Added Powder
(2 Tbsp)
35 calories
1 g fat
(.5 g saturated)
3 g sugars

Crystal Light® On The Go
(1 packet)
10 calories
0 g sugars
Check the serving size on the box, because they're almost always listed as ½ packet, while everyone will use the whole packet.

Crayons® All Natural Fruit Juice Drink
(1 can/8 oz)
90 calories
19 g sugars

Horizon® 2% Milk (1 container/ 8 oz) with 2 Tbsp Nesquik® Chocolate No Sugar Added Powder
155 calories
5.5 g fat
(3 g saturated)
15 g sugars

Tropicana® Light 'n Healthy (8 oz)
50 calories
10 g sugars

Tropicana® Fruit Squeeze™ Tropical Tangerine
(1 bottle)
35 calories
7 g sugars

Not That!

Capri Sun® Roarin' Waters® Tropical Fruit Water Beverage
(1 pouch)
35 calories
9 g sugars

Capri Sun® Sport™ Lightspeeed Lemon Lime with Electrolytes
(1 pouch)
60 calories
16 g sugars

Nestlé® Juicy Juice® Harvest Surprise™ Orange Mango
(1 bottle, 8 oz)
130 calories
27 g sugars

Sunny D® Tangy Original
(1 bottle, 6.75 oz)
80 calories
16 g sugars
Basically diluted HFCS: All of the ingredients combined, aside from water and HFCS, make up less than 2 percent of the drink.

Nesquik® Chocolate Milkshake
(1 bottle/16 oz)
340 calories
10 g fat
(6 g saturated)
26 g sugars
Exercise portion control by making your own 8-ounce glass of chocolate milk.

Hi-C Blast® Strawberry
(1 pouch)
100 calories
26 g sugars

Country Time® Lemonade On The Go
(1 packet)
70 calories
18 g sugars
The first ingredient is sugar.

Hershey's® Lite Syrup
(2 Tbsp)
50 calories
0 g fat
10 g sugars
Even this is a step above regular Hershey's, which lists high-fructose corn syrup as its main ingredient.

Grains

Eat This

This pilaf is the ultimate blend of whole grains, and it's far more flavorful than white rice.

Kashi® 7 Whole Grain Pilaf
(½ c dry)
170 calories
3 g fat (0 g saturated)
6 g fiber

Uncle Ben's® Fast and Natural™ Whole Grain Instant Brown Rice
(1 c prepared)
170 calories
1 g fat
(0 g saturated)
2 g fiber

Lundberg® Long Grain Brown (¼ c dry)
170 calories
1.5 g fat
(0 saturated)
3 g fiber
Slightly higher in calories, but it's worth it to get the extra fiber.

Near East® Whole Grain Blends Roasted Garlic
(1 c, prepared with olive oil)
220 calories
5 g fat
(0.5 g saturated)
5 g fiber

Arrowhead Mills® Quinoa
(⅓ c dry)
160 calories
2.5 g fat
(0 g saturated)
3 g fiber
One of the world's most perfect foods, quinoa has a remarkable balance of protein, healthy fats, and fiber.

Lundberg® White Basmati Rice (¼ c dry)
170 calories
.5 g fat
(0 g saturated)
1 g fiber
Basmati rice has a lower glycemic index than jasmine, so it better regulates blood sugar levels.

Uncle Ben's® Long Grain & Wild Rice, Roasted Garlic & Olive Oil
(1 c prepared)
180 calories
1 g fat
(0 g saturated)
3 g fiber

Not That!

Minute® Premium White Rice
(½ c dry)
190 calories
0 g fat
0 g fiber

White rice is the black sheep of the grain family. It has high levels of carbohydrates and no fiber to slow digestion, which means that white rice will spike kids' insulin levels dangerously high.

Rice-A-Roni® Lower Sodium Chicken Flavor Rice
(1 c prepared)
270 calories
5 g fat
(1 g saturated)
2 g fiber
This side will cost one-third of the day's sodium.

Golden Star® Jasmine Rice
(¼ c dry)
200 calories
.5 g fat
(0 g saturated)
0 g fiber

Lundberg® Quick Wild Rice
(¼ c dry)
150 calories
0.5 g fat
(0 g saturated)
2 g fiber
Wild beats white every time, but still can't compete with a superfood like quinoa.

Near East® Toasted Pine Nut Couscous
(1 c, prepared with olive oil)
230 calories
6 g fat
(1 g saturated)
2 g fiber

Minute® Brown Rice
(½ c dry)
150 calories
1.5 g fat
(0 g saturated)
2 g fiber

Uncle Ben's® Whole Grain Brown Ready Rice®
(1 c prepared)
220 calories
4 g fat
(0 g saturated)
2 g fiber
Faster prep time means that the rice is more processed.

Noodles

Eat This

Ronzoni® Healthy Harvest® Whole Wheat Blend Thin Spaghetti (2 oz)
180 calories
2 g fat
(0 g saturated)
6 g fiber
Tons of fiber and protein.

Kraft® Tangy Italian Spaghetti Classics® (2 oz prepared)
200 calories
1.5 g fat
(0.5 g saturated)
610 mg sodium

For prepackaged pasta meals, Kraft Spaghetti Classics outshines Kraft Macaroni & Cheese by 3 grams of protein and 14 grams of fat.

Ronzoni® Healthy Harvest® Whole Wheat Blend Extra-Wide Noodle Style Pasta (2 oz)
180 calories
1 g fat
(0 g saturated)
15 mg sodium
6 g fiber

Thai Kitchen® Bangkok Curry Instant Rice Noodle Soup (1 package)
190 calories
3.5 g fat
(0.5 g saturated)
870 mg sodium
Low-calorie rice noodles are a decent alternative to ramen.

Simply Asia® Roasted Peanut Noodles (105 g)
383 calories
14 g fat
(1 g saturated)
936 mg sodium
Kids will love the simple, familiar flavors of this dish.

SpaghettiOs® Plus Calcium (1 c)
170 calories
1 g fat
(0.5 g saturated)
620 mg sodium
Additional vitamin D and calcium come along with less fat.

Chef Boyardee® Cheesy Burger Macaroni (1 c)
200 calories
5 g fat
(2.5 g saturated)
820 mg sodium
It's better than Beefaroni, but still very high in sodium. Proceed with caution.

SpaghettiOs® Princess Fun Shapes (1 c)
170 calories
1 g fat
(0.5 g saturated)
630 mg sodium
Look for cans that say "plus calcium." Besides the calcium boost, they're lower in calories and sodium.

Not That!

Kraft® Macaroni & Cheese Dinner prepared with margarine and 2% milk (1 c prepared)

410 calories
19 g fat (5 g saturated, 4 g trans)
710 mg sodium

Was there ever any doubt that "The Cheesiest" was not the healthiest?

Barilla® Angel Hair Pasta (2 oz)

200 calories
1 g fat
(0 g saturated)
2 g fiber

With less fiber than its whole wheat counterpart, white pasta moves through the stomach quickly and raises blood sugar levels.

SpaghettiOs® A to Z's with Meatballs (1 c)

260 calories
9 g fat
(3.5 g saturated)
990 mg sodium

Small additions can tip the scale in a big way. The addition of meat means nine times the fat per serving.

Chef Boyardee® Beefaroni® (1 c)

260 calories
10 g fat
(4.5 g saturated)
990 mg sodium

SpaghettiOs® Raviolio's® (1 c)

270 calories
8 g fat
(3.5 g saturated)
1,090 mg sodium

Canned pastas have dangerously high levels of sodium. A whole can contains more than half the RDA for sodium.

Maruchan® Yakisoba Teriyaki Flavor (1 bowl/113 g)

520 calories
20 g fat
(10 g saturated)
1,260 mg sodium

The teriyaki flavor brings with it more than half a day's worth of sodium.

Maruchan® Top Ramen® Oriental Flavor (1 package)

380 calories
14 g fat
(7 g saturated)
1,760 mg sodium

This starving-student staple contains 77 percent of your kid's recommended daily sodium intake.

No Yolks® Cholesterol Free Egg White Pasta (2 oz)

210 calories
0.5 g fat
(0 g saturated)
3 g fiber

Don't fear the yolks—they're loaded with healthy fats and protein.

Sauces

Eat This

Stubb's® Mild Bar-B-Q Sauce (2 Tbsp)
15 calories
0 g fat
210 mg sodium

You don't have to bathe a wing in butter and fat to make it good. Stubb's is spicy and delicious without all the junk.

Classico® Fire Roasted Tomato & Garlic (½ c)
50 calories
0.5 g fat
(0 g saturated)
320 mg sodium
There's a reason Classico doesn't have a line of light sauces: It doesn't need one.

Kikkoman® Less Sodium Soy Sauce (1 Tbsp)
10 calories
0 g fat
575 mg sodium
With half a day's sodium in a tablespoon of regular soy sauce, you can't afford not to make this simple swap.

Ragú® Old World Style® Flavored with Meat (½ c)
70 calories
3 g fat
(0.5 g saturated)
570 mg sodium
You won't find a meat sauce with less calories or fat in the supermarket.

Ragú® Double Cheddar (¼ c)
100 calories
9 g fat
(3 g saturated)
450 mg sodium
Break glass in case of emergency! Otherwise, leave all cheese-based sauces out of your pantry.

Classico® Roasted Red Pepper Alfredo (½ c)
120 calories
10 g fat
(6 g saturated)
620 mg sodium
Far from a nutritional superstar, but this is the best of the Alfredo sauces.

Cibo Naturals® Artichoke Lemon Pesto (¼ c)
210 calories
21 g fat
(2.5 g saturated)
260 mg sodium
An antioxidant-packed sauce that's perfect tossed with hot spaghetti.

Not That!

Kraft® Original Barbecue Sauce
(2 Tbsp)
50 calories
0 g fat
440 mg sodium

Beware of high levels of sodium in steak and BBQ sauces—even a drizzle or a dunk can carry a huge salt load.

Ragú® Light Tomato & Basil, No Added Sugar
(½ c)
60 calories
1.5 g fat
(0 g saturated)
330 mg sodium
Even Ragu's lightest effort still loses to Classico.

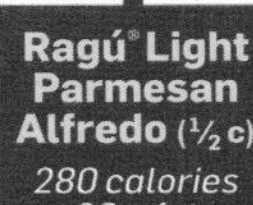

Melissa's® Italian Style Basil Pesto
(¼ c)
340 calories
34 g fat
(6 g saturated)
230 mg sodium
True, most of the fat comes from olive oil, but the calorie load is too great to justify.

Ragú® Light Parmesan Alfredo (½ c)
280 calories
20 g fat
(12 g saturated)
1280 mg sodium
Despite being "light," this version has more calories and sodium.

Kraft® Cheez Whiz®
(¼ c)
180 calories
14 g fat
(3 g saturated)
880 mg sodium

Prego® Flavored with Meat Italian Sauce (½ c)
100 calories
4 g fat
(1 g saturated)
580 mg sodium
Prego almost always has more calories than the other popular brands.

La Choy® Soy Sauce
(1 Tbsp)
10 calories
0 g fat
1,160 mg sodium
La Choy has more sodium than any of the other major soy sauce brands.

Soups

Eat This

Campbell's® Chunky™ Grilled Steak Chili with Beans
(1 c)
200 calories
3 g fat (1 g saturated)
870 mg sodium

Each serving is lower in calories and loaded with protein and fiber.

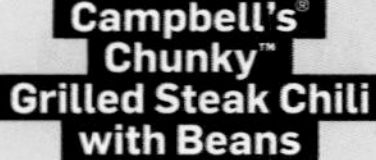

Campbell's® Tomato Soup with 25% Less Sodium
(1 c prepared)
90 calories
0 g fat
530 mg sodium
Of the soup aisle's many takes on tomato, this classic can is tops.

Imagine® Organic Sweet Potato Soup
(1 c)
110 calories
1.5 g fat
(0 g saturated)
400 mg sodium
One-third of kids ages 12 to 19 are vitamin A deficient. This soup has 270 percent of the RDI.

Campbell's® Dora Fun Shapes
(½ c prepared)
70 calories
2 g fat
(0.5 g saturated)
580 mg sodium

Campbell's® Healthy Request® Select™ Mexican Style Chicken Tortilla (1 c)
130 calories
2.5 g fat
(1 g saturated)
480 mg sodium

Lipton® Soup Secrets® Noodle Soup with Real Chicken Broth
(1 c prepared)
62 calories
2 g fat
(0.5 g saturated)
720 mg sodium

Campbell's® Healthy Request® Homestyle Chicken Noodle Soup
(½ c prepared)
60 calories
2 g fat
(0.5 g saturated)
480 mg sodium

Campbell's® Chunky™ Grilled Sirloin Steak (1 c)
130 calories
2 g fat
(1 g saturated)
890 mg sodium
Contains 40 percent of your child's daily vitamin A requirement.

Not That!

Bush's Best® Homestyle Chili (1 c)

250 calories
17 g fat
(10 g saturated, 4 g trans)
810 mg sodium

Dangerous amounts of trans fats in every serving.

Amy's® Organic Low Fat Light in Sodium Cream of Tomato Soup (1 c)

100 calories
2 g fat
(1.5 g saturated)
690 mg sodium

Amy's also adds in 11 grams of sugar.

Dinty Moore® Beef Stew (1 c)

210 calories
10 g fat
(4 g saturated)
970 mg sodium

After more than 70 years in American pantries, this ubiquitous stew has been lapped by more nutritionally minded newcomers.

Campbell's® Chicken Noodle Soup (1 c prepared)

60 calories
2 g fat
(0.5 g saturated)
890 mg sodium

This can may be iconic, but it's also a sodium bomb. Make Healthy Request your go-to soup.

Wyler's® Mrs. Grass® Soup Mix Extra Noodles (1 c prepared)

110 calories
2 g fat
(0.5 g saturated)
700 mg sodium

Wolfgang Puck® Organic Tortilla Soup (1 c)

160 calories
3.5 g fat
(1 g saturated)
980 mg sodium

Progresso® Traditional 99% Fat Free Chicken Noodle (1 c)

100 calories
2 g fat
(0.5 g saturated)
950 mg sodium

99% fat free, but saltier than 99% of soups out there.

Campbell's® Select™ New England Clam Chowder (1 c)

160 calories
8 g fat
(2 g saturated)
870 mg sodium

Chowder is generally a bad choice. This one is mixed with vegetable oil, butter, and cream.

Canned & Frozen Produce

Eat This

Ore-Ida® Potatoes O'Brien with Onions and Peppers
(¾ c)
60 calories
0 g fat
20 mg sodium

More flavor, fewer calories. It's a simple swap that will save your family big on weeknights and weekend breakfasts.

Del Monte® Mandarin Oranges No Sugar Added
(½ c)
45 calories
0 g fat
6 g sugars

Great as a snack, or tossed with a simple dinner salad with almonds and vinaigrette.

Del Monte® Sliced Peaches in 100% Juice
(½ c)
60 calories
14 g sugars

Never buy a can of fruit with the word "syrup" on the label. 100 percent real fruit juice is always the way to go.

Del Monte® Sweet Peas No Salt Added (½ c)
60 calories
6 g sugars
10 mg sodium

Peas offer the same natural sweetness kids love about corn, but with a much better nutritional payoff, including big doses of B vitamins, fiber, and vitamin C.

Bush's® Dark Red Kidney Beans
(½ c)
105 calories
3 g sugar
260 mg sodium

Dark red kidney beans are high in fiber, folate, and a surprise powerhouse in the antioxidant department.

Birds Eye® Broccoli & Cauliflower
(1 c frozen)
25 calories
0 g fat
25 mg sodium

Because vegetables are picked and flash frozen immediately, they retain most of the same nutrients fresh vegetables offer.

Not That!

Roasted potatoes should never have trans fats. On second thought, no potatoes should.

Ore-Ida® Roasted Potatoes
(3/4 c)
130 calories
4.5 g fat (1 g saturated; 1.5g trans fat)
380 mg sodium

Del Monte® Mandarin Oranges in Light Syrup (1/2 c)
80 calories
0 g fat
19 g sugars
Few fruits are sweeter than mandarins, so why have them preserved in a sugary syrup?

Green Giant® Broccoli Spears & Butter Sauce
(1 c frozen)
40 calories
1.5 g fat
(1 g saturated)
330 mg sodium

Bush's® Original Baked Beans
(1/2 c)
140 calories
12 g sugars
550 mg sodium
With all the sugar, bacon, and salt cooked into baked beans, you're better off seasoning the beans yourself.

Del Monte® Whole Kernel Corn No Salt Added (1/2 c)
60 calories
7 g sugars
10 mg sodium

Del Monte® Sliced Peaches in Heavy Syrup
(1/2 c)
100 calories
23 g sugars
Warning: Once your kids get hooked on sugar-spiked fruit, it'll be a challenge to get them to eat the real thing.

Frozen Breakfast Entr

Eat This

The 3 grams of fiber aren't as much as you'd get from a good bowl of cereal, but it's still a decent breakfast.

Eggo® Nutri-Grain® Low Fat Waffles
(2 waffles)
140 calories
2.5 g fat (0.5 g saturated)
410 mg sodium

Jimmy Dean® D-lights® Canadian Bacon, Egg White, & Cheese Sandwich
(1 sandwich)
230 calories
6 g fat
(3 g saturated)
790 mg sodium

Jimmy Dean® Ham Breakfast Skillets
(¼ package)
130 calories
4 g fat
(1 g saturated)
430 mg sodium

The simple swap of breakfast meat makes a difference of 11 grams of fat and 90 calories.

Amy's® Strawberry Toaster Pops
(1 toaster pop)
150 calories
3.5 g fat
(0 g saturated)
8 g sugars

Amy's filling is made from strawberry puree and strawberry juice concentrate.

Eggo® Toaster Swirlz™ Cinnamon Roll Minis
(4 mini rolls)
120 calories
3 g fat
(0.5 g saturated)
6 g sugars

One of the only cinnamon rolls you should feed a kid.

Quality Kangaroo® Cheese Omelet Pita (1 pita/106 g)
200 calories
7 g fat
(3 g saturated)
445 mg sodium

This pita a protein powerhouse with four times the fiber of the Toaster Scrambles pastry.

ées

Not That!

Eggo® Nutri-Grain® Whole Wheat Waffles
(2 waffles)
180 calories
6 g fat (1.5 g saturated)
420 mg sodium

Pillsbury® Cheese, Egg, and Bacon Toaster Scrambles®
(2 pastries/94 g)
360 calories
24 g fat
(7 g saturated, 2 g trans)
660 mg sodium

Rhodes® Anytime Cinnamon Rolls
(1 roll with icing/5 oz)
310 calories
9.5 g fat
(2.5 g saturated)
21 g sugars
High in fat and sugar, low in protein and fiber, this is the worst of breakfast formulas.

Pillsbury® Strawberry Toaster Strudel™
(1 pastry)
190 calories
9 g fat
(3.5 g saturated, 1 g trans)
9 g sugars
Be skeptical of toaster pastries—they're usually loaded with fat.

Jimmy Dean® Sausage Breakfast Skillets
(1/4 package)
220 calories
15 g fat
(5 g saturated)
590 mg sodium

Aunt Jemima® Sausage, Egg & Cheese Biscuit Sandwich
(1 sandwich)
340 calories
21 g fat
(7 g saturated, 3 g trans)
830 g sodium
Ban biscuits!

Frozen Snacks

Eat This

El Monterey® Chicken and Cheese Grilled Quesadillas
(1 quesadilla/85 g)
190 calories
7 g fat (3 g saturated)
460 mg sodium

More protein and fewer calories.

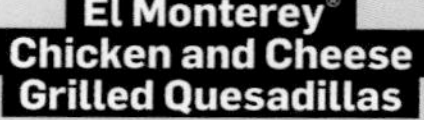

Green Giant® Broccoli and Cheese GiantBites™
(3 nuggets/85 g)
150 calories
7 g fat
(1 g saturated)
460 mg sodium
A sneaky way to get your kids to make friends with broccoli.

Bagel Bites® Supreme
(4 bites/88 g)
200 calories
6 g fat
(2.5 g saturated)
370 mg sodium
Not an ideal snack, but you could do a lot worse than four of these mini pizzas.

Alexia® Oven Reds
(12 pieces/85 g)
120 calories
3.5 g fat
(0.5 g saturated)
270 mg sodium
These fries are cut from red potatoes and cooked with olive oil.

Ore-Ida® Mini Tater Tots®
(19 pieces)
170 calories
9 g fat
(1.5 g saturated)
430 mg sodium
Not a substitute for fresh vegetables by any stretch of the imagination, but decent in a pinch.

Freschetta® PizzAmoré® Garlic with Savory Marinara Stuffed Breadsticks
(1 stick/51 g)
110 calories
3.5 fat
(1.5 g saturated)
330 mg sodium

Alexia® Breaded Mushrooms
(6 pieces/80 g)
110 calories
6 g fat
(0.5 g saturated)
280 mg sodium
The same rich, fried taste kids crave for half the calories and fat.

Not That!

Cedarlane™ Three Cheese Quesadillas
(1 quesadilla/85 g)
250 calories
11 g fat (6 g saturated)
420 mg sodium

Microwave your own whole wheat quesadilla with low-fat cheese at home.

Alexia® Onion Rings
(6 rings/85 g)
230 calories
12 g fat
(1 g saturated)
230 mg sodium
At 2 grams of fat per piece, these rings are best left frozen.

Alexia® Mozzarella Stix
(2 stix/37 g)
120 calories
7 g fat
(1 g saturated)
220 mg sodium

T.G.I. Fridays® Cheddar and Bacon Potato Skins (3 pieces)
210 calories
12 g fat
(4 g saturated)
480 mg sodium
Better than the bombs they serve in the restaurant, but still pretty awful.

Ore-Ida® Golden Twirls
(1⅓ c/84 g)
160 calories
6 g fat
(1 g saturated)
400 mg sodium
Choose a better potato cooked in a better oil, and you'll get a fry with half the fat.

Totino's® Pepperoni Pizza Rolls
(6 rolls/85 g)
220 calories
10 g fat
(3 g saturated, 1.5 g trans)
510 mg sodium

Van's® Ham & Cheese Stuffed Sandwiches
(1 pocket/121 g)
330 calories
18 g fat
(11 g saturated)
470 mg sodium
Contains more than half a day's saturated fat.

Frozen Beef Dishes

Eat This

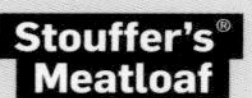

Stouffer's® Meatloaf
(1 package)
340 calories
18 g fat (8 g saturated)
780 mg sodium

Meatloaf trumps meatballs, with a fraction of the calories and saturated fat.

Michelina's Lean Gourmet® Salisbury Steak with Gravy and Mashed Potatoes
(1 package)
190 calories
6 g fat
(3 g saturated)
760 mg sodium
A lighter take on a normally heavy classic.

Smart Ones® Roast Beef in Portobello Vermouth Sauce with Broccoli and Cauliflower
(1 package)
190 calories
8 g fat
(2.5 g saturated)
680 mg sodium

José Olé® Shredded Steak Taquitos
(in corn tortillas)
(3 taquitos/113 g)
190 calories
7 g fat
(1.5 g saturated)
440 mg sodium
Serve with a scoop of salsa for a solid after-school snack.

Banquet® Crock-Pot Classics® Beef Pot Roast
(⅔ c)
150 calories
3.5 g fat
(2 g saturated)
660 mg sodium
A safe bet for a quick meal, even if they come back for seconds.

Hot Pockets® Philly Steak & Cheese Soft Baked Subs
(1 sub)
270 calories
9 g fat
(2.5 g saturated)
870 mg sodium
Surprisingly, this is the safest selection in the Hot Pockets section.

Not That!

In the battle of the beefy comfort dishes, the mountain of pasta and cream-drowned meatballs loses everytime. All told, this entrée has more than half a kid's daily allotment of saturated fat.

Stouffer's® Swedish Meatballs (1 package)
560 calories
27 g fat (12 g saturated)
1,250 mg sodium

Hot Pockets® Philly Steak and Cheese Croissant Crust (1 pocket)
340 calories
18 g fat
(9 g saturated)
550 mg sodium
The combo of margarine and dense croissant adds up to nearly half a day's worth of saturated fat.

Banquet® Crock-Pot Classics® Meatballs in Stroganoff Sauce (2/3 c)
300 calories
14 g fat
(5 g saturated)
800 mg sodium
The serving size is small, even for a kid, so count on higher calorie count.

José Olé® Steak & Cheese Chimichanga (1 chimichanga/142 g)
350 calories
15 g fat
(4.5 g saturated)
580 mg sodium
The only thing worse for your kid than a burrito is a fried burrito.

Lean Cuisine® Steak Tips Dijon (1 package)
280 calories
7 g fat
(2.5 g saturated)
650 mg sodium
If you're going to feed the little ones something lean, you can do much better than this.

Lean Cuisine® Salisbury Steak with Macaroni & Cheese (1 package)
280 calories
9 g fat
(4.5 g saturated)
610 mg sodium

Frozen Poultry Dishes

Eat This

Corn tortillas are lower in calories and carbs and higher in fiber than flour tortillas.

José Olé® Chicken Taquitos in Corn Tortillas
(3 taquitos/85 g)
190 calories
8 g fat (1 g saturated)
390 mg sodium

Kashi® Chicken Pasta Pomodoro
(1 package)
280 calories
6 g fat
(1.5 g saturated)
470 mg sodium

Multigrain penne pasta contributes to the 6 grams of fiber and 19 grams of protein in this skinny pasta.

Swanson® Boneless Fried Chicken with Mashed Potatoes and Corn
(1 package)
230 calories
11 g fat
(2.5 g saturated)
790 mg sodium

Gourmet Dining Chicken Stir Fry
(8 oz)
200 calories
1.5 g fat
(0 g saturated)
870 mg sodium

Instead of white rice, this stir-fry uses lo mein noodles, which consist mostly of niacin-enriched durum semolina.

Lean Pocket® Mexican Style Chicken Fajita
(1 pocket)
240 calories
7 g fat
(3 g saturated)
660 mg sodium

Tyson® Any'tizers™ Buffalo Style Boneless Chicken Wyngs™
(3 pieces/84 g)
150 calories
7 g fat
(1.5 g saturated)
680 mg sodium

Banquet® Crock Pot® Classics Chicken and Dumplings (⅔ c)
200 calories
8 g fat
(2 g saturated)
940 mg sodium

Basically, this is just the guts of a potpie. There's a ton of trans fats living in the buttery-biscuit skin.

Not That!

The perfect example of how one word can nearly double the calorie, fat, and sodium counts.

José Olé® Chicken & Cheese Taquitos in Flour Tortillas
(2 taquitos/85 g)
240 calories
10 g fat (2.5 g saturated)
500 mg sodium

Lean Cuisine® Sesame Chicken
(1 package)
330 calories
9 g fat
(1.5 g saturated)
650 mg sodium

Many "lean" entrées replace fat with sugar. This one packs 14 grams of sugar, mostly found in the sauce.

Marie Callender's® Chicken Pot Pie
(1 pie/10 oz)
670 calories
41 g fat
(14 g saturated, 2 g trans)
1,000 mg sodium

Potpies are consistently one of the worst foods you can feed to a kid.

Tyson® Chicken Nuggets
(5 nuggets/91 g)
280 calories
18 g fat
(4 g saturated)
480 mg sodium

Breaded with bleached wheat flour and fried in vegetable oil.

José Olé® Chicken & Cheese Chimichanga
(1 chimichanga/5 oz)
330 calories
12 g fat
(3 g saturated)
550 mg sodium

Tyson® Chicken Stir Fry Meal Kit
(1.8 c frozen)
290 calories
4 g fat
(1 g saturated)
1,130 mg sodium

A majority of American's sodium intake comes from packaged foods; this is one of the worst offenders.

Kid Cuisine® All Star Chicken Breast Nuggets with Corn, Mac & Cheese, and Chocolate Pudding (1 package)
430 calories
17 g fat
(4 g saturated)
640 mg sodium

Frozen Fish Dishes

Eat This

Kashi® Lime Cilantro Shrimp
(1 package)
250 calories
8 g fat (2 g saturated)
690 mg sodium

Sea Pak® Jumbo Breaded Butterfly Shrimp (4 shrimp/84 g)
210 calories
10 g fat
(1.5 g saturated)
480 mg sodium

While it's best to get your kid used to non-fried seafood, these numbers are super reasonable.

Van de Kamp's® Crispy Fish Portions
(1 portion)
140 calories
7 g fat
(2.5 g saturated)
440 mg sodium

Microwave a potato and serve it with the fish for a complete meal.

Ian's® Fish Sticks
(4 sticks/93 g)
190 calories
6 g fat
(1 g saturated)
310 mg sodium

When it comes to the normally perilous fish sticks, these are as good as it gets.

Gorton's® Roasted Garlic and Butter Grilled Tilapia
(1 fillet)
80 calories
2.5 g fat
(0.5 g saturated)
150 mg sodium

Grilled means good in the world of frozen foods.

Not That!

Bertolli® Shrimp Scampi & Linguine
(½ package)
560 calories
25 g fat (11 g saturated)
670 mg sodium

Gorton's® Crunchy Breaded Tilapia (1 fillet)
250 calories
12 g fat
(3.5 g saturated)
480 mg sodium
That thin layer of breading might seem innocent, but it effectively triples the calories and quadruples the fat found in this fish fillet.

Van de Kamp's® Crunchy Fish Sticks
(6 sticks/114 g)
230 calories
11 g fat
(4 g saturated)
370 mg sodium
Tartar sauce will tack on another 200 calories to the total. Dunk in cocktail sauce or ketchup, instead.

Kid Cuisine® Deep Sea Adventure Fish Sticks
(1 meal)
390 calories
12 g fat
(2.5 g saturated)
500 mg sodium
The abysmal sides included in Kid Cuisine meals (see: mac and cheese and gummi bears) make them consistently dubious picks.

Sea Pak® American Shrimp Scampi
(6 shrimp/4 oz)
330 calories
29 g fat
(10 g saturated)
460 mg sodium
The shrimp itself is innocent, but scampi is Italian for a heavy dose of oil and butter.

Frozen Vegetarian
Eat This

Boca® Meatless Chili
(1 package)
150 calories
1 g fat (0 g saturated)
650 mg sodium

Super-packed with fiber and protein.

Amy's® Mexican Tamale Pie
(1 pie)
150 calories
3 g fat
(0 g saturated)
590 mg sodium
Beneath the cornmeal crust lies a rich deposit of fiber-packed vegetables.

MorningStar Farms® Meal Starters™ Chik'n Strips
(12 strips/85 g)
140 calories
3.5 g fat
(0.5 g saturated)
510 mg sodium
Great low-cal treat with a massive dose of soy protein.

Cedarlane™ Garden Vegetable Enchiladas
(2 enchiladas)
280 calories
6 g fat
(3 g saturated)
620 mg sodium

Boca® Meatless Cheeseburger
(1 patty)
100 calories
4.5 g fat
(1.5 g saturated)
320 mg sodium

Boca® Chunky Tomato and Herb Meatless Lasagna
(1 package)
290 calories
5 g fat
(2 g saturated)
880 mg sodium

MorningStar Farms® Original Veggie Dogs®
(1 hot dog)
80 calories
0.5 g fat
(0 g saturated)
580 mg sodium

Not That!

Amy's® Chili & Cornbread Whole Meal
(1 package)
340 calories
6 g fat (2.5 g saturated)
680 mg sodium

MorningStar Farms® Veggie Corn Dogs
(1 corn dog)
150 calories
4 g fat
(0.5 g saturated)
500 mg sodium

Amy's® Cheese Lasagna
(1 package)
380 calories
14 g fat
(8 g saturated)
680 mg sodium

MorningStar Farms® Grillers Prime®
(1 patty)
170 calories
9 g fat
(1 g saturated)
360 mg sodium

Amy's® Black Bean Vegetable Enchilada
(2 enchiladas)
360 calories
12 g fat
(1 g saturated)
780 mg sodium

Quorn™ Meatless and Soy-Free Garlic & Herb Chik'n Cutlets
(1 cutlet/100 g)
200 calories
9 g fat
(1 g saturated)
570 mg sodium

Amy's® Country Vegetable Pie
(1 pie)
370 calories
16 g fat
(9 g saturated)
580 mg sodium
We've yet to find a healthy potpie anywhere in America.

Frozen Pasta

Eat This

Stouffer's® Spaghetti with Meatballs
(1 package)
350 calories
12 g fat (4 g saturated)
660 mg sodium

Trade alfredo for marinara and meatballs and ditch the bread and you'll cut the calories and sodium in half.

Mama Rosie's® Cheese Lasagna
(1 package)
290 calories
7 g fat
(3 g saturated)
680 mg sodium

Kashi® Pesto Pasta Primavera
(1 package)
290 calories
11 g fat
(2 g saturated)
750 mg sodium

Michelina's® Authenitico™ Macaroni & Cheese
(1 package)
230 calories
3.5 g fat
(2 g saturated)
540 mg sodium

Michelina's® Lean Gourmet Spaghetti & Meat Sauce
(1 package)
300 calories
6 g fat
(2 g saturated)
540 mg sodium

Not That!

Marie Callender's® Fettuccini Alfredo & Garlic Bread
(1 package)

770 calories
46 g fat (16 g saturated, 1 g trans)
1,300 mg sodium

Alfredo sauce means a rich, buttery, artery-clogging cream sauce, and this garlic bread adds an extra dose of high-fructose corn syrup and partially hydrogenated oils.

Stouffer's® Five Cheese Lasagna
(1 c/237 g)

330 calories
14 g fat
(8 g saturated)
870 mg sodium

Amy's® Pesto Tortellini Bowl
(1 package)

430 calories
19 g fat
(8 g saturated)
640 mg sodium

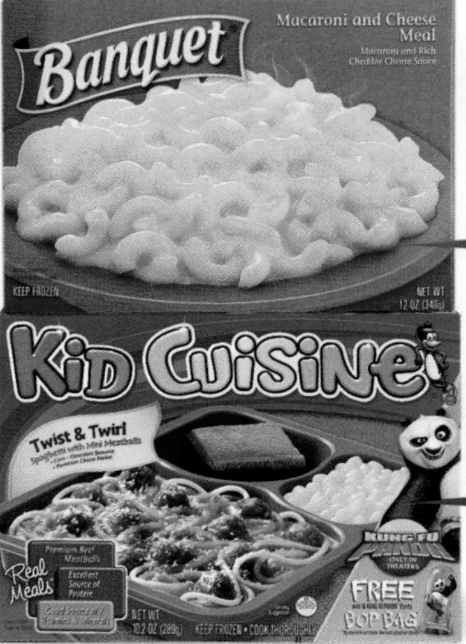

Banquet® Macaroni and Cheese Meal
(1 package)

390 calories
11 g fat
(6 g saturated)
1,100 mg sodium

Kid Cuisine® Twist & Twirl Spaghetti with Mini Meatballs and Brownie
(1 package)

420 calories
12 g fat (4 g saturated)
690 mg sodium

Frozen Pizza

Eat This

Lean Pockets® Whole Grain Supreme Pizza (1 pizza)

220 calories
7 g fat (2.5 g saturated)
490 mg sodium

Hot Pockets can be a great way to exercise portion control, as long as you avoid the oily crust used for their regular line of products. Lean Pockets replace the oil with 20 grams of whole grains.

Dole® Hawaiian Style Pizza (⅓ pizza)

290 calories
13 g fat
(7 g saturated)
800 mg sodium

Ham proves the perfect lean meat topping for a pizza, trouncing pepperoni and sausage in the fat and calorie categories.

Earth's Best® Sesame Street Frozen Whole Grain Cheese Pizza (1 pizza)

190 calories
6 g fat
(3 g saturated)
380 mg sodium

This is one of the few TV-backed products worth buying.

Kashi® Mediterranean Pizza (⅓ pizza)

290 calories
9 g fat
(4 g saturated)
640 mg sodium

Instead of vegetable oil, Kashi uses olive oil, which makes much of the fat here the heart-friendly kind.

Kid Cuisine® KC's Primo Pepperoni Pizza with Corn & Brownie (1 package)

480 calories
15 g fat
(5 g saturated)
710 mg sodium

Not That!

Red Baron may call this a pizza for one, but it contains a full day of saturated fat and nearly a full day of sodium.

Red Baron® Classic Crust Singles Pizza 4 Cheese
(1 pizza)
720 calories
38 g fat (19 g saturated)
1,470 mg sodium

Banquet® Pepperoni Pizza Meal with Corn and Brownie
(1 package)
550 calories
29 g fat
(5 g saturated, 0.5 g trans)
890 mg sodium

DiGiorno® Thin Crispy Crust Pepperoni Pizza
(⅕ pizza)
320 calories
15 g fat
(7 g saturated)
790 mg sodium
The thin crust keeps the carbs down, but the fatty meats jack the calories and sodium up.

Lean Cuisine® Four Cheese Pizza (1 pizza)
360 calories
8 g fat
(3.5 g saturated)
690 mg sodium
Four cheeses and lean are mutually exclusive terms.

Wolfgang Puck's® All-Natural Uncured Pepperoni Pizza
(⅓ pizza)
360 calories
19 g fat
(7 g saturated)
870 g sodium

Ice Cream

Eat This

Edy's/ Dreyer's® Loaded Chocolate Peanut Butter Cup (½ c)
140 calories
6 g fat
(3 g saturated)
12 g sugars
The main ingredient is skim milk.

"Double Churn" is Breyer's code word for low-fat, which is good news for you and the unsuspecting family.

Breyer's® Double Churn Extra Creamy Vanilla Bean Ice Cream (1/2 c)
100 calories
3 g fat (2 g saturated)
13 g sugars

Stonyfield Farm® Nonfat Vanilla Fudge Swirl Frozen Yogurt (½ c)
120 calories
0 g fat
22 g sugars

Blue Bunny® No Sugar Added Fat Free Caramel Toffee Crunch (½ c)
90 calories
0 g fat
4 g sugars
You won't find an ice cream with less sugar than this one.

Soy Dream® Non-Dairy Chocolate Fudge Brownie (½ c)
130 calories
7 g fat
(1.5 g saturated)
12 g sugars
A great sweet option for lactose-intolerant little ones.

Breyers® A&W™ Root Beer Float (½ c)
130 calories
4.5 g fat
(3 g saturated)
16 g sugars
Not a bad scoop, considering a real Root Beer float has about 400 calories.

Life Savers® 5 Flavor Real Fruit Sherbert (½ c)
110 calories
0 g fat
21 g sugars
Generally speaking, fruity sherberts make for a relatively safe fat-free scoop.

Not That!

Häagen-Dazs® Extra Rich Light Vanilla Bean Ice Cream (1/2 c)

200 calories
7 g fat (4 g saturated)
25 g sugars

While we applaud Häagen-Dazs for the simplicity of their ice cream—only seven ingredients in this scoop—their "light" ice creams are worse than most brands' regular lines.

Ben & Jerry's® All Natural Peanut Butter Cup™ (½ c)

360 calories
26 g fat
(13 g saturated)
23 g sugars

One of Ben & Jerry's most dubious flavors, with nearly a full day of saturated fat per serving.

Häagen-Dazs® Vanilla Raspberry Swirl Low-Fat Frozen Yogurt (½ c)

160 calories
1.5 g fat
(0.5 g saturated)
25 g sugars

Ben & Jerry's® All Natural Phish Food® Light (½ c)

210 calories
6 g fat
(4.5 g saturated)
23 g sugars

Made with skim milk, but liquid sugar and corn syrup are still the second and third ingredients.

Tofutti® Vanilla Milk Free Premium Frozen Dessert (½ c)

180 calories
11 g fat
(2 g saturated)
8 g sugars

Blue Bunny® Homemade Turtle Sundae (½ c)

180 calories
9 g fat
(5 g saturated)
19 g sugars

Take advantage of Blue Bunny's slimmer line of ice creams.

Rice Dream® Vanilla Swiss Almond (½ c)

190 calories
10 g fat
(2.5 g saturated)
18 g sugars

Frozen Treats

Eat This

Edy's/Dreyer's® Slow Churned® Vanilla with Nestlé Crunch® Bar
(1 bar)
150 calories
8 g fat (6 g saturated)
10 g sugars

Fudgesicle® Triple Chocolate
(1 fudgesicle)
60 calories
1.5 g fat
(1 g saturated)
9 g sugars

A good rule of thumb: Stuff with "sicle" in the name makes for a safe indulgence.

Edy's/Dreyer's® Strawberry Fruit Bars
(1 bar)
80 calories
0 g fat
20 g sugars

Popsicle® Orange, Cherry and Grape Ice Pops
(1 popsicle)
45 calories
0 g fat
8 g sugars

Classic, and still one of the best frozen treats you can use to reward your kids.

The Skinny Cow® Low Fat Chocolate Peanut Butter Ice Cream Sandwich
(1 sandwich)
150 calories
2 g fat
(1 g saturated)
15 g sugars

Breyers® Oreo Ice Cream Sandwiches
(1 sandwich)
160 calories
6 g fat
(2 g saturated)
13 g sugars

Your kid's better off eating this than three regular Oreos.

Blue Bunny® Orange Dream Bar
(1 pop)
80 calories
1.5 g fat
14 g sugars

Blue Bunny has some of the best and some of the worst products in the freezer. Be sure to read the label.

MolliCoolz™ Incredible Banana Split Ice Cream Beads (1 c/71 g)
129 calories
10 g fat
(7 g saturated)
5 g sugars

The smartest choice in the bite-size dessert category.

Not That!

Eskimo Pie® Vanilla Ice Cream Bar with Nestlé Crunch® Coating
(1 bar)
210 calories
14 g fat (10 g saturated)
12 g sugars

Rice Dream® Vanilla Bar
(1 bar)
230 calories
14 g fat
(9 g saturated)
16 g sugars
They may be lactose-free, but they still contain half a day's worth of saturated fat.

Edy's/Dreyer's® Strawberry Dibs®
(26 pieces/105 g)
370 calories
26 g fat
(16 g saturated)
22 g sugars
The "chocolate" coating is made with coconut and palm oil.

Edy's® Fruit Bars All Natural Creamy Coconut (1 bar)
120 calories
3 g fat
(2.5 g saturated)
15 g sugars
Keep your kid's popsicles under 100 calories.

Klondike® Dark Chocolate Bar
(1 bar)
250 calories
17 g fat
(12 g saturated)
17 g sugars
The "dark chocolate" is actually a "chocolate flavored coating," which lists vegetable oils as its first ingredient.

Snickers® Brownie Ice Cream Sandwich
(1 sandwich)
210 calories
9 g fat
(4.5 g saturated)
18 g sugars

Nestlé Push Ups® Shrek®
(1 push up)
80 calories
1 g fat
(0.5 g saturated)
13 g sugars
Not a terrible choice, but still has nearly double the calories of a Popsicle.

Blue Bunny® The Champ!® Strawberry Cone (1 cone)
220 calories
12 g fat
(9 g saturated)
21 g sugars

5

AT SCHOOL

Conquering the Cafeteria

There are few places on earth as terrifying as the school lunchroom.

First, there's the social intrigue over who's sitting with whom, who's not sitting with whom, and who gets picked on if they sit with the wrong whom. It's sort of like *Lord of the Flies* with spaghetti sauce, with tribes and cliques huddled together in a tremulous social pecking order. Add in grumpy, graying lunch ladies, stringent hall monitors, and the stress of trying to eat your lunch while dodging flying chicken fingers, and lunch can be a serious hazard to a kid's social standing.

School lunches shouldn't be hazardous to your child's health. Yet the lunchroom is, in most of America's school districts, a nutritional minefield.

Sure, the National School Lunch Program (NSLP), instituted in 1946, has made some positive strides toward improving the nutritional quality of school lunches. Under the program's guidelines, a proper school lunch must derive on average 30 percent or less of its calories from fat and must serve two or more fruit and vegetable items each day. So if your child sticks with the prescribed school lunch—mushy green beans and all—he or she will supposedly get a meal that at least hews to some modicum of nutritional responsibility, lacking though it might be in palate appeal. And the program does seem to be making a difference in some quarters: According to one study, students who report eating NSLP meals consume greater amounts of all nutrients except vitamin C, compared with students who eat meals from other sources.

But sending your child to school with a couple of dollars for lunch certainly doesn't guarantee that he's going to come home with a belly full of goodness. Despite the NSLP guidelines, many school districts are having a heck of a time measuring up to its standards. In a recent study by the National Institutes of Health, the average lunch got 35.9 percent of its calories from total fat and 12.6 percent from saturated fat, exceeding the guidelines of 30 and 10 percent, respectively. The problem? Funding. A recent analysis found that federal reimbursements cover only about half of the real cost of providing healthy meals for our children, and almost 85 percent of school food service programs receive no financial support from their school districts.

And in addition to the breakdown in the school lunch program, there are other hazards lurking in the school cafeteria.

SCREWY LUNCH SCHEDULES

First, the school day usually revolves around coordinating a fleet of buses, an army of students, and a complex schedule of academics—a schedule made ever more complicated by the increasing federal regulation of school course loads. Trying to fit time for lunch into that complex web can be difficult. Indeed, a survey conducted by Penn State University found that, of 228 high schools, one in four schools scheduled lunch periods before 10:30 A.M. Who wants to eat lunch at a time when most parents are still finishing their coffee? And researchers found that an earlier lunch start predicted that a larger number of students would be buying their food not from the school lunch program, but from . . .

THE SNACK BAR

About 90 percent of public schools now offer à la carte items, or as your kids might know them, "snack bar" foods. A study in the *Journal of the American Dietetic Association* found that middle-school students with access to snack bar foods consume significantly fewer fruit and vegetable servings than students who eat only NSLP meals. And a study at the University of Minnesota found that when students had access to snack bars at school, their consumption of both fat and saturated fat ballooned. Why do schools offer these less-healthy, à la carte foods? One word: money. To compensate for a lack of adequate funding, schools need to finance the feeding of our children in other ways, and à la carte foods offer an easy solution. The Penn State study found that the average school in Pennsylvania earned almost $700 a day—or nearly $14,000 a month—from à la carte food sales. And beyond the snack bars, there's another hazard lurking in your local school.

THE VENDING MACHINES

In addition to snack bar offerings, contracts from soft-drink manufacturers and vending-machine companies (and incentives from soft-drink bottlers based on sales) are another significant way that schools have found to finance their activities. Consider these eye-opening statistics:

- ✖ The average secondary school in America now has 12 vending machines on its property. Research shows that the greater the number of vending machines on the property, the fewer the fruits and vegetables students ate, and the fewer the students who took advantage of the school lunch program.
- ✖ During the past 2 decades, soft drink consumption among adolescents ages 11 to 17 has increased 100 percent. No wonder: In a survey of 228 high school food service directors in Pennsylvania, two-thirds reported having soft-drink advertisements in their school.
- ✖ A study of 2,000 middle school students in Texas found that 72 percent of the sweetened beverages, 80 percent of the soft drinks, and 39 percent of the candy they consumed came from vending machines.

Sadly, all of this could be avoided if schools were willing to intervene. In a 2008 study at the Center for Obesity Research and Education at Temple University, five Philadelphia-area elementary schools replaced high-sugar, high-fat vending machine snacks with juice, water, low-fat milk, and healthy snacks; provided nutritional education to the students; and gave away raffle tickets for wise food choices. The result: Over a 2-year period, the obesity rate in those five schools fell to half of what it was in similar elementary schools.

But until healthy eating becomes a priority, it's up to you, the parent, to make the smart choices. To help your child navigate the nutritional no-man's-land of the school cafeteria, arm him or her with this easy-to-follow guide. It may take a little coaxing—putting a kid with a little cash in his pocket next to a vending machine is like putting a local politician next to an empty podium—but by explaining that he'll not only look and feel better, but also become better at sports, at school, at play, and at all the things he enjoys doing, you'll inspire him to make the right choices.

How Our Schools Are Failing Our Kids

Established in 1946, the National School Lunch Program (NSLP) was supposed to guarantee that all public school children in America received a proper school lunch that averaged 30 percent or less of its calories from fat and 10 percent or less from saturated fat and offered two or more fruit and vegetable items each day. But as governments at every level have been draining funds away from our schools, one essential element of our children's lives—nutrition—has gotten the short end of the breadstick. Under the NSLP, the federal government reimburses school districts just $2.47 per day for every meal for children who qualify for free lunches, $2.07 per day for students who qualify for reduced-price fare, and a whopping $0.23 for students who pay full price. Ann Cooper, director of nutrition services for the Berkeley Unified School System, estimates that schools spend about $1.68 per meal on payroll and overhead. For actual food costs, that leaves cafeteria managers with all of 72 cents for each meal. Here is just a small sample of numbers underscoring the need for reform in our school lunch programs:

- In February 2008, 37 million pounds of meat were recalled from school lunches.

- In a recent study by the Center for Science in the Public Interest, 46 percent of states received an F on their School Food Report Card.

- In a study on school lunches in Harwich, Massachusetts, 50 percent of lunches were found to come from leftovers.

- In a study of 22 of the largest 100 elementary school districts in the United States, the Physicians Committee for Responsible Medicine rated the lunches students received based on how well those programs helped protect against obesity and chronic disease, promoted healthy nutrition, and taught children about healthy eating. Sadly, less than half of school programs rated an A or B. Nearly one in four received an F, including school districts in Missouri, Utah, Texas, West Virginia, and Alaska.

Breakfast

Eat This

Scrambled eggs and bacon

250 calories
10 g fat (4 g saturated)
550 mg sodium

A study from St. Louis University found that people starting their day with eggs consumed 264 fewer calories than people eating bagels for breakfast. The reason? Protein and good fat are important elements of satiety, working diligently to keep your kid's belly full and prevent those midmorning cravings that lead to empty calorie consumption.

Apple-cinnamon oatmeal

280 calories
3 g fat
(0 g saturated)
5 g carbohydrates

True, the calories from oatmeal come mostly from carbohydrates, but with each bowl comes a dose of soluble fiber, which helps slow the absorption of the carbs, keeping kids' blood sugar levels—and thus their energy and concentration levels—more stable.

Pancake on a stick

220 calories
13 g fat (4 g saturated)
350 mg sodium

The same concept as a sausage biscuit: carbs wrapped around a fatty piece of meat for a portable breakfast. Neither are paradigms of nutrition, but pancakes pack a fraction of the calories and fat found in the dreaded biscuit. Warning: If your kid has a penchant for syrup-dipping, the calories here can jump quickly.

Ham and egg on an English muffin

240 calories
8 g fat
(3 g saturated)
610 mg sodium

Not even the most malicious cafeteria cook could mess this one up: low-calorie bread, an egg, and a few slices of lean ham. Protein and healthy fat are two great ways to wake up; the only thing that's missing is fiber, and that can be corrected easily enough by using a whole grain English muffin.

Not That!

Blueberry muffin
360 calories
14 g fat (2 g saturated)
32 g sugars
2 g fiber

Bagel with jelly
390 calories
12 g fat (1 g saturated)
385 mg sodium

Bagels may look harmless, but behind each bite is a mouthful of refined carbohydrates. When a flood of quick-burning carbs enters the bloodstream, blood sugars rise rapidly and your body panics and begins to store fat. Jelly only makes matters worse, since most jellies found in school cafeterias have more sugar in them than fruit.

French toast with syrup and margarine
450 calories
18 g fat
(5 g saturated)
67 g carbohydrates

The only thing vaguely nutritious about French toast is the egg in which the bread is battered, but even that is drowned out by a flood of melted margarine and sugary syrup.

Sausage biscuit
400 calories
22 g fat
(12 g saturated,
3 g trans)
1,100 mg sodium

Here's the standard biscuit recipe: flour, lard, buttermilk. So it's not hard to imagine how this greasy, sausage-stuffed breakfast sandwich packs such a wallop. The fact that biscuits are one of the biggest transporters of trans fats only makes the need to avoid this breakfast bomb all the more vital.

Is blueberry pie healthy just because it packs a serving of fruit? Same problem here. Don't be fooled by the fruit façade: Muffins consist primarily of highly refined flour and sugar—hardly the breakfast of champions the masquerading muffin purports itself to be.

Lunch

Eat This

Roast beef and gravy

240 calories
11 g fat
(4 g saturated)
625 mg sodium

Bean burrito

300 calories
12 g fat
(3 g saturated)
650 mg sodium

The tortilla is a less-than-ideal vehicle for anything, but in this case, the benefit of the beans trumps the troubles of the tortilla. The ½ cup of beans inside this burrito pack massive amounts of fiber, protein, and—as one of nature's best sources of antioxidants—plenty of disease-fighting phytochemicals.

Made from a lean cut of beef, a few slices of roast beef prove to be a relatively low-fat, low-calorie source of protein. And since cafeteria gravies are invariably of the "instant" variety, the only minor threat they pose is of adding a bit of extra sodium to the meal.

Mashed potatoes

170 calories
8 g fat (3 g saturated)
300 mg sodium

Chances are this pile of potatoes comes from a box of instant mashed potatoes, which are made from potato flakes.

Green peas

75 calories
0 g fat
120 mg sodium

Peas are a great source of vitamin K, an important bone strengthener, which makes them a perfect segue to the type of playground high jinks that normally follow school lunch. They're also packed with thiamin, niacin, and riboflavin, all vital for energy production, which means kids might actually be able to keep their eyes open once recess is over.

Not That!

Turkey wrap
375 calories
14 g fat
(5 g saturated)
575 mg sodium

Corn niblets
100 calories
0 g fat
135 mg sodium

Not exactly a nutritional nightmare—in fact, corn does provide some meaningful nutrients like B vitamins and fiber. But corn is also one of nature's sweetest vegetables, which is why most of our packaged foods are sweetened with various forms of this processed staple crop. Save it for the summer barbecue.

Carrots with ranch
230 calories
16 g fat
(5 g saturated)
400 mg sodium

If it takes ranch dressing to get your kids to eat their vegetables, it's just not worth it. Two ounces of the stuff has more calories than an entire scoop of mashed potatoes.

Wraps start with the dreaded tortilla, to which the lunch ladies add fatty dressing (usually ranch or Italian), cheese (usually processed), and produce (usually token shreds of lettuce). What your kid is left with is something healthy in name only.

French bread cheese pizza
440 calories
19 g fat
(8 g saturated)
930 mg sodium

The thick, doughy crust used by most school cafeterias packs on a heavy carb and sodium load, plus it provides the structural integrity for a haphazard application of cheese, which doubles down on the calorie count.

Lunch

Eat This

Chili with shredded cheese
300 calories
12 g fat
(4 g saturated)
570 mg sodium

This cheesy, gooey mess is actually good for your kid? Hard to believe, but beyond being packed with enough protein to keep her full and focused the rest of the school day, a bean-laced bowl of red gives your kid plenty of fiber and disease-fighting antioxidants. Tastes great, more filling, fights against cancer. What more could you want?

Hamburger
350 calories
15 g fat
(5 g saturated)
650 mg sodium

Topped with ketchup, mustard, and hopefully a few pieces of produce (lettuce, onions, tomatoes, pickles), the humble hamburger proves to be a relatively reasonable choice, especially when compared to some of the hidden dangers lurking in the cafeteria.

Tater Tots®
150 calories
7 g fat (1 g saturated)
200 mg sodium

Cafeteria tots are invariably of the frozen variety. The upside is that they usually avoid the harsh fry treatment in favor of a simple bake, which keeps the calorie count down.

Red grapes (1 c)
104 calories
0 g fat
23 g sugars

Perhaps the most dependable fruit in the cafeteria. With tight budgets, cafeterias are often forced to buy fruit—apples, peaches, and pears, especially—in cans, which means they come with a thick coating of sugar syrup. Grapes, on the other hand, are dependably fresh and loaded with the same healthy antioxidants mom and dad enjoy in a glass of red wine.

Not That!

Grilled cheese

350 calories
16 g fat
(7 g saturated)
650 mg sodium

Cinnamon apples

200 calories
6 g fat (2 g saturated)
30 g sugars

Cinnamon apples are the perfect example of taking a perfectly good thing like an apple and messing it up with a load of unnecessary sugar and often butter or margarine. In the words of Pink Floyd (sorta): Hey, teachers, leave our fruit alone!

French fries

310 calories
18 g fat
(7 g saturated)
400 mg sodium

French fries probably won't be lucky enough to avoid the boiling oil, which is where they soak up most of their saturated fat. They might be America's favorite side dish, but more often than not, they contain as many calories, or more, than the entrée sharing the plate with them.

Crispy chicken sandwich

400 calories
19 g fat
(7 g saturated)
735 mg sodium

If they're going to take an innocent chicken breast, bread it, deep-fry it, and cover it in mayo, your kid may as well opt for the hamburger. When it comes to chicken sandwiches, if it ain't grilled, then it ain't worth eating.

Bread and cheese fried in butter? Kinda hard to imagine how this would be good for anyone. At least at home you can pair it with a cup of tomato soup and make sure your kid gets something nutritious out of the meal.

Candy

Eat This

Welch's® Fruit Snacks, Mixed Fruit
(1 package)
195 calories
0 g fat
37.5 g sugars

High in sugar, yes, but much of that sugar comes from actual fruit. All told, chewy snacks contain 100 percent of the recommended daily intake of vitamin C.

Good & Plenty®
(1 box)
170 calories
0 g fat
27 g sugars

Seems like licorice fell out of favor with the little ones a while back, which is too bad, since as far as candy goes, it's a pretty good go-to.

Nutter Butter® Bites (1 package)
170 calories
7 g fat
(2 g saturated)
10 g sugars

Guaranteed to become instant friends with peanut-butter fans young and old—which isn't such a bad thing, if your regular fix is of the Reese's variety.

York® Peppermint Pattie (1 pattie)
140 calories
2.5 g fat
(1.5 g saturated)
25 g sugars

The most reasonable of all the mainstream candies, with half the calories of a Snickers® bar.

Kit Kat® Bar
(1 package)
220 calories
11 g fat
(7 g saturated)
22 g sugars

In the wide world of crunchy, sweet chocolate bars, Kit Kat is as low-cal as they come. Plus, breakable pieces means you can save some for later.

Nestlé® Crunch® Bar (43.9 g)
220 calories
11 g fat
(7 g saturated)
24 g sugars

Give up two grams of saturated fat and get a load of crunch in return. Who wouldn't want to make that swap?

Not That!

Few products on these pages contain any hint of real nutritional value, and if you can help remove vending machine grub from your kid's diet altogether, all the better. If you're like us, though, and believe that the occasional indulgence is understandable, if not helpful, then the least you can do is make sure your kid is ready to indulge smartly.

The main ingredient in Skittles is sugar, but unlike the natural kind found in real fruit, the added sugars in Skittles will cause an attention-depleting energy crash before school lets out.

Original Fruit Skittles®
(1 package)

250 calories
2.5 g fat
(2.5 g saturated)
47 g sugars

Hershey's® Milk Chocolate Bar
(43 g)

230 calories
13 g fat (9 g saturated)
22 g sugars

Get your kid hooked on dark chocolate at an early age. It contains less sugar than milk chocolate and also has a higher concentration of antioxidants.

Twix® Cookie Bars (1 package)

280 calories
14 g fat
(11 g saturated)
27 g sugars

Both bars offer chocolate and cookie crunch, but the layer of fatty, corn syrup–based caramel is what makes Twix a clear "Not That!"

Reese's® Peanut Butter Cups
(1 package)

230 calories
13 g fat
(4.5 g saturated)
20 g sugars

If only the peanut butter weren't so riddled with sugar, the healthy spread might redeem these.

Reese's® Pieces®
(1 package)

220 calories
11 g fat
(7 g saturated)
23 g sugars

Same peanut flavor, but with a heavy dose of saturated fat and more than twice the sugar found in the Nutter Butter Bites.

Twizzlers® Pull-n-Peel™ Cherry
(1 package)

210 calories
1 g fat
(0 g saturated)
29 g sugars

Nearly fat-free, but these kid favorites are essentially dyed ropes of high-fructose corn syrup.

Crunchy Snacks

Eat This

Chex Mix® Traditional Snack Mix
(1 oz)
130 calories
4 g fat
(0.5 g saturated)
380 mg sodium

This mix of Chex cereal, pretzels, and rye chips has 60 percent less fat than regular potato chips, but beware of the high sodium counts and the misleading serving sizes on the pacakges. Keep consumption down to one ounce at a time.

Baked! Lay's® Potato Chips (1 oz)
110 calories
1.5 g fat
(0 g saturated)
150 mg sodium

Baked Lays chips offer all of the crunch without any of the saturated fat. This is as guilt-free as chip munching gets.

Rold Gold® Tiny Twists Pretzels (1 oz)
110 calories
1 g fat
(0 g saturated)
580 mg sodium

Pretzels are low in calories, but because of the high sodium count, keep your kid's intake to an ounce at a time.

Nacho Cheese Doritos® (1 oz)
150 calories
8 g fat
(1.5 g saturated)
180 mg sodium

Made from whole corn instead of corn meal. Shed another 20 calories switching over to Baked! Doritos.

Lays® Wavy Potato Chips (1 oz)
150 calories
10 g fat
(1 g saturated)
180 mg sodium

When it comes to snacking, portion control is key. An ounce of chips is more than enough for an afternoon snack.

Goldfish® Pretzel Baked Snack Crackers (1.3 oz)
140 calories
1.5 g fat
(0 g saturated)
530 mg sodium

Yes, high in sodium, but the fat and calorie advantage makes up for the saltiness.

Goldfish® Baked Snack Crackers (1.25 oz)

160 calories
6 g fat
(1.5 g saturated)
290 mg sodium

Goldfish beat out potato chips nine times out of ten, but when it comes to crackers, there are better options.

Sun Chips® Original (1.5 oz)

210 calories
10 g fat
(1.5 g saturated)
180 mg sodium

Low in saturated fat, but not quite the paradigm of health it pretends to be. The extra half-ounce serving size pushes this snack north of 200 caloires.

Crunchy Cheetos® (2 oz)

320 calories
20 g fat
(4 g saturated)
590 mg sodium

An unfortunate favorite in school halls across America, conisdering it's one of the saltiest, fattiest snacks in the vending machine.

Gardetto's® Snak-Ens Original Recipe (1 oz)

150 calories
6 g fat (1 g saturated, 2 g trans)
310 mg sodium

This bag contains enough partially hydrogenated oil to contribute 2 grams of trans fats to each serving.

Fritos® Original Corn Chips (1 oz)

160 calories
10 g fat
(1.5 g saturated)
170 mg sodium

The fried corn chips may have been the standard when you were in school, but a new, healthier legion of baked chips have since emerged.

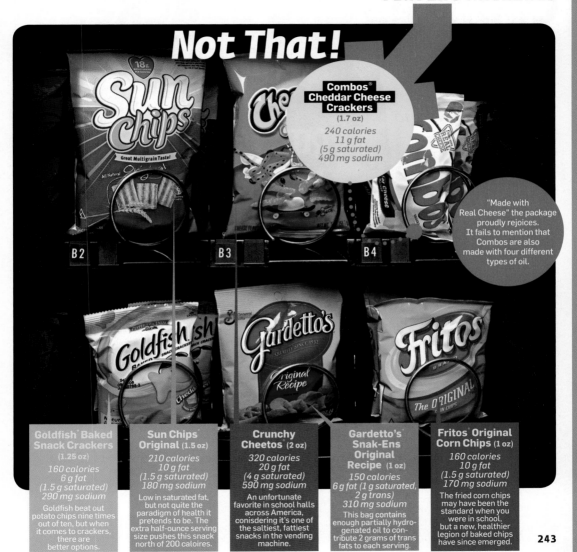

Cookies and Crackers

Eat This

Ritz Bits® Peanut Butter Sandwiches (1 package)
170 calories
10 g fat (2 g saturated)
280 mg sodium

Make Ritz the peanut butter cracker of choice. The Ritz taste better and have 15 percent fewer calories than the Austin variety—and no trans fats!

Pepperidge Farm® Milano® Cookies (1 package)
180 calories
10 g fat
(5 g saturated)
11 g sugars

The thin chocolate cookies are the best in the Pepperidge Farm line.

Austin® Vanilla Cremes (1 package)
170 calories
7 g fat
(2.5 g saturated)
11 g sugars

This is one of the safer packages of Austin crackers. It's trans fats–free and has 30 fewer calories than almost every other variety.

Rice Krispies Treats® Bar (1)
150 calories
3.5 g fat
(1 g saturated)
12 g sugars

Rice Krispies Treats are deceptively decent, mostly because the bulk of the bar is made from a fairly innocuous cereal.

Kraft® Cinnamon Bagel-fuls (1)
200 calories
4 g fat
(2.5 g saturated)
8 g sugars
190 mg sodium

Not one of Kraft's bagel-and-cream-cheese fusions has more that 200 calories or 6 grams of fat. Sweet!

Nabisco® Barnum's Animals® Crackers (1 package)
120 calories
3.5 g fat
(1 g saturated)
7 g sugars

As far as cookies are concerned, Barnum's Animals are a tame bunch.

Not That!

Austin® Cheese Crackers with Peanut Butter
(1 package, 39 g)
200 calories
10 g fat (1.5 g saturated; 2 g trans)
400 mg sodium

Far too many of Austin's prepackaged crackers contain trans fats. This small package contains 2 grams, which is why you should never fail to look over the label before passing a snack down to your child.

Mini Chips Ahoy!® Chocolate Chip
(1 package)
170 calories
8 g fat
(2.5 g saturated)
10 g sugars

The cookies might be smaller, but their caloric load is just as big.

Pop-Tarts® Brown Sugar Cinnamon
(2 pastries)
420 calories
14 g fat
(4.5 g saturated)
31 g sugars

The caloric equivalent of two doughnuts, loaded with HFCS and partially hydrogenated vegetable oil.

Little Debbie® Double Decker Oatmeal Creme Pie (1)
470 calories
18 g fat
(5 g saturated,)
39 g sugars

As densely caloric as anything your kid will encounter in the vending machine.

Keebler® Vanilla Sugar Wafers
(1 package)
400 calories
21 g fat
(4 g saturated,
8 g trans)
34 g sugars

The trans fattiest vending machine snack we've seen. A single serving has three times a safe daily intake.

Mrs. Fields® Semi-Sweet Chocolate Chip Cookie (1)
330 calories
16 g fat
(10 g saturated)
28 g sugars

The cookie queen has a thing for saturated fat—this cook has more than half a day's worth.

Beverages

Drink This

Dasani® Water

0 calories
0 g fat
0 g sugars

If you're really concerned about your kid's nutrient intake, give her a children's multivitamin—she can wash it down with a cold glass of H_2O.

Hershey's® Chocolate Drink
(8 oz)

130 calories
1 g fat
(0 g saturated)
26 g sugars

This chocolate drink has two advantages over Yoo-Hoo: Milk is higher up on the ingredient list, and the portion size is smaller.

Dole® 100% Orange Juice
(15.2 oz)

210 calories
0 g fat
42 g sugars

100% fruit juice will never lose a nutritional contest to psuedo juice. Still, OJ intake should be limited in favor of eating the actual fruit.

Propel® Fitness Water, Grape
(16.9 oz)

25 calories
0 g fat
4 g sugars

If your family is going to drink "fitness" waters or "functional beverages," make sure they have less than 50 calories and 10 grams of sugar per bottle.

Honest Ade® Orange Mango
(16.9 oz)

100 calories
0 g fat
25 g sugars

Learn to love the Honest line of drinks in your household: They offer a kid-pleasing sweetness with a lower concentration of sugar than most major brands.

Glaceau Vitamin Water® Endurance (20 oz)

125 calories
0 g fat
33 g sugars

Functional beverages make big promises and pack a variety of nutrients. But they also bring a flood of sugar. In the case of Vitamin Water, a 20-ounce bottle carries nearly as much sugar as a can of Coke.

Sobe® Lizard Lava™ (20 oz)

310 calories
1 g fat
75 g sugars

Sobe hooks your kids with clever advertising and hooks you with the promise of "a blend of aloe vera and vitamins." Truth is, it's a blend of water and high-fructose corn syrup.

Gatorade® Rain® Berry (20 oz)

130 calories
0 g fat
35 g sugars

Gatorade pushes a lot of science to help sell their spin on the sweetened beverage, but in reality it's not much more than salt, sugar, and potassium blended into water.

Snapple® Mango Madness Juice Drink (16 oz)

220 calories
0 g fat
54 g sugars

Snapple is 5 percent juice, 95 percent sugar water, so this drink brings with it little to no nutritional benefit.

Yoo-Hoo® Chocolate Drink (15.5 oz)

252 calories
2 g fat (1 g saturated)
52 g sugars

Yoo-Hoo isn't really milk in the true sense. The main ingredient is water, followed by whey, high-fructose corn syrup, and sugar. Then comes milk.

How to Pack the Perfect

Concerned that the sludge they're slopping at the cafeteria is ruining your kid's appetite, and maybe even his waistline? Then it's time to take control of the midday meal by packing a heroic lunch for your loved ones each morning. Not only will you ensure optimum nutrition, you'll also be able to cater to his likes and dislikes, which means there's a darn good shot he'll actually eat this lunch, rather than leaving it behind in the rush to get to the playground.

A good lunch is a balanced one, formed around a dependable main course and punctuated with a solid supporting cast of nutrient-packed sides, a low- or no-calorie drink, and even a little treat. Mix and match like you would when ordering Chinese takeout—though, unlike General Tso's chicken and sweet-and-sour goop, this stuff is actually good for your kid. Master the mix and your kid will be the envy of every mystery meat-eating student in the second grade. Here are the four elements to a perfectly packed lunch.

DEPENDABLE DRINK

This is a high-stakes decision that few parents really think about. Considering the fact that many kids' beverages have nearly as much sugar per ounce as soft drinks, tossing the wrong drink in the lunch-box could translate into 3 to 5 extra pounds by the end of the school year. Drinks should be either zero- or low-cal (water, diet drinks), high in nutrition (milk, 100 percent juice), or both (tea). Here are the best picks, in descending order.

- Water
- Lightly sweetened iced tea, like Honest Tea®
- Low-fat milk
- 100 percent juice drinks
- Low-calorie kids' drinks, like Minute Maid® Fruit Falls™ and Tropicana® Fruit Squeeze™

School Lunch

STURDY ANCHOR

Avoid a lunch built on refined carbohydrates, as the intake of quick-burning carbs will leave your kid with an energy and attention deficit for the rest of the day. Focus instead on protein, fiber, and healthy fats that will help keep your kid satisfied, keep his metabolism running high, and provide some meaningful nutrition along the way.

FOR SANDWICHES

Meats should be lean (no salami or bologna), breads should be whole wheat, and condiments should be used sparingly.

- Turkey or roast beef and Swiss sandwich on wheat bread (sans mayo, but loaded with produce, if you can get away with it)
- Sliced ham, cheese, and Triscuits®
- PB&J (made on whole wheat bread with a pure-fruit jelly like Smucker's® Simply Fruit®)
- Thermos of hot soup
- Grilled chicken breast
- Hard-boiled eggs
- Tuna or cubed chicken tossed with light mayo, mustard, celery, and carrot

SIDES WITH SUBSTANCE

Only one in four kids consumes the recommended five servings of fruits and vegetables daily, so pack a lunch sans produce and you're missing a golden opportunity to slip some much-needed nutrients back into their diets. As long as you have at least one piece of fruit or a serving of vegetables, adding a second crunchy snack is fine.

- Carrot sticks
- Celery sticks
- Apple slices with peanut butter
- Fruit salad
- Banana, pear, peach, or any other whole fruit
- Grapes
- Olives
- Almonds and raisins (mixed 50-50)
- Triscuits®
- Small bag of pretzel sticks or Goldfish® pretzels
- Baked! Lay's®

LOW-IMPACT TREAT

You've gotta give them something they can brag to their friends about, right? Some general rules of the lunchtime reward: A treat should have no trace of trans fats (many cookies and pastries do), less than 12 grams of sugar, and no more than 100 calories. If you can eke some extra nutrition out of it, all the better.

- Fruit leather
- Squeezable yogurt
- Low-fat, low-sugar chocolate pudding
- Sugar-free Jell-O®
- Rice Krispies Treats®
- A square of chocolate (the darker the better)

6

AT HOME

You, in Charge!

In the sanctity of your own kitchen is where you have the most control over your children's nutritional well-being. But while in your mind you may envision lazy Sundays spent lovingly cooking up a kitchen full of homemade chicken soup, the reality of our lives is often less Martha Stewart, more Speed Racer: Weekends are about charging through chores, plowing through paperwork, and chauffeuring the kids from soccer practice to sleepovers. That's American family life in the 21st century, and there's no evidence that things are going to slow down anytime soon.

Indeed, the notion of the home-cooked meal is beginning to fall by the wayside. Between 1977 and 1998, the percentage of our food calories consumed at home dropped precipitously—from 82 percent to less than 65 percent. Meanwhile, among children ages 2 to 18, intake of salty snacks and pizza has increased 132 percent. And a lack of home cooking and set mealtimes means that our children have become habitual snackers: In 1977, the average child had one snack a day, but by 1996 that number had doubled. Twice the snacks? Twice the calories.

So knowing what to prepare at home—and finding recipes that are both satisfying and nutritious—can be a challenge. The following food choices will help you cook up foods that make sense for your family—and keep your family out of the grasp of fast-food marketers.

- Saucing your noodles with a meaty marinara instead of creamy Alfredo will cut 200 calories from the dish—72 of which come from saturated fat.
- Upgrading from an Idaho to a baked sweet potato will save more than just a few calories: The swap will double the amount of fiber and save your kid from a vitamin A deficiency.
- Whipping up a pot of chili instead of a pot of mac 'n cheese will skim 110 calories and 9 grams of fat from your child's dinner.

Sneaky Parent! These Tricks Are for Kids!

How puppies, ice cream, and monkey runs can help you save your children (and yourself!) from obesity.

BREAK THE FAMILY FAST. University of Massachusetts researchers found that skipping breakfast makes you 4.5 times more likely to be obese. And waiting longer than 90 minutes after waking to break your fast can increase your chances of obesity by nearly 50 percent. "To keep your family's metabolisms stoked all day, serve them whole grain waffles drizzled with melted peanut butter and a sliced banana in place of syrup," says Cynthia Sass, RD, CSSD, and former spokesperson for the American Dietetic Association. That will ratchet up the fiber, cut down on sugar, and keep them coming back for more.

JOIN IN THE TEAM PRACTICE. When you take the kids to a sports practice, bring along your gym shoes and jog the track while they're playing, says Jen Mueller, MEd, CPT, the in-house personal trainer for sparkpeople.com. When there's a game, "follow the action on the field by walking up and down the sidelines," says Mueller. You'll not only keep yourself fit, but you'll also set an example for the kids to follow into their own adulthood.

BUY SMALLER PLATES. A recent study found that when presented with large portions, people consume 30 percent more food—and calories. Another study revealed that children don't regulate their food based on how much they've eaten during the day, which means that portion size is critical to how many calories they consume. Use smaller plates, and make sure that your kids eat the same foods that you eat.

SIT UP STRAIGHT. Teaching your kids good posture will encourage a sense of assurance—and protect them against back pain later in life. When sitting at the dinner table, have everyone imagine that there's a string tied from a shirt button at heart level to their belt buckle. See who can sit for the longest without collapsing the string. Do this for 5 minutes a few times each day, and you'll straighten up slumping shoulders.

BE STRICT ABOUT BEDTIME. A University of Chicago study found that people who don't get enough sleep have lower levels of the hormones that control appetite, putting them at risk for obesity. A follow-up study of 9,588 Americans found that those who slept for 4 hours or less per night were 234 percent more likely to be obese. The National Sleep Foundation recommends that children ages 5 to 12 get 10 to 11 hours of sleep each night and that adolescents get 8½ to 9½.

SPRING FOR A PUPPY. Kids won't exercise with you? Make your child walk the dog every morning. A recent study from Northwestern Medical School, in Chicago, found that people who walked their dogs for 20 minutes a day, 5 days a week, lost an average of 14 pounds during the course of a year.

INSTITUTE A 15-MINUTE RULE. Make it a family rule that there will be 15 minutes of roughhousing between the time Mom and Dad get home from work and the kids go off to bed. Researchers from the University of Bristol measured the activity of 5,500 12-year-olds and found that just 15 minutes a day spent doing moderate physical activity (equivalent to a brisk walk) reduces the chances of being obese by up to 50 percent. Keep playing for another 15 minutes, and you'll burn 240 calories—about the same amount you would burn on a moderate bike ride, according to a study in the *Journal of Sports Medicine and Physical Fitness.*

● **PUSH SMALL PEOPLE AROUND.** Researchers at Texas A&M University found that running with a jogging stroller can push your heart rate up 10 beats per minute higher than when you run solo. Try the Baby Jogger Switchback Quick-Fold Trailer/Jogger, $600. rei.com

● **REWARD THEM WITH ICE CREAM.** British researchers conducted MRI scans and found that a single spoonful of ice cream triggers the pleasure centers in the brain. Plus, $\frac{1}{2}$ cup of vanilla ice cream gives you 17 milligrams of choline, which recent USDA research showed lowered blood levels of homocysteine by 9 percent. That translates into protection from cancer, heart attack, stroke, and dementia. Best pick: Dreyer's® Slow Churned® Rich and Creamy Light. One serving has only 2 grams of saturated fat.

● **PUT THEIR STOMACHS IN SUMMER SCHOOL.** A new study in the *American Journal of Public Health* surveyed 5,380 kindergartners and first graders and found that they were gaining weight at twice the rate over the summer months that they do during the school year. Researchers speculate that increased calorie consumption is to blame. A moderately active child should consume about 1,400 calories a day. In summer, continue to structure their meals just like a school day: breakfast by 9, lunch at noon, and a snack at 3.

● **KICK THE CAN.** Soda is the single largest source of calories in the American diet, according to a 2005 study conducted by the Center for Science in the Public Interest. And popular energy drinks like Red Bull® are so packed with sugar that they completely inhibit your ability to burn fat, negating any metabolism-boosting effect the caffeine might have had. Swap water for sugary beverages and your kid will consume 150 fewer calories a day and drop an average of 15 pounds a year.

● **ENTER THE FAMILY OLYMPICS.** If you're serious about getting your kids moving, here are some parent-kid exercises put together by Michael Mejia, MS, CSCS, advisor to the Center for Sports Parenting.

6- TO 8-YEAR-OLDS:
Monkey runs. Shuffle sideways for 10 yards and back. Turn around and repeat, leading with the other foot.

9- TO 11-YEAR-OLDS:
Driveway shuttles. Place six objects—tennis balls on red plastic cups, for instance—at the end of the driveway. Take turns sprinting to retrieve the objects.

12- TO 16-YEAR-OLDS:
Timed suicides. Sprint as fast as you can for 5 yards, then turn and sprint back to the starting line. Turn around and sprint for 10 yards, and then back. Continue sprinting, increasing the distance by 5 yards each time. Cover as much ground as you can in 30 seconds.

A Week of Perfect Eating

First of all, if you're cooking at home, congratulations. You've just made one of the most important decisions you can make with regard to your family's health and well-being. Besides the ineffable joy that is (or should be) the family meal, by cooking and eating as a unit, you ensure ultimate control over every last piece of food that hits the plate. A study from the *Journal of the American Dietetic Association* found that the more family meals a kid consumes, the higher his or her intake of fruits, vegetables, grains, and nutrients will be. The fewer packages you use, the more control you have.

Still, some of the most explosive calorie landmines may be lurking in your dusty old recipe books. A study from New York University found that classic recipes in the *Joy of Cooking* have grown in serving size significantly over the years. And though it's easy enough to figure out what tastes good to your family, it's never quite as simple to know what's good for them. When the difference between potpie and pot roast could mean more than 400 calories, it's clear parents could use a hand on the home front. That's what this chapter is all about, helping you decide which of your weeknight standbys should be stood by, and which deserve to be deserted.

All of the numbers in this section are for kid-size portions—4 to 6 ounces of the entrée and ½ cup for side dishes, unless otherwise noted. If some of these numbers on the Not That! side are cause for concern, just consider that mom- and dad-size portions will have about 50 percent more calories, fat, sodium—everything. Stick to 5 or 6 days of "Eat This"–worthy meals throughout the week, and you'll earn the right to a night of indulging outside of the kitchen.

Find more tips, tricks, and savvy strategies for feeding your family well at **eatthis.com**

Sunday

Eat This

Meat Loaf Dinner

with baked sweet potato and roasted asparagus

540 calories
13 g fat
(3 g saturated)
850 mg sodium

The ketchup-covered loaf proves to be a fairly innocent weeknight standby. If the cook uses ground beef with anything more than 10 percent fat content, though, the fat and calorie counts begin to grow substantially.

The numbers in this section do not include desserts. While we wanted to give you dessert options for each night, it's not necessary (or advised) to end every meal with a bowl of ice cream or a slice of pie. Sometimes, a piece of fruit or nothing at all should be enough.

Baked Sweet Potato
(1 medium)
160 calories
0 g fat
100 mg sodium

Lower in calories and carbs and higher in fiber than an Idaho potato, sweet potatoes have a gentler effect on kids' blood sugar. Plus, they're loaded with vision-protecting beta-carotene.

Meat Loaf
280 calories
10 g fat
(3 g saturated)
600 mg sodium

Roasted Asparagus
100 calories, 3 g fat (0 g saturated), 150 mg sodium

Make asparagus kid-friendly by dusting them with fresh grated parmesan cheese before roasting in the oven.

Jell-O® (½ c)
80 calories
0 g fat
19 g sugars

In the world of sugar-clotted desserts, Jell-O proves to be a reasonable indulgence. But if you're the type of parent to let the kids get trigger happy with the whipped cream canister, then double the calories and add 10 grams of fat.

Not That!

Chicken Casserole Dinner

with baked potato and roasted asparagus

660 calories
20 g fat (6 g saturated)
1,220 mg sodium

This everything-but-the-kitchen-sink approach to dinner has been a perennial favorite of busy moms for decades. Problem is, casseroles include starchy pasta, salty broth, and plenty of cream or butter or both. Kill the dairy and the pasta, increase the veggies, and use low-sodium broth, and you'll have a casserole worth concocting.

Italian Ice

130 calories
0 g fat
30 g sugars

Ice might sound innocent, but not when it's packed with more sugar than most candy bars. If your kid wants something cold and icy, try a classic Popsicle®, which has about 50 calories and 15 grams of sugar.

Roasted Asparagus

100 calories, 3 g fat (0 g saturated), 150 mg sodium

Chicken Casserole

380 calories
17 g fat
(6 g saturated)
1,020 mg sodium

Baked Potato (1 medium)

180 calories
0 g fat
50 mg sodium

Still not a bad option for your family, assuming that you can keep them from stuffing the potato full of cheese, sour cream, and bacon bits. The best topping of all? Salsa: It adds just 10 calories, plus a host of nutrients.

Monday
Eat This
Chili Dinner
with buttered dinner roll and sautéed broccoli with almonds

530 calories
21 g fat (7 g saturated)
925 mg sodium

Make a batch from lean ground beef, onions, tomatoes, and plenty of beans, and you'll be doing your family a favor, packing their bellies full of fiber, protein, and antioxidants.

Buttered Dinner Roll (1)
130 calories
5 g fat (2 g saturated)
210 mg sodium

A small pat of butter actually helps lower the glycemic impact of high-carb foods like rolls and baked potatoes, which means they produce less of a spike in your kid's blood sugar.

Chili
300 calories
10 g fat (4 g saturated)
625 mg sodium

Sautéed Broccoli with almonds
100 calories
6 g fat (1 g saturated)
90 mg sodium

Broccoli is packed full of fat-soluble vitamins, which means they're better absorbed through your body when paired with a bit of fat. Skip the steaming and sauté the vegetable in a bit of olive oil.

Peach Cobbler
240 calories
10 g fat (4 g saturated)
22 g sugars

This Southern favorite has one major virtue: It's made primarily from fresh peaches, which bring the antioxidant beta-carotene to table. Use crushed almonds and rolled oats for the topping instead of flour and butter and you'll cut another 80 calories.

Not That!

Macaroni and Cheese Dinner

with biscuit and sautéed broccoli with almonds

730 calories
36 g fat (10.5 g saturated)
1,220 mg sodium

Pasta with milk, butter, and a small mountain of cheese: How could it possibly be healthy? Either adapt the recipe on page 268, or save more decadent versions of mac and cheese for a reward or a special occasion, rather than letting it to become a staple in your child's diet.

Banana Pudding

with wafers and whipped cream

350 calories
15 g fat (6 g saturated)
42 g sugars

This common comfort dessert is fruit-based in name only. Most of the sugar is added sugar, not naturally occuring sugar from the banana.

Sautéed Broccoli

with almonds

100 calories
6 g fat (1 g saturated)
90 mg sodium

Mac 'n Cheese

410 calories
19 g fat
(5.5 g saturated)
710 mg sodium

Biscuit (1)

220 calories
11 g fat (4 g saturated; 3 g trans fats)
420 mg sodium

Between the refined flour, the lard, and the copious amounts of salt, there's nothing in a biscuit that belongs on your dinner table.

Tuesday

Eat This

Pot Roast Dinner

with creamed corn and tomato soup

520 calories
22 g fat (7 g saturated)
885 mg sodium

This classic wintertime one-pot wonder brings big, hearty flavor to the table with little empty nutrition cluttering up the plate. Plus, what better way to get your kids to eat their carrots and onions than to cook them low and slow, until they no longer taste like something grown in the ground?

Pot Roast

320 calories
12 g fat (4 g saturated)
410 mg sodium

Tomato Soup (1 c)

80 calories
3 g fat (1 g saturated)
300 mg sodium

A study from Penn State found that people who ate soup before a meal consumed 135 fewer calories than those who went straight into the meal. If you're using canned soup, just be sure to score the reduced sodium version.

Creamed Corn

120 calories
7 g fat (2 g saturated)
175 mg sodium

Most of the creaminess in creamed corn doesn't come from the fatty dairy product, but from the corn itself, which releases its starch to thicken the dish and give it a rich taste and texture.

Scoop of Vanilla Ice Cream
with chocolate sauce

200 calories
10 g fat (6 g saturated)
26 g sugars

As far as desserts go, this is a pretty safe indulgence, especially if you use Breyer's® Creamery Style Vanilla to make it.

Not That!

Beef Stroganoff Dinner

with creamed spinach and iceberg salad

875 calories
44 g fat (17 g saturated)
1,320 mg sodium

This is a clear case of the good (mushrooms, onions, lean beef), the bad (cream, sour cream, buttered noodles), and the ugly (most renditions look like a car crash on a plate).

Slice of Chocolate Cake (4" slice)

400 calories
20 g fat (12 g saturated)
38 g sugars

Decadence defined. Too bad part of that definition includes more than half a day's worth of saturated fat and a small bucket of sugar.

Creamed Spinach

200 calories
10 g fat (4 g saturated)
240 mg sodium

Yes, spinach is nutritionally superior to corn, but each serving comes with up to a quarter cup of heavy cream. Cut the calories dramatically by using milk-and-flour-based bechamel sauce instead.

Iceberg Salad with Carrots, Tomatoes, and blue cheese dressing

200 calories
14 g fat (6 g saturated)
330 mg sodium

It's tempting to use any means necessary to get your kids to eat vegetables, but blue cheese dressing cancels out any possible benefits gleaned from the carrots and tomatoes.

Beef Stroganoff

475 calories
20 g fat (7 g saturated)
750 mg sodiumv

Wednesday

Eat This

Spaghetti Dinner

with mixed green salad and Pillsbury breadstick

550 calories
19.5 g fat
(6.5 g saturated)
1,005 mg sodium

Learn to adjust the pasta-to-sauce ratio in your house to skew heavily toward sauce. It might not be traditional, but it will cut calories and carbs dramatically.

Mixed Green Salad
with light balsamic vinaigrette

100 calories
6 g fat (1 g saturated)
270 mg sodium

Made of a variety of baby lettuces, prewashed mixed greens make the perfect staple for quick weeknight salads. Pick up a bag in the refrigerator section of the produce aisle.

Spaghetti and Meatballs

380 calories
12 g fat
(5 g saturated)
550 mg sodium

Pillsbury® Breadstick
(1)

70 calories
1.5 g fat (0.5 saturated)
185 mg sodium

One of the only times that one of those twist-and-pop cans yields something nutritionally reasonable.

Sliced Strawberries
with whipped cream

120 calories
6 g fat (2 g saturated)
16 g sugars

The simplest dessert on the planet is also one of the healthiest and most adored. Whip the cream fresh at home, adding just a touch of sugar for a bit of sweetness.

Not That!

Fettuccine Alfredo Dinner

with Caesar salad and garlic bread

1,040 calories
52 g fat (25 g saturated)
1,625 mg sodium

What do you expect from a sauce made entirely of cream, butter, and cheese?

Creamy Strawberry Yogurt (4 oz)

140 calories
5 g fat (3 g saturated)
18 g sugars

The strawberry in most flavored yogurts is more high-fructose corn syrup and food coloring than actual fruit. If you want a fruity yogurt, start with vanilla nonfat yogurt and add fresh fruit at home.

Garlic Bread (two 2" pieces)

200 calories
11 g fat (7 g saturated)
350 mg sodium

Whether store-bought or homemade, this perennial pasta sidekick is a sponge for the oil and butter that usually accompany the garlic coating.

Fettuccine Alfredo

540 calories
24 g fat (10 g saturated)
700 mg sodium

Caesar Salad

300 calories
17 g fat (8 g saturated)
575 mg sodium

Strip away the token greenery and consider the unnatural disaster you're left with: a downpour of egg- and oil-based dressing, a blizzard of Parmesan cheese, and a maelstrom of fried bread.

Thursday

Eat This

Roast Chicken Dinner

with Stove Top Stuffing and peas and pearl onions

412 calories
13 g fat (4 g saturated)
874 mg sodium

You can cut extra calories here by removing the chicken skin, but what many fat-fearing nutritionists won't tell you is that animal fat, like the kind found in chicken skin, actually contains many of the same heart-healthy fats found in olive oil and avocados.

Roast Chicken

225 calories
10 g fat (4 g saturated)
350 mg sodium

Stove Top® Stuffing, Chicken Flavor

(½ c prepared)

107 calories
1 g fat (0 g saturated)
429 mg sodium

Not exactly an ideal side, especially because of the high sodium levels, but it's good in a pinch and vastly superior to Rice-A-Roni.

Peas and Pearl Onions

80 calories
2 g fat (0 g saturated)
95 mg sodium

A great freezer staple. The fiber in the peas and the chromium in the onions both help to regulate blood sugar levels.

Chocolate Pudding

120 calories
3.5 g fat (2 g saturated)
16 g sugars

Made primarily from milk and chocolate, you could do worse than serve the occasional post-dinner scoop of pudding. It doesn't hurt that a serving of pudding also offers your kids a nice dose of bone-strengthening vitamin D.

Not That!

Chicken and Dumplings Dinner

with Rice a Roni and peas and pearl onions

670 calories
24.5 g fat
(7 g saturated)
1,465 mg sodium

Soul-soothing though it may be, the creamy, buttery base for this dish offers little comfort for the waistline. Making matters worse, those bloated dumplings, being just flour, salt, and water, offer nothing more than a heaping helping of quick-burning carbs.

Chocolate Chip Cookie

200 calories
14 g fat (4 g saturated)
15 g sugars

Every kid deserves a warm, homemade chocolate chip cookie on occasion, but it's just too high in calories—a function of the butter, sugar, and refined flour used to make these treats—to make for a reliable weeknight dessert.

Peas and Pearl Onions

80 calories
2 g fat (0 g saturated)
95 mg sodium

Rice-A-Roni® Rice Pilaf (½ c prepared)

155 calories
4.5 g fat (1g saturated)
600 mg sodium

This is no treat, not even for San Franciscans. The stratospheric sodium count is bad enough, but the 1.5 grams of trans fats (trans fats in rice? why?!) just adds insult to injury.

Chicken and Dumplings

435 calories
18 g fat
(6 g saturated)
770 mg sodium

Friday

Eat This

Blackened Catfish Dinner

with black beans and glazed carrots

370 calories
8 g fat (1 g saturated)
615 mg sodium

Catfish is a lean, omega-3–rich fish with few contaminants and a very mild taste—pretty much the best fish imaginable to serve a kid. The blackening seasoning serves two important functions: It boosts the mild flavor (and makes fish-phobic kids forget what they're eating) and because most spices contain active compounds, it adds an armory of antioxidants.

Blackened Catfish

180 calories
6 g fat (1 g saturated)
470 mg sodium

Glazed Carrots

80 calories
1 g fat (0 g saturated)
140 mg sodium

Make your carrots extra appealing by cooking them slowly in a bit of chicken stock and honey until they're tender, but still firm. Your kids will crave them!

Black Beans

110 calories
1 g fat (0 g saturated)
5 mg sodium

No, this isn't a mistake. Wild rice might have fewer calories than black beans, but it also offers considerably less nutrition. A cup of cooked black beans provides 15 grams of fiber, 15 grams of protein, and a huge dose of antioxidants.

Applesauce (1 c)

90 calories
0 g fat
18 g sugars

Make sure you stock your pantry with a good brand free of added sugars. How can you tell? Just read the back label. It should have apples, maybe cinnamon, maybe citric acid to help prevent spoiling. But no added sugar!

Not That!

Crab Cake Dinner

with wild rice and glazed carrots

565 calories
22 g fat (5 g saturated)
845 mg sodium

The crab isn't the problem with these cakes—it's the binding of mayo, bread crumbs, and eggs, followed by face time with an oily frying pan, that does them in. Add tartar sauce to the equation, and you're looking at an extra 200 calories and 10 grams of fat. Want to have your crab cake and eat it, too? Cut the mayo, add an extra egg white to the mix, and bake the cakes in a 400°F oven for 20 minutes.

Fruit Cocktail (1 c)

160 calories
0 g fat
40 g sugars

"Cocktail" is the food industry's euphemism for "soaking in a viscous sugary syrup."

Wild Rice

85 calories
1 g fat (0 g saturated)
5 mg sodium

Wild rice ain't all that it's cracked up to be. While it's better than plain white rice, it still only offers 3 grams of fiber per cup and little other nutritional value. Make the switch to quinoa, which is rich in fiber and healthy fats and contains all vital amino acids.

Glazed Carrots

80 calories
1 g fat (0 g saturated)
140 mg sodium

Crab Cakes

400 calories
20 g fat
(5 g saturated)
700 mg sodium

10 Kid Favorites Made Healthy

Good food and good nutrition don't have to be mutually exclusive. Grab a little sous chef and redefine the fatty foods they love.

From cheese-covered mountains of mac and cheese to hulking helpings of sloppy joes, it just so happens that kids' favorite foods to eat are also some of the worst things they could be putting in their bodies. Coincidence? Not likely. So what's a parent to do, ban them from eating these foods? You'll make enemies faster than a Yankees fan at Fenway. Allow them to eat with impunity? No way.

To help you out, we've recast 10 of the most troublesome kid favorites in a healthier light. All scream out for a young sous chef's help, so enlist your kid to bread the chicken fingers or melt the cheese for the mac. Getting them involved will only further solidify these recipes as staples in your household.

MAC 'N CHEESE

½ Tbsp butter
2 Tbsp all-purpose flour
1 c 1% low-fat milk
1 ½ c reduced-fat extra sharp Cheddar cheese
¼ c fresh grated Parmesan cheese
4 c cooked whole wheat macaroni or penne
¼ c bread crumbs (preferably panko)

Preheat the oven to 400°F. Melt the butter in a large saucepan over medium heat and add the flour, cooking and stirring until it's fully incorporated and lightly golden. Add the milk slowly, whisking constantly to work out any lumps that may form. Cook for 3 to 5 minutes, until the mixture thickens slightly. Stir in the Cheddar and Parmesan, and cook until fully melted. Toss the sauce with the pasta, place in a large baking dish, and top with the bread crumbs. Bake for 30 minutes, until the bread crumbs are toasted and a crust has formed on top. Makes 4 servings.

Per serving: 340 calories, 9 g fat, 412 mg sodium

FETTUCCINE ALFREDO

1 Tbsp butter
¼ c minced onion
1 Tbsp all-purpose flour
1¼ c skim milk
1 c freshly grated Parmesan cheese
2 Tbsp reduced-fat cream cheese
Pinch of nutmeg
Salt and pepper
4 cups cooked whole wheat fettuccine

In a large saucepan over medium heat, heat the butter. Add the onion and cook for 2 minutes. Add the flour and cook for another 2 minutes, stirring constantly, until the flour gives off a nutty aroma. Add the milk gradually, whisking as you do to prevent the flour from clumping. Simmer for 5 to 10 minutes, until the sauce has thickened, then add the Parmesan, cream cheese, nutmeg, and salt and pepper to taste. (Remember, Parmesan is already really salty.) Toss the sauce with the cooked fettuccine and serve right away.

265 calories, 5 g fat, 128 mg sodium

NACHO AVERAGE NACHOS
Mozzarella stands in for fatty cheddar, and black bean chips boost fiber and slice calories. Add a big scoop of black beans and salsa for a blast of antioxidants.

PEPPERONI PIZZA

1 c tomato sauce
4 whole wheat English muffins, split open to make 8 halves
1 tsp dried basil
½ tsp onion powder
1 c low-moisture mozzarella cheese
8 slices of turkey pepperoni

Preheat the oven to 400°F. Spread the tomato sauce evenly on the English muffin halves. Top with the basil, onion powder, cheese, and pepperoni, in that order. Bake for 15 to 20 minutes, until the cheese is fully melted and lightly browned. Makes 4 servings.

260 calories, 9 g fat, 750 mg sodium

NACHOS

1 bag black bean chips
1 can black beans, drained
1 ½ c shredded, low-moisture mozzarella cheese
1 c cooked shredded or chopped chicken
1 c favorite tomato salsa
½ c chopped fresh cilantro

Preheat the oven to 400°F. Arrange the chips in a single layer on a large nonstick baking sheet. Cover evenly with the beans, then the cheese. Cook for 15 minutes, until the cheese is slightly melted. Remove from the oven, spread the chicken evenly over the nachos, and return the nachos to the oven. Cook for another 10 minutes, or long enough to warm up the chicken and brown the cheese. Remove and top with your family's favorite salsa and the cilantro. Makes 6 servings.

350 calories, 15 g fat, 660 mg sodium

SLOPPY JOES

1 tsp olive oil
1 lb lean ground turkey
1 medium onion, diced
1 carrot, peeled and diced
1 medium green bell pepper, diced
2 cloves garlic, minced
½ c ketchup
1 Tbsp chili powder
2 tsp Worcestershire sauce
Salt and pepper, to taste
4 whole wheat hamburger buns, warmed

Heat a large nonstick skillet over medium heat. Add the olive oil, turkey, onion, carrot, pepper, and garlic. Sauté, stirring occasionally, until the turkey is cooked and the onions are translucent, 7 to 10 minutes. Add the ketchup, chili powder, and Worcestershire. Reduce the heat to low and simmer for at least 15 minutes. Serve with the buns. Makes 4 servings.

300 calories, 4.5 g fat, 720 mg sodium

NOT YOUR AVERAGE JOE
Lean turkey downsizes the caloric impact, while a slew of vegetables up the nutrition without arousing suspicion.

CHEESE FRIES

1½ lbs russet potatoes (about 2 medium), washed, dried, and cut into ½-inch wedges
1 Tbsp olive oil
Salt and pepper
1 c shredded low-fat Cheddar cheese
½ bunch green onions, thinly sliced

Preheat the oven to 450°F. Toss the potatoes with the oil and a few pinches of salt and pepper. Arrange the potatoes in a single layer on a baking sheet. Bake for 25 minutes, until lightly browned. Remove the sheet from the oven, sprinkle the potatoes evenly with the cheese, and return to the oven. Bake until the cheese is fully melted, another 10 to 15 minutes. Top with the green onions and serve. Makes 4 servings.

217 calories, 6 g fat, 220 mg sodium

APPLE CINNAMON PANCAKES

½ c all-purpose flour
½ c whole wheat flour
1 Tbsp sugar
1 tsp baking powder
½ tsp baking soda
½ tsp salt
½ tsp ground cinnamon
1 c low-fat buttermilk
½ Tbsp vegetable oil
1 large egg
½ c crushed walnuts
1 Granny Smith apple, peeled and diced
Cooking spray

Combine both flours, sugar, baking powder, baking soda, salt, and cinnamon in a large bowl. In a separate bowl, combine the buttermilk, oil, and egg. Combine the wet and dry mixtures and add in the walnuts, stirring until blended but still slightly lumpy.

Coat a griddle or nonstick skillet with cooking spray and place over medium heat. When it's hot, spoon about ¼ cup of the batter per pancake onto the griddle. Place small chunks of apple on the raw pancake batter. Turn the pancakes over when the tops are covered with bubbles and the edges look cooked. Serve with syrup and butter. Makes 4 servings.

246 calories, 9 g fat, 344 mg sodium

SWEET SENSATION
Not fit for nightly consumption, but with low-calorie ice cream, a flurry of fresh banana, and a sprinkling of healthy fats, this makes for a great occasional treat.

ICE CREAM SUNDAES

2 c vanilla ice cream
2 c sliced banana
¼ c chopped walnuts
¼ c hot fudge sauce
4 maraschino cherries

Place one large (½ cup) scoop of ice cream in each of four bowls. Divide the bananas and walnuts among the bowls, drizzle a tablespoon of hot chocolate sauce on each, and top with a maraschino cherry. Makes 4 servings.

268 calories, 9 g fat, 31 g sugars

CHICKEN STRIPS WITH HONEY MUSTARD

½ tsp salt
½ tsp pepper
½ tsp chili powder (optional)
1 c panko bread crumbs
1 lb boneless, skinless chicken breast tenders
2 eggs, lightly beaten
¼ c of your family's favorite mustard
2 Tbsp honey

Preheat the oven to 375°F. Combine the salt, pepper, and chili powder with the bread crumbs, and mix. Dip the chicken in the egg, then in the spiced bread crumbs. Place on a nonstick baking sheet and bake for 12 to 15 minutes, turning once, until the chicken is firm and the bread crumbs are browned. While the chicken cooks, mix together the mustard and honey. Makes 4 servings.

238 calories, 4 g fat, 583 mg sodium

FRENCH TOAST STICKS WITH HOT BANANA DIP

2 very ripe bananas
1 tsp brown sugar
¼ cup orange juice
2 tsp vanilla extract
4 egg whites
¼ cup skim milk
½ tsp ground cinnamon
Pinch ground nutmeg
8 slices whole wheat bread
Powdered sugar

Combine the bananas, brown sugar, orange juice, and half of the vanilla in a small sauce pan and cook over medium-low heat for 3 to 5 minutes. Mash the banana with the back of a fork until the sauce is mostly smooth and set aside.

Combine the egg whites, milk, remaining vanilla, cinnamon, and nutmeg in a large, shallow dish. Whisk. Warm up a nonstick pan or skillet covered with nonstick spray over medium heat. Lay individual slices of wheat bread in the mixture, then transfer to the pan or skillet. Cook for 2 to 3 minutes a side until brown and crispy. Remove the toast and slice into ½" thick sticks. Dust with powdered sugar and serve with the hot banana dip for dunking. Skip the syrup!

260 calories, 2.5 g fat, 16 g sugars

Thanksgiving

Eat This

White Meat Turkey Dinner

with homemade cranberry sauce, mashed potatoes and gravy, green bean casserole, and dinner roll

575 calories
22 g fat
(4.5 g saturated)
1,010 mg sodium

Americans consume more calories on Thanksgiving than on any other day of the year, but that's no reason to abandon all sense of proportion. Match 4 ounces of white meat with a few ½-cup servings of vegetables and you can keep the calorie count well under 1,000, an appropriate threshold for this yearly gorgefest.

Pumpkin Pie (1 medium slice/ ⅙ pie) with low-fat whipped cream

335 calories
15 g fat
(6.5 g saturated)
42 g carbohydrates

A relatively safe play when it comes to pies.

Green Bean Casserole (½ c)

100 calories
6 g fat
(1 g saturated)
200 mg sodium

Higher in fat and calories than corn, but also higher in nutrients. Can the Cream of Mushroom and fried onions and make it with fresh green beans and sautéed onions.

Turkey Breast (4 oz) with homemade cranberry sauce (2 Tbsp)

225 calories
4 g fat (0 g saturated)
250 mg sodium

You won't find leaner meat than turkey breast. And homemade cranberry sauce allows you to control the sugar content.

Mashed Potatoes (½ c) with turkey gravy (¼ c)

140 calories
7 g fat (2 g saturated)
340 mg sodium

Homemade mashed potatoes aren't nearly as bad as most people think, especially if the cook uses 2% milk and has a light hand with the butter.

Dinner Roll (1)

110 calories
5 g fat
(1.5 g saturated)
220 calories

While it would be ideal to cut bread out of the meal entirely, this special occasion might require a sturdy vessel for sopping up gravy.

Not That!

Dark Meat Turkey Dinner

with jellied cranberry sauce, candied sweet potatoes, corn, and stuffing

780 calories
31 g fat (15 g saturated)
1,285 mg sodium

This is no different from millions of plates that will come together on Turkey Day this year, but unfortunately, this seemingly average spread nearly satisfies an 8-year-old's requirements for calories, fat, and sodium for an entire day.

Stuffing (1/2 c)

175 calories
14 g fat (6 g saturated)
420 mg sodium

Flecked with butter and doused in salty broth, stuffing might be essential to your feast, but make sure to serve tiny portions. Cooking it inside the bird only makes matters worse.

Candied Sweet Potatoes with Marshmallow Topping (1/2 c)

225 calories
8 g fat (5 g saturated)
270 mg sodium

This dish suffers from an unecessary tidal wave of sugar. Sweet potatoes are sweet enough; drop the marshmallows and brown sugar.

Dark Turkey Meat (4 oz) with jellied cranberry sauce (1/2" slice)

310 calories
8 g fat (4 g saturated)
320 mg sodium

Leg meat will always be fattier than breast meat. And a slice of canned cranberry sauce adds 22 grams of sugar.

Corn (1/2 c)

70 calories
1 g fat (0 g saturated)
275 mg sodium

In November, corn usually comes in the canned variety, which can be long on sodium and short on nutrition.

Pecan Pie (1 small slice/1/8 pie)

450 calories
21 g fat (4 g saturated)
65 g carbohydrates

Much of the fat in this pie is of the heart-healthy variety found in pecans and other nuts. But the rest of the calories come from the thick slick of corn syrup.

Christmas

Eat This

Beef Tenderloin Dinner

with roasted new potatoes, green beans with almonds, and dinner roll

535 calories
24 g fat (7 g saturated)
800 mg sodium

Beef makes a surprisingly lean centerpiece for this holiday extravaganza. Just make sure it's tenderloin or sirloin and not fatty ribeye or strip steak. Beef in any form packs plenty of iron and zinc, two nutrients many kids, especially girls, don't get enough of.

Roasted New Potatoes (½ c)
100 calories
5 g fat (1 g saturated)
170 mg sodium
One of the healthiest ways to prepare any vegetable.

Beef Tenderloin (4 oz)
210 calories
10 g fat
(4 g saturated)
300 mg sodium

Green Beans with Almonds (½ c)
95 calories
4 g fat (0 g saturated)
120 mg sodium
Add crunch and a dose of heart-healthy fats to plain vegetables.

Dinner Roll with butter
130 calories
5 g fat
(2 g saturated)
210 mg sodium

Chocolate Fondue (1 oz) with fruit (½ c)
200 calories
8 g fat
(4 g saturated)
18 g sugars

760 calories
38 g fat
(14 g saturated)
2,190 mg sodium

Not That!

Honey Baked Ham Dinner

with mashed potates with gravy, salad, and cornbread

Don't make this the saltiest holiday ever! From the sodium-soaked ham to the Italian dressing and cornbread, this meal collectively has more salt than six large orders of McDonald's French fries.

Cheesecake
(1 slice/ 1/8 cake)
370 calories
19 g fat
(9 g saturated)
28 g sugars

Cornbread
with butter
190 calories
9 g fat (4 g saturated)
360 mg sodium
Simultaneously sweeter and saltier than a normal dinner roll.

Salad
with croutons and Italian dressing
240 calories
12 g fat
(4 g saturated)
390 mg sodium

Glazed Honey-Baked Ham (4 oz)
190 calories
10 g fat
(4 g saturated)
1,100 mg sodium
Fairly lean, but way too high in sodium.

Mashed Potatoes
with gravy (1/2 c)
140 calories
7 g fat (2 g saturated)
340 mg sodium
It beats other potato treatments, but can't contend with roasting.

Fourth Of July

Eat This

Hot Dog Meal

with beans, cole slaw, and fruit salad

615 calories
21.5 g fat (4 g saturated)
1,095 mg sodium

Want to cut this calorie count in half without arousing any suspicions in a discerning kid's palate? Swap out the normal beef or pork frank for an Applegate Farms® All Natural Turkey Dog.

Fruit Salad ($^1/_2$ c)
55 calories
0 g fat
5 mg sodium

Baked Beans ($^1/_2$ c)
150 calories
1.5 g fat (0 g saturated)
250 mg sodium

Cole Slaw ($^1/_2$ c)
170 calories
10 g fat (2 g saturated)
210 mg sodium

Hotdog
with ketchup, mustard and relish
240 calories
10 g fat
(2 g saturated)
630 mg sodium

Not That!

Cheeseburger Meal

with corn on the cob, potato salad, and iceberg salad

1,025 calories
54 g fat (18 g saturated)
1,670 mg sodium

For a truly healthy burger, start with 95% lean ground beef. Use skim-milk mozzarella for cheese and pack as much produce as you can possibly fit in between a toasted whole wheat bun.

Cheeseburger
500 calories
25 g fat (9 g saturated)
850 mg sodium

Potato Salad (1/2 c)
190 calories
12 g fat (3 g saturated)
430 mg sodium

Corn on the Cob
with butter
160 calories
6 g fat (4 g saturated)
150 mg sodium

Iceberg Salad
with honey mustard dressing
175 calories
11 g fat (2 g saturated)
240 mg sodium

Birthday Party

Eat This

Beef Taco Meal

(2) with chips and salsa and a virgin daiquiri

610 calories
24 g fat
(8 g saturated)
1,140 mg sodium

Make it a taco party this year. Sauté lean ground beef with taco seasoning, then lay out an assembly line of fresh tomato and onion, shredded lettuce, and low-fat cheese. The kids will love building their own meal, and you'll save them calories and yourself some cash.

Virgin Daiquiri (8 oz)

80 calories
0 g fat
16 g sugars

Blend together a can of pineapple chunks and their juices, a bag of frozen strawberries, the juice of two limes, 1 tablespoon of sugar, and a few cups of ice. This is enough to keep six kids from the soda.

Tortilla Chips
(1 oz) with salsa (1/8 c)

130 calories
5 g fat (1 g saturated)
390 mg sodium

Get your kids hooked on salsa at an early age. It's the ultimate condiment—loaded with disease-fighting lycopene, just 10 calories a serving, and 100% fat-free.

2 Beef Tacos
with cheese, lettuce, and tomato

400 calories
19 g fat
(7 g saturated)
750 mg sodium

Ice Cream Cake (1/8 cake)

330 calories
18 g fat (8 g saturated)
30 g sugars

Why give kids a huge serving of cake and a separate scoop of ice cream, when you can combine the two? They'll be so excited they won't notice that they're getting a smaller serving of each.

Not That!

Pepperoni Pizza Meal

with baby carrots and pink lemonade

860 calories
45 g fat (18 g saturated)
1,740 mg sodium

Whether for parents or kids, pepperoni piled on thin crust or thick, with extra cheese or not, is a pizza topping profoundly lacking in nutrition. A single disk has 10 calories and 1 gram of fat, adding up to 70 calories and a sheen of grease to each pizza slice.

Chocolate Cake with Ice Cream

420 calories
24 g fat (10 g saturated)
39 g sugars

The standard birthday closer is a certifiable trainwreck of calories, fat, and sugar. If they must have their cake and eat it too, cut the slices small.

Pepperoni Pizza (2 slices of 14" pie)

600 calories
30 g fat (14 g saturated)
1,450 mg sodium

Baby Carrots (1/2 c) with ranch dip (2 Tbsp)

160 calories
15 g fat (4 g saturated)
290 mg sodium

Don't let a perfectly healthy snack become a mere utensil used to bring fatty ranch from plate to mouth. Carrots are fine on their own.

Pink Lemonade (8 oz)

100 calories
0 g fat
28 g sugars

No, this is not juice. Most lemonades consist of 10% lemon juice and 90% sugar water. If not for the bit of vitamin C from the lemon, your kid might as well drink a soda.

The Holiday Candy Scorecard

Not all candy was created equal.
It's your job to steer kids to the lesser of all evils.

FARLEY'S® SUPER BUBBLE BUBBLE GUM
(3 pieces, 15 g)
45 calories, 0 g fat, 9 g sugars

WONKA NERDS
(1 small box, 13 g)
50 calories, 0 g fat, 6 g sugars

JOLLY RANCHER® HARD CANDY
(3 pieces, 14 g)
50 calories, 0 g fat, 7 g sugars

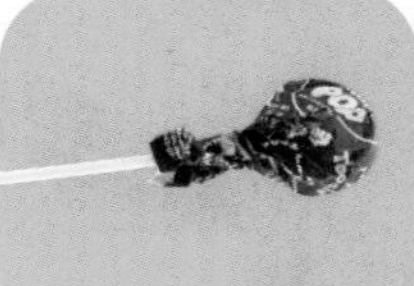

TOOTSIE® POP
(1 pop, 17 g)
60 calories, 0 g fat, 10 g sugars

NECCO® SWEETHEARTS
(½ box, 14 g)
55 calories, 0 g fat, 13.5 g sugar

CHARM'S® BLOW POP®
(1 pop, 18 g)
60 calories, 0 g fat, 13 g sugars

BOB'S® CANDY CANES
(1 piece, 14 g)
60 calories, 0 g fat, 14 g sugars

Americans consume nearly 8 billion pounds of candy a year, and much of that can be attributed to the collective appetite of sugar-happy kids. From Halloween handouts to convenience store chocolate bars, the difference between a smart choice and a perilous one could mean pounds to your kid's waistline. Just to be extra clear: Nothing you see on these four pages has even a trace of redeeming nutritional value. Even the lowest-calorie options here will pack on major pounds if consumed recklessly. But knowing the relative winners and losers should help your kids save thousands of calories over the course of a year.

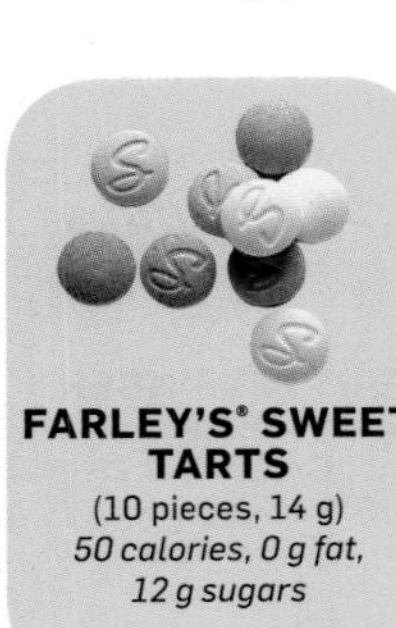

FARLEY'S® SWEET TARTS
(10 pieces, 14 g)
50 calories, 0 g fat, 12 g sugars

SMARTIES®
(2 rolls, 14 g)
50 calories, 0 g fat, 12.5 g sugars

SPANGLER® DUM DUM POPS®
(2 pops, 13 g)
51 calories, 0 g fat, 10 g sugars

NOW AND LATER®
(4 pieces, 18 g)
54 calories, 0.5 g fat (0 g saturated), 11 g sugars

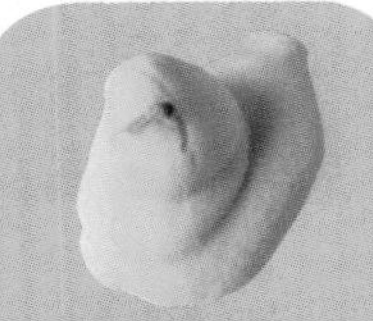

JUST BORN® MARSHMALLOW PEEPS®
(2 chicks, 17 g)
64 calories, 0 g fat, 14.5 g sugars

SWEET'S SALT WATER TAFFY
(3 pieces, 18 g)
69 calories, 1 g fat (0.5 g saturated), 10 g sugars

3 MUSKETEERS®
(1 "fun" size bar, 15 g)
63 calories, 2 g fat (1.5 g saturated), 10 g sugars

BRACH'S® CANDY CORN
(13 pieces, 20 g)
70 calories, 0 g fat, 14 g sugars

SEE'S® ASSORTED VALENTINE'S CHOCOLATES
(1 piece, 14 g)
70 calories, 4 g fat (2 g saturated), 7 g sugars

Bad

TOOTSIE ROLL®
(3 pieces)
70 calories, 1.5 g fat (0.5 g saturated), 9.5 g sugars

DOTS® CANDY
(1 box, 21 g)
70 calories, 0 g fat, 11 g sugars

SNICKERS®
(1 "fun" size bar, 17 g)
80 calories, 4 g fat (1.5 g saturated), 8.5 g sugars

STARBURSTS®
(4 pieces, 20 g)
80 calories, 2 g fat (1.5 g saturated), 11.5 g sugars

SKITTLES®
(1 "fun" size pack, 20 g)
80 calories, 1 g fat (1 g saturated), 15 g sugars

BUTTERFINGER® BAR
(1 "fun" size bar, 19 g)
85 calories, 3.5 g fat (2 g saturated), 8.5 g sugars

REESE'S PEANUT BUTTER CUPS® MINIATURES
(2 pieces, 16 g)
84 calories, 4.5 g fat (1.5 g saturated), 7.5 g sugars

HERSHEY'S® MINIATURES
(milk chocolate, Special Dark®, Krackel®, and Mr. Goodbar®)
(2 pieces, 17 g)
84 calories, 5.5 g fat (2.5 g saturated), 8.5 g sugars

CADBURY® MILK CHOCOLATE MINI EGGS
(6 eggs, 20 g)
90 calories, 5 g fat (3 g saturated), 12 g sugars

M&MS®
(1 "fun" size bag)
100 calories, 4.5 g fat (2.5 g saturated), 13 g sugars

JELLY BELLY® 40 FLAVORS JELLY BEANS
(20 beans, 23 g)
70 calories, 0 g fat, 14 g sugars

JAWBREAKERS
(3 pieces, 17 g)
70 calories, 0 g fat, 16 g sugars

FERRERO ROCHER® FINE HAZELNUT CHOCOLATES
(1 piece, 13.5 g)
73 calories, 5 g fat (1.5 g saturated), 4.5 g sugars

MILKY WAY®
(1 "fun" size bar, 17 g)
75 calories, 3 g fat (2 g saturated), 10 g sugars

Worst

BRACH'S® MILK MAID® CARAMELS
(2 pieces, 19 g)
80 calories, 2.5 g fat (2 g saturated), 18 g sugars

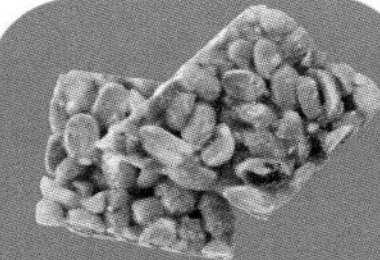

PEANUT BRITTLE
(1" chunk, 20 g)
90 calories, 3 g fat (1.5 g saturated), 7 g sugars

BRACH'S® AIRHEADS®
(2 pieces)
90 calories , 1 g fat (0 g saturated), 12 g sugars

HERSHEY®'S MILK CHOCOLATE KISSES®
(4 kisses, 18 g)
101.5 calories, 5.5 g fat (3.5 g saturated), 9 g sugars

RUSSELL STOVER® CHOCOLATE BUNNY
(½ bunny, 21.5 g)
115 calories, 7 g fat (4 g saturated), 11.5 g sugars

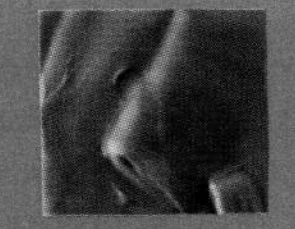

HOMEMADE FUDGE
(one 2" cube)
119 calories, 1.5 g fat 1.5 g saturated), 23.5 g sugars

CADBURY® CREME EGG
(1 egg, 34 g)
150 calories, 5 g fat (3 g saturated), 22 g sugars

The Ultimate Smoothie

Hopefully one of the major nutritional shortcomings of the average American kid's diet has become apparent in these pages: Kids don't consume enough fruits and vegetables. Parents need to find as many strategies as possible for boosting the presence of produce in their loved ones' diets. Luckily, the fruit failing is an easy fix: Toss it in a blender—or better yet, let them load it up with their favorite fresh and frozen fruits—add ice and juice and blast away. Each of the following liquid concoctions has between 200 and 300 calories (perfect for breakfast or a snack), can be made with fresh or frozen fruit, and takes about 60 seconds to make.

THE BRAIN BOOSTER

Try this one before a big test. Blueberries and raspberries are both loaded with antioxidants that help protect the brain from free-radical damage, which can improve cognitive processing. The berries here aren't just super food for your brain; they also offer an important cancer-fighting bonus.

½ c fresh or frozen blueberries
½ c fresh or frozen raspberries
¾ c pineapple orange juice
½ c low-fat vanilla yogurt
1 c ice (about 6 cubes)

270 calories, 2 g fat (0 g saturated), 57 g carbohydrates

THE METABOLISM CHARGER

Kids already have an edge over adults in the metabolism department, but that doesn't mean you shouldn't get their bodies into full calorie-burning mode early on. This smoothie employs the help of protein-packed yogurt and green tea, which contains antioxidants called catechins that are known to boost metabolism.

½ c brewed green tea, cooled to room temperature
½ c nonfat vanilla yogurt
1 c mango
½ Tbsp honey
1 c ice (about 6 cubes)

260 calories, 0 g fat, 61 g carbohydrates

Selector

THE IMMUNIZER

Beyond the vision-protecting capacity of beta-carotene, found abundantly in orange fruits and vegetables, researchers also believe the powerful carotenoid is vital for fortifying the immune system, which means this beta blast could be the first line of defense against sickness.

1 c ice (about 6 cubes)
1 apricot, sliced and pitted
½ c papaya, frozen in chunks
½ c mango, frozen in chunks
½ c carrots
1 Tbsp honey

250 calories, 1 g fat (0 g saturated), 63 g carbohydrates

THE SMOOTH OPERATOR

The yogurt aids digestion, while the mango and juice boost immune response.

¼ c pitted cherries
½ c mango
½ c nonfat vanilla yogurt
½ c pineapple orange juice
1 c ice (about 6 cubes)

260 calories, 0 g fat, 59 g carbohydrates

THE SANDMAN

Melatonin is nature's Ambien®, bestowing on even the most restless rug rat a set of heavy eyelids. Cherries, bananas, and grapes are all great sources of this sleep-inducer, and they make for a healthy encore to dinner.

¼ c pitted cherries
½ banana
½ c grape juice
½ c nonfat vanilla yogurt
1 c ice (about 6 cubes)

270 calories, 0 g fat, 59 carbohydrates

THE MOOD MAKER

This one's an all-fruit smoothie, packed with carbs to boost serotonin levels. Add a handful of flaxseeds for an extra dose of mood-boosting omega-3 fatty acids.

½ c fresh or frozen blueberries
½ c fresh or frozen mango
½ c orange juice
½ c nonfat vanilla yogurt
1 c ice (about 6 cubes)
1 Tbsp ground flaxseeds (optional)

269 calories, 1 g fat (0 g saturated), 61 g carbohydrates

11 Foods That Cure

RASH RELIEVER: PAPAYA
Vitamin C and flavonoids are known to help prevent infection and the spread of rashes. They also act as a natural antihistamine that reduces swelling. Nothing on this planet carries more of both than papaya.

COUGH AND COLD CURE: CHICKEN NOODLE SOUP
More than just comfort food. Researchers at the Nebraska Medical Center proved that the compounds in chicken soup lessen inflammation, a cause of cold symptoms.

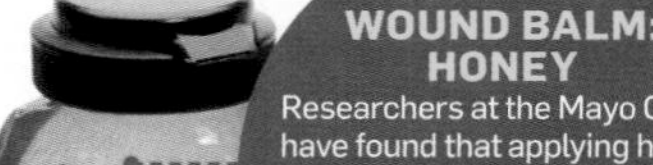

BURN AND WOUND BALM: HONEY
Researchers at the Mayo Clinic have found that applying honey directly to a wound protects it from outside contaminants. It also contains enzymes that have been shown to prevent infection and speed healing.

ATTENTION RETAINER: FLAXSEED
A 2006 study looked at the effects of flaxseed oil on children and reported that after 3 months of supplementation, children were found to be 18 percent less hyperactive and 19 percent more attentive.

CAVITY FIGHTER: CHEESE
Researchers found that eating less than a quarter ounce of Jack, cheddar, or mozzarella will boost pH levels to protect teeth from cavities. Cheese also contains casein, which combines with calcium to fill cracks in teeth.

TOOTHACHE TREATMENT: CLOVES
Cloves contain eugenol, a natural antiseptic that can be released by lightly chewing on a clove in the area where the pain is coming from. If your kid won't chew, try applying clove oil directly to the sore area.

NATURAL RELAXANT: POULTRY
Chickens and turkeys contain an amino acid called tryptophan, which is important for the production of serotinin, a brain chemical that helps regulate sleep cycles.

If some doctors had their way today, our kids would be more medicated than feedlot cattle. What most parents don't realize is that the first line of defense is found in the aisles of the supermarket, not in the drug store. Here are 11 research-backed quick cures in the form of fresh produce and reliable pantry products. Add them to your next grocery list and you might be able to save some space in your medicine cabinet.

NAUSEA FIGHTER: GINGER
Mother Nature's answer to Pepto-Bismol®. Studies have shown that ginger supplements can reduce the frequency, intensity, and duration of nausea. Add to stir-fries, or steep a few slices in hot water for a potent ginger tea.

CHICKEN POX CHALLENGER: SWEET POTATOES
There's a trio of good stuff at work here: beta-carotene, vitamin C, and flavonoids. Together they heal skin tissue, stimulate the immune system, and aid in keeping a fever down.

ACNE ATTACKER: BEEF TENDERLOIN
A lean steak might provide relief for prepubescent kids fighting off the early signs of acne. That's because beef is loaded with B vitamins and zinc, two nutrients known to combat facial blemishes.

HEADACHE RELIEVER: SHRIMP
Studies have shown that both fish oil and copper are helpful in fending off headaches. Double down on the defense with a dinner of lean shrimp—rich in both omega-3s and copper.

7

A FITNESS LEGACY

A Fitness Legacy

I've just spent the last 297 pages telling you that it's the food our children are eating—and not a lack of exercise—that's the main culprit that's making them fat. It's true: Remember, we burn only about 15 percent of our calories by actually moving. The rest goes to digesting food and maintaining our life functions.

Still, adding exercise to a sensible diet is like adding lighter fluid to a backyard barbecue—it lights things up, big time! So by increasing the time your children spend being active, you'll turbocharge the weight-loss effect of ***EAT THIS, NOT THAT! FOR KIDS!***

Only one minor problem: Kids don't want to exercise, because exercise feels like work. And as the song goes, girls (and boys) just want to have fun.

But aha: Therein lies the key.

Exercise for kids shouldn't be primarily about burning calories and losing weight. Those are just the fringe benefits. And it shouldn't be about sets and reps, or targeting specific body parts, either.

No, first and foremost, exercise for kids is about fun.

You might think that sounds overly idealistic. ("Come on, kids, strap on those sneaks! Jogging is way more fun than 'Grand Theft Auto!'") But it's not as crazy as it sounds. Children, bless their goofy little hearts, are nothing if not impressionable; the fact is, when exercise is called "fun" or "play," 83 percent of overweight children will do it consistently, report UK researchers. In a 10-week study, the scientists discovered that kids who switched their view of exercise from negative ("Exercise is work!") to positive ("Exercise is fun!") felt more confident and were more likely to engage in fitness activities again.

It doesn't take a rocket scientist (or an exercise scientist, for that matter) to conclude that you're more likely to stick with an activity if you enjoy doing it. So it's not a leap to suggest that learning to love exercise when you're young will make you far more likely to find time for it as an adult.

Unfortunately, it seems most of us missed out on this message as kids, and we're not passing it on to our children either. The evidence: Only 19 percent of Americans participate in "high levels of physical activity," according to the National Center for Health Statistics. The President's Council on Physical Fitness and Sports defines this as just three intense, 20-minute workouts per week—hardly an unrealistic time commitment.

So along with making smart nutritional choices, we can't underscore the importance of regular physical activity enough—for both you and your children. Case in point: A student who enters high school overweight has only a slight chance of reaching a normal weight by adulthood, report researchers at Baylor College of Medicine who studied more than 800 people, at age 10 and again between the ages of 19 and 35. High-school freshmen with a healthy weight, on the other hand, are four times as likely to stay slim as adults. The bottom line: Help your kids develop healthy habits early, and you'll help them grow into healthy adults.

FIT BODY, FIT MIND

Besides the ultimate payoff of a leaner, healthier body, exercise also makes kids smarter. That's not hyperbole; it's hard science from researchers at the University of Illinois at Urbana-Champaign, who studied the impact of regular physical activity on elementary-school students. Turns out, physically fit kids had a couple of advantages over those who were sedentary. Measurements of brain activity revealed that highly active children were not only able to process information faster, but that they also showed greater ability to focus. "Parts of your brain don't develop until late teenage years," says Charles H. Hillman, PhD, the study's lead author. (This may explain a lot of the dents in your car.) "These data show that those who are fit are better able to use what they have."

And it's not just teens who can muscle up their gray matter with exercise. In fact, the younger a child is, the more she may have to gain from regular activity. In a review of 44 studies examining the relationship between physical activity and cognition in children of varying ages, researchers at Arizona State University found that the youngest kids (grades one through five) improved cognitive development the most, followed by middle-school students. The California Department of Education found that the fittest students in the state scored best on academic tests. For instance, the average reading score of students who achieved one of six goals on the statewide fitness test was 38; students who achieved all six fitness goals averaged a reading score of 52.

The research is clear: Regular physical activity not only fosters a fit body, but also a fit mind. By ensuring that your child is exercising regularly, you're helping provide him with more opportunities to succeed in every aspect of his life—now and in the future.

MAKE EXERCISE A REWARD, NOT A PUNISHMENT

If you've ever watched "fat-to-fit" reality shows, you've witnessed running and pushups performed as punishment. But think of it this way: If you punish kids with exercise, how can they ever love it? Remember, exercise is something your kids should do for fun. Your dog wags his tail before a walk; build that sense of anticipation into activities you pursue and suggest to your kids. How? Use these simple guidelines—no matter what age your child is—to instill a love for activity that will linger for a lifetime.

GUIDE, DON'T PUSH.

What's your child interested in? Watch him in his free time and suggest new forms of active behavior. In a study of fifth and sixth graders, University of Missouri researchers found that parental encouragement is the second most important factor in determining whether or not kids exercise. Enjoyment of activity ranked first. So pick an activity your child already shows aptitude toward. If your daughter likes climbing trees, high-five her when she gets down, then take her to a rock-climbing gym. If your son is a one-man home-destructo unit, channel that excess energy into mixed martial arts.

CAP TV TIME.

Television is the enemy of activity: Studies show kids are half as likely to exercise if the tube roots them in place for more than 2 hours a day.

THINK OUTSIDE THE GYM.
Exercise doesn't have to be confined to a strict daily regimen. Gardening or driving to a local farm and picking berries, for instance, are active learning experiences. Plot your Sunday-afternoon bike ride on a map and build in extensions and diversions for the trip.

HANG A NERF HOOP.
Children are 38 percent more likely to exercise 60 minutes or more a day when exercise tools are available at home, report Australian researchers. But that doesn't mean your house has to be a jungle gym: Just make sure toys are visible and kids are allowed to move freely.

SET A GOOD EXAMPLE.
Kids are a whopping six times more likely to exercise when both mom and dad are active, according to a study in the *Journal of Pediatrics*. You could even exercise as a family. In fact, 76 percent of children say they'd like to exercise with their parents, according to a survey run by *Prevention* magazine. So get moving. Try this fun workout that you can do with your kids.

DIRECTIONS: Complete all sets of each task before moving to the next.

1. **RABBIT RACE:** Allow your kid a 5- to 10-yard head start for a 40-yard race, chasing him from behind. Rest 90 seconds, then repeat five times.

2. **DRIVEWAY SHUTTLES:** Place six objects—tennis balls, for instance—at the end of the driveway. Your kid starts, retrieving an object as fast as possible. You get the next one. Alternate until all of the objects have been retrieved. Rest 90 seconds, then repeat three to five times.

3. **TAG:** Mark off a 20-foot-by-20-foot area and play tag. (You're it!) Go continuously for 60 seconds, then rest for 60 seconds. Go five rounds.

The Fit Kids Toolbox

You've already discovered that this book is about giving you tools—powerful tools that will help you raise a happy, healthy child. And that's why we asked Brian Grasso, CEO of the International Youth Conditioning Association and a member of our FitSchools faculty (see "How Fit Is Your Child's School?" on page 300 to learn more), to provide you with your own toolbox of "fit kid" activities.

They'll sound like games to you—and they are. Your child will have loads of fun. But these activities will also boost your child's strength and improve her cardiovascular fitness. What's more, they'll stimulate your kid's central nervous system, the key to all bodily movements and coordination. For instance, our ability to throw and catch, kick, balance, and produce force are all dependent on our central nervous system. They're also all critical factors to develop from the ages of 5 to 12, since that's the period of life when our central nervous systems are the most "plastic," or adaptable. Help a child develop coordination, and he'll retain it for the rest of his life.

Of course, a nice side effect of participating in these games—in addition to a healthier heart, stronger muscles, and greater coordination—is that they also burn tons of calories. Paired with good eating habits, this can help any child achieve a healthy weight. So what are you waiting for? Open up your toolbox—and a world of fun and fitness for your kids.

AGES 2 TO 4

Kids are most active in their early years, between the ages of 2 and 4, since figuring out all the cool things their bodies are capable of is no small task. Unless you somehow stop them (and good luck trying), your children will be frenetic balls of relentless energy—and you'll be the one looking to take a breather.

AGES 5 TO 7

It's around age 5 that SpongeBob begins to exert his unholy pull. Don't get me wrong—I love SpongeBob, too (darn you, Mr. Krabs!). But it's now when a little parental coaching can make a difference. Here are some games that will keep your child active.

Balloon Up

DIRECTIONS FOR KIDS:
Blow up 8 to 20 balloons (depending on how many kids are participating). Start by throwing one balloon up in the air—the objective is for you to keep all the balloons from touching the ground. Every 10 seconds, throw another balloon into the mix. This is a great game to do with a group of kids.

TO INCREASE DIFFICULTY AND ADD FUN, INCORPORATE THE FOLLOWING PROGRESSIONS:
In groups, each participant is allowed to touch a balloon only once. Someone else must hit the balloon before they are allowed to hit it again.

You can use only your right hand, left hand, left knee, right elbow, and so on.

THE BENEFITS
Better Hand-Eye Coordination
Improved Agility
Cardiovascular Fitness

Tag Variations

DIRECTIONS FOR KIDS:
Standard tag isn't the only way to play the game. Try these variations:

One-Legged Tag: All participants must be on one foot the entire time.

Small Area Tag: Make the playing field a small area, so that participants must stay within close quarters during the game. Less running, but much more tactical thinking.

Monkey Tag: Each participant must squat down and stay in that position the entire time. They can run, jump, and side skip to move and avoid being tagged, but they must do so from this deep squatted position.

Crawling Tag: Each participant must be on all fours and bear crawl during the entire game.

THE BENEFITS
Cardiovascular Fitness
Improved Agility
Speed
Greater Strength and Flexibility

Wall Ball

DIRECTIONS FOR KIDS: This game is best played in groups of three or four kids. Start by facing a wall and designate an order: player 1, 2, 3, 4. Player 1 throws a tennis ball against a wall and then moves out of the way. Player 2 then tracks the ball, runs to retrieve it, and from that spot, throws it against the wall. Players 3 and 4 follow suit. Each player must retrieve the ball after only one bounce.

TO INCREASE DIFFICULTY AND ADD FUN, INCORPORATE THE FOLLOWING PROGRESSION:
Kids should learn to throw with both hands. This improves coordination, increases bodily strength, and helps avoid overuse injuries on one side of the body. So every other game played should be based on each participant throwing with their nondominant hand. Not only is this difficult, but tremendously fun to master.

THE BENEFITS:
Cardiovascular Fitness
Tactical Thinking
Greater Strength

Dynamic "Simon Says"

DIRECTIONS FOR KIDS: Just like tag, this conventional game is fun, but can also be a great fitness-oriented experience when played with certain rules. "Simon" should create the game so that the commands incorporate one of the following:

Running
Jumping
Crawling
Climbing
Skipping
Throwing or
Kicking

DON'T JUST STAY IN PLACE. Make the participants move from one place to another. For example, "Simon says: Run to the nearest tree," or "Simon says: Skip for 10 seconds." Also, play the game at "warp speed." That is, have each Simon command come right after the other so that the participants are constantly moving and changing direction.

THE BENEFITS:
Cardiovascular Fitness
Improved Coordination
Greater Strength

THE FIT KIDS TOOLBOX: AGES 8 TO 12

By age 8, many children begin to develop passions of their own: They may have rooted for the same team Mom and Dad did, but only because it was a family activity. Their musical taste was dictated by whatever you listened to. And their hobbies and favorite sports were whatever you signed them up for. But as their minds grow more independent, a slightly more targeted —and more challenging—fitness plan might be in order, one that begins to develop their skills in a variety of areas and prepares them for the challenges of organized sports and other group activities. Here are some of the most effective—and most fun!

Scramble to Balance

DIRECTIONS FOR KIDS: Start face down on the ground with your eyes closed. Have someone yell, "Go!" As soon as they do, stand up and balance on one leg (keeping your eyes closed). Hold that position for 5 seconds and then drop straight back to the ground. Repeat, this time standing on your opposite leg. Do this a total of 8 to 10 times per leg.

TO INCREASE DIFFICULTY AND ADD FUN, INCORPORATE THE FOLLOWING PROGRESSIONS:

While balancing on one foot, hold your hands over your head and pretend that you're reaching for something high up on a shelf.

After balancing for 5 seconds, open your eyes and perform 8 to 10 one-legged bunny hops before returning to the ground.

Rather than someone yelling, "Go!", use different auditory cues. For example, snap fingers, whistle, or clap hands.

THE BENEFITS:

Improved Reaction Time
Better Balance
Cardiovascular Fitness
Greater Strength
Tons of Fun

Obstacle Course

DIRECTIONS FOR KIDS: This can be done in a variety of ways and virtually anywhere. For example, your backyard, the local park, or the school playground. Simply use what's available to you—stairs, swing sets, jungle gyms, playground slides, tennis balls, and so on. Then make the obstacle course diverse, fun, and spirited. Think of it in terms of shapes: That is, create a course that goes in a square or triangle pattern.

HERE ARE THREE SUGGESTIONS:

Triangle:
Side 1: Run
Side 2:
Crab Walk
Side 3: Bunny Hop

Square:
Side 1: Skip
Side 2: Somersault
Side 3: Backward Jog
Side 4: Monster Walk

Playground:
Run from a tree to a bench—do 10 step-ups (each leg) on a bench
Run to the slide—climb up and slide down
Run to the swing set—do 15 swings as high as you can

THE BENEFITS:
Cardiovascular Fitness
Movement Skills
Greater Strength and Flexibility
Speed

Target Throws

DIRECTIONS FOR KIDS: Set up cones or some other type of target—for example, empty aluminum cans. Stand 10 to 20 feet away from the targets and be ready with various size balls, such as tennis balls, soccer balls, footballs, and so on. Using different kinds of throws, try to hit each target with a different ball. The throws could be overhead, underhand, a two-hand chest pass, or one-handed—it's up to your imagination. As soon as you throw the ball, chase after it and then run back to the cone and throw again. To increase difficulty and add fun, stand farther away from the targets.

THE BENEFITS:
Greater Strength
Accuracy
Cardiovascular Fitness

Hand Walks

DIRECTIONS FOR KIDS: Start in a push-up position—your hands set just wider than your shoulders, your arms straight, and your body forming a straight line from head to your ankles. Without bending your knees or back, walk forward on your hands and toes for a few feet. To make it harder, walk sideways or backward.

THE BENEFITS:
Greater Strength

How Fit Is Your Child's School?

Taking control of your kids' fitness at home is just a start. That's because most children 5 and up will spend the majority of their days from September to May not at home, but in school. Unfortunately, fewer than 10 percent of US schools offer daily physical education classes to their students, according to the Centers for Disease Control and Prevention. And in those schools that do offer regular PE, teachers and coaches around the country tell us that they simply don't have enough time, space, or equipment to provide an effective program for their students.

That's why *Men's Health* magazine established the FitSchools Foundation, a nonprofit organization designed to rescue physical-fitness programs from the budget cuts that are crippling public schools in America. We began the program in 2007 at Gettys Middle School in Easley, South Carolina, and have since instituted the FitSchools curriculum in schools across the nation. And the fact is, FitSchools works. In a recent pilot study, University of Southern California researchers found that our program significantly improved kids' fitness levels and love for physical activity. So they're not just getting healthier, they're enjoying the process—which will help them stay fit for a lifetime.

What's more, FitSchools is 100 percent free. Our ultimate mission: To inspire and enable kids, parents, and teachers to improve their lives and the world around them.

Ready to join the team? Go to ***eatthis.com/FitSchools*** *for more information on how you can help support this initiative.*

Index

Boldface page references indicate photographs.
Underscored references indicate boxed text and tables.

F

G

H

I

J

K

L

M

N

O

P

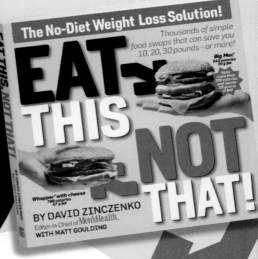